1998

The Selfhood of the Human Person

John F. Crosby

The Selfhood of the Human Person

The Catholic University of America Press
Washington, D.C.

The paper used in this publication meets the minimum requirements
of American National Standards for Information Science—
Permanence of Paper for Printed Library materials, ANSI Z39.48-
1984.
∞

Library of Congress Cataloging-in-Publication Data

Crosby, John F., 1944–
    The selfhood of the human person / John F. Crosby.
        p.   cm.
    Includes bibliographical references and index.
    1. Self (Philosophy) 2. Philosophical anthropology. I. Title.
BD450.C73 1996
126—dc20
ISBN 0-8132-0864-5 (cl : alk. paper).
ISBN 0-8132-0865-3 (pa : alk. paper)
                                                            96-30424

*In grateful memory
of my revered teacher and friend,
Dietrich von Hildebrand*

Contents

Acknowledgments

This work was born of my encounter with the personalism of Karol Wojtyla in the early 1980s. I began writing in the sabbatical semester granted to me by the University of Dallas in the fall of 1983. From then until the fall of 1994 this book stood at the center of my research and writing, and at the center of a good deal of my teaching.

It is a pleasant duty to thank those who helped me during the eleven years in which the ideas matured. I solicited and received critical reactions to various chapters from Pia Crosby, William Frank, Damian Fedoryka, Katryna Fedoryka, Josef Seifert, Barry Smith, L. Stafford Betty, Jorge Gracia, Patrick Lee, and Alice von Hildebrand. Each of the three readers of my typescript who were engaged by The Catholic University of America Press, William Frank, Bernard Gilligan, and Deal Hudson, made helpful critical observations.

In a particular way I thank Josef Seifert, founder of the International Academy of Philosophy, for his unflagging encouragement throughout the years of my work. Though he could never quite understand why my book should take so many years to be born, he never lost an opportunity to urge me on. His own work in the metaphysics of personal being provided a basis for many of my own investigations. I build on this work of Seifert's more than the footnotes indicate, for I have absorbed it over the many years of our collaboration.

I also owe special thanks to William Frank. He read the entire manuscript in 1988 and besides giving me helpful criticism he gave me much encouragement at a moment when I thought I had attempted too much and should leave such a work to others. I also want to remember Rocco Buttiglione, who gave me moral and intellectual support in my work on the book during our years together at the International Academy of Philosophy.

My wife, Pia, has been an important collaborator from the beginning. In many discussions she has helped me with her keen philosophical intelligence to clarify the issues of personalist philosophy that I was writing about. She read many early drafts of my chapters, pressing her questions and objections and challenging me to think more clearly and more concretely about human persons.

My students, too, have contributed to the maturation of my work. I thank all those to whom I taught my Philosophy of the Person course over the years at the University of Dallas, at the John Paul II Institute at the Lateran University in Rome, at the International Academy of Philosophy in Liechtenstein, and at Franciscan University of Steubenville. My book has grown in teaching them this and kindred courses; I largely rewrote it each time I taught about the human person. I might make particular mention of Nicholas J. Healy, my student at Steubenville, who thought that my study of personal selfhood tended to depreciate the interpersonal vocation of human persons and whose critical probing led me to do more justice to it.

Some of my students have collaborated in the production of the book. Celeste Gregory ably served as copyeditor and typesetter. Richard Gordon prepared the bibliography and, with Irene Lagan, the index.

The Thomist has kindly granted permission to reprint much of my study, "The Incommunicability of Human Persons," 57/3 (1993), 403–442. Chapter 2 is simply a more developed version of this study. The *Journal of Medicine and Philosophy* has given permission to reprint much of my study, "The Personhood of the Human Embryo," 18 (1993), 399–418. Chapter 4 is a development of this study.

Introduction

What does it mean to say that each human being is a person? Almost every answer to this question begins in terms of a certain *independence in being and acting.* Whether it is the definition of personhood deriving from Roman law, *persona est sui iuris et alteri incommunicabilis* ("a person is a being which belongs to itself and which does not share its being with another"), or Aquinas' teaching that a person is never a mere part in any whole but a whole of its own, or Kant's teaching that each person is an end in himself, or any of the many accounts of personhood in terms of freedom: wherever we look we find some variation on the theme of independence, autonomy, belonging to oneself, existing for one's own sake, living out of one's interiority, acting through oneself, determining oneself—in a word, some variation on the theme of *selfhood.* It is this selfhood proper to the human person that is the subject of this study.

Let me explain more concretely how I have approached my subject.

The idea of personal selfhood that I will develop in the first chapters is often thought to stand in contradiction to other fundamental dimensions of personal being. For example, those who affirm that we persons are beings of our own and belong to ourselves, are often unable to do justice to the way in which we exist for and with other persons, just as those who insist on the importance of the interpersonal are often unable to do justice to the selfhood of individual persons. To take another example, those who affirm that persons are incommunicably their own often deny that they stand under the judgment of an objective order of truth and right which is the same for all persons, just as those who are glad to stand under the judgment of the one moral order of the world are liable to adhere to some version of "natural law" that is not entirely adequate to the personhood of human beings. One more example: those who affirm that persons are ends in themselves may rebel against the idea of being subject to God and may be too quick to suspect heteronomy in the religious existence of human persons, just as those who are glad to exist under God may be too slow to assert the selfhood that is their birthright as persons and may even incline to a kind of religiously motivated nihilism with regard to human things and human values.

In this study I have sought out those aspects of personal being that seem to stand in contradiction to selfhood, such as interpersonal communion, contingent existence, and dependency on God (theonomy), and have tried to show that they are in fact grounded in selfhood, or that selfhood is grounded in them, or that they serve to specify the exact sense of human personhood. Thus having dealt in Part I with personal selfhood, I deal in Parts II and III with some apparently antithetical aspects of personhood, trying to understand the unity that they form with selfhood. In this way I will try to develop a *comprehensive* view of personal selfhood, not asserting it at the expense of everything else in human beings, but rather letting it be qualified and rendered more concrete by showing the polarities in which it stands. In fact, earlier on I was inclined to call this study *The Dialectical Structure of Personal Being,* and so to put into the title this intention towards comprehensiveness.

I mean, then, to study personal selfhood, not just according to some seminal text or tradition, but according to itself. I mean to turn in good phenomenological fashion to "the things themselves" and to ask what it is to exist as person, making bold even to try to glimpse some of the truth about personal selfhood. Such a project may seem extravagant to many, but I hope to justify it by the results that I gain in the course of my investigations.

Of course, I have been working in dialogue and debate with certain thinkers and movements of thought, and the reader will learn a great deal more about this book by learning who these are.

The idea of personal selfhood expressed above certainly owes much to the moral philosophy of Kant, who was the first to teach that persons should be respected as ends in themselves and should never be used as instrumental means. And yet my primary intellectual home is not the Enlightenment; I stand in the *philosophia perennis,* in the broad tradition of Western philosophy originating with Plato and Aristotle and passing through St. Augustine, St. Thomas Aquinas, Duns Scotus, Suarez, and reaching up to Newman. It is a philosophical tradition existing in the closest relation to the Judeo-Christian revelation. I would like to offer a contribution towards the "reception" of personal selfhood within this tradition. I want to show how far one can go along the lines of personal selfhood and how much one can learn from Kant without departing from the *philosophia perennis*. We do not have to accept the whole Kantian teaching on autonomy; we can let ourselves be challenged by Kant to develop a personalism more congenial with the deepest aspirations of this philosophical tradition.

By the way, one sees on the theological level a parallel work of reception in the teaching of the Second Vatican Council on religious liberty. It is a deeply personalist idea that believers, even when they err, have a right to their belief and to the public expression of it and even to attempts to share it with others. The old *cuius regio eius religio* ("the religion of a principality is to be determined by the faith of the prince") is profoundly depersonalizing, however much it may serve to promote social solidarity. And yet the reception by the Catholic Church of this personalist idea has not been without friction. Some say that the idea is more congenial to the religious individualism of Protestantism than to the Catholic tradition with its stress on the social and corporate dimension of salvation. Others do not see how it is consistent with being fully committed to revealed truth. Catholic theologians are still working at the task, not yet completed, of showing how the Council's teaching on religious liberty springs from the deepest sources of the Church's faith and how it coheres with all that the Church wants to say about social solidarity as well as about our duty to uphold revealed truth. This is akin to the properly philosophical task of receiving within the *philosophia perennis* the personal selfhood of which I will speak.

Actually it is only in Part I that I speak about the reception of selfhood within this tradition. I change perspectives in Part II and explain how the modern tradition of freedom and autonomy can and must receive within itself the idea of transcendence towards truth and good. I address here the fear of heteronomy awakened by the talk of such transcendence, and I develop the idea of the "transcendent autonomy" proper to the human person.

There is also an issue of political philosophy that has been constantly on my mind in the writing of this work. Some speak of a crisis in the Western democracies that derives from people understanding themselves more and more as autonomous subjects of rights and thus losing the sense of being co-responsible for the common good of their communities. The individualism of rights seems to be an irresistible solvent of all deeper senses of social solidarity. I am well aware that much of what I say in my first chapters sounds like this very individualism; but I hope to show that my understanding of personal selfhood provides the *only possible basis* for all deeper forms of community. This means that the defenders of community and the common good should beware of certain proposals of restoration, such as those that reject the idea of the person as subject of rights. There is a core of personalist truth in the individualism of rights, and this has to be preserved in all attempts at renewing the bonds of social solidarity.

In writing this book I have also thought long and hard about an idea of Karol Wojtyla. He has spoken, mainly with reference to the Aristotelian tradition of philosophy, of a predominantly "cosmological" understanding of man, and has welcomed the emergence in modern philosophy of a more "personalist" understanding of man. The former characterizes man in terms taken from the philosophy of nature, such as matter and form, terms that can just as well be used to characterize sub-personal beings; it runs the risk of reducing man to the world. The latter wants to vindicate that which makes man irreducible to the world; Wojtyla says that it gives special attention to personal subjectivity and develops categories applicable only to persons, such as interiority, self-presence, self-donation.[1] The philosophical anthropology of Max Scheler has provided me, as it provided Wojtyla, with one main source for the development of this personalism.

And yet, as Wojtyla also says, the real mission of the personalist view is not simply to replace the cosmological but to complete it. I, too, make my own a personalist vision of man, but without announcing an abrupt break with all pre-modern philosophy; I would like to retain the many truths contained in the more cosmological approach, such as the substantiality of the human person (which Scheler rejected), and to show how these truths are in fact understood more deeply through the personalist approach.

My hope is that my study will be intelligible to an audience wider than that of trained philosophers. In what I have said so far I surely address myself to a broad educated but non-specialist audience. But perhaps the following concern which I have also had in my writing this study will address primarily fellow philosophers.

---

1. "Subjectivity and the Irreducible in the Human Being," in Wojtyla, *Person and Community* (New York: Peter Lang, 1993), 209–217. This essay will provide us with our point of departure in Chapter 3.

I was formed in phenomenological philosophy with its stress on the intentionality of consciousness. Every conscious act, the phenomenologists have said ever since Brentano, is directed to some object; joy is always joy *over something,* doubting is always doubting *about something,* perceiving is always the perceiving *of something,* etc. In our conscious lives we do not have to do with ourselves, but with another; consciousness in this sense is objective, that is, object-directed. My own master in philosophy, Dietrich von Hildebrand, developed this objectivity of consciousness through his original idea of *value-response,* which is the idea that in our responding to the world we do not always bend things towards our needs but can transcend ourselves to the point of giving things their due. But the phenomenologists to whom I am most indebted—von Hildebrand, Scheler, and the other realist phenomenologists—did not explore the selfhood and subjectivity of the person with the same zeal that they showed for the objects of consciousness and for the acts in which we are directed to these objects. They were put off by the development of Husserl who, when he turned to the subjectivity of acting, was betrayed into an idealism according to which the objects of acting ultimately depend on our subjectivity not just for their being-cognized but for their very being. It was only natural for the realist phenomenologists to feel some reserve about the issue of personal subjectivity and to prefer to insist on the mind-independence of many of the beings that we encounter. But eventually one needs to return to subjectivity and to explore it more closely than they did. Husserl was after all right to call it "das Wunder aller Wunder" ("the wonder of all wonders"); and we can make his expression our own even if we share none of his subjective idealism. And in fact I hope to be able, on the basis of this study of selfhood and subjectivity, to contribute something towards understanding how it is possible for persons to achieve the different forms of transcendence (again the dialectical idea).

I will just add that it was my encounter with the philosophy of Karol Wojtyla that drew my attention in a new way to personal subjectivity and led me to balance my appreciation for the transcendence of the human person with a deepened appreciation for the interiority of the person. This study owes much to the so original personalism of Wojtyla.

The reader should not expect more from my study than it in fact offers. It is ambitious enough, but it is not a philosophical anthropology or a comprehensive philosophy of the person. Personal selfhood is indeed not a peripheral but a fundamental issue in the philosophy of the person, and in developing it I am led to other fundamental issues in the philosophy of the person; but what I have written is written in the form of an essay. For example, the discussion of the embodiment of the human person would have to occupy a much more prominent place in a philosophy of the person than it does in this study; I do not treat it in its own right, according to its own importance, but mainly as revealing the contingency of the human person. A related task of philosophical anthropology is to make philosophical sense of the empirical sciences of man, such as biology and genetics; there is almost nothing in the present study that answers to this task. In a systematic philosophy of the person the interpersonal and communitarian dimension of human persons would have to be a subject all its own; it could not be treated primarily from the point of view of selfhood, as I treat it here. There are even important aspects of personal selfhood that I do not treat; for example, "personal identity" in the ontological sense in which it has been much discussed by recent authors falls somewhat outside the primarily existential focus of my analysis (only in dealing with the substantiality of the human person do I come close to some of the "personal identity" literature). I say none of this by way of apology, but simply by way of focusing the expectations of my readers.

PART I

Selfhood

Persona est sui iuris et alteri incommunicabilis.

—The Roman jurists

CHAPTER ONE

The Selfhood of Human Persons as Revealed in Moral Consciousness

It is in the moral life that we have one of our primary experiences of persons; in understanding right and wrong ways of dealing with human beings we encounter them precisely as persons. This is why some of the deepest reflections on human personhood are found in ethical writings, such as in Kant's *Foundations of the Metaphysics of Morals*. I begin, then, with our moral consciousness, looking for the personhood of human beings in our experience of their moral relevance for our acting. I propose this moral point of departure because it lets me begin with intuitions that are widely shared, and so lets me gain a common ground with as many readers as possible. Strangely enough, we could not develop as broad a consensus about the person by discussing the person directly; the consensus seems to be broader if we begin with what is implied about persons in our experience of their moral relevance for our acting.

1. Our point of departure in moral experience: depersonalizing ways of treating human beings

It is a well-known psychological fact that a thing often shows itself with particular clarity when we are deprived of it, or when we see the thing being violated or ignored where it should be noticed. Recall the moving passage in *The Brothers Karamazov* in which Zosima strikes his servant in the face: as he is later tormented by the humiliated, bloody face of the boy, he is overwhelmed with a sense of the dignity, the preciousness of the boy as a human being; this sense is so strong that it is the beginning of his conversion. I shall make my first approach to the nature of persons by exploring our moral judgments on various kinds of depersonalizing treatment of human beings.

1. In a racially mixed community a crime has been committed by a member of one race against a member of the other, and the criminal has escaped, nothing more being known of him than his race. Racial violence is imminent, and nothing can avert this except finding the criminal and bringing him to justice; only this, it is assumed, will allay the outrage of the offended race and prevent it from turning into an angry mob looking for revenge on all the members of the other race. But since the criminal is nowhere to be found, it occurs to the authorities, who are not willing to sit by and watch many lives be lost in the race riots that are about to be unleashed, to look for a scapegoat. They decide to accuse, condemn, and punish someone (of the same race as the criminal) whom they know to be innocent. They resolve on this course of action with much regret, but they cannot think of any other way to defuse the potentially explosive social situation.

No one can fail to see that the scapegoat is violated *as person.* Although we may sense nothing wrong with sacrificing him as long as we think of him as a *thing* rather than as *person,* and speak of him as *something* rather than as *someone,* we are struck forcibly by the wrongness of sacrificing him as soon as we realize that he is a person, a *who* rather than a *what.* And it is not just any violation of him as person but a grievous violation, so grievous, in fact, that the action of framing him seems morally unacceptable even if innumerable lives will be saved by it. Even those who say that they want to have nothing to do with absolute, exceptionless moral norms will almost always see to it that they come to the conclusion that one ought not to frame the innocent. Even if their first principles would under certain circumstances allow for the framing of the innocent, their intuitions are usually stronger than their first principles, which they bend until these principles seem to support the position that the innocent ought under no circumstances to be framed.

Our question, then, is: in understanding that the proposal to frame an innocent man violates him as person, what are we understanding about the being of a person?

2. Almost everyone understands that the prostitute degrades herself by selling herself, and that her customers degrade her by buying her. We understand why she typically has no self-respect: she lives by throwing herself away. The new factor in this case is the absence of the coercion that was found in the case of the scapegoat: she willingly sells herself.

But we all think that her consent only keeps her from undergoing the violence of rape, not that it suffices to clear her and her customers of responsibility for committing grievously depersonalizing actions. We do not think that we have to do violence to *others* in order to do violence to persons; we can as well do violence to *ourselves* as persons, or at least make ourselves accomplices of such violence.

We ask: what must the personhood of a woman be if a prostitute throws away her birthright as person?

3. Suppose that someone wanted to breed human beings as animals are bred, and wanted to destroy before birth or at birth all human beings that did not promise to be excellent specimens of the human species. Clearly our moral sensibilities are offended by the killing of the unfit human beings; indeed, they are offended by the very idea of "unfit" or "defective" human beings. Why is this? What is it about persons that makes us recognize a kind of self-contradiction in the idea of a "defective human person"?

Notice that we are also offended by the breeder keeping and nourishing the promising human beings; we find something deeply depersonalizing in the treatment of human beings who are allowed to live and are cared for simply because they promise to be exemplary specimens of the human species and who would have been eliminated or ignored if they had been defective specimens, or simply inferior to better specimens. Though these breeders of human beings *commit a crime* only when they destroy their fellow humans and not when they keep them, nevertheless their approach to their fellows is hardly less depersonalizing when they keep them than when they destroy them. But why is this? What is the truth about human persons that they fail to recognize in treating persons as specimens?

We find the same kind of depersonalization in other ways of treating membership in the human species as the main thing about human beings. If, for instance, one minimizes the death of someone by saying that at least the human species did not die with him or her, as if the immortality of the species more than compensates for the mortality of any individual, then one would radically depersonalize each individual. But why is this? Why is personhood driven out of our experience of human beings as soon as their species membership is thought to predominate in them?

It is not only species membership that can threaten personhood; the qualities and excellences of a person that go beyond species membership can threaten it as well. Suppose that you were grieving over the

death of someone dear to you, and a friend tried to comfort you with the
thought that the particular excellences of the deceased, which awakened
your love, also exist in other human beings who are still living, as if you
could continue to love in them what you had loved in the deceased.
Again, everyone understands that if we treat people having excellences
as if they were replaceable specimens of those excellences, then we lose
our grip on them as persons, and even depersonalize them. Why is this?
Why is personhood driven out of our experience of human beings as
soon as their particular excellences are thought to predominate in them
to the point of making them only specimens of the excellences? How
must human persons be if they disappear for us as persons as soon as
they become in our eyes mere bearers of qualities and excellences?

According to our moral consciousness, these closely related forms of
depersonalization are independent of the subjective intentions of persons. The mere fact that I willingly function as specimen and understand myself as nothing but a specimen does nothing to protect me from
being depersonalized; it simply makes me a collaborator with the en-
emies of my personhood.

What must the structure of the person be if a human being is ignored
as person, and disappears as a *someone,* when cast into the role of a
mere specimen or instance and treated as entirely replaceable by other
specimens?

4. Let us take another case of radical depersonalization, the case of
slavery, in which one person claims to own another. It is not difficult to
see that one violates the other as person in trying to hold the other as
one's property. Even if the master were to treat his slaves with a view to
the slaves' real welfare, and thus not merely use them for his own welfare, he would nevertheless stand in a morally intolerable relationship to
the slaves, a relationship that does violence to the personhood of those
held as slaves. And even if the slaves were gladly to cooperate in becoming slaves, this cooperation cannot redeem the relationship morally;
it just makes them accomplices of their master in the violation of their
own personhood.[1] We find here an absoluteness just like we found in the
wrongness of framing the innocent man. It does not matter how great a

1. We have of course an entirely different case if a person quite understands the
degradation of being enslaved but refuses to offer violent resistance to the master, thinking that it is better to endure his degradation rather than engage in the violence of fighting it. We would hardly say of such a slave that he or she is an accomplice of the master
in the violating of his or her own personhood. We would instead say that in this case the
only one who violates persons is the master, but not the slave who acquiesces.

good could come from holding a person in slavery; the prospect of ever so much good, whether for the slave or for others, does not even begin to overcome the wrongness of holding a person as a slave, does nothing to create an exception, a case of slavery justified by its consequences.

There is not just the moral condemnation that we pass on American slavery; I want also to call attention to the judgment that we might pass on slavery as it existed in the ancient world, long before it occurred to anyone to question the moral soundness of slavery. We are perhaps not inclined to express the same moral indignation over the slavery of the ancient world as we might express over the slave trade as it was practiced at the beginning of the last century. We instead marvel at the immaturity in the understanding of the person that ancient peoples had who simply took slavery for granted; we think that it is as if they had hardly awakened to the personhood of human beings.

Observe that it is not just any belonging of one person to another that offends our moral sensibilities; the belonging of a child to its parents, or of spouses to each other, seems to us to be morally in order. What offends us is rather the particular kind of belonging which obtains between an owner and his property. A person cannot belong to someone in the sense of being owned by that person, owned the way his property is owned by him.

Our question then is: what do we understand about persons when we understand the moral immaturity of those periods in history in which slavery was taken for granted? What do we understand about persons when we see slavery as radically depersonalizing? And is it so very different from what we understand in grasping the violence committed against the man who is framed?

5. The violence against persons that offends our moral sensibilities can be much subtler. Everyone knows the experience of encountering other persons only under the aspect of how they intersect with our projects, and of noticing them only insofar as we have to notice them in order to interact with them as we pursue our goals. But from time to time we realize more keenly that the other with whom we are dealing is a person, and then we feel the irreverence and the arrogance of our attitude. We become aware of a certain violence with which we have been treating other persons; we realize that we have to draw back and grant them a space in which to be themselves as persons, and that we have to cease seeing them exclusively in relation to our projects. This violence is nothing like the violence of condemning an innocent man, and it will usually not even involve any physical violence or infringement of their

rights; but though it is a subtler violation of the person, it is nevertheless keenly felt by us as soon as we awaken to the fact that we are dealing with a person. The question is: what is the truth about persons to which we awaken?

2. *The selfhood of persons thrown into relief through these ways of depersonalizing human beings*

It goes without saying that in these opening pages I do not intend to record our moral intuitions and moral condemnations as so many sociological facts; I think, as almost all of my readers will think, that we are right to make these condemnations, and that these intuitions contain real moral knowledge, so that in unfolding the personalist assumptions of these intuitions we are beginning to develop real knowledge of the human person.

I proceed now to try to answer the questions raised in the previous section. I will do this by developing four statements about the personal selfhood that is co-experienced in human beings when we experience their moral relevance for our acting: or rather I will make one statement in four variations.

1. Persons are ends in themselves and never mere instrumental means. Why does it do violence to human persons to condemn them and to destroy them unjustly for the sake of maintaining civil order? Because as persons they stand in themselves and do not exist merely for the sake of another (or even of many others, or of a community of others), *but rather exist in some sense for their own sake.* It is because I am *so strongly anchored in myself* that I cannot, without being violated as person, exist as a mere instrument in the service of something outside of myself, not even in the service of ever so noble a goal, or of ever so great a benefit for ever so many people. This is the fact about the person that is disregarded when the innocent man is framed as scapegoat: he is treated as if he exists merely for the sake of his community. We could appropriate the well-known Kantian phrase and say that persons are *ends in themselves*[2] and are not mere instrumental means; it is precisely the fact of being one's own end that is flouted when the innocent person is made a

2. Schopenhauer thought that the famous Kantian expression, "end in itself," was self-contradictory on the grounds that an end is always an end for someone, and therefore never an end in itself. In reality, however, the Kantian expression is not at all contradictory, for to say that persons are ends in themselves is equivalent to other expressions in which the logical point on which Schopenhauer plays is not present, expres-

scapegoat and is used instrumentally for the attainment of a certain result.

Here we have at least part of the reason for the degradation of the prostitute: as person she is an end in herself, but as prostitute she lets herself be used as a mere means for the gratification of her customers.

When I look at others only insofar as they intersect with my projects, then of course I lose them as persons, because I am not willing to let them exist for me as ends in themselves.

This independence in being that belongs to persons seems to be understood by us as something metaphysically ultimate, for we think that it exists even before God: the idea of God using us and discarding us as an instrumental means is no less offensive to our moral consciousness than the idea of other human beings using us and discarding us. We think we would be right to rebel against God in the name of our personal selfhood if we thought that His relation to us were nothing but a relation of using. It is not only thinkers like Nietzsche and Sartre who have made this point; already Aquinas said something that implies it. In speaking of divine providence in Book III of the *Summa Contra Gentiles,* he argues in Chapter 111 "that rational creatures are subject to divine providence in a special way"; he specifies in Chapter 112 "that rational creatures are governed for their own sakes, while others are governed in subordination to them."[3] In my own terms, in which I speak of persons rather than of rational creatures, I would express the thought of Aquinas like this: God respects our personal selfhood by dealing with us on our own account, and precisely does not treat us as a mere instrumental means for serving other beings or even for advancing His designs.

It is, by the way, remarkable that in this passage, in which Aquinas approaches more closely than in any other (as far as I know) to persons existing for their own sakes and as ends in themselves, he speaks of human beings not in themselves but in their relation to God, and indeed in their being subject to divine government. I shall return later to this

---

sions such as that human persons belong to themselves, are *sui iuris,* are beings of their own, are beings which in a certain sense exist for their own sake; there is in these affirmations no obvious contradiction such as Schopenhauer thought he had found. And, as I think, there is no contradiction at all.

3. He explains himself with an analogy taken from human government: "under every sort of government, provision is made for free men for their own sakes, but for slaves in such a way that they may be at the disposal of free men. And so, through divine providence provision is made for intellectual creatures on their own account, but for the remaining creatures for the sake of the intellectual ones" (Chapter 112, para. 2).

unity formed by selfhood and theonomy. Thomas takes it for granted, but many modern thinkers since Kant have found it extremely problematical.

There is a weighty and plausible objection that many will want to raise to the idea of the person as existing in some sense for his own sake. It will be said that we sometimes find ourselves morally admiring persons who "lay down their lives for another." They do not seem to be asserting themselves as beings that exist for their own sakes, for they make a supreme sacrifice for another's sake. Does our moral consciousness contradict itself? Does it consistently reveal persons as ends in themselves? Or is it divided against itself when it reveals persons as beings for others? Or does the selfhood that we are now exploring form the basis of acts of self-donation? I will return to these questions in section 3 of this chapter, and above all in the chapters of Part II.

2. *Persons are wholes of their own and never mere parts.* We can bring out another aspect of persons "existing for their own sakes" if we consider the following justification which might be given for making a scapegoat. The authorities might say that each individual human being is, in relation to society, nothing but a part, a being whose whole *raison d'être* lies in building up the whole which is society; that each is related to society like an organ is related to the organism to which it belongs. Then they might argue: just as we remove an organ from the body, even a healthy organ, if its removal serves to promote the health of the whole body, so, since the individual member of a community is related to the community as organ to body, we of course remove those individuals whose removal promotes the common good of the community, and even if they are healthy, that is, innocent individuals.

And so when we understand that it is morally intolerable to frame the innocent man, no matter what good can thereby be secured for the community, we understand that the person is *not* a mere constituent part of the community, or for that matter of any whole; he exists for his own sake in so strong a sense that he cannot exist merely to build up some whole; he is his own center, and so cannot find his center in any community or in any other larger whole; he is a whole in his own right, and so forever repels the category of a mere part. A person is not a relative totality, like a bodily organ, which is indeed a unity in its own right, but which, considered in relation to the more encompassing totality of the human body, is a part. A unity such as a bodily organ is as it were relativized on being incorporated into the totality of the body. But there is no totality that can encompass a person in such a way as to relativize the totality that he or she is. Persons stand in themselves in such a way as to be absolute, that is, unsurpassable, unrelativizable totalities. Persons can no more be mere parts than they can be instrumental means.

A person can of course be incorporated in a community as a member of it; this life in community in no way threatens the personal selfhood of the member, and in fact can profoundly serve the flourishing of himself as person, as is obvious. But it is one thing to participate as person in a community; it is quite something else, it is quite a further step beyond such participation when one understands oneself as related to the community as an organ is related to its organism, that is, as having one's whole reason for being in building up the community. In this case one abandons oneself as a being existing for its own sake and accepts oneself as existing entirely for the sake of the community; one does violence to oneself as person, and one throws away a certain selfhood that is one's birthright as person, and lets one's life in the community become a source of destructive heteronomy.

But perhaps one will object that in many communities, such as in the political community of the state, one participates by playing some partial role complemented by other partial roles (such as "citizen," "official," "judge," "commander," "soldier," etc.) Though one might admit that certain communities such as mankind or a nation are not so structured as to give rise to complementary roles, one might still say that in those communities so structured the individual person is clearly cast into the role of a part, and this without any harm to the person; therefore, concludes the objection, the individual person is not a totality in as strong a sense as was claimed above, and in fact really has something like the being of a part, at least in relation to the totality which is a community.

Our answer is clear. It is only on one condition that persons are not harmed by playing partial social roles: on the condition that they do not identify their whole being as persons with those social roles. If they do identify themselves with their roles and think that they gain their whole reason for being in playing the partial social roles, then playing the roles does violence to them as persons.[4] The experience of this violence against oneself is widespread in our time. It may be the experience of being

---

4. I am speaking of *real* totalities, which have an inner unity and a center. If one speaks of *logical* classes such as the class of "all persons," then the belonging of a person to the class naturally represents no threat to the selfhood of the person, not even if one considers persons as belonging with all the depths of their personal being ("all

degraded, used, violated as person; or it may be a sense of meaningless-
ness in one's existence, or a painful loneliness. If we were to probe all
such experiences we could see anew that each person is indeed a kind of
totality of his or her own and never exhausts his or her whole being in
fulfilling some partial function, however noble or indispensable the function may be. For we would see that the pain and distress in these experiences come from a false self-understanding, from trying to understand
our being as having a partiality radically at odds with existing as person.
Only by understanding each partial social function as a kind of mask, as
something that does not contain without residue the depths of one's personal being; only by understanding it as something which, however important, even for a person's development as person, can never provide
the person with his whole reason for being, absorbing him or her as a
part of the community; only by understanding a society or community
as a "whole composed of wholes":[5] only then can a person remain intact
as person in performing the function.[6]

If one aspect of personal selfhood is thrown into relief by saying that
the person is not an instrumental means, then another aspect of the same
selfhood is thrown into relief by saying that the person is never a mere
part.[7]

This inability to be a part seems to have the same metaphysical
ultimacy that we noticed above. For our moral consciousness it seems to
matter little whether one tries to make human beings parts of society or

---

personal subjectivities"). When, however, we consider one person in relation to the class
of all other persons, we very easily lose sight of an important aspect of the selfhood of
the person; I shall speak of this in the next chapter when I discuss a certain "absoluteness" of the person (Chapter 2.3). But the mere fact of the membership of a person in a
logical class has in itself nothing depersonalizing about it.

5. In the felicitous phrase of Maritain, *The Person and the Common Good* (New
York: Charles Scribner's Sons, 1947), 47.

6. When Aquinas says (*Summa Theologiae*, I-II, a. 21, q. 4, ad 3), "homo non ordinatur
ad communitatem politicam secundum se totum, et secundum omnia sua" ("man is not
ordained to the body politic according to all that he is and has"), he seems to be saying
exactly what I mean to say in response to the objection.

7. This seems to be the teaching of Aquinas, too, who says (in *In III Sent.*, d. 5, 3, 2,
among many other places) that the *ratio personae* is opposed *(contrariatur)* to the *ratio
partis*. He is in fact so insistent on persons not being parts that he is led to deny (ibid.)
that the separated soul after death is still a person. Since it lacks the wholeness that it
can have only as embodied, it takes on a partiality that prevents it from being a person
any longer. We can hardly accept this conclusion of Aquinas, though his argument is in
part based on a sound personalist premise.

parts of God; the depersonalization inflicted on them is no less grievous in the latter than in the former case. Whatever the larger whole, even if it is God Himself, persons can never function as mere parts in it. Pantheistic religion not only exalts but also degrades human beings: by making them parts *of God* it makes them divine, but by making them *parts* of God it abolishes them as persons.

3. Persons are incommunicably their own and never mere specimens. Why does one do violence to persons in treating them as a mere specimens of the human species, or of some ever so great excellence? Why does the status of an instance or specimen seem to be incompatible with the personhood of human beings? I have to give the same answer that I gave to the previous question: it is because persons stand in themselves and are anchored in themselves, each existing as incommunicably his own, that they can never exist as mere specimens or carriers of anything. Actually there are two different respects in which the status of a specimen is opposed to personal selfhood. First, in relation to the ideal of which persons are supposed to be specimens: as specimens they would exist for the sake only of instantiating the ideal, whereas as persons they exist for their own sakes. Secondly, in relation to other specimens: they would be replaceable by all other equally good specimens, and this replaceability would destroy the standing in themselves and having a being of their own which belongs to them in virtue of their personal selfhood.

As far as violating persons goes, it seems to make little difference whether one uses them as an instrumental means or treats them as specimens, esteeming them only insofar as they fulfill some type or ideal; in either case one does not let persons stand in themselves but tries to draw them off their center in the direction of something other than themselves. Of course at first it seems that in the first case (framing the innocent person for the sake of preserving civil order) there is a greater violation of the person as a being that stands in itself than in the second case (esteeming a human being only insofar as he or she exemplifies some ideal). After all, if the ideal is that of humanity or personhood or femininity, or is some moral ideal, then that for the sake of which persons are said to exist is nothing outside of themselves but rather something internal to themselves; for the ideal of humanity is not external to a human being, nor is femininity external to a woman, in the way the civil order of a given town is external to the individual who gets sacrificed for it as scapegoat. For this reason the persons taken as mere specimens do not seem to be used as a mere instrumental means, for there is here no end which, once reached, will lead the breeder to discard the exemplary person; the end for which he strives is inside and not outside the exemplary person. And yet this difference between the two cases, though in the abstract it seems to be a considerable difference, does not seem to make so very much moral difference; for even when we keep the difference in mind we still find something radically depersonalizing in the attitude of breeding human beings as one breeds animals. That persons are beings who stand in themselves, are anchored in themselves, indeed, in a certain sense exist for their own sakes, is conveyed to the mind by the negation of personal being in the present case almost as effectively as by the negation of personal being in the case of using the innocent man as scapegoat.

It is commonly thought that this aspect of persons—I will call it the incommunicability of the human person—was recognized only in modern thought; in fact it was recognized by Aquinas, even though it does not play the central role in his thought that it merits.

> Now, a rational creature exists under divine providence as a being governed and provided for in himself, and not simply for the sake of his species, as is the case with other corruptible creatures. For the individual that is governed only for the sake of the species is not governed for its own sake, but the rational creature is governed for his own sake, as is clear from what we have said (ch. 112). And so, only rational creatures receive direction from God in their acts, not only for the species, but for the individual.[8]

Notice that Aquinas teaches the metaphysical ultimacy of this aspect of personhood, too; it exists even before God in the sense that it determines Him (so to speak) to a different kind of providence than He exercises towards non-persons. It is not primarily the human species that appears before God, as if human persons only appeared before Him

8. Aquinas, *Summa Contra Gentiles,* Chapter 113, para. 1. By the way, Chapters 111–114 seem to me to constitute the most "personalist" passage in the entire corpus of St. Thomas. The modern reader sees to his amazement that St. Thomas here has already made his own the Kantian idea that each person in a sense exists for his own sake (is an end in himself), as well as the Kierkegaardian idea that each individual person exists in a sense "above" the human species. On the other hand, one has to admit, as I just remarked in the text, that these personalist insights do not yet occupy the place of prominence in the philosophical anthropology of St. Thomas that they deserve. In Chapter 6 we will even find a train of thought in St. Thomas that stands in contrast to genuine personalist philosophy. It is as if he glimpses in these chapters a new world whose time had not yet come.

insofar as they belong to the species, but individual persons appear before Him in their own right as individuals who are more than species-members. This ultimacy, though expressed here in theological language, seems to belong to the understanding of personhood implied in our moral consciousness.

I am well aware that on speculative grounds unrelated to our moral consciousness some have challenged the incommunicability of human persons, or at least that ultimacy of it which I am just now stressing. In Averroism, in Buddhism, in German Idealism, in the thought of Schopenhauer, the young Nietzsche, and others, it has been said that the distinct individuality of human persons is a kind of human appearance, and that at the level of ultimate reality this distinctness gives way to a oneness that excludes a plurality of incommunicable persons. Sometimes this oneness of ultimate reality is explained in terms of something universal or general, which forms a contrast with real concrete beings. In the last chapter I will defend our moral consciousness against all of these thinkers, arguing with Aquinas that human persons are incommunicable and unrepeatable even in relation to God.

In the next chapter I will explore more closely this incommunicability and unrepeatability that I have affirmed in my third statement about personal selfhood.

4. Persona est sui iuris et non alterius iuris: each person belongs to himself and not to any other. What underlies our judgment about the moral immaturity of historical periods in which slavery was taken for granted, or our indignation over the practice of slavery in our times? Nothing but this, which is my fourth statement about the person: persons exist for their own sakes in the sense of belonging to themselves, of being *sui iuris,* of possessing themselves, and can therefore never belong to another as the property of the other.

This is closely related to my previous statements about the person. The person exists for his own sake not only in the sense of not being an instrument in the hands of another, and not being a part of another, and not being a specimen replaceable by another specimen, but also in the sense of not belonging as property to another.[9] Each of these negations brings out another aspect of the person's existing for his own sake and standing in himself. The present negation seems to point to something

9. See the profound discussion of personhood in Romano Guardini, *The World and the Person* (Chicago: Regnery, 1965), 103–131. On page 114 Guardini expresses well the antagonism between being a person and being owned by someone.

de iure in the selfhood of the person: a person belongs to himself and is his own *(sui iuris)*, and so cannot belong to another as that other's property *(alterius iuris)*.

The person as subject of rights. It is this belonging of persons to themselves that underlies something strongly rooted in our moral consciousness: it underlies our sense that in many (though not all) of the cases presented above *basic rights of persons* were violated. We would all say that the *rights* of people sold forcibly into slavery are violated by their owners. It is also natural to say this about the scapegoat; his rights are violated by those who frame him. And these rights seem to be closely related to the personhood of the right holder: in respecting the rights of others we respect them as persons, and in violating their rights we violate them as persons. Indeed, the growing awareness of the basic rights of human beings seems to be nothing but an aspect of the growing awareness of them as persons. Now that we have attained to our fourth statement we can explain why violence against persons is commonly a violating of the rights of persons, and why persons are subjects of rights.

But let us first specify which rights we mean. When we say that the rights of the scapegoat or of the slave are violated, we obviously speak of the fundamental rights that the person has as person and not of the rights acquired by contract or conferred by the positive law. These latter rights also give evidence of the personhood of the right holder, but for my present purposes I set them aside, focusing on the former rights, which have a special relation to the personhood of the right holder in that they spring directly from this personhood and without the mediation of any acts of contracting or conferring.

It seems that to violate these rights of a person is nothing other than to try to dispose over what is that person's own, or to commit a kind of theft against the very being of the person. The authorities treat the innocent man as if his being were theirs to dispose over, when in fact it belongs to him; it is this arrogant interference in the realm of what is his own which seems to make the action of framing him a violation of his rights. It is, then, especially our fourth statement about the person which we understand when we consider the person as a subject of rights.[10]

---

10. I do not make bold to assert that the belonging of the person to himself is the *exclusive* ground of rights in the human person, and to deny that considerations of good, and of the common good, also play a role in the grounding of rights. My task is not to give a full account of the ground of rights, but to refer to them only insofar as we can see in them the belonging of the person to himself; this we can see even if it should turn out that the self-belonging of the person is not the only factor that gives rise to rights.

Here is a kind of indirect confirmation that rights of the person derive precisely from the belonging of persons to themselves. These rights have the peculiarity that they cannot be violated, or for that matter respected, by the person who has them, *but only by some other person.* If I freely take my own life, I do not violate my own rights; only someone else who takes my life against my will violates my rights. Let us assume that I do what is wrong and immoral in taking my life; still the wrongness, though it can be explained in terms of the respect I owe myself as person, cannot be explained in terms of my violating the rights I have as person. I can no more violate my own right to life than I can steal my own property or commit adultery with my own spouse. It is different with the *worth* or *dignity* of the person; I can respect or violate my own dignity no less than that of another; but my rights are essentially more social, needing *another* person to respect or violate them.[11] Now this peculiarity of such rights seems to be explained precisely by their being grounded in the belonging of persons to themselves; for it is entirely understandable that the belonging of persons to themselves will create for others moral obstacles that do not exist for the persons themselves, just as the belonging of property to its owner creates for others moral obstacles that do not exist for the owner. I repeat that this is not to say that there are *no* moral restraints on what I do with myself; this no more follows than it follows from the structure of property that owners cannot act irresponsibly in disposing over their own property.

The selfhood and solitude of the human person. I have attempted, then, by means of four statements about what the person is *not,* to make four statements about what the person is, or rather to vary four times one statement about the selfhood of persons. Perhaps I could say that what emerges from this fourfold statement is "the selfhood and the solitude of the person."[12] I speak here of solitude not in a subjective or experiential sense but in the sense of a person being set off from everything other than himself: because persons are gathered so strongly into themselves,

11. It follows that the man who freely offers himself as scapegoat effectively removes his rights from the situation; those who proceed to condemn him and punish him do not violate any right of his. This of course does not mean that they do not do him any violence as person, nor that he does not do himself any such violence; it only means that this violence does not take the particular form of violating rights.

12. This talk of solitude is entirely consistent with a claim that will emerge in the course of our study, namely that there can ultimately be no such thing as a solitary person, and that personal being is such that it can only exist in the form of persons existing together with others.

we can say that they preeminently *are themselves and are not another.* We see in the inability of the person to be a part in some whole, or the property owned by someone, or a replaceable specimen, just different aspects of what I mean by the solitude of the person.[13]

It is remarkable how our results, derived from our moral conscious-ness, converge with the understanding of personhood that has emerged in Western thought. Maritain says that "the metaphysical tradition of the West defines the person in terms of independence, as a reality which, subsisting spiritually, constitutes a universe unto itself, a relatively inde-pendent whole within the great whole of the universe, facing the tran-scendent whole which is God."[14] Thus our results point directly to the classical definition of the person given by Boethius: *persona est sub-stantia individua naturae rationalis* ("a person is an individual substance of rational nature"). A being is a substance in virtue of standing in itself, of existing neither as a part nor as a property of another, and it is just this moment of independence which emerges as the essence of personal selfhood.

I know of course that many contemporary philosophers have weighty objections against speaking of the person in terms of substance. We have first to study the subjectivity of the person in Chapter 3 in order to un-derstand why they think that subjectivity excludes substantiality; in Chapter 4 I will respond to them and argue for the substantiality of the person, thus justifying more critically than I can now my acceptance of the old Boethian definition.

But there is another "definition" of personhood in the tradition with which our investigations coincide even more closely than with that of Boethius. I mean the principle deriving from Roman law, *persona est*

13. Cf. Guardini's talk of the solitude of the person in his op. cit.: "'Person' means that I cannot be penetrated by another but in relation to myself am alone with myself, that I cannot be replaced by any one else, but stand on my own, that no one can substi-tute for me, but that I am unique. All this remains valid, even if the sphere of reserve is disturbed profoundly by interference and publicity. What is lost is only the psychologi-cal condition of being respected and at peace, not *the solitude of the person as such*" (114). (I have modified in a few places the English translation, and have added the italics.)

14. Maritain, op. cit., 30. Josef Pieper says the same thing: personal being is charac-terized by "an unlimited capacity of living in oneself, the gift of self-reliance and inde-pendence that, *in the philosophical tradition of Europe,* have always been regarded as the attributes of the human person, of being a person" (Pieper, "The Philosophical Act," in *Leisure* [New York: The New American Library, 1963], 91 (my italics).

sui iuris et alteri incommunicabilis, which we might freely render in this way: a person is a being of its own and does not share its being with another. *Persona est sui iuris* expresses what I have called the selfhood, *alteri incommunicabilis* expresses the resulting solitude of personal being.[15]

3. The acting proper to persons

Having given our attention so far to the being of persons, it is only natural to turn now to their characteristic acting. This is entirely in accordance with the Scholastic axiom *"agere sequitur esse:* acting follows being," or, as we could just as well translate, "as a being is, so it acts." Karol Wojtyla thinks that there is no more promising approach to the person than the approach through acting; hence the title of his major work in philosophical anthropology, *The Acting Person.*

Two opposites of personal acting. Let us continue the strategy of looking for a thing through its state of being repressed or denied.

In some of the cases presented above persons were coerced in their acting, forced against their will; this is what we find in the typical case of the scapegoat and of the slave. This coercion seems to violate such persons in their acting as persons.[16] The violation cannot be explained simply by saying that the coerced persons are being used for some end

---

15. I come here in the present section to the same conclusion as Ismael Quiles, S.J., in his "La Esencia del Hombre," in *Antropologia Filosofica In-sistencial* (Buenos Aires: Editiones Depalma, 1983), 330–360. After posing with great precision the question of "the essence of the essence" of man, he argues that it lies in his inner center, his standing in himself (hence Quiles' new term, in-sistence, and his designation of his own position as an "in-sistential" philosophical anthropology). It seems that what he calls "in-sistence" is very close to what we have called the selfhood of the person. He then surveys all the main attempts to capture the essence of the essence of man in other terms, as for example in terms of rationality, or freedom, or self-transcendence, and shows convincingly that all such powers or characteristics presuppose in-sistence and are grounded in it, and are therefore not as fundamental as it. It is not, of course, as if these other dimensions of personhood were less important than selfhood or even were mere accidents of in-sistence; it is just that there is one sense of "fundamental" in which they are not as fundamental as in-sistence.

16. Which is not to say that all coercion of persons is morally unjustified; it is, for example, undoubtedly morally in order to deprive criminals of their liberty. Even in their case we might study the acting proper to persons. But in what follows I will be thinking of *unjustified coercion.*

foreign to themselves, for there is after all a kind of coercion undertaken with a view to the well-being of the persons coerced. A paternalistic ruler, for example, may coerce his subjects into ways of acting that he thinks are in their best interest and that really may be in their best interest. He may insist that they profess religious and moral beliefs that are indeed true, just as he thinks they are true. And yet the coercion can violate the subjects of the ruler in their acting as persons. Even though human persons are made to live in the truth and even though they thrive as persons only in the truth (more on this in Chapter 6), still they do not thrive but rather undergo violence when they are coerced into the truth. What must the acting of the person be if even such "benevolent" coercion violates it? And how is properly personal acting related to the personal selfhood which we have been discussing?

We will return later to the second of these two questions. At present I answer the first by saying that persons act as persons by *acting through themselves,* that is, *acting with an acting which is radically their own.* My acting as person is not an undergoing, or an enduring, or a transmitting of what originates outside of myself; it is I, I myself who act when I act as person, and no one else. Aquinas expresses it with precision when he says of the acting of persons: "*non aguntur, sed per se agunt:* persons are not acted on but act through themselves."[17] When persons are coerced, some other is acting through them: but as persons they act through themselves.

This is clearly implied by the violence that is done to slaves by being owned. The acting of slaves is nothing but the prolongation of the acting of their master; as Aristotle said in his discussion of slavery, the slave originates nothing but transmits and executes only what originates in the master. A large part of the reason why slaves disappear as persons is that they are reduced to a condition in which they cannot act through themselves or act with an act which is radically their own.[18]

17. *Summa Theologiae,* I, q. 29, art. 1. Of course, St. Thomas does not mean that persons can never or should never be acted upon, but only that being acted upon does not reveal them as persons.

18. It is not only we human beings who respect each other as persons by abstaining from coercion; God, too, respects us in this same way, as Wojtyla indicates in the following: "Nobody can use a person as a means towards an end, no human being, nor yet God the Creator. . . . Therefore, if God intends to direct man towards certain goals, he allows him, to begin with, to know those goals, so that he may make them his own and strive towards them independently" (*Love and Responsibility* [New York: Farrar, Straus, Giroux, 1981], 27).

One opposite of personal acting, then, is coercion, a rather obvious opposite. The other is a certain *blindness* of acting.[19] By reflecting on this opposite, too, we can come to understand personal acting.

Consider any example of what Max Scheler called "emotional infection."[20] Suppose that panic has broken out in a crowd and is spreading through it. The panic does not spread by each new panicky person *understanding* some danger and *responding* to it by fearing it. No, the transmission of the panic bypasses all understanding and responding; panic engenders panic without any reasons being given or understood. Panic spreads through the crowd by a kind of psychic causality, not essentially different from the transmission of fear in a herd of animals. As the people seized by panic run for safety, they do not act in a properly personal way. They are only transmitting what comes from others; they are not acting through themselves. And why do they disappear as acting persons? Not because of coercion, but rather because of the blindness of their acting. Each would have to *understand some danger* if he or she were to act as person in seeking safety. We can say on the level of philosophical principle that my action becomes entirely my own only when I act *on the basis of my own understanding of the point of my action.* Thus for personal acting it is not enough to be free of coercion; I also have to act on the basis of this understanding.

It follows that the personalistic opposite of unjustified coercion is a certain kind of persuasion. If I want to move another to act, and to move the other in such a way as to respect his or her personhood, then I give the other reasons that can be understood; I convey the point of the proposed action and help the other person to see it for himself.[21] In all attempts at such persuasion I enable the other to go in a certain direction, not as an extension of my willing, but with a willing that is as truly his own as mine is my own. All authentic education has to use as much persuasion and as little coercion as possible, and has thus to aim at the greatest possible independence of the educated from the educator. Real

19. Max Scheler distinguishes these two opposites in distinguishing between two forms of heteronomy; see his *Formalism in Ethics and Non-Formal Ethics of Values,* tr. Frings and Funk (Evanston: Northwestern University Press, 1973), 495.

20. See Scheler, *The Nature of Sympathy,* tr. Heath (Hamden, CT: Shoe String Press Inc., 1973), 14–18.

21. I repeat that when all such persuasion fails, the resort to coercion need not in every case be depersonalizing; in fact coercion can be exercised in such a way as to take people very seriously as persons, as when they are held accountable for their crimes by some legitimate authority.

educators understand the paradox of eliciting in their students independence from themselves.[22] This distinction between coercion and persuasion lies deep in our moral consciousness.

The talk of a kind of persuasion that is entirely worthy of the person to whom it is addressed brings out the significant fact that persons can act through themselves even while being dependent on others in various ways. Perhaps someone gives me reasons that I, left to myself, would have never discovered. As a result I depend on the other in my acting on the basis of these reasons: but at the same time I can act entirely through myself *as long as I understand for myself these reasons* and do not just repeat them without understanding them. In the same way we could show that my dependency on some tradition need not have anything to do with emotional infection or interfere in any other way with my acting as person through myself. I do not have to break all the ties of human solidarity in order to act through myself; I do not have to act with the originality of doing what no one else has ever thought of doing. It does not matter that I act as others have acted *as long as I understand what others have understood.*

From its beginning Western philosophy has recognized the *rationality* of man. I can appropriate this insistence on rationality for my present purposes, saying that only those who have reasons for their acting, and *have* them in the sense of understanding them for themselves, can really act through themselves. Thus I can make entirely my own that part of the Boethian definition of the person which says that a person is an individual substance *of a rational nature.* Even though, as we will see, the Greeks failed to do justice to the personhood of man, they nevertheless provide some of the elements of a philosophy of human personhood.

A more modern way of expressing this thing of understanding the point of some action is in terms of the *intentionality* of acting. We can say that people infected with panic and fleeing out of panic are not in-

22. Needless to say, this paradox is not much in evidence in very small children, with whom the discipline that would otherwise be depersonalizing coercion can be entirely in order. Indeed, such discipline can be exercised in such a way as to aid them in acting well when they come of age as persons, as both Plato and Aristotle wisely teach. This is all quite consistent with my claims in the text. Since small children, while undeniably persons, have as yet little power of acting as persons, the main impediments to personal acting, such as coercion, or failure to understand the point of an action, in a sense do not yet exist for them.

tentionally related to some danger, they are not *motivated* by it: this is just another way of saying that they flee lacking any *understanding* of danger. In Chapter 5 I will study more closely the rationality contained in all intentional acts of the person. The only point that I will stress more than the Greeks is that in all intentional acting the rationality is my own, is immanent in my acting, is necessarily known to me acting.[23]

We will at this point be asked whether we can make sense of actions performed in obedience, which frequently are actions different from the ones we would have performed had we acted on the basis of our own insight. If we think of a soldier obeying his commander, or of Abraham obeying God, or simply of a citizen obeying a law that he would himself have never enacted, we find cases of obedience that do not offend our most fundamental moral sense, even though they seem to be at odds with what I have just said about properly personal acting.

It seems that we can indeed make personalistic sense of such actions of obeying. The one who obeys must at least understand for himself why the person in authority is worthy of being obeyed. Abraham does not see the point of sacrificing his son, but he does see the point of obeying the God who commands him, for he knows that He is trustworthy. This element of understanding lets Abraham's action of preparing to sacrifice his son be an act of himself as person. But if the action were entirely blind, blind even as regards God's claim on his obedience, then it would surely be impossible to act as person in performing the action. Or take a citizen in relation to a law by which he abides even though his own judgment suggests a much better law that might have been enacted in its place. His conforming behavior may indeed be nothing but a matter of emotional infection. But it might be an entirely personal action. The citizen might understand the practical impossibility of the best personal judgment of every citizen being enacted into law; he might also understand the necessity of one law being enacted to the exclusion of other possible laws; he might further understand that the enacted law is not absurd, and is even reasonable, even if not the one he would have chosen; in addition, he might understand something of the legal authority that was exercised in enacting the law in question: understanding all

---

23. But we can even discern something of this immanence in these words of Aristotle: "This [human reason] would seem, too, to be each man himself. . . . It would be strange, then, if he were to choose not the life of his self [the life of contemplative understanding] but that of something else." And above all this: ". . . since reason more than anything else *is* man" (*Nichomachean Ethics,* X, Chapter 7, 1178a, 2–9).

these things he surely stays fully intact as person while he obeys the law which does not entirely correspond to his own understanding of right.[24]

Of course, my present talk of not acting blindly but "seeing the point" of an action is still extremely vague; later I will have to distinguish different kinds of "points" and, as a result, different kinds of ownership of our actions. Above all, I will examine in Chapter 6.3 the particular perfection of ownership of which I become capable as soon as I see some *objective validity*, some *objective justification* in my action.

In the acting of persons through themselves we catch sight for the first time of the person as subject, and so of the subjectivity of persons. Insofar as persons are acted on by another and made to transmit what originates outside of them, they do not appear in their subjectivity, but rather as objects. With this I touch on an aspect of personhood to which all of Chapter 3 is devoted.

We also catch sight of the corresponding theme of the objectivity of persons, by which I mean the transcendence of persons in their acting. Notice that I was unable to discuss how we act through ourselves as persons without saying something about the *reasons* we have for acting and about the *motivating objects* to which we are directed in acting. This means that I was unable to discuss the acting of persons in a purely immanent way; almost from the beginning I had to take account of the transcendent reference of personal acting. In fact, we have even gotten a first glimpse of a theme that will occupy us throughout the chapters of Part II: a certain interpenetration of immanent and transcendent in personal acting. We own our actions *on the very basis* of having some reason for performing them, or being motivated by some object in performing them.

The archaic sense of social solidarity. It seems that this sense of persons acting through themselves was very weak in certain premodern forms of social life. For example, when the chieftain of a tribe converted to a religion he would decree that the entire tribe should join him in his new religion, and the entire tribe acquiesced without question. It did not occur to anyone to ask each member of the tribe if he or she really believed the new religion, and to take precautions lest any member of the tribe be pushed to profess what he or she did not really believe. Each apparently had so strong a sense of solidarity with the group that decid-

---

24. This is exactly the way in which Scheler deals with the question of obedience and insight in *Formalism in Ethics*, 498–501.

ing for oneself about one's religious beliefs and commitments was un-
thinkable; such a decision was a decision for the group and not for the
individual, and could therefore be made only by the group acting through
its leader. If one were to try to say exactly *who* underwent the conversion, one should not say, "each of the members of the tribe," but rather
"the tribe"; it seems to have been more a corporate or collective subject
that underwent the conversion than a number of individual subjects. One
sees why I say that we have here a situation that cannot be characterized
in terms of coercion; the members of the tribe do not have to be re-
strained from leading their own religious lives, since such "individualism" in acting apparently lies entirely beyond the horizon of their existence.

This archaic sense of social solidarity, as we might call it, is not found
only among "primitive" peoples; it lived on in Europe into the seven-
teenth century (Peace of Westphalia, 1648), when German princes took
it for granted that they might govern their subjects according to the principle *cuius regio eius religio* (the religion of a principality is to be determined by its prince). It perhaps even lingers into fairly recent times in
the "establishment" of churches in certain states. In another way it lingers wherever Christianity is held and lived in a merely *conventional*
way, that is, as a "totem of the tribe," or in other words out of loyal
solidarity with tribal fellows.

I mention religion and in particular Christianity not because I mean
to limit our study of personal acting to religious acting, but because I
take the socialization of even Christian faith as indicating the complete
socialization of human existence. The archaic absorption of the individual into the group strikes our moral sensibilities as particularly inap-
propriate in all that concerns religious existence.

We have been speaking of the archaic sense of social solidarity as
something which characterizes primarily premodern social life, and has
begun to break down in the modern world.[25] But we can also point out
this sense of solidarity in a perennial form, occurring in all times, in
modern no less than in premodern times. I refer to the mentality of young
children, who seem to begin their lives with an overwhelming sense of

25. Cf. the discussion of this breakdown in the writings of Glenn Tinder. I am personally much indebted to his early work, *The Crisis of Political Imagination* (New York:
Chas. Scribner's Sons, 1964), Part I, "The Ordeal of Personal Existence." Tinder was
the first author I read on the questions of selfhood under discussion in the present section.

being immersed in their social group. They seem to share the life of their group rather than lead much of a life of their own. When they begin to enunciate opinions they typically speak in such a way that we can hear their family or larger social group speaking through them. Of course this childlike mentality does not awaken our moral indignation as certain kinds of coercion do, and neither does the archaic sense of social solidarity, little as we want to return to it.

And why could we not want to return to it? Because we think that people who experienced their whole existence as tribal, and did not know how to reserve any realm of existence as personal and not tribal, had not yet discovered themselves as persons; they lived lost in the social totality as mere parts of it.[26] We find again in our moral consciousness what we found above in it, namely that human beings, insofar as they are persons, are more than parts. They have a being of their own that is so strong as to make them wholes or totalities in their own right. Persons express this strength of selfhood, in virtue of which they are persons, by acting through themselves, that is, acting with an acting that is understood by each person for himself and that is, therefore, centered in each person and not centered in any group to which they belong. But as soon as they yield the primary agency to the group, they tend to disappear as persons.[27]

Suppose that some leader arises who wants to restore the old archaic solidarity, and that he finds plenty of followers who are only too glad to dissolve into his group and to escape the burdens of individual exist-

26. Cf. the fascinating discussion which Hegel gives of the place of Socrates in human thought. Hegel seems to interpret Socrates as one of the first to break through to this understanding of the individual person. Perhaps he would say that the condemnation of Socrates was, among other things, a revolt of the old archaic sense of social solidarity against the Socratic assertion of the individual relation to truth that each human being has. Hegel, *Vorlesungen über die Geschichte der Philosophie*, II, in *Sämtliche Werke* XVIII, Jubiläumsausgabe, 42–122. English: *Lectures on the History of Philosophy* (London, 1892), tr. Haldane, vol. I, 384–448.

27. One may ask whether a Christian practice like infant baptism is a residue of archaic social consciousness. Is this a modern-day case of a tribal leader bringing his tribe with him in converting to a religion? I answer that this practice need have nothing to do with a sense of the family members as mere parts of the familial whole. One can do for a child what it cannot yet do for itself on the basis of fully respecting the distinct selfhood of the child. As long as the parents would not dream of trying to do for their older children what they do for their small children, as long as they would not dream of requiring baptism of the former without their consent, then they give evidence of providing for their small children without any hint of any depersonalizing sense of the children as mere parts of the family.

ence. Our moral sensibilities are more seriously offended by this retrogression, and we respond to it with disapproval and censure. For these people would be trying to return to the archaic solidarity at a time when individual personal existence has become possible; they cannot really return to it, and by trying to do so are indulging in a reprehensible escapism. In this case it becomes even clearer that persons act as persons only by acting through themselves, each having his or her own existence.[28]

Selfhood and solidarity. There is an objection which I can feel rising again in the minds of many otherwise sympathetic readers. They will say that the disintegration of social solidarity that has occurred in recent centuries in religion and in other realms of life seems a great loss. They will say that the rootlessness and isolation under which so many modern people suffer is a social catastrophe, and that there is something in the solidarity of traditional premodern societies that we urgently need to recover. If in order to find ourselves as persons we have to be shaken out of all traditional bonds and roles and become free-floating and disoriented selves, then perhaps something has gone wrong in the analysis of selfhood—perhaps there is too much individualism in our understanding of the human person.

How can we not feel the appeal of such an objection, we who often live in circumstances of the most painful social disintegration? But I do not see that the truth in the objection needs to be in opposition to my claims. For not even those who plead the cause of social solidarity really want to restore what I have been calling the archaic sense of social solidarity, that is, the complete absorption of the individual in the group. They and I agree that the task of social philosophy is to find new forms of social solidarity *on the basis of the personal selfhood* that we have found in our moral consciousness, or in other words, to preserve the truth of the old social solidarity in a new personalist social order. After the discovery of personal selfhood, we can no more return to the archaic socialization of life than an adolescent who grieves over the passing of his childhood can return to being a child.

28. One might think that I am offering a Protestant idea of religious existence, and that if I were to develop an ecclesiology to go with what has been said in the text, I could only allow for a loose and unstructured community of believers. But one should think twice before assuming that the "higher" ecclesiology of the Catholic tradition cannot deal with individual religious existence. Certainly I go no farther with my religious individualism that Vatican II did in its "Declaration on Religious Liberty."

I could perhaps also say in response to the objection that the discovery of personal selfhood is not simply a movement away from social solidarity, but rather presupposes a certain solidarity within which it takes place. I mean that it was apparently not possible for just any dweller in, say, ancient Mesopotamia to discover himself or herself fully as person; it is only by being caught up in a mysterious world-historical development that human beings discover themselves as persons. So there is a certain social support even for the disintegration of the old archaic sense of solidarity. In suffering under this disintegration we do not find ourselves simply thrown into a social void; we rather find ourselves undergoing something together, one with another.

This is the place to offer a first response to the objection posed above, namely that in our moral consciousness we sometimes grasp not the selfhood of the persons with whom we deal, but rather their power of self-transcendence, as when we admire them for generously spending themselves for the sake of others. This objection would seem to call into question the usefulness of our moral consciousness as a point of departure for studying personal selfhood; it would say that if we really do grasp selfhood in certain moral intuitions, then our moral consciousness must be divided against itself, since other moral intuitions seem inconsistent with selfhood.

I do not deny that our moral consciousness contains other insights into personhood besides our insight into selfhood; but whatever we implicitly understand about self-transcendence when we admire persons *does not exclude but rather presupposes* what I have been saying about selfhood. For if an act of generously spending myself on behalf of another is not *my own* act, if I am coerced, or neurotically driven, to act for the other, or if my act is too conditioned by convention and by what "one does," so that I cannot really say, "It is I, I myself who will the good of the other," then I forfeit the moral admiration of others. We do not see any admirable self-transcendence in such acting, because we do not see any awakened selfhood at the basis of it. This means that in our admiration for someone's self-sacrificing generosity we can find all of that selfhood which is our subject here. It also means that our moral consciousness is entirely coherent, confirming our sense of selfhood even when it seems at first glance to contradict it.

Personal acting is grounded in personal selfhood. It is easy to see how this power that persons have of acting through themselves is related to the selfhood and solitude in which they exist as persons. It is only because persons are gathered into themselves in the sense explained above, that is, only because persons stand in themselves, and exist for their own sakes, and in an incomparable sense are themselves and are not any another, and belong to themselves—it is only because of this selfhood that persons can act through themselves. Or to express the dependency more succinctly: only because persons have a being radically their own, can they act with acts radically their own. Only because persons are autonomous in their being are they capable of autonomy in their acting. If persons were really nothing but instrumental means or pieces of property, or if they were nothing but parts in some whole, or were nothing but specimens of some type, then they could not possibly act through themselves: they would lack the centering in themselves without which they cannot act through themselves. Their *esse* could not support the *agere* of acting through themselves. We would have the reverse impossibility, so to speak, if persons had indeed the selfhood described above in our four statements, but could in principle not act through themselves; there could not possibly be a being that was gathered into itself as person but was in principle incapable of acting through itself (and not just hindered by extrinsic factors from so acting).

We have here the reason why it is that, as I observed above, we show respect for persons as ends in themselves by limiting all coercion in their regard and using as much as possible that persuasion which works with reasons and which enables them to act through themselves. If we reach persons as ends in themselves by respecting their acting through themselves, then this acting must be grounded in and be expressive of their being ends in themselves.

Notice that when we approach personal selfhood through the acting of persons we do not just discern the same selfhood with which we are already acquainted. We understand it with a new depth and concreteness as a result of seeing how it grounds the acting of the person. We find something similar when we move in the opposite direction, namely from selfhood to personal acting; we understand in a new dimension the acting of the person through himself when we understand it through the selfhood that makes it possible. It is a question of "rubbing two stones together," as Socrates said of the justice of the individual soul and of the justice of the whole city.

The range of personal acting. I want to say a brief word on how various the activities are that count as personal acting. It must be admitted that when I first approached personal acting through the coercion of

persons, I was thinking of acting mainly as *performing actions;* for coercion interferes not just with any kind of acting, but above all with
action. But in fact personal acting is in no way limited to the performing
of actions *(praxis);* there are all kinds of inner acting that lack the outer
aspect that belongs to all action. The experience to which I will appeal
in the following is no longer limited to our moral experience of respecting and violating persons; I now reach beyond this experience, which,
after all, only provided a point of departure for this study.

First of all, then, we recognize persons acting through themselves in
their knowing and understanding, as one can see from our discussion of
the harm inflicted by the excessively paternalistic educator, and above
all from our discussion of the place of *one's own insight* in all properly
personal acting. Of course, if we were to misconceive knowing and understanding as something merely passive, as a mere passive exposure to
the objects of cognition, analogous to the exposure of camera film to
light, then it could not possibly involve acting through oneself. But if all
deeper forms of knowing and understanding are distinguished from mere
sensation, or from the blind repetition of the opinions of others, precisely by the fact that they are not passive as these are passive; if they
involve what has been called "active receptivity"; if they can be performed more or less authentically: then it follows that persons act through
themselves even in their knowing and understanding, and this in a sense
entirely consistent with the receptivity intrinsic to all knowing and understanding.[29]

There is also the receptivity of listening to other persons, receiving
the self-disclosure that they address to us. One is fully alive as acting
person in all such interpersonal receiving.[30]

In the affective life, too, there is full personal acting. This is at first
surprising; the way in which some affective moods and states befall us

29. In *The Acting Person* (Dordrecht: D. Reidel Publishing Co., 1979), Karol Wojtyla
asks (in Chapter 3, section 9) whether acting through oneself can be found even *within*
the cognitive life of the person, that is, whether there is a way of man acting through
himself that is not yet specifically volitional but rather cognitive. He answers in the
affirmative, and claims that the cognitive agency of the person is found above all in the
act of forming a judgment or statement.

30. For one of the best recent affirmations of this receptivity, see Norris Clarke in his
Person and Being (Milwaukee: Marquette University Press, 1993), Chapter 2, section 5,
"Receptivity as Complementary to Self-Communication." In fact, Clarke argues, suc-
cessfully I think, that personal receptivity should be understood not as a mixed but as a
pure perfection, that is, as a perfection in the idea of which there is no intrinsic relation
to finite being.

prevents them from being acts in which we act through ourselves; in them persons seem more *aguntur* than *per se agunt*. Even affective experiences that are meaningfully motivated, such as love for another, and so seem to be more susceptible of being forms of personal acting, often well up with so strong a spontaneity of their own as to seem to prevent us from acting through ourselves. And yet we find in our moral experience the possibility of what von Hildebrand has called *sanctioning* such affective responses, that is, incorporating them into ourselves in such a way as to act through ourselves in the responses.[31] In sanctioned affective experiences, which do not originate in our arbitrary freedom and yet are eminently forms of personal acting, the reader sees how far we are from having to think of personal acting exclusively in terms of performing actions and making things.

We also find in our moral experience that persons act through themselves even in living in basic attitudes such as generosity, or reverence, or selfishness. It is true that these attitudes, being distinct from particular acts, are withdrawn from our arbitrary freedom (that is, the mere wanting to change such fundamental attitudes usually does not suffice to change them), and yet in them we have one of the most significant ways, perhaps *the most significant* way, in which persons act through themselves. But this is not the place to develop the distinction between act and attitude that is required for the fuller explanation of this mode of acting through oneself.

One important consequence of doing justice to the range of personal acting is the recognition that women are no less persons than men. It may seem at first glance that acting through oneself, especially if it is narrowed to the performing of actions, has a specifically masculine sense, so that men would be persons in a more proper sense than women. Only in surveying the full range of acting through oneself, and the full range of the selfhood manifested through such acting, does one see that, even assuming certain long-recognized psychic and even spiritual differences between men and women, the personhood of which we speak is no more masculine than feminine. There is nothing in my analysis that inclines me to the Aristotelian view of woman as a "deformed male." On the other hand, it does not follow that human personhood is genderless; it may well be, for all we have said, that there is a specifically masculine

31. See von Hildebrand, *Ethics* (Chicago, Franciscan Herald Press, 1972), Chapter 25. We will return to von Hildebrand's profound analysis of personal affectivity towards the end of Chapter 6.3.

personhood and a specifically feminine personhood. But if there is such a difference within human personhood, it is not equivalent to the difference between more and less authentic personhood. The equally authentic personhood of man and woman can, of course, be maintained on the basis of holding personhood to be genderless, but it can just as well be maintained on the basis of affirming that human personhood always exists as masculine or feminine.

"Person" and "nature." Wojtyla has pointed out personal acting by contrasting it with a certain opposite: he contrasts "what merely happens in man," such as feeling hunger or thirst, with "what man does himself"; in other words he contrasts undergoing or enduring with acting through oneself (very much as Aquinas contrasts *aguntur* with *per se agunt*). He calls the former "activations" and reserves for the latter the term "acting." This leads him to follow many recent authors in distinguishing between "person" and "nature" in the makeup of human beings, person being the principle of acting through oneself, nature the more passive principle of undergoing. We, too, want to make our own this contrast of person and nature. It is a personalistic way of expressing the peculiar "mixed" character of man, that is, the fact that in him there is something coming from above and something coming from the earth, something of "spirit" and something of "matter."[32]

By the way, this distinction is not as modern as one might think. It is directly parallel to an old Scholastic distinction with respect to sin: *peccatum naturae* and *peccatum personae,* the former referring to original sin, the sin into which human beings are born, the sin that they contract without doing anything to contract it: the latter referring, by contrast, to the sin which I, I myself commit.

It is important to notice that "person" in the sense of the person-nature distinction does not exactly mean what person means for Boethius when he defines a person as a certain kind of individual substance, nor does it mean what person means for us when we speak of this or that individual person. Person in the sense of person-nature does not express a substance, a distinct being, it expresses rather a pole of human acting, a fundamental dimension of the human person. How can we recognize

32. It seems that Maritain, with his well-known distinction between man as person and man as individual (op. cit., Chapter 3), is aiming at a distinction in many ways like ours between person and nature. But I do not approve of Maritain's use of the term "individual" in this context, since there is a fullness of individuality precisely in personhood, as we shall see in the next chapter.

this difference? First of all linguistically; person in the sense of person-nature is not used with an article, definite or indefinite, and is never used in the plural; whereas with regard to individual persons we typically speak of *a* person, or of *the* persons, or of *this one.*

But we can also recognize the difference through the fact that *within any individual person* one can distinguish between person and nature, which one could not do if person had only one meaning. We can say that it is the same person who now acts through himself, and now experiences things happening in himself. When I feel desires, cravings, urges springing up on their own, outside of my freedom, and thus happening in me, I do not just *perceive these desires and urges as objects,* as springing up in another being which however close to me is still other than me; I experience them subjectively and not just objectively (to use terminology that will be introduced in Chapter 3), as belonging to myself as subject; I experience myself as the one who lives in them and has them as his own. When I express the urges that spring up in me, saying for example, "I fear this," "I desire that," I use "I" in the same sense in which I say, expressing my acting through myself, "I will," "I refuse," etc. We have, then, to say with Wojtyla[33] that person and nature, sharply as they contrast in idea, nevertheless do not express two different subjects of being; it is one and the same subject of being that now acts through itself, and now undergoes what happens in itself. When we call this subject of being *a person,* then we have the new meaning of person that has to be distinguished from the one that emerges from the contrast with nature. On the other hand, the two meanings are not unrelated; a person is obviously called a person with a view to the fact that he is not all nature but is also person (in the sense of the person-nature distinction).

Conclusion. Will some say our notion of personal selfhood is simply a modern product of Western culture and is unknown in the great cultures of the East, or even say that it is the product of the individualism of Western bourgeois societies, a kind of metaphysical reflection of the economic and social conditions of a definite historical period? Will "postmodernist" thinkers say that there is no universally valid truth about the human person? I respond simply by saying that even after the passing of this historical period it will remain true, and will continue to be widely understood, and to be readily understandable, and to be really the case,

33. See the discussion of this in *The Acting Person,* 71–90.

that persons should not use each other as instrumental means, or treat each other as mere parts, or as specimens, or as thing-like property, but should rather treat each other as ends in themselves. Even the one who raises the objection will understand this; but in understanding this the objector understands, at least in a virtual way, all that I have wanted to say about personal selfhood. And if some in non-Western cultures were really to think that persons can be instrumentally used or treated as mere parts of some whole, then they would err, and even the most ecumenically-minded people will agree that they err. There is, of course, such a thing as a Western individualism that disrupts the deeper forms of community; various historically contingent products go by this name; but my affirmation of personal selfhood is not any such product. It cannot be denied that my notion of selfhood is more at home in the Western world than elsewhere, indeed that it has clearly recognizable roots in Western experience and thought; Scheler is surely right when he says that this notion is "the *magna carta* of Europe, as against Asia."[34] But nobody who understands personal selfhood thinks that it is merely an historically contingent product lacking universal validity. To think this is like thinking that geometry lacks universal validity because of its Greek origins. Indeed, if we ask whether there is any such thing as universally valid truth, any truth which is not just relative to some particular tradition but which is intelligible to people of the most various traditions, then there is no better way of satisfying most people with an affirmative answer, no better way of showing the universality that is still possible in the pluralistic, "post-modern" world of the late twentieth century, than by referring to the moral principle that persons, since they exist in some sense for their own sakes, are never rightly used as a mere means.

I now proceed to more controverted aspects of personal selfhood; but I first wanted to gain a common ground with as many readers as possible. When they object to some of the claims that I will be making in the following chapters, I will often try to trace these claims back to the common ground of our moral consciousness.

34. Scheler, *On the Eternal in Man* (Hamden, CT: Archon Books, 1972), 383.

CHAPTER TWO

Incommunicability

I now proceed to explore the structure of personal selfhood by examining more closely my third statement above: persons do not exist as replaceable specimens or as mere instances of some ideal or type, but exist rather for their own sakes, each existing as incommunicably his or her own.

Needless to say, when I speak of personal incommunicability I do not speak of any impossibility that persons have in communicating with each other; for the purpose of the discourse of the present chapter I return to an older, more metaphysical sense of the term. It is the sense already familiar to us from our examination of the axiom of Roman law, *persona est sui iuris et alteri incommunicabilis.* It is the incommunicability that is nothing but an aspect of personal selfhood.

The terms we will be using in the present chapter, unrepeatability and incommunicability, express something relational and negative, at least at their most literal level; they set a person in relation to other persons and affirm that this person is *not* able to be repeated in some sense or other by the other persons, and does *not* share his being with them in some sense or other. What I am above all interested in, however, is that entirely positive core of persons *in virtue of which* they are unrepeatable and incommunicable. But these terms, since they are not confined to their most literal meaning, quite naturally serve to express both this positive core of a person as well as the resulting negative relation of a person to other persons. It is, by the way, not at all unusual to find a negative form in a concept through which we also aim at something entirely positive, as when we express the concrete being and the inner unity of a thing by speaking of the in-dividuality of the thing,[1] or when a theologian speaks of the divine fullness and plenitude as the in-finity of God; and in the same way the im-mortality of the soul expresses a fullness of life in the soul and thereby something entirely positive.

1. The distinction between communicable and incommunicable in general

We begin by exploring the distinction between what is *communicable* and what is *incommunicable* in a being. Let us take the classic example of the human nature of Socrates. If we say that the human nature of Socrates is communicable, we mean that Socrates does not possess human nature as radically his own, absorbing it into his own being, but rather has it in such a way as to leave room—metaphysical room—for other human beings. He does not monopolize human nature, but he has it in such a way as to be able to have it in common with others, and thus to be able to be one among many human beings. On the other hand, there is something incommunicable in Socrates; he has something that exists only in him and not in any other. His being Socrates is radically his own, it *is* monopolized by him; Socrates has it in such a way as to exclude the possibility of another Socrates.

But it is much more difficult than it at first seems to draw this distinction with precision, and especially to capture that which is communicable in a being. For there is clearly some sense in which each human being has his or her own human nature, so that the humanity of Socrates is not the humanity of Plato. In fact there seems to be nothing at all in the being of Socrates that is literally held in common with other human beings; everything that belongs to his real being, and hence also his humanity (and not just his being Socrates), is incommunicably his own. Even his accidental features, such as his hair color, seem to be incommunicably his own. Sometimes one speaks as if only a being's act of existence were incommunicably the being's own and as if all the being's essence were something general or universal and so were shared or held in common with others of the same essence. But this will not do, for the humanity of Socrates belongs to his essence, and yet it is, as I say, in some sense incommunicably his own and not to be confounded with the humanity of Plato. And besides, it seems impossible for something gen-

1. In his *Individuality: An Essay on the Foundations of Metaphysics* (Albany: State University of New York Press, 1988), 54–55, Jorge Gracia ably brings out the positive core of individuality.

eral or universal to enter into a real being so as to form a constituent of it;[2] a real being can be through and through real only in all of its properties and accidents. What remains, then, of the communicability of Socrates' humanity? How can we avoid saying that everything in Socrates is incommunicable and nothing is communicable? How do we explain the way in which he has humanity in common with other human beings so that we can speak of their "common humanity"?

It is all-important to distinguish *the concrete humanity* of Socrates or of Plato from *the universal form of humanity*.[3] The former is indeed incommunicably Socrates' or Plato's own, but the latter introduces us to their common humanity, for which we are looking. For the universal form of humanity *is* identically the same for Socrates and for Plato, and in fact is common to them. Of course it does not enter into the real being of either of them so as to constitute a real part of their being; as we just remarked, no real being can possibly have *general* or *universal* constituents of itself. It is rather the case that the being of each human being is "formed according to" the universal, humanity, and so "participates" in it, to speak Platonically. The communicability of humanity, then, would lie primarily in the universal form; humanity does not coincide with anyone's concrete humanity but in some sense transcends all human beings so as to be able to be common to them all.[4] In an analogous sense, however, one can speak of something communicable even in the

2. With this I distance myself from Aristotelian hylomorphism, at least in the interpretation according to which a general form and individuating matter unite to form a concrete substance. In the text I am saying that no concrete substance has anything general as one of its real, concrete ingredients.

3. In his important monograph, "Essence and Existence" (*Aletheia*, I [1977/78], 17–157 and 371–459), Josef Seifert makes this distinction between concrete and general essence with a greater sharpness and precision than most previous attempts at the distinction (see especially 37–114). He is thereby enabled to explain the impossibility of something general or universal entering into a real being as a constituent of it, and also to explain in a new way the "participation" of real beings in general essences. He comes to a position on essence and existence which combines in the most original way Platonic and Aristotelian elements.

4. I see from the learned studies of Jorge Gracia that my use of communicable and incommunicable coincides with the main meaning of the medieval *communicabile* and *incommunicabile*. See, for example, his *Introduction to the Problem of Individuation in the Early Middle Ages* (Munich: Philosophia Verlag, 1984), 24–25, or his work already cited, *Individuality*, 45–46. By the way, of the six fundamental issues regarding individuality (or incommunicability) that Gracia so helpfully distinguishes, our discussion in this section deals primarily with the central issue of the intension of incommunicability, and to some extent with the extension of it.

concrete humanity of Socrates and in the concrete humanity of Plato, rather as one can speak of "healthy" not only with respect to living beings but also with respect to diets and to environments. If we speak of something communicable in the concrete humanity of Socrates, we are referring to *his humanity insofar as it participates in the universal form of humanity and insofar as it is modified by this participation, being reduced in its incommunicable being.* In fact, I will usually be speaking of communicable being in this more concrete, if less proper, sense, just as I spoke of it when I began analyzing the communicable and the incommunicable.

It follows that the humanity of Socrates is communicable in one respect and incommunicable in another. It is communicable in the secondary sense just explained, but it is incommunicable insofar as it is Socrates' own and is therefore to be distinguished from Plato's humanity.

It follows, furthermore, that "incommunicability" expresses individual being by means of an antithesis to what is *general* or *universal.* "Unrepeatable," by contrast, expresses individual being by means of a certain antithesis to *other individual beings of the same kind.* Though we sometimes use these terms interchangeably, there is in fact this distinction between them. This distinction is also found in "communicable" and "repeatable" or "replaceable": "communicable" is said primarily of what is general, whereas "repeatable" or "replaceable" is said exclusively of what is concretely real.

Now it seems that this talk of incommunicability is deeply expressive precisely of persons. And yet one cannot help noticing that *every* real being is unrepeatable and incommunicable, and not just persons. We say of the person *"persona est sui iuris et alteri incommunicabilis:* a person is a being which belongs to itself and does not share its being with another." And yet the principle of identity seems to say much the same thing of *every* real being: every being is itself and is not another. It follows that every being has a certain selfhood in virtue of which it is incommunicably itself. If a being were through and through communicable, having nothing incommunicable in itself, having nothing of its own, then it would not even amount to "a being" but would resolve itself into a general idea. When, then, I insist on the incommunicability of human persons, meaning to say thereby something strongly expressive of them precisely as persons, I must be claiming to find a *particular fullness* of self-identity and of incommunicable being in the person; I must be claiming that the incommunicable selfhood proper to every being is raised, in personal being to a higher power. But how are we to understand this higher power, this particular fullness of incommunicable being?

2. *The distinction between communicable and incommunicable with respect to the human person*

I will now distinguish different ways in which a being can be incommunicably itself.[5] In particular I want to identify the greatest conceivable incommunicability and contrast it with the poorest possible incommunicability, and then situate human persons with respect to these two extremes. I speak first of supreme incommunicability.

The very fact that a being is subject to a universal, and thus has something in common with other beings of its kind, weakens or blurs the contrast between that being and those other beings; this weakens the force with which it "is itself and is not another." A being would be gathered far more perfectly into itself and set off more sharply against others if it had all its nature and its attributes as incommunicably its own, and in such a way that no metaphysical room remained for a second being of its nature, or for a second being having its attributes as it has them. It is a limitation on the incommunicable being of Socrates that he has human nature in such a way as to have it in a certain sense in common with other human beings. Socrates would be incommunicably himself in a far more proper way—indeed, his incommunicability would belong to a different order of being—if he had his humanity in the same way as he has his being Socrates, being it instead of participating in it, and if he were, as a result, the only possible human being. This supreme incommunicability, which neither Socrates nor any other human being has, is in fact proper to God. God does not just share in divinity, leaving room thereby for other Gods, but *He is His divinity*, that is, He has all His divinity as incommunicably his own,[6] eliminating thereby the possibility of other Gods.[7]

5. This question as to *fundamentally different kinds of incommunicability* does not seem to be included among the six basic questions about incommunicability distinguished by Gracia, op. cit., chapter 1, and yet it would seem to be as important as any of his six. I could as well characterize this new question of mine by saying that the present study aims at clarifying the *analogical* character of incommunicability.

6. Thinking about the arguments that have been made for the divine unicity, especially the argument based on the divine incommunicability, has been particularly important in developing the analysis of the present chapter.

7. I do not call into question the communicability of the divine nature in relation to creation; God's is not an incommunicability that prevents any being from bearing any

Now let us look for the weakest possible incommunicability—that incommunicability without which a being would cease to amount to a determinate being. Consider a copy of today's newspaper, of which, we will assume, millions of copies have been printed. Any copy is of course incommunicably itself and is not any other. But notice that it is unreasonable to take any interest in the incommunicable being of the one copy. Whatever interests me in the one copy would interest me equally in any other copy; no one copy has anything of possible interest to me that I could not as well find in any other copy. The incommunicable being of each copy exists entirely for the sake of that which is common to them all; it is there only for the sake of instantiating and multiplying the communicable. This is what makes each copy of the paper a mere instance or specimen,[8] and as repeatable as could be. Only in the most minimal sense can we say that each copy of the paper "is itself and is not another"; for the predominance of the communicable in each copy greatly weakens the contrast between each copy and the others.

This predominance is reflected in the impossibility of discriminating between one copy of the paper and another. If I step away from my desk, on which sits today's paper, and then return, I cannot tell if the paper I find on my return is the one I left or a substitute. If I see two copies next to each other I can discriminate between them, but not if I see them one after another; in this case I cannot tell whether there is one or two. This curious *indiscernibility of the individual* reflects the strong dominance in the copies of that which is common to all of them, and the extreme weakness of the incommunicable being of each.

---

resemblance to Him (in the last chapter we will study the resemblance between God and human persons). I say only that it is an incommunicability that prevents the existence of other Gods. There is an analogy to this among finite beings: the incommunicability of Socrates prevents the existence of a second Socrates, but it does not prevent the followers and admirers of Socrates from imitating Socrates and patterning themselves on him and so becoming Socratic thinkers.

8. The reader will see why I am less than enthusiastic about Gracia's proposal to call incommunicable individuals by the name of "instances," entities that instantiate but cannot be instantiated (Gracia, 1988, 43–56). Though of course I accept that each individual human person is an instance of person considered as a universal, nevertheless "instance" suggests to many the particularly poor individuality of the *mere specimen* and thus seems to be dangerous in a discourse about persons. Furthermore, we will see in section 5 that not all aspects of a person can be taken as instances of some universal. We will see that there is in each person something so radically the person's own that the distinction between "instance" and "instantiated universal" has no place anymore—just as it has no place with God.

Let us suppose that one day the presses broke down after printing only one copy of the paper, resulting in a great interest in the one copy and a great demand for it. There would still be no more interest in its incommunicable being than on any other day. The one copy is still desired only for the sake of its communicable content; the focusing of everyone's attention on the one copy comes only from the accident that there is only one, and not from any discovery of some hitherto unsuspected incommunicability of being in the one copy.

It is hard to imagine how any being could possibly be weaker than the newspaper in "being itself and not another." We can, therefore, say that such a mere specimen-being forms the extreme opposite to the being that has its nature as so incommunicably its own as to be the only possible being of its nature. Here is the contrast between the barest minimum of incommunicable being and the absolute fullness of it. We need now to inquire whether there are not, between these extremes, different possible "measures" of incommunicable being, and which measure the human person has.

It seems that the incommunicability of being gets stronger as we "ascend" in the system of being, moving as it were in the direction of the being that has an absolute incommunicability of being in itself. Thus even the most elementary living being, existing as it does out of an inner center, is incommunicably itself beyond anything on the order of the newspaper; we can say of it far more properly than of the newspaper that it is itself and is not another. Of course we find communicable natures and a far-reaching repeatability among the individuals of a common nature, and yet we can hardly speak here, as with the newspaper, of mere specimens, of individuals existing for no other reason than to instantiate universals. A professor of biology may treat a given insect as a mere specimen of its species, but we sense right away that he is taking a particular approach, determined by his scientific and pedagogical concerns, and that his approach, legitimate as it may be, is not entirely adequate to the being of the insect and thus does not acquaint him with the insect as it is in its own right. But there is no lack of objectivity in taking the newspaper as the mere bearer of a communicable content; this is simply to take the paper for what it really and objectively is.

We can also say that the metaphysical "space" between each copy of the same newspaper is much smaller than the "space" between each individual living being of even the most elementary species. The communicable nature of each living being is incorporated, as it were, into the stronger incommunicable being that each has, and this reduces the communicability of its nature. The communicable content is almost "free-floating" in the case of the newspaper; it becomes much more a being's own in the case of a living being. This explains our sense that individual insects are less "abstract" and more "concrete" in their being than the copies of the newspaper.[9] The copies are in their being "closer" to an ideal type and are subjected more strictly to it as a result of existing only to instantiate it; thus they share in the abstractness of it.[10]

Still stronger is the incommunicability of being in *conscious* living beings; precisely the factor of consciousness strengthens the inner center out of which the being lives and so strengthens the incommunicability of the being, which we experience when we sense the greater concreteness of conscious living beings. In the case of the animals that play a role in the life of human beings, one experiences so strong an incommunicability of being that one is even inclined to speak, for the first time in our ascent to ever higher levels of being, of a certain unrepeatability.

The incommunicability found in human persons, however, is incomparable with any order of being below the person. In the realm of our direct experience the human person goes farthest beyond the specimen-being of each copy of the newspaper, even though, as we saw, the human person does not have the greatest conceivable incommunicability.

There will of course be those who find, with respect to unrepeatability, no essential difference at all between human persons and the higher animals that play a role in the lives of persons. Perhaps we should ask such persons whether they really think that it is immoral to *own* animals as property or to *use* them for one's own ends (we assume a use that is made without pain being wantonly inflicted on them). But if no one can reasonably object to using them or owning them, then they are not *sui iuris,* they do not have a being of their own as persons have: but then one can hardly say that they are incommunicably their own in the sense of personal incommunicability.

9. It is an interesting question why the element of incommunicability never seems to become as weak in nature as it does in some things of human design—why mere specimens seem to exist only in the realm of human making.

10. But this loose and almost metaphorical talk of "abstract" in no way means to suggest that there is anything abstract or general or universal that really enters into the makeup of any one copy of the newspaper. I have not forgotten what I said in the previous section, namely that all the parts, properties, features, moments of a real being are in some sense incommunicably the being's own and are therefore concrete and real as it is concrete and real.

It may also help to distinguish between the incommunicability proper to persons and the derived incommunicability that can be acquired by interacting with persons. The higher animals can in various ways be drawn into the world of persons, living with them and participating in their world; through this participation they sometimes get raised above themselves, receiving a spiritual refinement that they could not develop out of themselves. And then it is not surprising—though how it happens is entirely mysterious—if something of the unrepeatability of persons begins to appear in the animals living with human persons.

There seems to be another and more direct way in which certain animals share in personal being: the very fact that they are dear to human persons lets them share in the dignity and unrepeatability of these persons. But it is an unrepeatability that they do not have in their own right; it exists primarily in the persons who care for them. It, too, is only a derived unrepeatability, not to be confused with the proper and intrinsic unrepeatability of persons.

The development of our reflection in the following section leads us particularly deep into the mystery of personal selfhood. It will show how surprisingly close the incommunicability of human persons approaches to the supreme incommunicability of God.

3. A certain "absoluteness" or "infinity" of the human person

Though there are many persons, each person exists *as if he were the only one.* With this expression I mean something very definite. When we consider the many copies of the same newspaper, or for that matter the many insects of the same species, and then consider any one copy of the paper, or any one insect, then the one seems to be inconsiderable in comparison to the many; it seems to be "relativized" by the many, to get smaller in the midst of them, and to be reduced to insignificance by them. We have here the quantitative relations of larger and smaller that Socrates so marvels at in the *Theatetus,* when he observes that 6 can become larger, not by becoming 7 or 8, but by being compared to 2, and can become smaller, not by becoming 5 or 4, but by being compared to 12. Since copies of a newspaper, or insects of a species, are governed by these laws of finite numerical quantity, it follows that if a large quantity of them gets reduced by one, or enlarged by one, nothing much seems to have happened to the quantity; the change is negligible. In relation to millions or billions, one is very small.

Now persons are not subject to these laws of numerical quantity. Or more exactly: the more we consider human beings according to what is "nature" in them, according to that which only happens in them, then the more they are subject to these laws; but the more we consider them as persons, then the less they are subject to them. According to one estimate, there have existed until now some 77 billion human beings. But no one person becomes small in the presence of all these other persons, or is relativized in their presence; no one comes to represent an inconsiderable quantity in the realm of personal being, and to be overwhelmed by the many other persons. Each rather has personhood as so incommunicably his own that, though he is not the only person, he nevertheless "appears in being" as if he were the only one. If we must speak of persons in terms of number, then it would seem to be vastly more appropriate to introduce infinite numbers, and to say that each person represents "infinitely many," so that when one person is added to another it is like adding one numerical infinity to another numerical infinity: just as the second infinity adds infinitely much to the first, and yet, paradoxically, adds nothing, since there is nothing more than infinitely many, so one person adds infinitely much to another, and yet in a way adds nothing. It seems to be a particularly "worldly" way of considering persons to subject them to the laws of finite numerical quantity and to think that each person gets smaller as the number of persons he is compared with gets larger. One recovers a sense of their personhood only by realizing that each person has a certain "absoluteness" of being, by which I mean not a divine self-existence *(esse a se et per se),* but rather a curious metaphysical "insensitivity" to the presence of other persons, an inability to be relativized by them in the quantitative sense just explained.[11]

It may seem as if we have lost track of the incommunicability of persons, for this "absoluteness" or "infinity" seems to express each person being a whole of his own and no mere part, and with this we seem to

11. One way of trying to find in St. Thomas something of this "absoluteness" of human persons is to consider whether it is not implied in his teaching that *ratio partis contrariatur rationi personae* ("the concept of a part is opposed to that of person"), which I cited in the previous chapter. If human persons were entirely subject to laws of finite numerical quantity, then they would be small parts of an immense whole. By reflecting closely on each person as a whole of his or her own and no mere part, one can find a way to the "absoluteness" of which I speak in the text. The reader will have already noticed that in the present section I am exploring not only the incommunicability of persons (the third statement about personal selfhood that I formulated in Chapter 1.2), but also that wholeness in virtue of which persons are never mere parts (the second statement).

be going back to our second statement about personal selfhood in the previous chapter. Recall that it is our third statement about personal selfhood that is expressed in terms of incommunicability. On the other hand, our four statements pick out aspects of selfhood that are interrelated in such a way that the discussion of one is bound to pass over into the other. This is just what we find here; this absoluteness or infinity seems almost to coincide with personal incommunicability. For each human person, through his absoluteness/infinity, approximates in an amazing way to the supreme incommunicability of the being that can only exist as one. Though human persons do not have this supreme, divine incommunicability, since each after all exists as "one among many others," each nevertheless stands in a unique negative relation to all the others, *having so strong a being of his own that he exists as if in a sense the others did not exist.* Guardini expresses this in a profound way:

> The one who says "I" exists only once. This fact is so radical that the question arises whether the person as such can really be classified, or what the classifications must be in order that man may be placed in them as a person. Can we—to take an elementary form of classification—count persons? We can count *Gestalten,* individuals, personalities—but can we, while doing justice to the concept of "person," speak meaningfully of "two persons"?... Here reason balks.[12]

In one of his writings John Henry Newman reflects on the very point that we are trying to understand here, namely that each person "is as whole and independent a being in himself, as if there were no one else in the whole world but he." He begins his reflection by dwelling on the difficulty of *realizing* this wholeness of each person. Thus he says,

> do you think that a commander of an army realizes it, when he sends a body of men on some dangerous service? I am not speaking as if he were wrong in so sending them; I only ask in matter of fact, does he, think you, commonly understand that each of those poor men has a soul, a soul as dear to himself, as precious in its nature, as his own? Or does he not rather look on the body of men collectively, as one mass, as parts of a whole, as but the wheels or springs of some great machine, to which he assigns the individuality, not to each soul that goes to make it up?

The commander looks upon his men precisely in terms of those laws of finite numerical quantity, according to which four or five men are really

---

12. Guardini, *The World and the Person* (Chicago: Regnery, 1965), 215–216. I have modified in several places this English so as to bring it closer to the German.

very few, and a hundred men are far more, and a thousand far more still. There is nothing in the commander's point of view that would let him think of any one of his soldiers as if the only one; he thinks in terms of substitutable parts and not in terms of incommunicable individuals. Newman offers another example of how we think about human beings in such a way as to lose the incommunicability of each of them:

> Or again, survey some populous town: crowds are pouring through the streets; some on foot, some in carriages; while the shops are full, and the houses too, could we see into them. Every part of it is full of life. Hence we gain a general idea of splendour, magnificence, opulence, and energy.

Again we have a way of looking which sees crowds rather than incommunicable persons. Newman proceeds to reverse this way of looking and to break through to the "infinity" of each incommunicable person. I continue quoting without any break.

> But what is the truth? why, that every being in that great concourse is his own centre, and all things about him are but shades, but a "vain shadow," in which he "walketh and disquieteth himself in vain." He has his own hopes and fears, desires, judgments, and aims; he is everything to himself, and no one else is really any thing. No one outside of him can really touch him, can touch his soul. . . . He has a depth within him unfathomable, an infinite abyss of existence; and the scene in which he bears part for the moment is but like a gleam of sunshine upon its surface.[13]

Newman powerfully expresses the contrast between persons and small replaceable parts in some vast whole; each person lives out of an "infinite abyss of existence" and exists as if the only person. Some readers, however, may think that Newman overshoots the mark in saying that "he is everything to himself, and no one else is really any thing." I will address this difficulty in the next section, "Incommunicability and Interpersonal Communion."

Now that we have explored the "infinity" and the "absoluteness" of human persons, we proceed to mention briefly a relatively new personalist argument for the presence of something immaterial in the being of the person. However one defines matter, is it not spread out in space in such a way as to be subject to what we have been calling the laws of finite numerical quantity? Given any one material something, is it not the case that it, together with a second material something just like it, is

13. Newman, "The Individuality of the Soul," *Parochial and Plain Sermons* (London: Rivingtons, 1869), IV, 81–83.

twice as much as it alone? Are not four such things four times as much as the first? Does it not become a negligible quantity when it becomes one of millions? In defying these laws of numerical quantity, do persons not step out of the realm of the spatial and the material and so give evidence of something immaterial in their being? Indeed, I might have asked this question at an earlier point in the present chapter; I might have asked in the previous section whether a purely material thing does not always admit of being copied in a second and a third material thing, and whether the unrepeatability of the person does not directly imply the presence of something immaterial in the person. If I express myself tentatively, it is because these arguments for immateriality could be completed only after the concept of matter has received more clarification than this study allows.

Before concluding this section, in which we have gone far in our affirmation of the incommunicability of human persons, I should add that human persons are of course *also* subject to the laws of numerical quantity. Our being really has a quantitative aspect in virtue of which we really are subject to those laws. It seems that this results from the fact that we are compositions of person and nature. We cannot simply identify ourselves without residue with the "infinity" and "absoluteness" of our being, as if our finitude and our quantitative smallness were illusions; no, we are as truly finite and as truly located in space and time as we are "infinite" in the sense explained. This means that it is not necessarily illegitimate to consider human persons in large groups and to consider each one as a small fractional part of the group, as when economists try to calculate how many people will have to sell some item before its price gets depressed, or as when a general considers how many men he needs to retake a hill. The quantitative view is not in itself erroneous; it just runs the great risk of obscuring the sight of personhood in each human being. This is why Buber said that in our relation to other persons, it is impossible always to live in the I-Thou relation; the I-Thou will often give way to the I-It.[14] This giving way is not necessarily a tragic fall into a depersonalized view; for Buber it need not involve any depersonalization. It may be nothing other than the recognition that we human persons are not pure persons, but rather have a mixed personhood, one composed of person and nature.

14. Martin Buber, *I and Thou,* tr. Ronald Gregor Smith (New York: Charles Scribner's Sons, 1958), 34.

4. Incommunicability and interpersonal communion

Though Newman reflects deeply on the mysterious "infinity" of human persons, he does so in such a way as to raise a disturbing question, as I have already acknowledged. In saying that "he is everything to himself, and no one else is really any thing," does Newman mean that persons, as they awaken to their incommunicability, break away from others and want to have nothing more to do with them? Do persons live their incommunicability only by renouncing all bonds of interpersonal communion? Does "incommunicability" imply a negation of communicating and sharing among persons? An important question, which expresses the unease that some readers may feel with all this talk about incommunicability and that they perhaps feel more strongly than ever on reading these lines of Newman.[15]

Various responses may be given to this serious and challenging objection.

1. The others whom Newman says are "nothing" are others taken in a very definite way; they are the others who form a quantitatively large totality in comparison with which any single human being almost disappears as a hardly noticeable quantity. When we come to ourselves as persons we have indeed to break away from the others who threaten to swallow us up like this, we have to turn away from them saying, "no one else is really any thing to me"; only in this way can we experience in ourselves our existing as persons. Of course on closer examination this turning away from others is really a turning away, not exactly from them, but from the view of them that exaggerates their quantitative aspect.

2. There is also a *turning towards others* on the basis of personal incommunicability. I can encounter another not only according to the laws of finite numerical quantity, but in his or her infinity, as if he or she

---

15. In the effort to find a place in the theory of personal incommunicability for the social nature of man, one should take care not to look for it only in the mixed character of human personhood of which we were just speaking. It is not just as compositions of person and nature, or of personality and individuality, as Maritain puts it, that we escape from our solitude and form groups. As I will try to show in the present section, it is precisely our incommunicability—not that which limits incommunicability, but incommunicability itself—which underlies and makes possible the deepest forms of interpersonal life. Norris Clarke insists on this in his *Person and Being* (Milwaukee: Marquette University Press, 1993), 75–76, when he says that it is not just through need and poverty but also through self-communicating abundance that we turn to others.

were the only person. This is to encounter the other deeply as person; it is the beginning of any authentic intersubjectivity. Thus we should not be surprised to find in Martin Buber's characterization of the Thou of an I-Thou encounter the very "infinity" that we are studying here. "The world of *It* is set in the context of space and time. The world of the *Thou* is not set in the context of either of these."[16] Buber seems to mean space and time in the sense of that quantitative realm where one human being is something very small, and many of them are something much larger. If he wants to affirm "infinity" of the Thou, then he does just what one would expect in refusing to think of the Thou as existing without residue in space and time. Buber comes even closer to this "infinity" when he says of my Thou: "But with no neighbour, and whole in himself, he is *Thou* and fills the heavens. This does not mean that nothing exists except himself. But all else lives in *his* light."[17] Notice that Buber has to guard against seeming to say that *only* the Thou exists; this invites us to think that in saying that the Thou has no neighbor and "fills the heavens," Buber is close to my own affirmation that the Thou as incommunicable person exists as if he or she were the only person. The point is that our discourse on incommunicability does not tend to solipsism, nor do the thoughts expressed above by Newman; the contrary is true. Incommunicability is found in others no less than in myself; and only if we encounter others in all their incommunicability do we encounter them as Thou and have the opportunity of entering into deep interpersonal communion with them.

3. The suspicion of solipsism can also be removed by considering what is required for one person to love another. If I see someone only as a specimen of lovable qualities that can in principle exist in the same way in other human beings, then I precisely do not love that someone; I love his or her qualities and excellences, but my love does not reach the other as person, nor will the other feel loved by me. I have to see in the excellences of the other his or her incommunicable selfhood; only then can I love with a love that reaches the other as person. This means that to encounter incommunicability in another is not to be separated from the other, but on the contrary to fulfill one of the conditions for loving the other.

4. If we now consider love from the point of view of the one who is loved, then we get a further reason why personal incommunicability

16. Martin Buber, op. cit., 100.
17. Ibid., 8.

does not exclude interpersonal communion. Persons can be known either according to some communicable form or known according to their incommunicable selves. I can be known as "a human being," as "a male," as "an American," as "a professor," or I can be known as the person I am beyond all such types and stereotypes, beyond even the sum of them all. Now each person has a profound need to be known in all of his or her incommunicable selfhood. John Henry Newman expresses the point quite forcefully in a religious setting when he says: "But men of keener hearts would be overpowered by despondency, and would even loathe existence, did they suppose themselves under the mere operation of fixed laws, powerless to excite the pity or the attention of Him who has appointed them."[18] What Newman says about our relation to God has its truth even among human beings; we would loathe existence if we were always known and dealt with by our fellows only according to some type which we (and others) instantiate and were never known according to what we (alone) incommunicably are. We see yet again how the logic of incommunicability, when thought through fully, leads into the interpersonal and does not impede it. For implied in what we are saying is that persons not only exist as incommunicable persons but that they need, profoundly need, to be recognized as such by others. More exactly: it is precisely the incommunicable in them that cries out for recognition by others. Perhaps they cannot even fully believe in their own incommunicability except on the basis of this recognition of it by other persons. My personal incommunicability does not isolate me from others but rather from the beginning looks to others who know me and love me in all my incommunicability.

5. I just mentioned in passing the encounter with God. Let us now consider why it is that the incommunicability of human persons makes it possible for there to be such a thing as an interpersonal encounter between them and God. Religious thinkers like Kierkegaard have often pointed out that a human person, precisely in virtue of that "infinity" or "absoluteness" of which I have spoken, can "appear" directly or immediately before God. It seems that a being exists at a much greater "distance" from God if it is only a small part of some finite totality, for then God would deal with that being only as part of the totality. Since persons cannot be completely encompassed by any totality and be made small by it, since they stand in being as wholes of their own, each existing as if the only person, it seems that their relation to God must also be

18. John Henry Newman, *Parochial and Plain Sermons*, III, 124.

an immediate one. With this hint, which of course has to be developed, we catch a glimpse of an entirely new way in which incommunicability can underlie the interpersonal.

6. Furthermore, we can say that not only individual persons *but also the encounters between persons, and interpersonal relations,* are incommunicable. They are not mere specimens of general kinds; they share in the mystery of personal concreteness that I am expressing here in terms of incommunicability. Ethicians have recently reflected on the uniqueness of each moral *situation* in which I find myself with other persons, and they have pointed out the limits of general moral norms in determining what I ought to do in a given situation (more on this in section 7 of this chapter). Something similar to the idea of a situation, but on a larger scale, is found in the idea of *an historical moment,* or *kairos,* which also expresses an interpersonal structure that shares in the unrepeatability of the persons who constitute it. And so we say: personal incommunicability does not imply that persons are isolated from each other; far from preventing interpersonal relations, it stamps them with itself. Not only that, but personal incommunicability seems to find in the interpersonal an irreplaceable way of expressing and developing itself.

7. I have been defending incommunicability against the objection by showing how it does not exclude but rather grounds interpersonal communion. I can offer a new kind of response by the reminder that our whole being is not incommunicably our own; there is that in each of us which is in some sense common to us all. We share human nature; it is not incommunicably mine, for you have it as well. Now our common human nature can become the basis for interpersonal communion. I know of fears and joys in myself, and I thereby know of them in fellow human beings, since they, too, have the same human nature susceptible to the same fears and joys. It is not as if I infer from what I know in myself to what I assume must be in others; it is rather the case that experiences rooted in my human nature are in a sense not exclusively my own in the first place; they are such as to enable me to experience others in myself, so to say. When one studies the profound things that Newman says about sympathy between persons one finds that he consistently bases our capacity for sympathy on our sharing a common nature.[19] Since our talk about personal incommunicability, then, in no way excludes all that is

19. See, for example, sermon 7 in Newman's *Sermons Preached on Various Occasions.*

common to human persons, we can do full justice to the interpersonal
life that is based on our common nature.

8. I will just mention an issue that will be discussed in Chapter 8.1 in
connection with our study of the contingency and finitude of human
persons. We will see that, though we persons are not mere parts in any
whole, we are nevertheless signed in our personhood by a certain partiality and are thus revealed as finite in our personal selfhood. Each of us
realizes human personhood in his own way, which is not another person's
way; there is a fullness of human personhood that exists in all human
persons taken together and that exceeds the capacity of any one person.
This partiality implies, as we shall see, a fundamental connectedness
with all other persons, for the human personhood proper to me is elaborated and developed in all other persons. Here the connectedness is not,
as in the previous argument, based on our *common* human nature but on
the *complementarity* of your personal being with mine.

9. If now for a moment we step beyond the bounds of philosophy
proper and look to the mystery of the Trinity, we can see anew that
personal incommunicability does not isolate. Each of the three divine
persons is incommunicably himself and is not any other divine person,
and yet they share among themselves the divine nature and the divine
being. Not only that, but we can say from the point of view of Christian
belief that each divine person has the divine nature *as if he were the only
divine person;* that is, none of them merely shares in the divine nature in
the sense of only partially having it and of being completed by other
divine persons who have it in a different way. And yet this supreme
possession of the divine nature in each divine person does not prevent
there being three persons in the unity of one divine nature and one divine being.

The incommunicability of human persons, then, does not undermine
any of the things that we might want to say about interpersonal communion and social solidarity: in part it precisely underlies these things,
in part it is open to being completed by them.[20]

---

20. I might mention one other source of the suspicion of solipsism felt in relation to
my understanding of incommunicability. One sometimes thinks of interpersonal unity
in terms of fusion, or amalgamation, and then, of course, personal incommunicability
appears to be the enemy of interpersonal unity. One needs to see that amalgamation
represents a metaphysically low and primitive form of unity, which can hardly be compared with other higher forms of unity that presuppose distinct individuals.

5. *Two aspects of the incommunicable selfhood of human persons: the existential and the essential*

Existential incommunicability. Many beings are defined only in terms of their communicable elements; and while it is understood that each individual being falling under the definition has something incommunicably its own, this moment of incommunicability is not taken into the definition. Even man has been defined in this way, as when Aristotle defines him as a rational animal. Though Aristotle knows that each individual human being has something incommunicably his own, his famous definition only alludes to this (*a* rational animal), expressing itself for the most part in terms of the communicable moments of rationality and animality. Now when it comes to man as person, this kind of communicable definition is no longer adequate, and the incommunicability of the person has to be named in any worthy definition. Boethius seems to be aware of this in his celebrated definition of the person, *persona est substantia individua naturae rationalis:* a person is an individual substance of rational nature. In taking "individual substance" into the definition, he takes the element of incommunicability into it, and this in such a way as to form a contrast with the Aristotelian definition.[21]

But there is another medieval definition of the person even worthier of mention here, since it explicitly names incommunicable existence. Richard of St. Victor says that a person, whether human or divine, is *rationalis naturae individua existentia,* and then proceeds to indicate that the *individua existentia* can as well be called *incommunicabilis existentia,* so that we can translate: a person is an incommunicable existence of a rational nature.[22] One would not define an animal as an in-

---

21. St. Thomas seems to stress this very excellence in the Boethian definition when he makes it his own in the *Summa Theologiae,* I, q. 29, a. 1: "although the universal and particular exist in every genus, nevertheless, in a certain special way, the individual belongs to the genus of substance. . . . Further still, in a more special and perfect way, the particular and the individual are found in the rational substances which have dominion over their own actions; and which are not only made to act, like others, but which can act of themselves; for actions belong to singulars. Therefore also the individuals of the rational nature have a special name even among other substances; and this name is *person*" (translation of the Fathers of the English Dominican Province).

22. Richard of St. Victor, *De Trinitate,* IV, 23. In *La Trinité* (Paris, 1959), Gaston Salet, S.J., ed., 282 and 284. Richard is of course looking for a definition of person that will hold for all persons, including the three divine persons. He has just (cap. 21) re-

communicable existence of an animal nature; though each animal is indeed incommunicably itself, it seems strange to give its incommunicable existence such prominence in the definition of the animal. It seems more natural to define the animal in communicable terms, as in terms of genus and species. The moment of incommunicable selfhood, then, seems more important in persons than in non-persons; this moment belongs more centrally to persons than to non-persons, and for this reason has to be explicitly named in any definition of personal being.[23]

In the following I think Guardini wants to insist on the inadequacy of defining the person exclusively in terms of communicable moments.

> To the question, "What is your person?" I cannot answer "my body, my soul, my reason, my will, my freedom, my spirit." All this is not as yet the person, but, as it were, the stuff of which it is made; the person itself is the fact that it exists in the form of belonging to oneself (*in der Form der Selbstgehörigkeit*).[24]

Guardini seems to be pleading for a definition, or better, for a philosophical account of personhood that explicitly includes the *incommunicabilis existentia* of Richard.

And so we hold for a kind of "existential" account of the incommunicable selfhood, which seems to be a certain fullness and intensity of concrete existence, as the definition of Richard suggests, and as Newman,

---

jected the definition of Boethius *(substantia individua naturae rationalis)* on the grounds that if a divine person were a separate substance, there could not be three divine persons in one divine substance. So in his preferred definition of person he replaces *substantia* with *existentia incommunicabilis,* adapting thereby to the Trinity the truth in the Boethian definition. In the text I am at present trying to find in our lived experience of persons that incommunicable existence at which Richard arrived by the path of theological speculation.

23. Cf. the excellent discussion of this in Hans-Eduard Hengstenberg, *Philosophische Anthropologie* (Munich-Salzburg: Anton Pustet Verlag, 1984), "Der Mensch als Individuum," 329–331.

24. Guardini, op. cit., 118 (I have corrected the translation in one place); German in *Welt und Person* (Würzburg: Werkbund Verlag, 1962), 128. It seems to us, by the way, that the notoriously difficult opening sentences of Kierkegaard's *The Sickness unto Death* are trying to say just what Guardini says here and what we have been saying in the text. I refer to the sentences: "Man is spirit. But what is spirit? Spirit is the self. But what is the self? The self is a relation which relates itself to its own self. . . . Man is a synthesis of the infinite and the finite, of the temporal and the eternal, of freedom and necessity. . . . So regarded, man is not yet a self." Kierkegaard seems to be saying that it is not enough to find the component elements or principles of the personal self; one has also to bring out "die Form der Selbstgehörigkeit" in which the self exists.

too, suggests, in speaking of the "infinite abyss of existence" in each person, and as Guardini suggests in speaking of the elusive factor in the definition of the person as a certain "form of existence." This puts us in a position to discern a faint analogy between human persons and God, or rather another aspect of the analogy that we have already discerned between the incommunicability of human persons and the divine unicity. Theologians say that God is that being whose essence is to exist, whose essence cannot be rightly thought apart from His existence, who *is* His existence; this is indeed the basis for the never-dying attempts to establish an ontological argument for the existence of God. It is something just like this that I am saying, with Guardini, regarding human persons; what persons are is not rightly conceived apart from the incommunicable selfhood of each of them. Of course, no concrete being is rightly conceived apart from its incommunicable selfhood, as we saw, for apart from this it is nothing at all. And yet incommunicable selfhood belongs in quite another way to persons; it enters with quite another intimacy and centrality into personal being than into non-personal being, as is especially clear in the definition of Richard of St. Victor. And though we cannot make an ontological argument for the existence of human persons, proceeding from the idea of the human person to the existence of such persons, we nevertheless grievously misconceive personhood whenever we think of it apart from the way in which each person is incommunicably himself or herself.

One last reflection, this on the particular difficulty of coming to know incommunicable existence in human persons. Guardini adds that the *Form der Selbstgehörigkeit* of which he speaks explains the "peculiar way in which the person eludes our grasp. The person eludes being uttered."[25] This perhaps helps us to understand why it is possible to make great progress in philosophically grasping the communicable parts of human nature but have an underdeveloped grasp of the incommunicable in man, and hence no adequate sense of man as person. It is in fact just this discrepancy that we seem to find in the philosophical understanding of man developed in Greek philosophy. In reading the *Republic* of Plato we can only marvel at the contrast between the profound analysis of the human soul, its levels and its ruling principle, on the one hand, and the proposal, in Book V, to dispose of defective newborns, on the other. This proposal does not rest in the first place on any *reductionistic* understand-

---

25. *Welt und Person,* ibid. This sentence is missing from the English translation cited above.

ing of man, on any materialism, or on any cynicism with respect to the spiritual in man; it does not seem to rest on any major error at all regarding the communicable principles of human nature. It seems rather to rest on the failure to grasp the incommunicable selfhood of each human person. Plato does not seem to know how to do justice to the amazing *concreteness* of persons, of the density and heaviness of their existence; insofar as all beings, including human beings, exist under the Ideas as specimens of them, they are abstract in their being.[26] Aristotle wants to vindicate the selfhood of every real being, but is impeded by all the Platonism that remains in his thought. The decisive breakthrough to grasping the selfhood of persons came only much later in the history of philosophy. But it costs even us no small effort to hold fast to this selfhood and not to let go of the incommunicability of the person, losing it amidst all the communicable elements of human nature.

Essential incommunicability. As just explained, it is an "existential" account of personhood for which I am arguing; the Platonic failure to do justice to incommunicable selfhood seems to be a certain "essentialist" excess. At first it may seem as if all incommunicability were by its very nature existential and as if the essential[27] were equivalent to the commu-

26. Cf. the judgment of the great Italian historian of philosophy, Giovanni Reale, on Plotinus: "Plotinus, though he teaches the necessity of drawing ourselves from external things into the inner part of ourselves, of our souls, so as to find the truth, nevertheless speaks of the soul and of the interiority of man only in the abstract, or rather in general, rigorously depriving the soul of its individuality and ignoring the concrete question of personality. Plotinus never spoke of himself in his writings and did not even want to speak of himself to his friends. Porphery writes: 'Plotinus had the appearance of someone who was ashamed to be in a body. As a result of this spiritual disposition, he was hesitant to tell about his birth or his parents or his country.'" Reale proceeds to contrast Plotinus with Augustine in a way that is revealing for our purposes. "Augustine, on the contrary, speaks constantly of himself, and his masterpiece is precisely the *Confessions,* in which he not only speaks at length of his parents and of his country and of persons dear to him, but exposes his very soul in all its most hidden folds and in all the intimate tensions of his 'will.'" Reale and Antiseri, *Il pensiero occidentale dalle origini ad oggi,* I (Brescia, 1985), 333; my translation. The contrast of Plotinus and Augustine is found in the chapter on Augustine, in a section entitled, "The Discovery of the Person and the Metaphysics of Interiority."

27. I assume that my talk of "essential" in contrast to "existential" is sufficiently clear without discussing the contrast as a subject of its own. I am, of course, distinguishing two concrete moments of a concrete being; thus our talk of "essential" in this context does not mean essential in a general or universal sense, but in a concretely real sense. With "essential" we refer to everything belonging to what or how a being is, and in particular to the what and the how which stands in a closer relation to the "identity" of the being.

nicable.[28] But closer reflection will, I think, lead us to agree with Scheler, who writes: "*Essence* . . . has nothing to do with *universality*. . . . Therefore there are essences that are given only in one particular individual."[29] This implies that we can discriminate between existential and essential aspects of incommunicability. I will (1) point out a kind of essential incommunicability which belongs to all beings, then (2) point out a kind of essential incommunicability proper to persons, and finally (3) suggest the existence of another and stronger kind of essential incommunicability in human persons.

1. As I said above, Socrates has his own humanity, which we must never confound with the humanity of Plato. Since humanity belongs to the essence of each, we find in each of them something of essential incommunicability. Of course, there is this kind of essential incommunicability in every person, as in every being; while participating in the general idea of humanity, each human being has his or her own humanity. And in fact, as we saw, every part and aspect of the essence of a concrete being is in some sense incommunicably that being's own.

2. When I spoke above of experiencing someone as if he or she were the only human being, I was speaking of a stronger incommunicability of humanity in that person. I was speaking of an experience in which the humanity of the person forms so close a unity with his or her incommunicability that the communicability proper to humanity is reduced and, as it seems, almost abolished. It is as if humanity were to an amazing extent incorporated into the incommunicability of a person. Of course, other aspects of the essence of a human being besides humanity can be incorporated like this into the incommunicable being of a person. Thus, for example, the womanhood of a woman can, in the eyes of the man who loves her, form such a unity with her personal incommunicability that she stands before him as if she were the only woman: "*che sola a me par donna,*" says Petrarch.

3. In saying that each angel *is* its own species and is thus the only possible member of the species, or rather that with the angels there is no distinction between one species and plural individuals in the species, Aquinas ascribes to each angel an essential content that is not communi-

28. Thus Josef Cardinal Ratzinger, speaking of Richard of St. Victor's definition of the person, says, "This definition correctly sees that in its theological meaning 'person' does not lie on the level of essence, but of existence" ("Concerning the notion of person in theology," *Communio* 17 [1990], 449).

29. Max Scheler, *Formalism in Ethics* (Evanston: Northwestern University Press, 1973), 489.

cable.[30] Is there, as Rahner and others have suggested, something similar, or at least something analogous, in human persons? Is there in each
person some essential content that is beyond the distinction between
universal form and concrete instance, so that the essential content is not
just participated in but rather completely possessed by the person, possessed in such a way as to eliminate the possibility of another person
participating in the same essential content? We ascribe this essential
incommunicability to God when we say that He does not participate in
His essence, but rather *is* His essence; our question is whether the human person resembles God in this respect by *being* in some analogous
way his own essence.[31] Does each human being perhaps exist as human
being *in his or her own way,* so that each does not just participate in but
is a sub-species of humanity? One should not be too quick to answer in
the negative on the grounds that being one's own essence is an exclusively divine way of relating to one's essence. Certainly one cannot give
this negative answer on Thomistic grounds, since St. Thomas holds, as I
just noted, that each angel—a non-divine being—*is* its own species and
so *is* a certain part of its essence. Our question can also be put like this:
is it enough to say that each human person has some essential content *as
if* he or she were that content (as I expressed it above in n. 2), or do we
have to go farther and say that each *really and literally* is that content?

In order to give an affirmative answer to this question it does not
suffice to point to the unrepeatability of the genetic makeup of a human
being, that is, of those traits of race, temperament, intelligence, etc.,
which depend on the genetic makeup of an individual. These traits are
indeed woven together in a given individual in a way that is not repeated
by other individuals, but this is only a relative unrepeatability. There is
after all no absurdity in exactly these traits being repeated in exactly
these interconnections in a second and a third individual—indeed, this
repeating is exactly what happens in the case of identical twins. But

30. I ought to add that Aquinas is not just trying to explain the particular perfection
of incommunicable being found in the angels, but is trying to draw the consequences of
the immateriality of the angels; he thinks that it takes matter in beings to ground the
possibility of a plurality of individuals in one and the same species. But it is not at all an
unnatural use of his thought to take it as also giving an account of the kind of incommunicable selfhood proper to angels, and as important for any discussion of personal
selfhood.

31. Whereas in discussing above the existential incommunicability of human persons I said that they resemble God insofar as He is His own existence or *esse,* I now
point out another aspect of their incommunicability by asking whether they resemble
God insofar as He is His own essence.

there is an absurdity in there being two copies of one and the same person. The incommunicability that we found above in a certain existential form, and into which we now inquire in asking about a possible essential form of it, lies at a deeper level in a human being. It lies in the depths of personal being; it is not a relative but an absolute incommunicability.

This essential incommunicability is also not found in beings such as "the last dinosaur," "the only daughter of the Smiths," "the first book written by Husserl." These phrases express, of course, a note that can be had only by one being and cannot be shared by that being with any other. But these one-of-a-kind beings do not have to have any particular strength or perfection of incommunicable being. This is why they include among themselves even non-persons and in fact even mere specimens ("the first copy of the *Times* printed today"). Their uniqueness seems to derive more from an intention of the mind that picks them out rather than from any inherent strength of their incommunicable being.

Having posed the question as carefully as possible, I say that I strongly incline to the answer that human persons do indeed possess the deeper incommunicability at which we are aiming in n. 3. Each person has an essential something that only he or she can have, or rather can be, an essential something that would be forever lost to the world, leaving a kind of irreparable metaphysical hole in it, if the person embodying it were to go out of existence altogether.

6. The value of human persons

Let us suppose that we misunderstood human beings as mere specimens of humanity. What value might we still experience in them? We could, it seems, still experience various values in them, such as values of "rationality" like intelligence, resourcefulness, and the like. But whatever the values, they would always be located in certain human qualities and excellences and not primarily in human beings themselves. A human being having intelligence could always be replaced by another human being having the same kind of intelligence; the value that we admire in the one we would continue to admire in the other; the exchange of human beings need have no consequences for the values that we admire. Now it is for our present purposes highly significant that the value called the dignity of the human person—the value in virtue of which persons merit unconditional respect—would no longer appear in our experience; whatever other values we would experience in the human specimens, this would not be one of them. As a result, there could be no moral objection to destroying a given human being, so long as his or her excellences lived on in other human beings. Nor would we be able to love persons; as I remarked above, we could only love the excellences of persons, but never the persons who have the excellences; the interchangeability of the persons prevents them from being loved as individuals.

Suppose now that in our apprehension of persons we were to undergo a great awakening to the incommunicable selfhood of each of them; suppose we were to become aware of the mysterious concreteness of human persons, and were to begin to experience each as if he or she were the only human person. What would change in our value consciousness? It would be immeasurably enlarged; no value would be lost and much value would be gained. In the incommunicable selfhood of human persons we would find value that is in a sense infinite value. In our new personalist perspective it would not be only qualities and excellences but rather also the subject of them, the one who has them, this or that particular human being, which would stand before us as worthy, good. Now for the first time the value datum called the dignity of the human person would appear, and it would appear as rooted in incommunicable selfhood. Moral imperatives to respect persons would also appear for the first time; we would no longer be bound just to respect worthy qualities and excellences, we would now be bound to respect this or that person, that is, to show a respect that is not transferable to other persons but which refers to each as incommunicable person. Love for other persons would also become possible for the first time, for it would now be possible to reach with our love beyond the qualities of persons and to attain to the persons themselves.[32]

Once again we see how far removed our understanding of personal incommunicability is from a social atomism according to which persons are ultimately isolated one from another. If it is the incommunicability of persons that grounds the moral imperative to respect them and that opens the possibility of loving them, then this incommunicability turns out to be a first principle of social solidarity and community.

---

32. It is remarkable that among the "definitions" of person found in the medieval masters there is one which defines person in terms of dignity; St. Thomas reports the definition according to which a person is a "*hypostasis proprietate distincta ad dignitatem pertinente:* a hypostasis distinct by reason of dignity" (cf. *Summa Theologiae*, I, 29, 3, ad 2).

Two aspects of the value of persons. One does not have to dwell long on the value in persons that is born of their incommunicable selfhood before noticing two distinct data. There is the dignity of each person in virtue of which we owe respect to persons;[33] but then there is the goodness or lovableness of a person which, once seen and experienced, awakens something like a love of friendship, or perhaps a spousal love, for that person. This lovableness is perhaps even more deeply rooted in the incommunicable selfhood of each person than the dignity of the person, because *every person* has this dignity, whereas the lovableness of a person is possessed only by that person and by no other. I am capable of recognizing the dignity of every person whom I meet and of showing him or her respect, but I am capable of recognizing the unique personal lovableness of only very few persons and I am capable of loving only these few. There is, strange to say, a certain communicability that remains in the dignity of the person, even though it is grounded precisely in the incommunicable selfhood of each person. The principle of incommunicability asserts itself more strongly, so to say, in the unrepeatable lovableness of a person. This is why we lack any general terms to express the lovableness of a particular person; we keenly experience here the ineffability, the unutterability of the incommunicable. But our language and concepts do not fail us in the same way when it comes to the dignity of the person; after all, "the dignity of the person" is a general term. It is as if I recognize a human being *as person* when I am mindful of his dignity and show him respect and abstain from all coercion and using, but recognize a human being *as this particular person* when I know him or her as friend or spouse. This of course seems paradoxical, for it seems impossible to recognize someone as person in any other way than as this particular person. And yet how can one deny that this distinction captures a real difference known to us all in experience?[34]

33. Sometimes people talk loosely about "dignity" and mean in fact "showing respect to a person," as when they say that someone was denied his or her dignity by being manipulated. I will not use the term like this, but will rather mean by dignity "that in virtue of which persons are owed respect." In this sense, dignity is not something that can be lost by persons when they are mistreated.

34. The difference is also shown in this, that the dignity of the person is very close to the person as subject of rights, so close that one can move back and forth between these two ideas without even noticing it (as Kant seems to do in Section II of the *Foundations of the Metaphysics of Morals*). But no one could confuse the unique personal preciousness of a person with that same person considered as a subject of rights; just as one could not confuse loving another with respecting the rights of another.

We can ask more questions about this curious distinction than we are equal to answering. Is it a distinction relative to our knowing in the sense that the value of the person appears as dignity when we know it only under a limited aspect, and appears as personal lovableness when we know it more fully and more concretely? Or does the distinction reflect some difference in reality? Could it be, for example, that the dignity of the person belongs more to what I called existential incommunicability, with the personal preciousness of each person belonging more to essential incommunicability?

Whenever in what immediately follows I do not need to discriminate between the dignity that commands respect and the more personal goodness that can elicit love, I shall speak simply of "the value of the person," meaning with this expression all value or goodness that is born of the incommunicable selfhood of a person and which is prior to the distinction between dignity and personal lovableness.

The value of every person in relation to the "greatness" of a few persons. A good way of testing whether people really understand the value of persons is to ask them to set it in relation to special abilities, talents, gifts of genius, and other such excellences which a few persons have but which most lack. Whoever does not understand that the value of the person completely overshadows these excellences and in a sense relativizes them does not really understand this value. Whoever does not understand how much worth persons have by being persons and what a relatively small value difference arises from one of them having some talent and another lacking it, does not really understand the dignity of persons. Of course even after one has grasped this in principle it can be difficult to hold fast to it in practice. How often it happens that, sensing our value as incommunicable persons and sensing at the same time that it is endangered by being ignored, we try to affirm it by *extraordinary achievements that set us apart from all others and that awaken their astonishment.* We thus confuse what is rare and unusual in the realm of the communicable with our incommunicable selves. We try to affirm our value as persons by trying to realize in ourselves values which, when compared with this fundamental value, are in a sense negligible. We think that, without special talents and achievements, we are in danger of being a defective person, a bad draft fit to be discarded and replaced; with this we absurdly overestimate the importance of special talents and at the same time underestimate the importance of simply being a person. We fall into this same confusion when we begin feeling a certain awe for geniuses and heroes and great men and women, and begin thinking (with Nietzsche) of all other human beings as forming an indistinct and uninteresting mass, as if real personal worth and dignity were found only in the realm of human "greatness."[35] There is a respect for the living and experiencing of the common man that is born of understanding the dignity of his personhood, and which has nothing to do with a democratic resentment against the aristocracy of human excellence. Thus it is, for example, a good personalist instinct that leads historians to relate wars not only from the point of view of the generals and the princes, but also from the point of view of the foot soldiers and the civilians. We touch here on the personalist foundations of genuine democracy, and we see how one could make personalist sense of the "equality" that is so prominent in the rhetoric of democracy; it is not an equality that has to deny the existence of real and important differences among human persons, but rather one that derives from the fact that persons already have a certain infinite worth in virtue of simply being persons.

The reader will readily understand why, from this point of view, I strenuously object to the "Beethoven-argument" against abortion, often made by well-intentioned people. They say that we are all immeasurably indebted to the mother of Beethoven for not aborting him, and they warn mothers who abort today that one of them may be depriving the world of a similar genius. This shifts the focus away from the value of

---

35. This point was seen and forcefully expressed by Josef Popper, an Austrian author who is no longer much read, in his *Das Individuum und die Bewertung menschlicher Existenzen* (Dresden, 1910), published under the pseudonym, Lynkeus. "The distinction between 'average' and 'outstanding' individuals must be completely rejected in the area of all these reflections. In public as well as in private life the loss of even the most insignificant—but harmless—human being must always be seen as something in itself terrible. The death of such a one leaves behind a 'hole in the world.' The tremendous number of deaths does nothing to reduce the significance of each individual" (161). Later we have an impressive account of the kind of experience out of which Popper's "ethical individualism," as it is called (see the article by Paul Edwards in the *Encyclopedia of Philosophy* on Popper and his ethical individualism), was born: "Some 30 or 35 years ago an enthusiastic admirer of the music of Wagner said in my presence to one of my dearest friends, who was not indeed an important personality but who was an extremely nice man: 'What is F. worth compared with eight measures of Wagner's *Tannhäuser*?' My friend became pale as a corpse and, wounded and bitter, protested against such a degradation of his existence. Such a way of thinking made on me so terrible an impression that to this day I have still not overcome it, and all that has been said in this book about the evaluation of human lives is just an outgrowth of this impression" (161, my translation).

the person to peripheral excellences, and trivializes the whole discussion. The loss of Beethoven would have been a terrible loss because the world would have been deprived of an incommunicable person; only quite secondarily would it have been a loss because the world would have been deprived of a musical genius. If we had to choose between having the music of Beethoven on the condition that we would lack Beethoven the person, and having Beethoven the person on the condition that he would be musically ungifted, we would have to choose him and forgo his music.[36]

Yet again we see how far removed our understanding of personal incommunicability is from a social atomism according to which persons are ultimately isolated one from another. For we have just seen how we are led by this understanding to relativize certain distinctions often made among human beings and which have the effect of positing a large distance between some of them and others of them.

In this whole train of thought I assume that the human excellences that are in a sense overshadowed by the value of the person are non-moral excellences. Musical genius is not a moral excellence; other forms of human greatness, too, need not include moral worthiness, as Kierkegaard teaches quite rightly in the *Postscript*. But if we think of moral goodness, or moral decency, or moral worthiness, however we call it, and, on the other hand, moral indecency, moral unworthiness, moral vileness, then we find a form of good and bad which, far from being overshadowed by the value of the human person, in a sense overshadows this value. One cannot say that the difference between Cordelia and Goneril (in *King Lear*) is inconsiderable on the grounds that they are both persons and both have the value of persons. It has been understood by almost everyone in the tradition of Western philosophy that a person becomes good as person by possessing moral worthiness, and

36. See ibid., 193, where Popper says that "the existence of one human being who wants to go on living is something so great, so irreplaceable...and a so significant fact in itself that the life of even the most unimportant individual has to count as something infinite in comparison with every technological or artistic accomplishment; in relation to such an individual every finite measure of value vanishes." In the next sentence Popper proceeds to develop a thought like the one which we developed above in section 3 of this chapter: "And just as an infinite quantity does not become more infinite by the addition of a finite number, so an individual personal existence is not enlarged or raised in its significance by the addition of any special quality, and even if this be the greatest gifts of genius" (my translations). It is as if the "absoluteness" that we found in each person in his relation to all other persons is found by Popper in each person in his relation to all possible "technological and cultural accomplishments."

becomes bad as person by being morally unworthy. I will return to this subject in Chapter 7; for the time being I simply want to point out that my affirmations about the almost infinite value of incommunicable persons have their limits, and that not everything which persons can become is overshadowed and "relativized" by this value.

Some readers may be pleasantly surprised that my analysis of selfhood has led in the direction of the dignity and worth of persons. These are the readers who fear that personal selfhood and the existing of each person as a being radically his own, when developed axiologically, can only lead to the human person as the subject of rights; since they deny that being a subject of rights is the most significant thing about being a human being, they are loath to make as much as I have of personal selfhood. What emerges from the present discussion, however, is that by probing the selfhood of the person we attain to a vastly deeper level in the person than the level at which the person has rights; for we attain to the level at which the person has dignity, ontological nobility,[37] and even to the level at which we find that preciousness in a person that can awaken the love of another, as we saw.[38]

This may be the best place to mention an important aspect of our subject which, however, I shall not examine more closely in the present study: the connection between the unrepeatability of each person and the immortality of each person. The connection seems to be best pointed out by assuming that human persons are only repeatable specimens of the human kind; on this assumption the immortality of any one of them seems to be in no way required or meaningful. If there is immortality in such a species it can be perfectly well secured by an unending succession of instantiating individuals, but it would not require immortal individuals. But persons are not repeatable specimens but are absolutely unrepeatable, so that with the destruction of any one of them something

37. If the reader hesitates to recognize any difference between being a subject of rights and having dignity, let him recall something that already came up in Chapter 1: I can violate my own dignity, throwing away my birthright as person, but I cannot violate my own rights; only another can violate my rights. I can no more violate them than I can steal out of my own property. Rights have a social reference that is foreign to dignity. Dignity inheres in a more absolute way in persons.

38. For a perfect example of an author who thinks that the axiological importance of personhood exhausts itself in having rights, and that the deeper axiological dimension of human beings expressed by notions such as inviolable dignity lies beyond personhood, see Simone Weil's essay, "Human Personality," in Rees (tr.), *Selected Essays, 1934–1943* (London, 1962). She goes so far as to say that our deepest dignity is tied to that which is impersonal in us—in my view, an utterly untenable position.

of almost infinite value would be irretrievably lost in the world, a gap that could never be filled would be left in the race of human persons. The loss of any person would not be a negligible loss on the grounds that so many persons remain, but would be an almost infinitely great loss, as if the only human person in existence had been lost. I do not claim here to have developed this into a finished argument for the immortality of persons, but the very least I can say is that their immortality is vastly more intelligible on the basis of their unrepeatability and of the value rooted in it than it would have been on the basis of specimen-like repeatability.

I will return to the value of the person at the end of Chapter 7, where I will examine the bearing of the moral vocation of the person on the value that persons have through their incommunicable selfhood.

7. Incommunicable personhood as expressed in the acting of human persons

It is natural to look to the acting of the person when exploring the incommunicability of the person. We saw above that Aquinas thinks that persons are *particulare et individuum* in a preeminent sense and that he finds this to be revealed especially in the power of persons to act through themselves *(per se agunt)* rather than to be acted upon by others *(aguntur)*. For in acting through themselves they act in freedom, and a being acting in freedom is not just instantiating a communicable type or kind, but is asserting its incommunicable self. In the strikingly personalist passage in the *Summa Contra Gentiles,* III, St. Thomas says that freedom is lost in human beings to the extent that their acting is dominated by that which is communicable in them.

> Whenever beings are directed in their acts solely on the basis of what pertains to the species, the capacity to act or not to act is not present in them. For things that are associated with the species are common and natural to all individuals contained in the species. Now, natural functions are not within our power to control. So, if man were able to direct his acts only in accord with what is suitable to the species, he would not have within him the capacity to act or not to act. Rather, he would have to follow the natural inclina-

---

39. One sees that this distinction between acting based on the communicable in us and acting based on the incommunicable seems to be directly parallel to the Scholastic distinction with respect to sin mentioned above, namely the distinction between *peccatum naturae* and *peccatum personae.*

tion common to the whole species, as is the case with all irrational creatures. Therefore, it is obvious that a rational creature has the ability to direct his acts, not only in accord with the species, but also in accord with the individual (Chapter 113; Bourke translation).

Instead of "in accord with the individual" St. Thomas might as well have said "in accord with its incommunicable being."[39]

Of course, it is commonly quite in order for me to step back as unrepeatable person and to let my acting be controlled by "common" principles, so that I act just as anyone else in my position would act. Thus a just judge wants to decide a case, and also to be perceived as deciding it, just as any other judge would have decided it. He wants to avoid any "respect of persons" and also to avoid a certain way of assertion of himself as incommunicable person. Similarly, in saying Mass a priest should not aim at putting his personal stamp on all his priestly actions, but should in a sense disappear into his priestly office, acting as a priest of the Church and not as this unique individual. There is nothing depersonalizing about this yielding to the requirements of an office that is not a personal possession but is shared in by many others. But our task at present is to explore those kinds of acting in which we emphatically express our incommunicable selfhood.[40]

I propose to proceed by considering first a form of acting that belongs to the intellectual life of the person, and then a form of acting that belongs to the moral life, and to search in each case for the expression of the incommunicability of the acting person.

1. In the course of explaining his theory of the "illative sense," John Henry Newman distinguishes between two kinds of reasoning that underlie our convictions. We can reason with clearly formulated grounds and by means of precise principles of inference, as we typically reason in mathematics. Newman lays great stress on the fact that this "formal inference," as he calls it, is impersonal; the mind is led to its conclusion

---

40. It would be interesting to study certain debates about whether in a given case the communicable should predominate or the incommunicable should assert itself. In his famous essay, "Tradition and Individual Talent," T. S. Eliot argues that the personal uniqueness of a great author is commonly a hindrance to the universality of truth expressed in his literary productions, and that the more of an impersonal medium he becomes, the greater his work. John Henry Newman (in his essay, "Literature," in *The Idea of a University*), in accordance with the personalism of his thought, holds just the opposite, namely that great literary artists express their unique selves in their works and write out of their own personal existence (as Newman himself did) in expressing something of universal validity.

"*ex opere operato,* by a scientific necessity independent of ourselves."[41] Everyone who starts from the same premises and who reasons well is bound to reach the same conclusion and to form the same conviction. But there is another kind of reasoning which is highly personal, and which is as legitimate in its own sphere as formal inference is in its. Newman is thinking of reasoning where "the personality (so to speak) of the parties reasoning is an important element"[42] in forming a conviction, and where the *ex opere operato* necessity of formal inference gives way to "the personal action of our own minds."[43] "Thus in concrete reasonings," where Newman thinks that we especially exercise this informal inference,[44] ". . . we judge for ourselves, by our own lights, and on our own principles; and our criterion of truth is not so much the manipulation of propositions, as the intellectual and moral character of the person maintaining them, and the ultimate silent effect of his arguments or conclusions upon our minds."[45] We discern clearly enough the incommunicability of the person who reasons, when Newman says of the "illative sense," as he calls this personal power of reasoning informally, that "it is seated in the mind of the individual, who is thus his own law, his own teacher, and his own judge. . . ."[46]

Naturally Newman does not mean that the illative sense sets aside the principles of formal inference, creating exceptions to them. Nor does he mean that it has reasons that are "incommunicable" in the sense of being unable to be conveyed to anyone. It is well known that Newman, by the exercise of his own illative sense, has profoundly influenced fellow inquirers, and has led many of them to share his own deepest convic-

---

41. Newman, *Grammar of Assent,* Chapter 8, section 2, "Informal Inference," para. 3.

42. Ibid., 253.

43. Ibid., 242.

44. Here is an example of informal inference taken from Newman's own life. Shortly after being received into the Catholic Church he wrote to a correspondent: "I do not know how to do justice to my reasons for becoming a Catholic in ever so many words— but if I attempted to do so in few, and that in print, I should wantonly expose myself and my cause to the hasty and prejudiced criticisms of opponents. This I will not do. People shall not say, 'We have now got his reasons, and know their worth.' No, you have not got them, you cannot get them, except at the cost of some portion of the trouble I have been at myself. You cannot buy them for a crown piece. . . . You must consent to *think.* . . . Moral proofs are grown into, not learnt by heart" (Letter of February 8, 1846, in *The Letters and Diaries of John Henry Newman* XI [London: Thomas Nelson and Sons, 1961], 110).

45. Ibid., 240.

46. Ibid., 279.

tions. He means instead that in exercising our illative sense in concrete matters, especially those touching our moral and religious existence, we think and reason not only according to universally valid forms of inference, but personally; that we live and exist in a particular way as incommunicable persons in all such thinking and reasoning; that when persons influence each other by means of their illative sense, the influence deserves to be called in a preeminent sense personal influence, and is to be contrasted with the "influence" whereby one discussant forces another to accept some formal demonstration.[47]

2. I now turn to our moral acting, in which we can study fruitfully the incommunicable element in our acting and the incommunicability of the acting person.

But I begin with a communicable aspect of moral acting, namely with the general moral norms to which persons are subject. I assume that there are such norms, some of which are not just formal but material norms, such as the norm prohibiting the direct killing of innocent persons. Such norms bind me indeed as person, and yet *they bind me as they bind any other human person.*[48] Now the question arises how the generality and universal validity of these norms cohere with the incommunicable selfhood of the moral subject. Often enough they seem to be asserted at the expense of individual selfhood. I recently came across a review of a study on divorce by the nineteenth century French traditionalist, de Bonald, who apparently developed a natural law argument against divorce. The reviewer quotes him asking, "What does it matter, after all, if a few individuals suffer in the course of this transient life, as long as reason, nature, and society do not suffer?" This seems to express a mentality far more concerned with preserving the communicable in human acting than with recognizing the incommunicably personal in acting. Other authors agree that there is an antagonism between universally valid laws and persons, but where de Bonald seems to opt for laws, they opt for persons. They typically maintain some kind of situation-ethics ac-

47. It is well said by Edward Sillem at the end of his excellent study of Newman the philosopher: "But he stands at the threshold of the new age as a Christian Socrates, the pioneer of a new philosophy of the individual Person and Personal Life." Sillem, *The Philosophical Notebook,* I (Louvain: Nauwelaerts Publishing House, 1969), 250.

48. Notice that when I speak of a communicable aspect of our acting, I mean something rather different from what Thomas means in speaking of our acting "only in accord with what is suitable to the species": Thomas is referring to instinctive acting that forms a contrast with properly personal acting (*Summa Contra Gentiles,* III, chapter 113, para. 2), whereas we take it for granted that we act freely, in the form of *per se agere,* when we act according to moral norms that bind all human beings.

cording to which the moral life is led in unrepeatable moral situations without reference to general norms.

But some have found a way to keep the general norms and yet show how the moral subject can live according to them in such a way as to assert himself in his personal incommunicability. Thus every morally awakened person knows that a general moral norm, for all its generality, *takes with ultimate seriousness the person who is bound by it.*[49] In recognizing what this norm requires of us in a particular situation, we do not feel treated as specimens, but—provided that we have some understanding of the goods out of which it grows—we are stirred up in our conscience, we are aware that our deepest personal integrity has been put at stake; we are aware that the moral good or evil that will result in us according as we do or do not respect the norm, will qualify us in our innermost selfhood. We find here a kind of paradoxical coinciding of the general and the incommunicable: the moral law, in all its generality, addresses us in the most existential way, enabling us to act out of our incommunicable selfhood.

When it comes to applying general norms to concrete situations, the incommunicability of persons enters in a further way into our moral existence. Thus Maritain, who wants to have nothing to do with situation ethics, says of the uniqueness that moral situations have as a result of the uniqueness of the persons entering into them:

> The same moral case never appears twice in the world. To speak absolutely strictly, precedent does not exist. Each time, I find myself in a situation requiring me to do a new thing, to bring into existence an act that is unique in the world, an act which must be in conformity with the moral law in a manner and under conditions belonging strictly to me alone and which have never arisen before. Useless to thumb through the dictionary of cases of conscience! Moral treatises will of course tell me the universal rule or rules I am bound to apply; they will not tell me how I, the unique I, am to apply them in the unique context in which I am involved. No knowledge of moral essences, however perfect, meticulous, or detailed it may be and however particularised those essences may be (though they will always remain general); no casuistry, no chain of pure deduction, no science, can exempt me from my judgment of conscience. . . .[50]

49. Cf. Josef Seifert, *Was ist und was motiviert eine sittliche Handlung* (Salzburg: Anton Pustet Verlag, 1976), 46: ". . . a moral duty contains a unique synthesis of historical concreteness, addressing the moral agent 'here and now,' and universality, addressing in the same way each human person who is in the same situation" (my translation). Cf. also 61–66.

50. Maritain, *Existence and the Existent* (New York: Doubleday, 1948), 60.

Of course this "judgment of conscience" is nothing other than Newman's illative sense as applied to the question of determining what I ought to do in a concrete moral situation.

Perhaps I can clarify the thought of Maritain by taking Montaigne's famous utterance about love and extending it to moral actions performed by unrepeatable persons in relation to other unrepeatable persons. He said: "If I am entreated to say why I loved him, I feel that this cannot be expressed except by answering 'Because it was he, because it was I.'" Montaigne does not deny that there is also a law of love, but he is taking seriously the fact that it is a law for the love between unrepeatable persons. Have we not had to say sometimes, without implying any disrespect for the general norms governing a moral situation, that we felt bound to certain actions "because it was he, because it was I" in the situation? Have we not said with Montaigne that the reason for a given duty lies "beyond all my discourse and whatever I can say distinctly about it," lying as it does in the incommunicable selfhood of the persons involved?[51]

But there is something else in the moral life that also displays the incommunicable selfhood of the moral subject, something other than the moral judgment required to bring general moral norms to bear on concrete persons. We can find this further factor in the seminal essay of Karl Rahner, "Über die Frage einer formalen Existenzialethik."[52] Rahner begins by assuming that our moral acting is subject to general moral norms, and in this he distinguishes himself from the position of situation ethics.[53] Then he asks whether a knowledge of the general norms relevant to a given situation together with a knowledge of the situation always suffice to determine what I ought to do in the situation. He answers that sometimes they do, but that often enough they leave open several actions each of which is in conformity with the relevant norms. Is it just an arbitrary choosing that I exercise with regard to these several actions? Is it morally indifferent how I choose? Rahner says no, for he recognizes what he calls an *Individualnorm* or an *Existenzialnorm* (I will call it an "individual norm"), which he contrasts with the general norms just mentioned. He thinks that I may find myself personally called

---

51. Montaigne, *Essays*, I, chapter 27.

52. Rahner, *Schriften zur Theologie*, II (Einsiedeln: Benzinger Verlag, 1955) 227–246. English: *Theological Investigations*, II (London, 1963), 217–234.

53. It exceeds the scope of this study to inquire why certain moral theologians (such as Josef Fuchs) who start from Rahnerian presuppositions are unable to hold fast to exceptionless material moral norms.

to one of the allowable actions and not to the others; that I ought to perform this action and none of the others. But this moral requirement cannot be derived from the relevant general norms; I also have to discern the individual norm addressed to me not as a human being but in the most personal way. Notice that for Rahner the individual norm does not set aside a general norm, creating an exception to it, but rather does its work *within* the realm of acting defined by the relevant general norms.[54]

When Rahner goes to reflect on the basis of such an individual norm he is led to the very point of concern to us, to the incommunicability and unrepeatability of each person. He suggests that the Thomistic teaching on the unrepeatability of each angel may admit of some application to human persons, who in no case should be understood as mere specimens of the human species. He seems to say that if we were just repeatable instances of our species, then the general norms would suffice; a knowledge of them, together with a knowledge of the concrete situation in which we must act, would suffice to determine what is morally required of us. But since we are not specimens but unrepeatable persons, it is only fitting, perhaps even necessary, that we also be subject to moral calls that speak to us personally and that call for actions proceeding in a special way from my incommunicable selfhood.[55]

Maritain, too, seems to be aware of these highly personal moral calls. He may be thinking of them in the passage just quoted, and he is certainly thinking of them when he writes:

> We are told, as if it were a novelty, that the motives which reason deliberates upon do not play the decisive part in the deepest, freest (indeed wisest) acts of moral option but that this role is reserved to that unforeseeable impulse of

---

54. There is a passage in the New Testament that seems to contain the distinction between general norms and individual norms. When the rich young man comes to Jesus asking about the attainment of eternal life, he is first told by Jesus to observe the commandments, and then he is invited by Him to a closer discipleship (Mt 19:16–22): the commandments represent general norms, and the special invitation seems to be a typical individual norm. By the way, it would be worth inquiring whether this invitation expresses an ought that binds in the same sense in which the general norms bind.

55. Rahner, who is always looking for Thomistic support for his positions, might have found some in the *Summa Contra Gentiles,* Book III, chapter 113, from which we have already quoted twice in this study. This chapter is entitled, "that the rational creature is directed by God to his actions not only by an ordering of the species, but also according to what befits the individual." And in fact when Aquinas proceeds in chapter 114 to speak of the law which God gives to man, he has a notion of law which seems to come very close to Rahner's *Individualnorm.*

one's inscrutable subjectivity, so often disconcerting for the intellect of the subject himself. How can it be otherwise, if it is true that the judgment of the subject's conscience is obliged, at the moment when judgment is freely made, to take account also of the whole of the unknown reality within him—his secret capacities, his deeply rooted aspirations, the strength or frailty of his moral stuff, his virtues (if he has any), the mysterious call of his destiny? He cannot formulate any of these things. They are unknown to him in terms of reason.[56]

And Maritain seems to recognize Rahner's individual norm in the lives of the saints when he goes on to say:

The saints always amaze us. Their virtues are freer than those of a merely virtuous man. Now and again, in circumstances outwardly alike, they act quite differently from the way in which a merely virtuous man acts. They are indulgent where he would be severe, severe where he would be indulgent. . . . What does that signify? They have their own kind of mean, their own kinds of standards. But they are valid only for each one of them. . . . This is why we utter something deeper than we realise when we say of such acts that they are admirable but not imitable. They are not generalisable, universalisable. They are good; indeed, they are the best of all moral acts. But they are good only for him who does them. We are here very far from the Kantian universal with its morality defined by the possibility of making the maxim of an act into a law for all men.[57]

This is extremely well said, including the comment about Kant at the end;[58] for my purposes I have only to add the connection (stressed more by Rahner than by Maritain) between this lack of generalizability in the best moral acts and the incommunicability of each person. It is because persons are incommunicable and unrepeatable in the sense explained in this chapter that they are capable of acting, and of being called to act, on

---

56. Maritain, op.cit., 62.

57. Ibid., 63–64. Though both Maritain and Rahner explicitly repudiate situation ethics, they are at the same time aware of vindicating the core of truth in situation ethics. For another important contribution towards distinguishing true from false with regard to the claims of situation ethics, see Dietrich von Hildebrand, *Morality and Situation Ethics* (Chicago: Franciscan Herald Press, 1966).

58. In his polemic against Kant, Scheler makes the same point (*Formalism in Ethics,* 490). He insists not only on the individuality of certain moral maxims, but also on the individuality of that which underlies them, namely the worth or value of individual persons. This thought, which completes the thought of Maritain in the text, is in accordance with the whole thrust of Scheler's ethics of "material" values and with his teaching of a certain priority of values over norms.

strictly personal maxims, which cannot be made into general laws valid for all human beings.[59]

We find, then, in our moral acting, a highly significant expression of our personal incommunicability. But at the same time we find, as we found above, that the human person does not have the supreme measure of incommunicability; for we human persons are not subject only to individual norms, we are also subject to many general norms that bind any one of us in the same way as they bind any other of us. We also find a certain re-emergence of the communicable in the midst of the incommunicable. Though the saints of which Maritain speaks act on highly personal maxims, they are after all exemplary for us. These are the very persons on whom we pattern ourselves; they are representative human beings. It is a universally valid moral truth which they live in their own incommunicable way and which they challenge me to live in my incommunicable way. Socrates does certain things that only Socrates is called to do; yet in doing these very things he makes me re-examine my own life and makes me ask myself why I am not more like him.

Throughout this section I have been speaking of the acting of persons. But persons not only act; they receive the acting of others. They hear what others say to them; they receive the looks and the attentions of others; they are known by others. By drawing into our study this more receptive mode of existence, we could explore more deeply the incommunicability of persons. We could show that there is something profoundly distressing for a person in always only being known through some general category or under some general rubric; every person has the most elementary need to be known by his or her proper name, and to be affirmed as the incommunicable person he or she is. Since I have already said something about this in section 4, I do not propose to explore it further here.

Conclusion. As I indicated at the end of the last chapter, the selfhood of human persons is an idea capable of being understood and accepted by philosophers coming from various points of view. Relatively few are

59. Perhaps we have here further evidence for that *essential incommunicability* for which we were searching above. Aristotle teaches that all moral acting leaves some trace on the character of the agent, and in fact that nothing else forms moral character but the acting of the agent. But if an action is performed in response to an individual norm, which appeals to a person in all of the person's incommunicability, is it not natural to assume that which is wrought in the character of that person shares in this incommunicability, and, since moral character belongs to the essence of the person, gives evidence of some essential incommunicability?

prepared today to maintain that human persons are indeed nothing but specimens of the human kind. The broad consensus that we can hope to achieve here is at first glance surprising when one considers the Christian origins of the idea of personal incommunicability. As Guardini says, in agreement with what I suggested above, ". . . antiquity did not have a true concept of the person—indeed, one does not find it outside of Revelation."[60] And yet, even though the idea of each person being incommunicably himself seems to have been gained within a particular tradition, and to be most adequately understandable within the theological presuppositions of that tradition, it has, nevertheless, no small intelligibility for contemporaries who do not share these presuppositions and who in fact are non-Christians. Whoever understands that a person is never rightly used as a mere means will be able to understand all that we have said about personal incommunicability.[61]

60. Guardini, op. cit., 115.

61. The author quoted above in section 5, Josef Popper, for all his deep insight into personal incommunicability, was, I believe, not a theist. This does not preclude that he was, if unwittingly, the beneficiary of Christianity, but he did not write as a theist. Even when one affirms personal incommunicability in connection with theism, the theism need not be Christian. A friend specializing in Hindu philosophy has called my attention to the thirteenth century Hindu philosopher, Madhva, who apparently maintained an irreducible plurality of incommunicable human souls. He seems to have used the incisive argument that I can immediately experience only myself and can never experience another with the same immediacy. I do not doubt that there is a different and deeper experience of incommunicability within Christianity; but incommunicability is not the exclusive reserve of Christians.

CHAPTER THREE

Subjectivity

In his seminal little essay, "Subjectivity and the Irreducible in Man,"[1] Karol Wojtyla claims that the Aristotelian metaphysics of human nature runs the risk of "reducing man to the world," of failing to do justice to the *proprium* of man, to what distinguishes him as person. Wojtyla says that there is a *cosmological* focus of the Aristotelian tradition that needs to be completed by a more *personalist* focus, which studies human beings not only in terms of substance, potentiality, rationality, and the like, but also in terms of subjectivity, that is, in terms such as self-presence, inwardness, self-donation. Only by probing the subjectivity of human beings can we understand them in all their personhood. He thinks that as a matter of historical fact the recourse to subjectivity in the last few centuries has enabled many thinkers to achieve a more adequate vision of man as person, and that this can be achieved, even if it has not always in fact been achieved, without any least concession to subjectivism. I agree entirely with Wojtyla, and I hope to show by the end of this chapter just how fruitful the study of personal subjectivity can be for the philosophy of the person.

We already caught sight of subjectivity in Chapter 1 in discussing the acting of persons. As long as human beings are merely being acted upon, undergoing what originates outside of their freedom and perhaps also transmitting it, they do not live out of their subjectivity; as long as "na-

---

1. In *Analecta Husserliana* VII (Dordrecht: D. Reidel, 1978), 107–114. It has been retranslated by Theresa Sandok, *Person and Community: Selected Essays* (New York: Peter Lang, 1993), 209–217. This statement of Wojtyla's philosophy, in which he boldly expresses what is specifically modern in it, seems to provide the best introduction to his thought.

ture" predominates in them to the relative exclusion of "person," they are indeed there as objective beings, but they do not appear in their subjectivity. Only in acting through themselves and living in freedom do they come alive subjectively. And yet in the previous chapters I did not make a point of referring directly to the self-experience of the person in trying to ground my claims about the selfhood and solitude of the human person. Since these claims are not fully understandable without recourse to personal subjectivity, and can in any case be understood more deeply through personal subjectivity, I propose now to thematize subjectivity.

I insist, however, that with this turn to subjectivity I am not lapsing from ontology into psychology, as if I were in this chapter attempting nothing more than to confirm the previous chapters with empirical observations drawn from introspection; I will instead show how much the metaphysics of the person has to gain from a "subjective" analysis of the person. My first task is to explain what I mean by subjectivity.

We begin by noting that the term subjectivity has a broader and a narrower meaning. The meaning is broader when it is controlled by the contrast with "cosmological," as in Wojtyla's essay. It is narrower when one distinguishes between subjectivity and intersubjectivity, or when one distinguishes between individual subjectivity and collective subjectivity, and lets the unqualified term, subjectivity, express the meaning of "individual subjectivity." This is a distinction *within* subjectivity in Wojtyla's sense. In my use of the term subjectivity I will commonly mean to express *both* meanings, that is, both the contrast with cosmological as well as the contrast with intersubjectivity.

1. Self-presence

When persons act as persons, that is, act through themselves, their act is *intentional* in the sense of Brentano and of many after him, that is, it lives as act through its relation to the object of the act. Thus to say that a person's act of understanding is intentional is simply to say that the understanding is an understanding *of something,* and could not exist as the act that it is apart from something that is understood. Or to say that the act of willing is intentional is simply to say that the willing is a willing *of something,* and collapses as act apart from the conscious relation to the object that is willed. In all such acts persons encounter something in front of themselves.

Now this intentionality, or object-directedness, or self-transcendence, is a fundamental dimension of personal consciousness; it is in fact so fundamental that Brentano takes it as *the* defining mark of consciousness. But I think that with this he goes too far, because there is another equally fundamental dimension of personal consciousness. In turning to an object outside of myself, I turn as one who is consciously anchored in himself. The *outward thrust* of the intentional act is anchored in the *interiority* of my personal being. I who turn to the object am present to myself in the turning. However far I go in losing myself in the object of my act, I can never lose my self-presence entirely; my consciousness-of can never completely repress my conscious self-presence. This relation of me to myself as subject, which constitutes the interiority of my existence and of my acting, is what I mean by subjectivity. I will return in Chapter 5 to the intentionality, or as I could also say, to the objectivity of consciousness; in the present chapter my theme is above all the subjectivity of consciousness.

In Chapter 1 we first encountered subjectivity through a contrast with nature, with that which happens in us, subjectivity coinciding with the person acting through himself; now we will approach subjectivity more closely through a contrast with the object-directedness of consciousness.

In the subjectivity of the human person I distinguish two fundamental dimensions; they correspond to the distinction between cognition and volition, or between knowing and willing. I call the first the self-presence of the person, and the second the self-determination, or subjective freedom, of the person.

One might ask whether the self-presence of an intentional act is perhaps another intentional act, one in which I am directed not to some being outside of myself but to myself as object. There undoubtedly are intentional acts in which I bend back over myself as object, as when I describe my inner life to someone; but these acts have to be sharply distinguished from self-presence, *in which I encounter myself not objectively but subjectively.* I will briefly explain some of the reasons for the irreducibility of self-presence to self-directed intentional acts.

1. If one says that the self-presence on the subjective pole of an intentional act is a new intentional act in which the person cognizes himself as object, then it follows that the person in performing one intentional act is in fact performing infinitely many of them, which is absurd. For in this new intentional act (in which the person cognizes himself as object), the person is present to himself performing the act of cognition. If

one says that the self-presence of this new act is also to be explained in terms of the subject-object polarity of intentional consciousness, then it follows that there is a third self-directed intentional act. And the third will generate a fourth as soon as one tries to explain in the same terms the presence of the person to himself performing the third act; and so on without end. As long as one recognizes that on the subjective pole of every intentional act there is a presence of the person to himself, then the attempt to explain self-presence in terms of an intentional relation of the person to himself as object inevitably generates the infinite series. But if one recognizes that the relation of the person to himself in self-presence is a certain dwelling of the person with himself that is not an intentional act, then the analysis stops with the self-presence of the person performing the first intentional act; there is nothing in the logic of self-presence that requires every self-presence to generate another self-presence.

2. Let us speak of the intentional acts directed to an object other than myself. We just said that I am present to myself in these acts. Now if the relation of me to myself in self-presence were an intentional relation towards myself as object, then I would be simultaneously performing two intentional acts, one towards the intentional object outside of me and one towards myself as intentional object (the infinitely many other intentional acts beyond these two do not concern us here). I do not say that this is impossible, but notice that the two intentions would at least compete with each other, so that the stronger my self-presence, the more I would be diverted from the object outside of me. But the experience of self-presence reveals the very opposite: *the stronger my self-presence, the more I can enter into the object outside of me; my self-presence does not compete with my transcendence towards the object but rather renders this transcendence possible and perfects it.* I am about to explain exactly what stronger and weaker self-presence means; when discussing the act of the person recollecting himself, we will see why one strengthens one's self-presence in recollecting oneself, and why as a result of recollecting oneself one's power of performing intentional acts is enhanced. But perhaps even now, in advance of the discussion of recollection, the reader can understand enough of self-presence and its possible degrees to see why self-presence grounds the performing of intentional acts. The relation of me to myself in self-presence has indeed a certain reflexivity, otherwise we could not speak of it as a relation of "me to myself," nor could we expressively call it "self-presence"; but it is not the reflexivity of making an intentional object of myself, other-

wise it would divert me from other intentional acts and would not serve to ground them and to perfect them in the way in which it in fact does.

I see this as one of the strongest arguments for the irreducibility of self-presence to a subject-object relation to myself.

Already here in the discussion of selfhood and subjectivity, before we have made transcendence our subject, we are led to transcendence by the very logic of subjectivity. I have just said that it is the strengthening of my subjectivity which empowers me to transcend myself: with this I touch on one of the main themes of this study, which becomes a subject of its own in Part II.

3. It seems that self-presence is primarily a way in which I am consciously related to myself. It is true that I can through empathy and sympathy enter the inner lives of other persons and can to some extent come to experience them as they experience themselves; but I can never become present to them in the same way as they are present to themselves and as I am present to myself. The fact that I am myself and not another has consequences for my self-experiencing in relation to my experiencing of others; it forever prevents me from being present to others in the same way as I am to myself, or as they are to themselves. On the other hand, an intentional relation to myself is by no means a relation that I have primarily to myself; others can also have me as the intentional object of their acting. In fact, there may be some sense in which it is primarily others who have me as intentional object. I can of course make myself the object of my acting and perhaps I can do this as truly as others can; but in doing so, do I not see myself and act towards myself as others see me and act towards me? What is this position outside of myself that I take up in making an object of myself, if not the position of another person? In bending back on myself as object, do I not emerge from a certain solitude of subjectivity and enter a certain social realm of my existence, even if I do not encounter another person? How is it that others provide me with such indispensable help in objectifying myself if this objectifying does not have something to do with the perspective of others? In any case, we see anew that one cannot reduce self-presence to an objective self-relation, as we might call the relation that I have to myself as to an intentional object. For one could not explain in this reductionistic way why it is that my presence to myself in what I am calling self-presence is a relation I have primarily to myself and cannot have in the same way to another.

4. This reductionism also flies in the face of the most basic facts of our self-experience. It would conceive of persons as always experienc-

ing themselves from without and would be unable to understand the sense of *inwardness* and *interiority* we find in self-presence. The truth is that we experience ourselves not only from a point outside ourselves, but also from within ourselves, not only *objectively* but also *subjectively*. Consider this analogy: I can experience my own body as the intentional object of my seeing, feeling, touching, and so forth; but it would be a mistake to try to explain without residue my entire body-experience in terms of such self-directed intentional acts; there is clearly also an experience of my body from within, an experience only I can have of my body, a kind of body-experience essentially different from intentional self-experiencing—something like a subjective rather than an objective body-experience.

It seems that the spatial metaphor implied in the talk of inwardness and interiority is extremely expressive of the subjectivity of the human person.[2]

It is of course very difficult to *conceive* how it is that in self-presence I should be consciously related to myself, which means related with a certain reflexivity, related in a sense cognitively, yet not as intentional object; related to myself as subject to subject rather than as subject to object. But this non-intentional reflexivity, this difference between experiencing myself subjectively and experiencing myself objectively, between experiencing myself from within and from without, is undeniably given, and all attempts at philosophical understanding have to hold fast to this given and to clarify it; and they must under no circumstances try to reduce self-presence to an objective, intentional self-relation.[3]

2. One should not overlook the striking grammatical expression of subjectivity that resides in the first person pronouns of the nominative case: "I" and "we." Here we express ourselves from within ourselves, or subjectively. The accusative forms, "me" and "us," are not expressive of subjectivity in the same way; it is with good reason that in English we call their case the "objective" case. Just as "I" is irreducible to "me" in terms of expressing subjectivity, so the conscious relation to myself as subject is irreducible to the conscious relation to myself as object.

3. This is the result to which Wojtyla comes in his profound analysis of consciousness in Chapter I of *The Acting Person* (Dordrecht: D. Reidel, 1979); see especially 41–50 and his discussion of what he calls the "reflexive" function of consciousness. It is a result that also converges with the Augustinian analysis of consciousness in *De Trinitate* X. Augustine's distinction between *se nosse* and *se cogitare* seems to express exactly my distinction between self-presence and reflecting on oneself as object. See the extremely competent discussion of the Augustinian distinction in Ludger Hölscher, *The Reality of the Mind: St. Augustine's Philosophical Arguments for the Human Soul as a Spiritual Substance* (London and New York: Routledge, 1986), Chapter 3. Of particular

2. Self-determination

The self-presence we have been discussing is a subjective relation of the person to himself with a certain *cognitive* character. In self-presence the person gets acquainted with himself as subject rather than as object. If one were going to confuse self-presence with an intentional act directed to oneself, then this intentional act would be some kind of act in which I cognize myself as object. Now the question arises whether there is also a more volitional way in which the person is subjectively related to himself—whether there is a less cognitive and more volitional form of personal subjectivity. I think that there is, and that we can find it in a way directly parallel to the way in which we found the self-presence of the person.

Consider an act of the will in which I affirm or reject something outside of myself which I apprehend as good or bad. The good or bad thing is the intentional object, and the act of the will is an intentional act. But in performing this act I not only have to do with the good or bad thing to which I am directed; I also have to do with myself. This is nowhere so clear as when I perform a morally good or bad action towards another: I am aware in my conscience of having to do not only with this other, but also, though in a different way, with myself. As I discern in my conscience the obligation to act in a certain way, I at the same time experience myself as handed over to myself. I know that in deciding whether or not to act in accordance with the dictate of my conscience I will at the same time decide about myself, I will dispose over myself. If I act as my conscience admonishes me, I am aware of affirming myself in a certain way, of willing my deepest human integrity. And if I act against my conscience I am aware of radically compromising myself. This is why persons who are caught up in a moral crisis will sometimes speak as if what binds them to do the right thing is not so much the good that they act to preserve, but rather the integrity of themselves—as if they would split apart as persons by acting against their conscience. We find, then, on the subjective pole of the moral action a being-handed-over to one-

---

interest for us is his "Excursion into Wojtyla's notion of consciousness," 161–167, where Hölscher connects Wojtyla's reflexive function of consciousness with Augustine's *se nosse*.

self, a being-subject to one's own freedom, which is directly parallel to the self-presence that is found on the subjective pole of all intentional acts, as we saw.

The parallel goes further. One will object, just as above, that this self-determination is an intentional relation of me to myself as object. And I will respond, just as above, that if this were really so, it would be difficult to explain how the affirmation of myself in conscience does not weaken but rather strengthens my inner resources for acting towards the object of the action. In willing my deepest integrity I am no more diverted from the other person towards whom I typically act than I am diverted by my self-presence from some thing that I want to understand. Just as my reaching out to something so as to understand it is not harmed but rather made possible by the strength of my self-presence, so my affirmation of another in a moral action is made possible by the strength of my self-affirmation. This is why in this self-affirmation I no more objectify myself than I do in self-presence. In being handed over to myself in conscience and in disposing over myself, I have to do with myself subjectively, living a more volitional dimension of my subjectivity, which can be distinguished from the more cognitive subjectivity of self-presence.[4]

The spatial analogy of inner and outer is even more applicable here than with self-presence. The determination of myself in conscience is a determination of myself *from within.* It is a determination that I can exercise only towards myself, never towards another. Thus the term conscience is often used to mean the innermost center, the inner sanctuary, of the human person. How would this inwardness of self-determination be possible if I had to do with myself only as with an object, if I were for myself nothing but another object on which I acted volitionally? The radical way in which I determine myself (and only myself) from the center of my being requires a subjective relation of me to myself and excludes an objective relation. And only this subjectivity of self-determination explains how it is that I can experience in it the supreme inwardness of my existence.

4. This, too, is in agreement with Wojtyla in *The Acting Person;* see above all Chapter 3, section 2. See also his 1975 paper, "The Personal Structure of Self-Determination" (in Sandok, tr., op. cit., 187–195). It is true that I seem to contradict him when, speaking of self-determination, he says, "I myself am the first and most basic object that I determine" (192). But the context makes abundantly clear that he does not mean object in the sense of intentional object; he simply wants to say *that I have to do with myself* in self-determination.

One can understand rightly this volitional subjectivity, or subjective freedom, only by distinguishing it from certain instinctive ways of being related to myself. When, for example, I sense that my life is immediately endangered, an instinct of self-preservation takes over in virtue of which I clutch desperately at my life. In this instinct I am related to myself, in contrast to other instincts in which I am related to others. And yet this instinct, since it belongs more to that which happens in me than to that which I do by acting through myself, is something sub-personal and has nothing more than an analogy with personal subjectivity. The volitional subjectivity of which I speak is a basic form of freedom. Thus a subjective self-affirmation or self-acceptance belongs to an entirely different realm in the existence of the person than does the instinct for self-preservation.

It is not difficult to recognize in the subjectivity of conscience the selfhood of the person. When conscience stirs and the inwardness of conscience opens up in us, we subjectively experience our standing in ourselves and our incommunicability; indeed, the subjectivity and inwardness of conscience is one of the primary sources out of which the philosopher can develop an understanding of the selfhood and solitude of the person. But with this I get a little ahead of myself; before attempting a "subjective" analysis of personhood I have to say more about subjectivity itself.

Now this volitional subjectivity, or subjective freedom, is not only found on the subjective pole of moral action, in conscience; it can also be found elsewhere in the inner lives of persons. Whether we speak of persons as having confidence in themselves, or lacking self-confidence, or pitying themselves, or being ashamed of themselves, or having self-irony, or self-hatred, or despairing over themselves, or accepting themselves—in all such cases we speak of a more than cognitive relation of the person to himself, and in most of these cases of a certain stance that the person takes towards himself. And it seems that in all these self-relations persons have to do with themselves subjectively and not only objectively. It is, for example, as subject and not only as object that I accept myself and will to be the self that I am.

On closer inspection we find that in some of these self-relations, such as self-hatred, I have a particular tendency to objectify myself, to deal with myself from without. It seems to take a loving or at least a love-like relation of me to myself in order to exercise fully my subjectivity in a volitional way. After all, it seems clear that I need to have a loving or at least a love-like relation to others in order to enter into their subjectivity and to experience them subjectively.[5]

The main point of concern for us at present is that my subjectivity, my lived relation to myself as subject, is by no means confined to the mainly cognitive subjectivity of self-presence; that there is also a subjectivity in which I have to do with myself, and dispose over myself, and which I will call volitional subjectivity, or subjective freedom.

The most fundamental exercise of subjective freedom. In his philosophy and theology of freedom Karl Rahner has the merit not only of recognizing the subjective dimension of our freedom; he also recognizes that we are capable of encompassing in our subjective freedom *our whole selves.* Thus he says, writing about earlier forms of this idea, that "the biblical and Augustinian concept of the heart, the concept of subjectivity in Kierkegaard, the notion of *'action'* in Blondel, etc., show understanding for the fact that there is such a *basic act of freedom which embraces and shapes the whole of human existence*" (my italics).[6]

Often I take a stance towards myself as subject which does not encompass my whole self, as when I am satisfied with myself for completing some particular project; this can cohere with being dissatisfied with myself for being unsuccessful in other projects. But I am also capable of, and in fact cannot evade, a fundamental stance towards myself in which I decide subjectively about all that I am; this stance does not have

5. This is surely the main reason why Sartre (at least the Sartre of *Being and Nothing*) failed to recognize our ability to encounter another in his or her subjectivity: he despaired of the love that renders it possible.

6. Rahner, "Theology of Freedom," in *Theological Investigations VI* (New York, 1974), 185. But I should also register a serious weakness which I see in Rahner's theory of fundamental freedom, a weakness that is connected with the strength of it. In his enthusiasm for the freedom in which we determine ourselves from within ourselves, he fails to do justice, as it seems to me, to the freedom exercised towards particular goods and evils. When, for instance, a judge is offered a bribe, he is challenged to decide not only about himself, but also about the guilty persons whom he would protect and the innocent persons whom he would wrong by accepting the bribe. One cannot say, as Rahner sometimes seems to say, that the whole point of these latter decisions is to develop one's fundamental freedom in relation to oneself; one has rather to recognize that these have their own moral meaning. Such concrete decisions are also more important for our fundamental freedom, and, when they are made badly, more capable of interfering with it, than Rahner seems to realize. Important as it is to vindicate our fundamental freedom in relation to ourselves, it is no less important to understand rightly its relation to that other aspect of freedom that is exercised in deciding about particular goods and evils.

the partial focus that the mentioned satisfaction and dissatisfaction have, but is instead all-encompassing. Kierkegaard seems to be aiming precisely at this most fundamental freedom in *The Sickness unto Death* when he says that each human person is challenged to choose between willing to be the self that he or she is, or refusing to be the self that he or she is. If I existed through myself as God does, I would not be faced with this choice, for then I would be so radically my own that it would not make sense to have to accept my being or not. But since I am in some sense given to myself, I come into the position of having to choose to accept myself or not.

Rahner thinks that this freedom is always performed on the subjective pole of acts in which I affirm or reject some finite good or evil. This is certainly often the case. It is the case whenever our acting becomes a matter of conscience; the subjectivity of conscience is surely a subjectivity in which I dispose over myself *simpliciter,* that is, over my whole self. But it also seems that this freedom is challenged in a particular way whenever I come up against some painful limitation in myself, often as a result of encountering in another person some excellence that I lack. As long as I just accept or try to overcome the limitation, I am not yet exercising my most fundamental subjective freedom; but if I accept *being such a person as has this limitation,* or if I refuse *to be such a limited person,* then my freedom takes on a fearful depth and breadth, and I dispose over my whole self in an ultimate way.

In an essay profoundly akin to the work of Kierkegaard but perhaps more accessible to readers, *Die Annahme seiner Selbst (The Acceptance of One's Self),* Romano Guardini explains as follows certain temptations to reject the self that one is.

> It is possible to rebel against having to be oneself. Why should I anyway? Did I ask to exist? There is the feeling that it is no longer worth it to be oneself. What does it profit me? I bore myself. I disgust myself. I cannot stand it any longer with myself. There is the feeling . . . of being locked in myself: I am only so much, and yet I want to be more. I have only this talent, and yet I want greater and more splendid talents. It is always the same thing which I have to do. I always run up against the same limits. I always commit the same mistakes, undergo the same failure.[7]

We can develop the reflection of Guardini by observing that the temptation to rebellion can go deeper; one can be dissatisfied with the fact that

---

7. Guardini, *Die Annahme Seiner Selbst* (Würzburg: Werkbund Verlag, 1960), 13 (my translation).

much of one's being is shared with others, or with one's corporeality, or with one's very contingency (the fact that one is not absolute, divine, but instead could as well not exist). But the temptation to rebellion need not come from the sight of my weaknesses and metaphysical limitations; it can as well come—surprising as this sounds on first hearing—from the sight of my dignity, my greatness, the seriousness of my responsibility. I can experience it as too great a "weight of glory" to have to exist as a free and responsible person. I can resent my destiny as person and run away from it.[8]

What concerns us here is that in the face of these temptations to rebellion[9] I come into a position in which I can dispose over my whole self: I can rebel against my self, refuse to accept my self and the terms of my existence, be scandalized at myself, disown myself, as it were, and accuse God; or I can accept myself, will to be myself, and in the face of my weaknesses and my guilt still preserve a certain *Treue zum eigenen Sein* (faithfulness to my own being), as Guardini says.[10] This faithfulness of course does not mean that we are passive with regard to defects that might be changed in us, but only that we criticize the defects out of a certain loyalty to ourselves rather than make the removal of them the condition for having loyalty to ourselves. We do not live our volitional lives only in relation to other beings around us, or only in relation to some limited aspect of ourselves; we are with our whole being a problem for ourselves. We have to come to grip with ourselves, to take a stance towards ourselves; we have to dispose in an ultimate way over all that we are. On the other hand, we should take care not to exaggerate this fundamental subjective freedom. It is almost never performed in one single act but is rather built up in and through many single acts over time. This is why Rahner says (though perhaps not without sometimes overstating it) that this freedom is to some extent mysteriously hidden from each person, escaping the full view of his or her intentional consciousness.

8. To my knowledge no one has expressed more powerfully than Kierkegaard (*The Sickness unto Death,* Part II, section 1, appendix) the despair over oneself that comes from refusing one's calling to greatness. He speaks here of refusing the Christian call to life with God, but what he says can also be said of the refusal to live as person.

9. In the light of this rebellion, Guardini attempts (ibid., 18–20) to interpret the object-less fear *(Angst)* from which so many modern men and women suffer from and which has been much discussed in modern philosophy. One usually says that this fear is a certain experience of our finitude and contingency, but Guardini holds that it in fact results from *refusing to accept our finitude and contingency.*

10. Ibid., 12.

This subjective freedom is particularly revealing of personal selfhood. In this freedom we can see our belonging to ourselves; we can dispose over ourselves only if we are handed over to ourselves in the sense of self-possession and of being *sui iuris,* of which I spoke above in unfolding what is contained in our moral consciousness. And we must be handed over to ourselves in a radical way, otherwise we could not dispose over our whole selves as we do in our fundamental freedom.

As we look for personal selfhood in our subjective freedom we right away notice that this selfhood is in one sense much more properly enacted in the acceptance than in the refusal of ourselves. In this accepting I take possession of myself, I make myself my own, and come to belong to myself in a new way, whereas in refusing to be the self that I am, I become estranged from myself, an object for myself, divided against myself; I *disown* myself, thus setting myself against my belonging to myself, impotently trying to undo it. In this disowning of myself I *presuppose* indeed my belonging to myself, but I do not *enact* it, I do not *live* it, as I do when I will to be the self that I am. I will resume below in section 4 this attempt to recognize selfhood in the subjectivity of persons, or in other words, to enrich subjectively our understanding of selfhood.

There are, then, two basic forms of subjectivity: self-presence and being handed over to oneself so as to be able to determine oneself. Though I distinguish them, I only distinguish them, and I have no intention of setting them against each other. It is clear that in being present to myself I am already to some extent handed over to myself so as to determine myself. And whenever we are handed over to ourselves in conscience, we are present to ourselves as being handed over. We will see later that the deeper forms of self-presence presuppose that I subjectively affirm and accept myself; they are possible only in conjunction with a certain subjective self-determination. And we will find still other ways in which these two forms of subjectivity interpenetrate. I have made a distinction between them, but not in such a way as to prevent a uniting of the things distinguished.

As I said at the outset, I am presently speaking, and through section 5 will continue to speak, of the subjectivity *of an individual person.* I am aware that there is also the collective subjectivity whereby a number of persons perform some act together with each other, as when they grieve together over some common loss. I will say something about this social dimension of subjectivity in section 6. It would, of course, be artificial to postpone like this the treatment of collective subjectivity if individual subjectivities existed only as mere parts in a collective subjectivity; in that case I would have to take individual and collective subjectivity as one issue. But given my understanding of each person as a whole of his own, it is surely in order to divide the subject matter as I have divided it, and to begin with individual subjectivity.

3. Can subjectivity be reflected on philosophically?

It has often been said that the subjectivity of the person, precisely in virtue of being subjectivity, cannot be reflected on philosophically, on the grounds that philosophical reflection is carried out in and through intentional consciousness, which objectifies. The objection is that one can only grasp subjectivity by making of it an object, but this is not to grasp it but to distort it. Thus Maritain says, speaking not only for himself but for many other philosophers as well:

> Subjectivity *as subjectivity* is inconceptualisable; is an unknowable abyss. It is unknowable by the mode of notion, concept, or representation, or by any mode of any science whatsoever—introspection, psychology, or philosophy. How could it be otherwise, seeing that every reality known through a concept, a notion, or a representation is known as object and not as subject?[11]

Maritain suggests that any attempt to philosophize about subjectivity inevitably distorts it:

> Philosophy runs against an insurmountable barrier in attempting to deal with subjectivity, because while philosophy of course knows subjects, it knows them only as objects.[12]

If subjectivity were really inconceptualisable, how comes it that "subjectivity," in Maritain's text no less than in mine, expresses a genuine concept, as genuine a concept as "objectivity"?

It is true that in uttering any of the statements in this study we make intentional objects of the things of which we speak; as a result, in this chapter we make the subjectivity of the person an object. But why should

11. Maritain, *Existence and the Existent* (New York: Doubleday, 1948), 69–70. On 71 Maritain renders his thesis more precise by recognizing three kinds of improper knowledge of subjectivity that we do have: moral, poetical, and mystical knowledge. It is knowledge in the most proper sense, "which is to say, by mode of conceptual objectisation," which he says we lack with respect to subjectivity.

12. Ibid., 72. Both of these quotations are taken from the section "Subjectivity as subjectivity."

it not be possible to unfold in philosophical discourse that which is first of all experienced subjectively by us? Let us take a concrete example of such discourse: the subjectivity of self-presence, of which I just spoke. Our discussion put it in the position of the intentional object of our philosophizing: but did we thereby distort the subjectivity of self-presence, did self-presence thereby appear as a relation in which I objectify myself as an intentional object? But of course not! The whole point of our reflection and our discourse—our objectifying reflection and discourse—was to find and to affirm precisely the subjectivity of self-presence. Or did this subjectivity disappear from view when we objectivized it in philosophical reflection? But then what was it which we had before our minds when we understood that self-presence is irreducible to any subject-object relation?

I am reminded of an objection that Aquinas once posed to himself and of his response to it. In discussing whether the mind can form propositions about God, he objects that God is simple and any proposition is something composite; our discourse about God would seem inescapably to present Him otherwise (compositely) than He really is.[13] Aquinas identifies with great precision the equivocation on which the objection rests: the composite form of our propositions does not require us to ascribe composition to that about which we speak in the propositions; the logical compositeness of our propositions does not require an ontological compositeness in the referent of them: "for our intellect understands in one way, and things are in another" (ad 3). When we say God is absolutely simple, our proposition, composed though it be of subject, predicate, and copula, precisely removes any such composition from God. Aquinas adduces a parallel case to support his distinction. Assuming the immateriality of the mind, he says:

> Thus it is clear that our intellect understands material things below itself in an immaterial way; not that it understands them to be immaterial things: but its way of understanding is immaterial. Likewise, when it understands simple things above itself, it understands them according to its own way, which is composite; yet not so as to understand them to be composite things (ad 3).

In a directly parallel way, we understand subjectivity in an objectifying, intentional way, yet not so as to understand it to be itself an objectifying, intentional form of consciousness; we can put subjectivity in front of us as object, yet understand it precisely as subjectivity.

13. Aquinas, *Summa Theologiae*, I, q. 13, a. 12, obj. 3.

And yet the criticized position must have its truth, for it has often been maintained. I would express its truth like this. Certain experiences cannot be reflected on as objects as long as we are living in the experiences; thus, for example, there is no quicker way to kill the act of prayer than to begin reflecting on it and examining it as an object. Perhaps there are not only acts but even enduring attitudes of the person that cannot be reflected on, or can be reflected on only partially, as long as the person lives in them. It seems that certain acts and attitudes require so strong a commitment from us to their motivating object that they cease to exist as soon as we step outside of them to examine them as objects. We can seriously interfere with the authenticity of our inner life by carrying self-observation too far; we have to live in our acts and not outside of them as observers of them. But this important fact about our inner lives is far from implying a general unknowability of personal subjectivity. It implies only that certain elements of *my own* subjective experiencing are unavailable to my objectifying act, it implies nothing about my apprehension of the experiencing *of others;* and it implies that these elements are unavailable to me only *as long as* I have the experience, but not *before or after* having the experience.[14] And it in no way tells against the possibility of understanding subjectivity in principle, that is, understanding philosophically what it essentially is.

I hope to overcome the objection not only by what I have just now said, but also by means of the investigations of subjectivity in the present chapter; I think that they will lead to enough results to convince everyone that, however one explains it, we are indeed able to reflect philosophically on subjectivity.

We will return to this subject in Chapter 5.2 when we test critically the thesis of Scheler that persons can never be made objects of anyone's acts. Scheler's claim has a more personalist basis than does Maritain's; it does not turn on the apparent impossibility of objectifying subjectivity, but on the apparent resistance of persons to being objectified.

---

14. This point is ably made by Josef Seifert in his excellent critique of the thesis of the unknowability of subjectivity in his *Leib und Seele* (Salzburg: Anton Pustet Verlag, 1973), 45–61. His analysis expands on other important points that I only mentioned in the text, such as the self-contradiction committed by all who say that subjectivity can never be made the object of an intentional act: they objectify it in the intentional act of making this assertion.

*4. How the structure of personal selfhood shows itself in
subjectivity, especially in recollected subjectivity*

Having clarified to this point the subjectivity of the person, and the
knowability of it, I can now put the question: how can we recognize in
personal subjectivity the structure of selfhood and incommunicability
that we were studying in the first two chapters? How can our previous
reflection be subjectively enriched? I have already made some observations in passing on this subjective enrichment, but I now make it my
subject.

Suppose that in our conscious lives we lacked all conscious relation
to ourselves. Suppose that we could indeed cognize all kinds of objects
and could act volitionally towards them, but that we lacked entirely any
conscious relation to ourselves. It seems that this lack of subjectivity,
assuming that it were possible at all, could only do violence to us as
persons. For to be entirely absorbed in the objects of our cognizing and
of our willing is surely a mode of existing at odds with being an end in
ourselves, a being of our own, standing in ourselves. The intentional
objects of our acting would become a cause of heteronomy for us if we
were to lose ourselves entirely in them; they would draw us off ourselves in a depersonalizing way.

It is only because in all of our cognizing we are present to ourselves,
and in all of our willing we have to do with ourselves, that we need not
live lost in things outside of ourselves, but can remain in ourselves even
as we encounter them, and so can encounter them as persons who are
ends in themselves and who belong to themselves. This is why we can
recognize in the subjectivity of the person the selfhood and solitude of
personal existence that we previously discussed.

But now suppose that we were indeed consciously related to ourselves, but related only *objectively*. We would not be entirely lost in
things in the way just described, we would still have a certain conscious
grip on ourselves, but we would not yet be living the selfhood of personal being. We would live strangely outside of ourselves; we would not
really live our being-established in ourselves and our standing in ourselves. We can live our selfhood and actualize it only if in all our acting
we have to do with ourselves subjectively, experiencing ourselves from
within ourselves. Here, then, is a further way in which we can recognize
in personal subjectivity the selfhood and solitude of the person.

We also find that our *experience of personhood in others* is rooted in our *experience of their subjectivity.* Suppose that we ignored the subjective self-experience of another, making no effort to feel ourselves into it but being content to look at him from the outside; we would do very little justice to the personhood of the other. But if we enter sympathetically into his subjectivity, we begin to experience him as person; as we come to understand the other *as he experiences himself,* we are confronted with the other as a being of his own, as an end in himself. This personalist significance of subjectivity was expressed by Newman in the previous chapter. After presenting the point of view according to which human beings are mere parts of larger social wholes, Newman suddenly changes his point of view so that human beings might be revealed as persons. Notice that the new, personalist point of view is a subjective point of view, for Newman introduces it like this: "But what is the truth? why, that every being in that great concourse is his own centre. . . . He has his own hopes and fears, desires, judgements, and aims; he is everything to himself. . . ."

I now propose to enter more deeply into the subjective disclosure of personal selfhood by distinguishing between stronger and weaker forms of subjectivity and by showing that the stronger the subjectivity, the more developed the selfhood. Let us consider what it is for our subjectivity to be weak, and for it to be strengthened by the act of *recollecting oneself.* It is the act in which persons recall not something *about* themselves in the past, but recall their very selves in the present, and recall themselves not as an *object* of cognition, but as *subject,* and not just as subject of cognition but of all kinds of acts. Though this experience has been discussed almost exclusively in the writings of spiritual masters,[15] it can be understood, or at least something of the deep revelation of the person that it contains can be understood, without any reference to the religious life.[16]

1. Two antitheses to recollected subjectivity. It is helpful to begin by considering the conscious condition of the person in which the person is

15. See for example Romano Guardini, *Prayer in Practice,* Chapter 1; von Hildebrand, *Transformation in Christ,* Chapter 6.

16. One of the few philosophers to bring recollection into his philosophy of the person is Max Scheler. See his talk of *Sammlung* in his essay, "Die Stellung des Menschen im Kosmos"; English in *Man's Place in Nature* (New York: Farrar, Straus, and Cudahy, 1962), 40ff. But *Sammlung* is here very unsatisfactorily translated as "concentration"; it is far more adequately rendered as "recollection."

precisely *not* recollected; this procedure, which is similar to the one used in Chapter 1.1, will enable us to find recollection through its conspicuous absence, and also to observe recollection as an event, as something that comes about where it had been lacking, and thus to display the actuality of personal selfhood in a dynamic way. In fact, I want to point out two different conscious conditions in which persons are not recollected.

a. There is a state of consciousness in which our subjectivity gets so weakened that we tend to lose ourselves in the things around us. We are so inwardly weakened that we lack a firm ground in ourselves on which to stand in dealing with the impressions that stream in on us and with the experiences that we undergo. This weakening can under certain circumstances go very far, as when persons watch television in a very passive way. The glazed look on their faces reveals the far-reaching loss of themselves in what they are looking at, it reveals how weak their self-presence has become. Such a state of consciousness approaches a mere succession of impressions, in which memory in all its deeper forms tends to be extinguished, and persons tend to live completely in their present impression. Such persons do not take a distance to what they experience in the present, they do not bring it into relation to previous experiences, they do not form a critical judgment on it; they do not amount to subjects consciously facing objects, and their self-presence comes close to being extinguished. This is why their sense of distinctness from other beings gets weakened and why they almost feel themselves to be "of one piece" with them.

In this description I am stressing the *passivity* of this reduced state of conscious self-presence; but I also want to call attention to something closely related to it, namely to the *loss of inner unity.* Such dispersed persons lose *one center* in themselves to which the objects of experience are referred; they undergo an inner fragmentation and cease to be the center of their world. They do not really have as their own their experiences, which seem rather to happen in them. Their inner life comes to be nothing but a reflex of the multiplicity of the objects they experience.

As a result of this passivity and fragmentation, they cannot really originate any life and activity of their own; they rather tend to be borne along by what happens to them and what happens in them. They live at the beck and call of their urges and instincts. This is why they cannot really act through themselves. Thus they lose the ability to understand deeply what they experience, for they are not sufficiently gathered into themselves so as to take that spiritual distance to things which is presupposed for knowing and understanding them. Not only that, but they lose their ability to make decisions and to perform moral actions that are radically their own. As soon as they encounter things with some character of goodness they are irresistibly attracted to them; they lack a threshold in themselves that the attraction must not cross. They are not subjectively handed over to themselves so as to be able to determine themselves in relation to them, they are instead determined by them. They have neither sufficient distance to them nor sufficient inner unity to preserve their freedom in the midst of them. Just as this distance and inner unity are presupposed for deeply understanding and knowing a being, so they are no less presupposed for acting towards it in freedom.

It is not difficult to see how persons of weakened subjectivity relate to other persons. They can be easily manipulated by others, they live too much in the expectations of others; they repeat the opinions of others without really making any opinions their own and without even realizing that they have no mind of their own. And if they were to repeat contradictory opinions this would only show their lack of inner unity. One could appropriate Heidegger's analysis of what "one does," "one thinks," etc., and even more Kierkegaard's analyses of conventional belief and of its lack of "subjectivity," for the purpose of characterizing the heteronomy in relation to other persons that is typical of dispersed subjectivity.

b. There is another way in which this self-loss occurs. I am thinking of persons who are always striving to realize some goal in the future—we assume that it is some worthy goal—but they strive in such a way that they never experience the present fully. They live in a state of restlessness conditioned by their tension towards the future. The present does not open up for them, and they do not expand to fill it; they never fully achieve presence. If perchance they try to dwell in the present, they are overcome by a certain spiritual malaise and listlessness, and seek relief by resuming their striving towards their goal.

This is a disorder of subjectivity that forms a remarkable contrast to that of dispersion. This one is not so passive as that one is; in fact it presupposes intense goal-directed activities. Nor does it involve the dispersion, the scatteredness that I described; the consciousness of the persons who sacrifice the present to the future is very definitely focused, and they might with great self-control turn away from every distraction that would divert them from their goal. And they have a very different relation to time; they do not lose themselves in the present moment, as does the person with dispersed consciousness; as I was just saying, they instead lose themselves in the future. This inability to live a fully actual present is a condition of subjectivity possible only in an adult; it has no analogy to a child's subjectivity, as does the scattered condition of consciousness. And yet this inability also involves a serious loss of personal life; those who suffer from it never achieve a real self-presence, they never really dwell with themselves.

It is their preoccupation with their goals in the future that keeps them from coming to themselves. This is why they cannot experience anything deeply and authentically, and why they typically feel that the events in their lives, for all their hectic activity,[17] pass by as in a dream, and that they themselves are phantastic and unreal. And they are aware that their acting, for all its intense directedness to some result, does not come from their inner center and is not radically their own, and indeed that they are more the slaves of their activity than its masters. They act almost as if they were a mere instrument for the completion of their projects; their power of acting through themselves has been wounded.

2. *Recollecting oneself.* But however reduced my self-presence, I always have the possibility of what is expressively called *recollecting myself.* In recollecting myself *I come to myself.* I recover the center of my being. I take a distance to what I experience, or to my projects, and I can awaken to them. I become a subject facing an objective world, and not just the shadow cast in consciousness by the objective world. In becoming recollected I actualize a certain self-presence and awaken as out of a stupor. Before recollecting myself I had lost myself in things around myself, or in my unfinished projects; I was possessed by them. Now I recover myself, retake possession of myself, come to dwell with myself, become present to myself, and not only present to myself but handed over to myself. As a result of thus coming to myself I become capable of those acts which I had previously been incapable of. Thus I have enough distance to things to be able to understand them, and to

17. One might recall here Josef Pieper's profound study of *acedia* and its modern forms and especially the form it takes in the modern obsession with productive work. He shows how this obsession derives from a fundamental "refusal to acquiesce in one's being." See his "Leisure, the Basis of Culture," chapter 3, in Dru, tr., *Leisure, the Basis of Culture* (New York: New American Library, 1956).

determine myself in freedom with respect to them. And as for the opinions of others, I can take a distance to them too, and returning to myself I can ask, But what do I, I myself, really think?

By recollecting myself I also gain a distance from my unfinished projects, and realize that even now, in the present moment, and before they are completed, I am a self, an unrepeatable self, and do not become one by means of completing them. Through recollection I recover a moment of inner rest, of dwelling in peace with myself, which had been disrupted by my preoccupation with my projects.

The self-possession achieved in recollection should not be limited to the mere ability to *concentrate intently* on some subject or task, or the ability to *control oneself;* nor is it necessarily expressed in such abilities. I can concentrate intensely on, say, driving and exercise great self-control in turning away from everything that could divert me from driving, and yet do this without living out of any particularly deep self-presence, without breaking out of that immediacy to my surroundings which I was describing. In recollecting myself I recover the unity of my being at the deepest level; this depth is in no way guaranteed by concentration or self-control, which may have a merely technical character and entirely lack the existential depth of recollection.

It is only natural to ask at this point how one goes about achieving recollection. I will not enter here into this new question, but will instead refer again to the authors just cited. I remark in passing that there seem to be two fundamental ways of recollecting oneself (which do not exclude each other). I can begin to do it directly, withdrawing myself by an act of the will from the multiplicity of things in which I am involved and collecting myself into myself. But this beginning of recollection has to be completed by a more indirect way: I can think of myself in relation to something ultimately important, such as my own death or the death of a beloved person, or think of myself before God, and I can let myself be recollected, not so much by my own act, as by the recollecting power issuing from things of ultimate significance. (In Chapters 6 and 7 I will have more to say about this second way of recollecting oneself.) This is why the best treatments of recollection have been written by religious writers. We could say, then, that there is the immanent way of recollecting oneself, and the more transcendent way. The fullness of recollection of which we have been thinking in the previous pages certainly presupposes the transcendent sources of recollection.

What is it, then, to recollect oneself out of a state of being lost in things or projects? We can answer with the famous utterance of St. Augustine, "*noli foras ire, in te redi, in interiore homine habitat veritas.*"[18]

3. Personal selfhood as enacted and manifested in recollected self-presence. It is clear that in the state of weakened subjectivity it is my personhood which tends to get submerged. Of course I do not cease to be a person absolutely, nor do I run the danger of going out of existence altogether, but the actuality of personal life is weakened in me. We recognize in this state of reduced subjectivity the specific lack of all the elements of personal selfhood that we studied above. When I am "ecstatically lost"[19] in the things and the people around myself, or in my projects, I precisely do not subjectively live my selfhood and especially my solitude, my having a being of my own. And far from experiencing myself as unrepeatable, I feel thrown among things, as one among many, as small and insignificant in the vast universe. Instead of possessing myself I am possessed by other beings. I lose the power of acting in a typically personal way, that is, through myself. The more I live in this state of being lost in things and projects, the more I lose the fullness of personal life.

We will perhaps recognize more readily this loss of personal life if we consider that we do not always just fall into it but that we often *want* to be in it. Often we cannot bear the selfhood and solitude of personal existence, we dread the burden of living as personal selves and in possession of ourselves, and we want nothing more than to lose ourselves, to immerse ourselves in things around us, whether by a passive exposure to them or by an active involvement with them. There are many addictive dependencies on food, drugs, other persons, which can only be understood as forms of fleeing in fear from the burden of personal selfhood.

One thinks here of the unforgettable words of Pascal in the *Pensées* on the itch for *divertissement* and on the use of *divertissement* to flee

18. St. Augustine, *De vera religione*, XXXIX, 72. "Do not go outside of yourself, return into yourself, in the inner man dwells truth." It is worth mentioning the next sentence in the text of St. Augustine, which points in the direction of our investigations in Part II of this study: "If you find that you are by nature mutable, transcend yourself." We, too, shall be discussing a transcendence intimately connected with interiority and recollection.

19. This expression of Scheler, which refers to a negative, depersonalizing ecstasy, should not prevent us from recognizing an entirely positive kind of ecstasy in which the person supremely lives as person.

from ourselves. And yet what I am saying here is in fact quite different from what Pascal says. Pascal says that we cannot endure the sight of our misery and mortality, and that this is what we are fleeing from when we distract ourselves. But my idea is that it is *not just the misery but the greatness* of the human person that makes us flee from ourselves. For the selfhood of the person is our strength and glory as persons, the source of our being *imago Dei* (more on this in the final chapter); it is in many ways opposed to our misery and mortality. Considering the matter in the abstract one might think that we could experience our mortality as a burden, but not our selfhood; and yet this too can be a burden for us, a too heavy "weight of glory," and then we want nothing more than to blunt our sense of selfhood by immersing ourselves and losing ourselves in many things.

In recollecting ourselves we recover ourselves as persons, and achieve, or move towards achieving, the fullness of personal life. The reader will easily recognize in recollected consciousness the presence, the conspicuous presence of all the aspects of personal selfhood discussed above. The more deeply I am recollected, the stronger my sense of my interiority, my inwardness. And what is this interiority if not the living from within of the selfhood and solitude of the person? What is it if not the "subjectification" of my self-possession and my belonging to myself?[20] The stronger my interiority, the more I subjectively experience my self-possession, and the more I in fact do possess myself.

Or consider the incommunicability of the person: the more recollected I am, dwelling with myself, the more I experience myself from within myself. With this intimacy and immediacy of my self-experience I experience myself as I can experience no other person, and I thereby experience myself as being myself and no other. Not only that, but the more recollected I am, the less I feel myself to be just one among many, an insignificant speck in comparison with all the other persons and with the immensity of space-time, and the stronger my sense of the mysterious "absoluteness" of my selfhood as well as of the dignity of myself as person. The more I am recollected, then the more I sense how "worldly" it is to affirm my personal unrepeatability through extraordinary achievements that set me apart from everyone else, and the more I will be se-

---

20. There is a priceless Spanish term that expresses this unity of recollection and selfhood: *ensimismamiento*. If I were to make an effort to translate the untranslatable, I might say something like "selfification." Ortega y Gasset often uses *ensimismamiento* in a sense akin to what I mean by recollection; see his "Ensimismamiento y alteracion," in *Obras Completas* (Madrid, 1958), V.

cure in my unrepeatability even while I am very like many others in my accomplishments and social position.

And the same holds for the power of persons to act through themselves on the basis of their selfhood: the more persons are recollected and gathered into themselves, then the more distance they have to things and the more they are able to assert themselves towards them, rather than to live under their spell and to act only at their prompting. This power of acting through oneself on the basis of one's selfhood is strongly experienced in recollection.

In Part II I will explain why the selfhood of human persons is a transcendent selfhood, a selfhood that becomes itself in transcending itself. This dimension of selfhood, too, can be found in recollection. It is above all in recollected subjectivity that persons are empowered to transcend themselves. I will say more on this later, but the attentive reader will recall that we already encountered this opening of subjectivity to transcendence at the beginning of our discussion of self-presence. I will also say more later about the transcendent sources of recollection just alluded to; here, too, we will find a subjective expression of the transcendent selfhood of human persons.

If we now return to the essay of Wojtyla from which we began in this chapter, we can understand better than before why he sees in personal subjectivity an indispensable source for the philosophy of the person.

5. How turning outward to other beings ("bad transcendence") can endanger selfhood and subjectivity

As I keep saying, I entirely recognize the transcendence of the human person, even though I will make it my subject only in the chapters of Part II. Human persons can go beyond themselves to participate by knowledge in that which is real, and to participate by willing and loving in that which is good and worthy. In Chapters 5 and 6 I will try to show the dialectical relations which obtain between selfhood and transcendence, that is, show how transcendence, far from excluding selfhood, is in fact grounded in it and is perfected by it. But at present it is not any such dialectical relations that concern me; I want instead to call attention to certain relations of exclusivity whereby a kind of turning outward to other beings—a kind of "bad transcendence"—is achieved at the expense of selfhood, or in other words is a cause of heteronomy for persons. In the following I lay no claim to systematic completeness; I simply offer a few specimens of such heteronomy, some taken from the cognitive, others taken from the moral acting of persons.

1. We have already encountered instances of such turning outward. When in dispersed consciousness I am "ecstatically lost" in things, my relation to these things is achieved at the expense of my selfhood. This heteronomy is all the worse if it is other persons in whom I lose myself. Their expectations of me can be so strongly felt by me that they block out my own expectations of myself. Perhaps I really do have expectations of my own for myself and suffer a temporary occlusion of them when I am in the presence of a strong personality who asserts forcefully his expectations of me. But the more extreme case is possible in which I am permanently prevented from leading my own life by some strong other in whom I am in a sense absorbed. This "heteropathic identification" with others, as Scheler called it in discussing it with great penetration,[21] is clearly a pathological form of personal existence. There is little consolation in the fact that I am not locked in myself but am related to others and transcend myself towards them: this relation to others is a relation of the most depersonalizing heteronomy. Of course it goes without saying that this "transcendence" towards others is no real transcendence; I cannot really transcend myself towards others as long as it is not *I* who transcend.

2. Let us consider a less grievous but perhaps more interesting case of how my relation to other minds can interfere with my subjectivity. As philosopher I not only have the objective task of attaining to what is in itself true, but also the subjective task of seeing to it that it is I, I myself who attain to the truth, and not someone else. One will at first ask: who are the philosophers so deranged that they do not realize that when they philosophize it is they and not someone else in them who philosophize? And yet I insist: it is a very difficult task, which only few succeed in, to search for the truth so that it is I, I myself who attain to it, and not someone else.

Consider the way in which thinkers often deal with objections raised to their positions. It is of course necessary to take seriously the most plausible objections and to develop one's own position in doing so. But it happens that intellectuals often think that they have no right to their own insight until they have silenced all possible objectors. They often

21. In his *Wesen und Formen der Sympathie*, Part I, Chapter 2. English: *The Nature of Sympathy* (Hamden, CT: Shoe String Press, 1973), 18–23, 42–44.

refer to the existence of all those who still do not agree with them, as if this obliged them in their philosophical conscience to suspend their own convictions. How many thinkers acquiesce, for example, in the thesis of value relativism, not because they are convinced that all values are relative, but because they do not know how else to take account of all those people who do not share their value intuitions. Now it is not at all exaggerated to say that such thinkers are in danger of confusing their own minds with those of others. For in the question of value, as in every other question, we have to come to the point at which we withdraw from the many others and their opinions about value and turn into ourselves, recollecting ourselves, and ask ourselves, as if before God, But what do I, I myself really think about value? Do I find that many things are endowed with real and intrinsic worth? And if, in this philosophical solitude, which belongs to me precisely as subjective person, I really do find intrinsic worth and excellence in things, then I have to cling fast to this, despite all the divergent value perceptions that other people say they have.[22] Of course I would do well to let myself be challenged by this divergency to test my perceptions anew, and to learn to hold them more critically; and I may want to try to explain the causes of others failing to see what I see. But still, I see what I see, and I must not deny my own mind. If, however, I am unsettled in my perception of value by the clamor of the many others, and lose my grip on what I have seen with my own mind, and think that the question of value has to stay open until everyone in the world comes around to reporting value perceptions that agree with what I see, then I am beginning to show confusion about where the boundary runs between my own mind and the minds of others. And in this confusion I am drawn off myself towards others; one could speak of a bad transcendence towards them that interferes with my subjectivity.

Or consider how difficult it is to avoid this confusion when reading great philosophical authors or hearing the lectures of great living philosophers. It is all too easy to feel ourselves into their intellectual world and to come to understand the unity and style of their thought, to relish the greatness of their thought, to understand with the greatest sympathy what they teach about truth, and yet to live so intensely in *their* thought

---

22. Cf. the words of Socrates to Callicles in the *Gorgias* (482 b): "Yet, I think, my good sir, that it would be better for me . . . that the mass of mankind should disagree with me and contradict me than that I, a single individual, should be out of harmony with myself and contradict myself."

that we cease to cultivate *our own*. As we make our way through the great works, we run the risk of a certain self-forgetfulness, of ceasing to exist as an independent center of thought; it is the risk of a certain spiritual passivity—which is entirely compatible with working ever so hard at our studies. Of course we all know that our own thought will not be worth much if we do not immerse ourselves in the thought of the greatest minds, but still, we fail to be not slaves but freemen in the kingdom of the mind if we do not know how to put aside our books and teachers and, entering into ourselves, ask ourselves what w*e, we ourselves* really think about the great issues. Once again we see that it is after all not so far-fetched to speak of the danger of losing one's own mind in other minds (but it is a danger subtler than the danger of Scheler's heteropathic identification with others).

Cardinal Newman says exactly what I want to say in a well-known passage in which he defends the principle that sometimes "egotism is true modesty."

> I begin with expressing a sentiment, which is habitually in my thoughts, whenever they are turned to the subject of mental or moral science . . . viz. that in these provinces of inquiry egotism is true modesty. In religious inquiry each of us can speak only for himself, and for himself he has a right to speak. His own experiences are enough for himself, but he cannot speak for others: he cannot lay down the law. . . . He knows what has satisfied and satisfies himself; if it satisfies him, it is likely to satisfy others; if, as he believes and is sure, it is true, it will approve itself to others also, for there is but one truth. And doubtless he does find in fact, that, allowing for the difference of minds and modes of speech, what convinces him, does convince others also. There will be very many exceptions, but these will admit of explanation. . . . This being the case, it causes no uneasiness to any one who honestly attempts to set down his own view of the Evidences of Religion, that at first sight he seems to be but one among many who are all in opposition to each other. But, however that may be, he brings together his reasons, and relies on them, because they are his own, and this is his primary evidence; and he has a second ground of evidence, in the testimony of those who agree with him. But his best evidence is the former, which is derived from his own thoughts; . . . and therefore his true sobriety and modesty consists, not in claiming for his conclusions an acceptance or a scientific approval which is not to be found anywhere, but in stating what are personally his own grounds for his belief . . . grounds which he holds to be so sufficient, that he thinks that others do hold them implicitly or in substance, or would hold them, if they inquired fairly, or will hold if they listen to him, or do not hold from impediments, invincible or not as it may be, into which

he has no call to inquire. However, his own business is to speak for him-self.[23]

This is exactly the point; in questions of truth my task is to inquire, to think, and to speak for myself, and not to feel my mind to be a mere part of some collective mind, as if I could come to a conclusion only by thinking in concert with the collective mind. This would establish me in a relation of bad transcendence towards other minds.

3. I have been speaking of a certain sacrifice of subjectivity to tran-scendence in the way some people lead their intellectual lives. I might inquire whether the same sacrifice sometimes occurs on a level more theoretical than practical. I would be inclined to see an example of its theoretical occurrence in a famous Aristotelian teaching regarding knowl-edge. In *On the Soul*, III, iv, Aristotle says that the mind has its whole being in the objects that it knows, so that the mind "is, before it thinks, not actually any real being" (429a 24, Ross translation), and has, after it thinks, only the intentional being of its objects, since to know them is in a certain sense to become them. If Aristotle is just stressing the all-im-portant actualizing function that the knowing of objects has for the mind, his teaching need not disparage the selfhood of the knower, who can still be understood to have a being of his or her own. But it is to be feared that Aristotle in fact, at least in these passages, reduces the actu-ality of the knower to the intentional actuality in the mind of the beings known, overlooking entirely the presence of the knower to himself; so that Aristotle opens himself to the charge of asserting the transcendence of knowing at the expense of the selfhood of the knower. Later in the Aristotelian tradition philosophers compared the mind to prime matter, saying that the mind is to its objects as prime matter is to material sub-stances: this seems to dissolve entirely the being of the mind into the being of its objects. Perhaps one could say that the position I find in some texts of Aristotle is the extreme opposite to any subjective ideal-ism: in the latter, subjectivity swallows up transcendence, but in this thought of Aristotle, transcendence swallows up subjectivity.

4. I have been speaking of how in the intellectual life transcendence can be either lived or theoretically asserted at the expense of subjectiv-ity; let us now examine a case of the same danger occurring in the moral life.

23. John Henry Newman, *A Grammar of Assent* (London: Longmans, Green, and Co., 1898), 384–85.

There is a certain extreme altruism that teaches that we must never look for our own happiness in loving another person and must do nothing but love the others for their own sake. As soon as we desire to be happy in loving others, we spoil our love with selfishness. A love free of selfishness is a love free of any desire to be happy in loving the other.

Von Hildebrand has shown in *Das Wesen der Liebe*[24] that the altruistic ideal of love is depersonalizing, that it tends to the elimination *not just of selfishness but of the personal selfhood* of the one who tries to love altruistically. Or in my language: those who transcend themselves towards another in love must also have to do with themselves subjectively in the sense of willing the happiness that flows from their loving. *This is not because in loving we inevitably make concessions to our selfishness, as if the mistake of altruism were to overlook the inevitability of a certain minimum of selfishness.* No; the reason, or at least part of the reason, why we will to be happy in loving is that we have to stay intact as persons in loving. We must not love in such a way that we cease to stand in ourselves and to belong to ourselves; we must not abolish ourselves in favor of the beloved person.

Of course it is possible to assert the desire for happiness at the expense of the self-transcendence of love, as in the eudaemonism according to which we love another only for the sake of becoming happy ourselves, and cannot transcend ourselves in the sense of loving another for his or her own sake. But this is not the only alternative to altruism,[25] as von Hildebrand has shown; one can desire to be happy in the beloved person without reducing the love to a means for one's happiness, without ceasing to love the other for his or her own sake. And in fact, as he has also shown, the desire to be happy in loving perfects the transcendence of love; only a fully intact person can act authentically, and so only such a one can love authentically. In addition, there are certain kinds of love, such as spousal love, where I love the other by desiring to be happy in the other; if I devalue my desire for happiness, then I make myself unfit for these loves and for the self-donation proper to them.

24. Von Hildebrand, *Das Wesen der Liebe* (Stuttgart: Kohlhammer Verlag, 1971), above all Chapter 9, but also 193–197. A kindred critic of the same altruism is Max Scheler in his *Ressentiment,* Holdheim, tr. (New York, 1972), 95–96, 124–126.

25. It seems that Ayn Rand's philosophy of selfishness draws much of its attractiveness from presenting itself as the only possible alternative to extreme altruism. As soon as one sees that the core of truth in her critique of altruism is far from implying her philosophy of selfishness, this philosophy loses all its plausibility.

But with this we touch upon the dialectic of subjectivity and transcendence and the way each perfects the other, and this subject belongs in Chapters 5 and 6; at present I simply want to say that we need the strength of subjectivity implied in desiring our own happiness in order not to lose ourselves in a depersonalizing way when we open ourselves to another in love.[26]

One has to understand rightly what I mean by "desiring one's own happiness," otherwise one will think that I greatly exaggerate its importance in the existence of the person. I obviously do not mean by happiness mere satisfaction or gratification: why should we have to cling to that in order to stay intact as persons? Nor do I mean an instinctive desire on the level of shrinking from pain or clutching at my life when I sense that it is immediately endangered. As we saw in section 2 above, there is an instinct of self-preservation that belongs more to what happens in the person than to what the person himself performs. It would make no sense to say that I have to be subject to such reactions in order to stay intact as person in my attempts at loving others. No, the desire for happiness of which I speak is performed by persons acting through themselves; it is an exercise of their subjective freedom. We all know that there are many seductive goods capable of diverting us from what we know to be our real happiness, and that it is a work not of instinct or natural appetite but of freedom to hold fast to our happiness and to continue to will it in spite of them.

5. One more example of "bad transcendence," this one also taken from the moral life: ethical consequentialism, the ethical teaching that the whole measure of right and wrong in actions lies in the consequences of the actions. This ethics often poses as particularly personalistic and polemicizes against what it takes to be a depersonalizing ethics of rules. And yet it supplies a perfect example of sacrificing personal selfhood to the pursuit of certain things outside of the person.

The consequentialists look at what happens in nature beyond our control, such as diseases running their course, earthquakes doing their dam-

---

26. Let us mention an important extension that Josef Seifert has made of von Hildebrand's philosophy of love. In analyzing the motivation of a morally good action, Seifert resists the view that the happiness which comes from a morally good action should play no role in the motivation of the action. Of course it should not play the main role; but moral action becomes depersonalized if happiness plays no role at all. Seifert goes so far as to speak of a certain self-annihilation of the moral subject who renounces any interest in his or her own happiness. See Seifert, *Was ist und was motiviert eine sittliche Handlung?* (Salzburg: Anton Pustet Verlag, 1976), 70–77.

age, the turning of the seasons. They hope, as we all hope, for the best possible proportion of good over bad results in the unfolding of these natural events. Thus they hope that a hurricane might destroy as few houses as possible, that a sick person might recover rather than die from his disease, etc. They hope for good results, and hope that they will prevail as far as possible over the bad ones that threaten to occur. Now consequentialism teaches that, to the extent that events *are* subject to our control, we should bring about just those results which, when events are not subject to us, we hope for. It teaches that a moral agent is just as much a natural cause as the causes beyond our control, and should distinguish itself from other natural causes by being as beneficent a cause as possible, intervening in the world out of the same beneficence that it feels in the form of wishing and hoping at those times when it can only look on helplessly. There seems to be in this ethical doctrine a strong element of transcendence, namely transcendence towards good results; the moral subject is supposedly not selfishly preoccupied with his own motives and intentions but is rather turned outward towards the world with the intention of improving it.

But this ethical doctrine has a strong element of self-forgetfulness. It forgets that the moral subject is not just another natural cause but is an acting person who can introduce things into the world that no other natural cause can introduce. Since I who act belong to myself and exist as an end in myself, my actions are not just instrumental means, existing only for the sake of their results; they reflect the selfhood from which they proceed and so are capable of having a meaning that goes far beyond that of instrumentality. Thus, for example, no natural cause, however destructive, can be said to respect or violate rights; when an earthquake swallows up a village, no rights are violated. But if I wantonly destroy the village, I violate the rights of all who are injured or killed. My actions, even though they produce the same effects as certain natural causes, have, in virtue of my personal selfhood and subjectivity, a meaning utterly impossible for a natural cause. Thus my actions towards others can have the meaning of using others in a depersonalizing way, or of letting them go in such a way as to stand before me as persons. No natural causes can have any such meaning. What ethical consequentialism typically fails to see is that I can stay intact in my moral acting only if I know in myself that as subjective person I am not a mere instrumental means for producing results, but am called to realize through my acting entirely non-instrumental meanings that express, among other things, my being an end in myself.

To these five instances of bad transcendence, or of transcendence-become-heteronomy, I could add many others. I realize that there is also the opposite deformity, what we might call a bad immanence, by which I mean that the subjectivity of persons becomes so intense as to interfere with their power of transcending themselves towards other beings. There are people who are absorbed in their inner lives in such a way as to be unable to get out of themselves; as Scheler shows, there is not only heteropathic but also idiopathic identification. This excess of subjectivity can also be more than just a personal failing; it can become a philosophical error. All those, for example, who maintain some kind of the just-mentioned subjective idealism commit such a mistake. In saying with Kant that we know reality when we make it conform to our minds rather than conforming our minds to reality, one asserts the subjectivity of the knower at the expense of the independence of the objects known. I am only claiming at present—and how can one reasonably deny it?—that it is also possible to assert transcendence at the expense of subjectivity, and ultimately at the expense of personal selfhood, in other words, to assert transcendence to the point of heteronomy.

But it is above all the investigations of Chapters 5 and 6 that will dispel any appearance of neglecting transcendence; as one enters into the dialectical relations obtaining between subjectivity and transcendence, one will see how necessary the work of the present chapter is for any philosophy of transcendence. Some readers may in fact want to proceed directly to Chapter 5, as this would be as good a way as any of reading this study.

But the talk of subjectivity not only leads to transcendence; it also leads in at least two other directions. It leads to questions about the being of the person, such as whether the subjectivity of the person excludes the substantiality that the *philosophia perennis* has ascribed to personal being. I will turn to these questions in the following chapter. The talk of subjectivity also leads to questions of intersubjectivity, to which I now turn.

6. Sharing in the subjectivity of others

As I indicated at the end of section 2, I have been speaking of the subjectivity of an individual person. If I do not proceed now to say something about intersubjectivity as well as collective subjectivity, I will seem to some readers to be tending towards some kind of solipsism. If it is in the first place myself I experience in my subjectivity, then I seem through my subjectivity to be enclosed in myself and cut off from others. I might express the concern of many readers like this: if Scheler warns, as we just saw, against what he calls a heteropathic identification with others, then surely he should also warn (as in fact he does) against an ideopathic identification of others with oneself, which is what we find in those people who seem to experience only themselves and who in encountering others can do no better than to project something of their inner lives into the others. You try to tell such people for instance about some suffering of yours, and all you can do is remind them of something similar in their own experience; instead of entering with sympathy and empathy into your suffering, they can only talk out of the experience of their own suffering. We could speak here of a kind of solipsism, even though such people do not formally deny the existence of other persons.

I turn, then, at the end of our discussion of subjectivity to the task of showing that we are as far removed as could be from anything that could be called solipsism. Following Wojtyla's lead I have tried to overcome a onesidedly cosmological image of man by consulting the evidence of personal subjectivity; but this has not had the effect of confining us to individual subjectivity. In fact, the subjective way proposed by Wojtyla would let us overcome a onesidedly cosmological approach to the social existence of man and develop a personalist philosophy of intersubjectivity and collective subjectivity. My results in the preceding sections are not at odds with such a philosophy, but receive their natural completion from it, and at the same time provide it with its true foundations. It cannot be my task in this study to develop a personalist social philosophy in proportion to its inherent importance, but only to show how my point of view in this study is altogether open for it. We have already seen in the previous chapter (Chapter 2.4) that my understanding of personal incommunicability does not leave persons isolated from one another, but rather underlies the most intimate forms of interpersonal life, and that in various ways. What I showed for incommunicability, I now propose to show for subjectivity.

The intersubjectivity of Nachfühlen and sympathy. Earlier in this chapter I said that, since we are ourselves and not any other, we experience ourselves from within ourselves more "naturally" than we experience others from within themselves. It typically costs us an effort to get into the subjectivity of another, an effort that we are spared when it comes to entering into our own subjectivity, given our identity with ourselves. It is true that the person suffering from Scheler's heteropathic identification with others seems to enter more easily into their experiencing than into his own experiencing of himself; but I regard this as a pathological self-loss because it reverses the normal priority of experiencing myself subjectively over experiencing others subjectively.

Now this priority does not mean that we can experience *only* ourselves subjectively. Though there is an inwardness and intimacy possible only in our self-experience, we are undeniably capable of experiencing others subjectively, that is, experiencing them to some extent as they experience themselves and their own world. This subjective experiencing of others has nothing to do with the pathological self-loss of heteropathic identification with others. We can enter into the subjective experiencing of others while remaining fully intact in our own self-experience. This subjective experiencing is not just any experience of their motives and desires; there is after all a way of experiencing these entirely as objects, as when I predict from long experience that a given situation will provoke, say, angry behavior in another. I refer instead to an experiencing of others whereby I, without blurring the distinction between myself and them, place myself at the center of their subjectivity and experience them to some extent in the same subjective way as they always experience themselves and as I always experience myself.[27] This is the experiencing of others on which all sympathizing and empathizing with them is based. It is also an indispensable element in any real love for another (though it can exist apart from any such love). In loving another you desire what is beneficial for the other, and this often leads you to consider what things mean to him and how he experiences them.

I said in section 4 that we experience others as persons in experiencing them subjectively; for in this way we experience them on their own terms, in their own being; and, as we know by now, persons are preeminently beings of their own. The pragmatic way of interacting with others that hinders me from doing justice to them as persons, equally hinders me from entering into their subjectivity. It often happens that as I take my pragmatic hands off another and release him to be himself, I begin wondering, "But how does this other person experience his or her life?" I begin saying with Newman, "He has his own hopes and fears, desires, judgements, and aims; he is everything to himself, and no one

---

27. The German words, *Nachfühlen, Nacherleben,* express better than any English words this sharing in the subjective experiencing of another. How can one say in English, "Ich kann Dir Deinen Schmerz gut nachfühlen"?

else is really anything." And with this I break through to the other as person.

But not only can I enter into the subjectivity of others and so find them as persons; something happens in my own subjectivity in and through this entering into others. Guardini has described this with great sensitivity. After speaking of approaching another as an object of my pragmatic interest, he considers the transformation whereby I encounter him or her as person.

> In the measure in which I release the being which at first I regarded only as an object, and consider it as a self meeting me from its own center, permitting it to become my "Thou," I pass from the attitude of a using or fighting subject into that of the "I."

A human being who uses others as things is not yet a real I; Guardini calls him merely a "using or fighting subject." He begins to exist as "I" only by letting the other "meet me from its own center."

> This process involves a risk. When confronting an object a man is only objectively interested. His personality is at rest. His interior countenance is not revealed. His hands are free for any desired movement. It is only what he possesses or can do that is involved, not his own self. But as soon as he confronts the other as an "I" something arises within him . . . he loses the protection which consists in the "objective quality" of the situation in which he is acting. When I glance at another as "I," I become open and "show" myself. . . . Personal destiny springs only from the unprotected openness of the "I-Thou" relation. . . .[28]

There is for Guardini a certain armored, fortified condition of the self in which it is not yet alive as a personal I; only in awakening to the subjectivity and freedom of others, and thereby living in a certain vulnerability in relation to them, does it quicken as personal I. This is not exactly a quickening in self-possession; indeed, vulnerability goes in a certain sense in the opposite direction of self-possession. We cannot fully explain this personal quickening in any of the terms of my analysis up to this point. Personal subjectivity evidently involves more than self-possession, a fact that we will encounter again and again throughout the chapters of Part II. What concerns us at present is that the act of entering into another person by feeling oneself into his or her subjectivity is an act in which the performing person thrives in a certain way in his own subjectivity. Persons must exist at a fundamental level of their being

28. Guardini, *The World and the Person* (Chicago: Regnery, 1965), 127–8.

with each other if the flourishing of one person's subjectivity is tied like this to sharing in the subjectivity of others.

Social dimensions of subjective freedom. 1. Let us return to the experience of a person being deeply recollected, which means being in possession of oneself and fully alive in what I called subjective freedom.

By recollecting myself I come to dwell with myself, but not only with myself. I also become open to others at the same depth in myself at which I dwell with myself. I begin to experience a certain solidarity with others, even if I am not in the company of anyone; and if I encounter someone, I find myself already open to him and disposed to welcome him as a fellow human being. In such an encounter I become aware of a certain deep receptivity in myself towards others that has grown out of my recollection. It is born of a sense of them and me belonging in some ultimate sense together. I am not drawn to others so as to use them or manipulate them; the lust to dominate is not a fruit of recollection. But as recollected, I am drawn to them as persons, I feel the need of living the solidarity in which I and they are already established as fellow human persons.

And there is the other social dimension of recollection that is well known: the deeper my recollection goes, the more I become aware of a divine Other in whom I live and am grounded. The opening into the other unfolds in recollection in relation to God as well as to human others.

Thus recollection reveals not only selfhood and solitude, it also reveals the social form of our existence; and this latter revelation is no less important for philosophy than the former.

2. In connection with subjective freedom I also spoke of the various ways in which a person can relate himself to himself as subject: he can be ashamed of himself, have confidence in himself, throw himself away in despair, have respect for himself, accept himself with all the limits imposed on him. I spoke of these as examples of acts of volitional subjectivity, or subjective freedom. Now, I spoke of these by referring to a solitary person dealing with himself; I have to overcome the abstractness of this point of view by noting that in many of these exercises of subjective freedom I am in fact subjectively disposing over myself *towards other persons,* as when I disclose myself to another, or bind myself in a promise or a vow to another, or when I enact my love for an-

other by performing in some way what is called a self-donation towards the other. In my subjective freedom, then, I can have to do not only with myself but *with myself in relation to some other.* In fact, some exercises of my subjective freedom that at first seem to involve only me in relation to myself, reveal on closer examination an opening to some other person before whom they are performed. Thus all being ashamed of oneself presupposes perhaps some other before whom one is ashamed. Certainly self-pity requires an audience. Kierkegaard thinks that the act of accepting or rejecting the self that I am can only be performed before God, so that it is inevitably a profoundly religious act.

3. But there is another, quite different social dimension of my subjective freedom. Other persons commonly empower me to perform certain acts of subjective freedom, including the most significant of them. The respect shown to me as person by others enables me to respect myself as person; their respect mediates me to myself, empowering me to respect myself. The unconditional acceptance of me by another person, or by the entire social milieu in which I live, is all-important in enabling me to accept myself. If all the significant others in my life refuse to accept me as the self that I am, then I will be crippled in my relation to myself. There is more here than an empirical psychological need for the confirmation of others. It seems rather that I exist from the roots of my personal being towards others and with others; *this* is why they play this large role in mediating me to myself. I cannot simply say to those who do not accept the self which I am, "You are wrong, I have in reality a self worthy of acceptance," and then proceed to live, unimpeded, a full self-acceptance—as if they were in error about the date of my birth and I were holding fast to what I know to be the true date. It is rather the case that I exist in such solidarity with them that their rejection of me is a real assault on me, it creates a serious (even if not an absolutely insuperable) obstacle for my relation to myself. I quote here the profound words of Martin Buber:

> Man wishes to be confirmed in his being by man, and wishes to have a presence in the being of the other. The human person needs confirmation because man as man needs it. An animal does not need to be confirmed, for it is what it is unquestionably. It is different with man: sent forth from the natural domain of species into the hazard of the solitary category, surrounded by the air of a chaos which came into being with him, secretly and bashfully he watches for a Yes which allows him to be and which can come to him

only from one human person to another. It is from one man to another that the heavenly bread of self-being is passed.[29]

Buber is suggesting that in the solitary subjectivity of a single individual there is an uncertainty, a fundamental self-doubt that impedes the subjective freedom of the individual; only in relation to other persons can this self-doubt give way to a subjective self-relation such as self-acceptance in the sense of Kierkegaard.

Collective subjectivity. In his great work on sympathy Scheler distinguishes from *Nachfühlen* (untranslatable) and *Mitfühlen* (to sympathize) what he calls *Miteinanderfühlen* (to feel or experience together with others).[30] Both parents of a dead child are grieving together at the funeral (Scheler's example). The grieving of the one is not a sympathetic sharing in the grieving of the other, rather they grieve together with each other. But they do not just grieve next to each other, as if they had in common only the motive for grieving, each grieving for the same reason for which the other is grieving but each having his or her own grieving; no, the grieving of each unites at the funeral with that of the other so that one shared grief results. Of course, under certain conditions there will be nothing but two griefs, one in each parent, as when the parents are estranged from each other. But the point of interest for us here is the undeniable possibility that the grieving of the one can at certain moments unite with that of the other to become a grieving-one-with-the-other. It is a unity not in the I-Thou-form, but in the we-form;[31] the sharers in grief do not face each other, but, without disappearing as individual subjects, form a new subject of grieving. If we speak of the *individual subjectivity* of the one who grieves by himself or herself, then we can speak of the *collective subjectivity* of those grieving *miteinander,* one with another. A collective subjectivity is of course not limited to two persons, but can be shared in by very many persons, as when we speak of a nation suffering over some national humiliation, by which we mean

29. Martin Buber, "Distance and Relation," in *The Knowledge of Man* (New York: Harper and Row, 1966), 71. The reader might recall my reflection at the end of Chapter 2.4 on the fundamental need of each human person to be recognized in all of his or her incommunicable selfhood.

30. Max Scheler, *The Nature of Sympathy,* 12–14.

31. For some deep reflections on the way in which Christian revelation promotes the study of the we-form of interpersonal life, see Josef Ratzinger, "Concerning the notion of person in theology," *Communio* 17 (1990), 452–454, where he warns against conceiving of our relation to Christ exclusively in I-Thou terms and points out the we-forms of union that we also have with Him.

that most of those making up the nation are suffering, not each for himself or herself and parallel with the others, but rather one-with-another.

There is something astonishing in the possibility of such collective subjectivity, especially after all that we have brought to light about individual subjectivity. Edith Stein expresses well this astonishment:

> It is altogether amazing how this I, despite its uniqueness and inalienable solitude, can enter into a community with other subjects, how the individual subject can become a member of a superindividual subject, and how in the actual life of such a subjective community, or communal subject, there is even a superindividual stream of consciousness which is constituted.[32]

And yet there can be no calling into question the fact of collective subjectivity. I want to have nothing to do with the individualism that would resolve such subjectivity into a number of individual subjectivities that are at the most united in the object of their acting but not in the very subjectivity of their acting.

This thing called collective subjectivity is already familiar to us from Chapter 1.3. When I spoke of the tribal conversion I remarked that the subject of the conversion seems not to be each and every tribal member; it seems rather to be a collective subject, the whole tribe, that converts. The tribal members convert together, one with another. It is a conversion that involves little individual subjectivity; it belongs mainly to the collective subjectivity of the tribe. Recall, too, the mind of the child who lives absorbed in his social milieu; his subjectivity is primarily the collective subjectivity in which he shares; he seems to be still immature as person because his individual subjectivity is so little developed.

It is clear from such examples that the collective subjectivity in which persons share can sometimes interfere with their individual subjectivity and so can impede authentic personal life. Who can deny this? What is the subjective life of a frenzied crowd if not a subjective life in which the experiencing of people one with another almost extinguishes any individual experiencing? We have to recognize, however, that this suppression of all individual subjectivity is not of the very essence of collective subjectivity, which in fact has an important and legitimate place in the social existence of persons. Individual subjectivity is not the only legitimate form of subjectivity. Who can deny the unique form of per-

32. Edith Stein, "Individuum und Gemeinschaft," in *Jahrbuch für Philosophie und phänomenologische Forschung* (1922), V, 119 (my translation). For more on collective subjectivity written from a point of view very close to my own, see her entire study, 116–283, especially 119–175.

sonal life that is found in grieving and rejoicing, in suffering and loving, *together with others?* Perhaps there is also a remembering that I can live together with others, and perhaps what we call a living tradition is nothing but a people remembering their past one with another. If we consider, for example, the way in which the Civil War lives in the consciousness of Americans, can we not discern a remembering that is performed not only by each for himself but also by all of us in the form of together-with-each-other? How could anyone say that there is something depersonalizing in this collective remembering that underlies a living tradition, and that it should yield to a remembering performed by each in the solitude of his or her individual subjectivity? Indeed, how could anyone deny that the selfhood incapable of any sharing in any kind of collective acting is a selfhood that is individualistically deformed?

There is, however, a thesis of Scheler's regarding the two kinds of subjectivity to which I have to take the sharpest exception. He says that individual subjectivity and collective subjectivity form the inner lives of two kinds of persons, individual persons and collective persons *(Gesamtpersonen),* the latter kind of person existing most typically in nations and in the Church. He proceeds to say that a collective person can be as truly and authentically a person as an individual person[33]— this is the point in Scheler that seems to be utterly mistaken. Real as collective persons are, unified as their subjectivities are, important as their role in human life is, still they are surely persons only in an analogous sense; they are not persons in the same proper sense in which individual persons are persons. When I speak of them in terms of consciousness, incommunicability, self-possession, subjectivity, I am speaking in a very derived sense. A community with a strong collective subjectivity at its center cannot recollect itself as individual persons can recollect themselves, cannot dispose over itself in subjective freedom as individual persons can. In Chapter 7 we shall discuss the central place of moral worthiness in the existence of persons; and we will see that it is primarily individual persons and not communities which are capable of becoming morally worthy. Furthermore, it is evident that collective subjectivity exists in a fundamental dependency-on-others that has no counterpart in individual subjectivity. For a collective subjectivity presupposes individual subjectivities and exists only in and through them, and apart from them is nothing at all. But an individual subjectivity does not in the same way exist in collective subjectivities or in anything else;

33. Scheler, *Formalism in Ethics,* 519–560.

much as it may owe them for the fullness of its life, it does not exist *in* them in the way in which they exist in individual persons.

It will be noticed that all of the ideas presented in this section on forms of interpersonal life come from a subjective study of persons in the sense of Wojtyla; not in a cosmological but in a personalist way have we explored some of the aspects of the social existence of persons.[34]

As I said earlier, it does not belong to this study to explore these superindividual and communitarian realities in their own right; I have only wanted to show the openness of our essay, or rather of the principles of our essay, to being completed by the truth about the interpersonal. I have also wanted to indicate that such truth is based on my results about the individual person. In Chapter 5.2 we will again be led by our study of selfhood to the theme of interpersonal relation.

34. And in this same personalist vein it could be further explored. For example, Wojtyla has shown in innumerable writings that the marital act has the meaning of spousal self-donation. From the cosmological point of view one noticed primarily the procreative possibility of the marital act; it is a specifically personalist advance to retrieve its meaning of self-donation and to understand the former meaning in terms of this latter one. Wojtyla is very clear about the fact that it is retrieved by consulting the evidence of spousal subjectivity.

CHAPTER FOUR

Subjectivity and Substantiality

1. Posing the problem of subjectivity and substantiality in the human person

Throughout the previous chapter I assumed that there is a certain distinction between the person and the subjectivity of the person. I have spoken of the selfhood of the person being disclosed and also actualized in the subjectivity of the person, and this presupposes that subjectivity is one thing, and the selfhood of the person something else. But many will want to challenge this assumption saying that the person is nothing but subjectivity and that there is no being of the person which may go unactualized in subjectivity, but that the being of the person *is* subjectivity and is nothing more besides. They will say that in the absence of any possibility of personal life, as in the embryo or in the irreversibly comatose, we have no person; we have indeed a living human being, but no human person. The issue is commonly expressed in terms of "subjectivity and substantiality." I accept these terms, and I understand by the substantiality of the person nothing else than a certain more-than-conscious being of the person, that is, a being which, while it actualizes itself in subjectivity, does not exhaust itself in subjectivity.

Of course there is far more to substantiality than that which emerges from the contrast with subjectivity. In fact, in Aristotle's metaphysics of substance this contrast plays no role at all; his whole account of substance is rather in terms of independence in being—in terms of an individual standing in itself, not belonging to another as part or property of the other, etc. These Aristotelian notes of substance are easy to verify in persons, and in fact persons have them far more perfectly than nonpersonal substances have them.[1] One could take the definition of person given above, *persona est sui iuris et alteri incommunicabilis,* and could replace *persona* with *substantia,* deriving thereby a valid definition of substance. If there were nothing more to Aristotelian substance than independence in being, then there would be little controversy over the substantiality of persons; almost everyone would concur in affirming that persons are substances. Controversy arises because Aristotelian substance is felt to be incurably "cosmological," to be inhospitable to personal subjectivity. When applied to human beings substance certainly does express something that cannot be reduced without residue to subjectivity. I propose to defend this irreducibility and to reconcile it with all that I want to say about personal subjectivity, thus clearing away the last obstacle to affirming the substantiality of persons. This is why, for our purposes in this chapter, I am willing to let "substantiality" express mainly the irreducibility of a person to his subjectivity.

Now those who would reduce persons to their subjectivity, denying to them any substantial personal being, can adduce certain plausible reasons for their position.

1. They will ask whether we find any difference between being annihilated as persons and being completely deprived forever of all conscious life. Is our loss in the latter case really any less than our loss in the former? Does not the one loss simply coincide with the other?

2. The next reason for reducing personhood to subjectivity can be explained by referring to one of the results of the previous chapter. I claimed in effect to find in the human person a certain coinciding of being and consciousness, or as some say, of being and knowledge. In recollecting myself I come to myself, I come alive as person, and thereby achieve, in one, both an experience of myself from within as well as the actuality of my being as person. The full actuality of personal being in the recollected person seems to coincide with the conscious self-presence and the other forms of subjectivity developed in recollection. Being and consciousness do not stand here in a relation of polarity, as if the being of the person were over against consciousness as its cognitive

---

1. See the important metaphysical treatise of Josef Seifert, *Essere e Persona* (Milan: Università Cattolica del Sacro Cuore, 1989), Chapter 9, in which Seifert shows in detail how personal being can be understood as substantial being that has been brought to its fullest and most perfect form. The metaphysics of substance is, Seifert argues, capable of a personalist development and completion.

object; rather the being of the person is itself a conscious being and is actualized in and through the presence of the person to himself. We notice this coinciding of being and cognition whenever we realize the unsurpassable immediacy and intimacy with which the person encounters himself in recollected self-presence. But if all of this is true, then it is plausible to interpret the coinciding of being and consciousness in the sense that the being of persons is their consciousness, or in other words that persons are nothing but their subjectivity.

3. And this identification is not only plausible; there are many who will go on to give a definite reason why the reduction of the person to subjectivity is the only tenable position. They think that if persons are not reducible to their subjectivity, then they must have some being in themselves that is objective in the sense of lying outside subjectivity, in the sense of being unable to be subjectively lived through. Once they think this, it is only natural for them to conclude that such substantial being is foreign to subjectivity, that it would, as Sartre says, introduce an opacity and obscurity foreign to the pure transparency of subjectivity.[2] Perhaps they will express themselves in terms used by Wojtyla and say that the category of substantial being is too "cosmological" a category for persons, and that a radically "personalist" approach to man has to reduce the human person to subjectivity.

They will, of course, be willing to recognize substantial being at another level in man; in the sense of the distinction between "person" and "nature" they can admit that much that belongs to nature in man is substantial. They can admit this because such substantial being can be contrasted with personal selfhood taken in a strict sense, and can in this way be kept outside of it. It is the introducing of substantial being *into* the heart of personal selfhood that seems to them to be the mistaken attempt to bring together categories of being that exclude each other. But the only way to avoid this mistake, they say, is to let the person be nothing but subjectivity.

Thus the reasons that lead very many thinkers to reduce personal selfhood to subjectivity. I will reply to each of them in section 5 of the present chapter.

We cannot avoid dealing with this issue in the present study of personal selfhood. We need to know whether this selfhood exists only as subjectively lived through, or whether there is also an ontological

2. Sartre, "La transcendence de l'ego, esquisse d'une description phénoménologique," *Recherches Philosophiques* 6 (1936–1937), 89–91. English in Sartre, *The Transcendence of the Ego* (New York, 1990), by Williams and Kirkpatrick, tr., 37–42.

selfhood, a selfhood actualized only in subjectivity but not reducible without residue to subjectivity—whether, in other words, there is a substantial selfhood at the ground of our subjectivity.

2. A *"subjective"* argument for the necessity of distinguishing in human persons between being and subjectivity

Introducing the argument. I propose to look for the fundamental distinction between the substantial being of the person and the subjectivity of the person, and to look for it in a place which at first seems very unpromising for our purposes, namely in my conscious experience of myself, in my subjectivity. It may seem that by probing my self-experience I will find only subjectivity and not some being of the person irreducible to subjectivity; it may seem that for attaining to the being of the person I would have to go outside of my subjectivity and attempt in some way or other to deduce the necessity of personal being underlying personal consciousness. But I will do without any such deductions; I will attempt to probe my subjectivity to the point *where the being of the person subjectively shows itself.* This subjective approach, demanding as it is, at least lets us pursue our question on the basis of the previous chapter. It also lets me join the argument with my interlocutors, who see nothing more in the person than conscious self-presence; since I want to engage them in discussion and not talk past them, I take my point of departure from this very conscious self-presence and try to show why the evidence of precisely our conscious self-presence forces us to go beyond consciousness to being.

Much will be gained for the understanding of my argument by recalling a famous Socratic-Platonic argument, to which my argument is in many ways directly parallel. In the *Theatetus* Socrates is dealing (152a–183c) with the Protagorean thesis that "man is the measure of all things, of the things that are, that they are, of the things that are not, that they are not." He interprets this thesis to mean that things are nothing more than we think they are, that they exhaust themselves in being thought by us. Against Protagoras Socrates argues that we can err, and with the help of a teacher can correct our error and can enlarge and deepen our knowledge, and that this presupposes an object of thought that is not measured by our thinking but is the measure of our thinking. How can there be any inadequacy in our thinking, or any overcoming of the inadequacy, if the objects about which we think are nothing more than we think they are (161c–162c)?

Now I want to argue that the human being qua person is just as little reducible to self-presence and the other forms of subjectivity as the objects of our thinking are, for Socrates, reducible to their being thought by us. Just as Socrates distinguishes between the being of an object and its being thought by us, and does so by arguing that the latter can fall short of the former, so I will distinguish between the being of ourselves as persons and our being consciously present to ourselves, and will argue for this thesis by showing that the latter can fall short of the former.

One might at first think that what I want to show is simply a part of what Socrates wanted to show against Protagoras, and that I will be trying to defend the Socratic position with respect to our cognition of ourselves. One might think that I simply want to show that when we go to cognize ourselves we encounter in the object of our cognition a being that is not reducible to its being cognized by us. But this is not exactly what I want to show. It is one thing to cognize myself as object, from without; it is another, as we know from the last chapter, to experience myself as subject, from within. When I speak of being present to myself as I perform conscious acts, I do not mean putting myself in front of myself in the performing of those acts; these acts have their own object, and I who perform them am not another object of my acts. In the self-presence found on the subjective pole of all object-directed acts, I experience myself not objectively but subjectively, as we have seen. Now it is in my subjectivity in the sense of this subjective self-experience that I will try to find a being of the person that is more than subjective self-experience. I want to probe my subjectivity to the point at which the distinction between being and subjective consciousness appears,[3] just as Socrates wanted to probe our experience of some object to the point at which the distinction between its being and its being cognized by us appears. We have, then, an instructive parallel between my thesis and the Socratic thesis against Protagoras, but not exactly a coinciding, not even a partial coinciding, of mine with his.

We are now in a position to make our argument for the distinction between personal being and personal consciousness.

The argument. Let us recall the state of dispersion of which we spoke in the previous chapter, the state in which we are distracted, preoccu-

---

3. This is just where I differ from Sartre in his well-known essay referred to in the previous note. He thinks that a more-than-conscious being of the person appears only when we make the person an object of consciousness; but I will try to find this being precisely in the subjective self-experience of the person.

pied with many things, in which we are an easy prey for new distractions and are buffeted back and forth by every influence brought to bear on us; in which we lack distance to the things we encounter, are immersed in them, perhaps even "ecstatically lost in them," and so are dominated by them. Is there anyone who will disagree that in this condition of reduced self-presence, of weakened self-consciousness, we fall short of what we really are as persons, that we live in a condition unworthy of ourselves as persons? It is easy to see the discrepancy between the conscious condition of dispersion and living fully as person, to see that when we are "ecstatically lost" in things and dominated by them we do not live as a being which is an end in itself, or which belongs to itself. How can our inner resources for acting through ourselves and for determining ourselves in freedom be as reduced as they are in this state of inner dispersion, without us thereby being somehow outside of, or estranged from, our real being as persons? Can we not say that, though we experience ourselves as immersed in the things around us, perhaps even as "of one piece" with them, we as persons are *in reality* not of one piece with anything but are rather incommunicably ourselves and not another, and that therefore the subjective self-experience that we have in the state of dispersion is at odds with what we *really* are as persons? But then we have our distinction between being and consciousness in the person, and have gained it, just as I proposed, from an examination of our subjective self-experience. The argument, however, is not yet finished.

When we emerge out of this state of dispersion, when we "come to ourselves" by recollecting ourselves and renew our inner resources for acting through ourselves in freedom, what exactly do we experience in ourselves? Are we not aware of beginning to *live consciously* what we *really are* as persons? When we experience subjectively our being incommunicably ourselves and not being continuous with anything other than ourselves, do we not subjectively experience more adequately our personhood? But how can there be a more and a less adequate subjective experience of ourselves as persons if there is nothing more to our personhood than subjective self-experience? Where is the measure of this "adequacy" if not in some being of the person that is now more, now less actualized, according to the condition of the self-presence of the person?

I can make the same argument by looking at our experience of personal development. Take the small child, who seems often to feel himself to be of one piece with his surroundings and with his social milieu. The opinions of the social groups in which the child lives flow through the mind of the child, who simply thinks with the group, or better, simply thinks as a part or extension of the group. But as the child grows he begins to experience himself as a being of his own, he begins to lead a life of his own and to form judgments of his own, thereby falling out of the sheltering social cocoon. Of interest for us is the fact the child is aware that in developing towards this kind of independence he is growing *as person*; that he used to be *immature* as person, and that he would have become *retarded* as person if he had remained immersed in his social groups. This seems to presuppose that a person cannot be reduced to his conscious condition, for how else explain the immaturity or retardation of a person except as a discrepancy between all that that person *really* is and the inadequate conscious condition in which he or she presently exists?

The same argument can be made with regard to certain pathological conditions of persons, as for example with the sense of isolation in autism. If autistic persons could recover from their affliction they would say that they were not *really* isolated from others as they felt themselves to be, and that they have recovered a *truer* self-experience in being healed of their pathological sense of isolation. How explain this except by recognizing in the person some being that is more than what the person experiences in himself or herself?

Just as Socrates claimed to find in *the objects* of our cognition the distinction between the being of the objects and their being cognized by us, and to find this distinction by showing the inadequacy, and the possibility of overcoming the inadequacy, of many of our attempts at cognizing them, so I claim to find in our *subjective self-experience* the distinction between the being of the person and the subjectivity (that is, the subjective self-experience) of the person. And I claim, in direct parallel to the Socratic argument, to find this distinction in the inadequacy with which our personal being is subjectively disclosed from within in the dispersed, or immature, or pathological forms of self-presence, and in the possibility of achieving subjective life in which our personal being is subjectively disclosed in a more adequate way.

One would think that this way of showing the irreducibility of personal being to personal subjectivity can in fact be carried out no matter what subjective condition I am in. For surely no human person ever consciously possesses himself in such a way that there is no residue of personal being outside of his self-presence and no possibility of further actualizing himself by further recollection. It is just that this irreducibility can be thrown into particularly sharp relief by starting, as I did, with a very weak state of subjectivity.

But suppose for the sake of argument that the self-presence of a person encompassed his entire being as person, there being no least residue of being that the person did not consciously live through. The thesis I am opposing would remain false even in this case. For the subjective condition of such a supremely recollected person would not be one in which *being is reduced to subjective consciousness;* my analysis of the condition of this person before he became so ultimately recollected tells us that in him *being and consciousness would remain distinct while completely interpenetrating.* The distinction that I claim to find between being and subjective consciousness in the person *consists in* the being of the person falling outside of conscious self-presence and other forms of subjectivity; it is merely that the distinction is *easier to bring to evidence* when we see such a discrepancy of being and consciousness.[4]

3. Developing this argument in response to the main objection that can be raised against it

Those who would reduce the person to personal consciousness will be resourceful in trying to explain in their own way the facts of self-experience to which I appeal, that is, to explain them without going beyond subjectivity to anything like a being of the person irreducible to subjectivity. The parallel to the debate between Socrates and Protagoras holds here too; for Socrates put into the mouth of Protagoras (who was not present in the discussion reported in the *Theatetus*) a plausible way of explaining how we might correct our conceptions of things yet without introducing any being of the objects of cognition which goes beyond their being cognized (166a–168c). I will state as forcefully as possible the strongest objection that can be made to us.

One might say that there are many ways of measuring the inadequacy of a thing without positing in the thing anything like the "being" that I just recognized in the person. For example, we say that the performance of a piece of music is deficient, that the piece ought to have been per-

4. One has to make a similar distinction in order to read correctly Section 1 of Kant's *Foundations of the Metaphysics of Morals.* Kant does not teach, as he is sometimes taken to teach, that an action from duty has to be performed in opposition to inclination, but only that the opposition to inclination manifests more clearly to our cognition the dutifulness of an action.

formed differently, and yet we do not dream of ascribing to the performance a mysterious "being" that was disfigured because of the defects of the performance. Or we say that a plane triangle is badly drawn: that the lines are crooked, and the inner angles more or less than 180 degrees. Here, too, it would be bizarre to assume a mysterious being in the drawn triangle that was obscured by the bad drawing. There is nothing more to the being of the bad performance than the bad performance, nor is there anything more to the being of the crooked triangle than the crooked triangle. The talk of adequacy and inadequacy in these things comes not from measuring them against a hidden being that they have but from measuring them against standards that are in a sense external to them. We measure the performance against the score of the composer or against other performances; we measure the triangle against the idea of the triangle. Why should it be different with the human person? Why can we not recognize inadequate states of personal subjectivity without assuming some being of the person that is not yet subjectively lived through? Why can we not explain this inadequacy simply by referring to standards? Do we not all have some ideal of personal life, and do we not measure ourselves against this ideal and usually find ourselves wanting? The objection, then, comes to this: it is easier to replace the *being* of the person, which I tried to introduce above, with some *ideal* of personal life; this explains all the evidence to which I appeal, but explains it in an ontologically more economical way. One could say that the objector is opposed to my too Aristotelian interpretation of this evidence, and is arguing for a more Platonic interpretation of it.

I respond to the objection as follows.

1. If we look more closely at the examples on which the objection is based, we find that they supply us with the materials for a new argument for the distinction between being and consciousness in the person.

Suppose the performance of a piece of music was poor one night, but better the next night: we would have here not one performance that improves but two performances, one of which is better than the other. Or suppose the badly drawn triangle is improved by erasing the crooked lines and drawing straighter lines: we would have not one triangle that becomes more like a triangle but rather two triangles, one of which replaces the other. But with a person it is different: a state of more centered consciousness in myself and a state of less centered consciousness, or a state of greater or of lesser personal maturity, are not two distinct entities, but rather only two conscious states *of the same person.*

With a person we have *one being* which is now dispersed, now recollected, or is now immature, now more mature. One cannot explain this oneness of being by referring different conscious states to the same ideal of personal consciousness; this reference to a common ideal is quite consistent with them being plural entities; it only unites them as members of one class, but not necessarily as modalities of one being. One must instead recognize what I have been calling the being of the person, which is that in virtue of which I am one throughout various conscious states. This being does not exhaust itself in consciousness, since it is, by its oneness, to be distinguished precisely from the plurality of conscious states in which it lives at different times.

I should not be misunderstood as trying to *prove* the being of the person, as if I were saying that we can make sense of the oneness or sameness of the person only by *assuming* the being of the person. I rather mean that by understanding the oneness or sameness of the person we can come *directly to see* the personal being. I no more mean to carry out an inference than Descartes did with his *cogito*, even though he expressed himself in one place with the somewhat misleading *ergo*.

2. We cannot say that the crooked triangle in being improved and made straighter *actualizes itself.* One reason for this has just been given: it is always one and the same being that actualizes itself; but we are dealing here with two entities one of which replaces the other. But there is another reason, which leads back to our main argument.

In order for a being to actualize itself by straightening out, it would have to be, while it is still crooked, more than just crooked; it would have to have some being in addition to its being crooked, and indeed would have to be in some sense straight (though not in such a sense as to contradict its empirical crookedness); it would have to be *potentially straight*, as Western philosophers have put it ever since Aristotle (meaning of course with this far more than "possibly straight"). Whenever, then, we speak of a being actualizing itself, we recognize that there is more to it than its present factual condition, and that the being in some sense already is that which, once it is actualized, it will be fully.

We do not find this potentiality in the crooked triangle or in the poor musical performance; we do not find enough being in these entities to allow for a dimension of potential being. But we do find it in the person. It is only natural for us when we come to ourselves (as by recollecting ourselves) to say that we *actualize* ourselves as persons, that we gain the actuality of that which we already somehow are. The alternative is to say that one posits oneself, constitutes oneself, creates oneself as person, simply replacing thereby one's previous conscious condition: but this is entirely foreign to the experience of emerging from dispersion and coming to oneself, which clearly shows itself to be the experience of reawakening, of recovering oneself, returning to oneself; it is the experience of actualizing oneself out of a potential condition, not positing oneself out of nothing. When I am once again alive as person, I can only say that I have gained, not my very personhood, but the conscious actuality of it, and that as dispersed I had lost, not my very personhood, but the conscious actuality of it. What is this something that is not lost in the worst state of inner dispersion and heteronomy, and that is not gained when one achieves strong conscious self-presence? Is it perhaps some ideal of personal life? No, because it is something *within* me, which could have no existence apart from me; the ideal, by contrast, is not tied to my existence and can perfectly well exist (in whatever way it can be said to exist) without me existing. That something is, instead, the being of the person; in considering what is implied in actualizing ourselves as persons we find anew our fundamental distinction between being and subjective consciousness in the person. The conscious life of the person is not the whole person; it is that in which the being of the person is actualized. This implies that a person is more than consciousness or subjectivity and that his being is to be distinguished from his subjectivity.

We can lend some support to this conclusion by pointing to something else in the world of the person that also shows the irreducibility of being to conscious experiencing. Certain communities of persons are fully themselves only as consciously experienced, and yet they clearly exist in advance of such experiencing; they are only actualized, not constituted in being for the first time, in the experiencing. This is perhaps nowhere so clear as with the community of mankind. When we wake up to our fundamental human solidarity with each other, we are aware of waking up to an already-existing solidarity.[5] Of course, it comes to exist much more properly through our awakening, but in this very awakening we experience it as existing independently of our experiencing. This is just like what we find with individual persons, whose personal selfhood, while it is actualized by being experienced, is experienced as existing even before it is experienced.

5. On this more-than-conscious solidarity of human beings in the community of mankind, see Dietrich von Hildebrand, *Metaphysik der Gemeinschaft* (Regensburg: Habbel Verlag, 1955), Teil I, Kapitel 8 and Teil II, Kapitel 6.

With this I conclude my first argument for the distinction between being and consciousness in the person.[6] Before passing on to the second, I think it important to say again that, in order to show that the person is not reducible to conscious self-presence, it was not necessary to abandon subjectivity and to consider the person more from without than from within, and more as object than as subject; even less did we have to go beyond subjectivity by resorting, say, to metaphysical deductions, or by considering the person from a "cosmological" point of view; no, *we found this irreducibility in conscious self-presence.* And so we were able to hold fast to the unity of being and subjectivity in the person at the very time that I distinguished them. Just as one can, as I think might be shown (elsewhere), bring to evidence the transcendence of the object of knowledge, that is, its being more than just an object for me, by attending closely to what is given in it, so one can bring to evidence the transcendence of the person, that is, his being more than self-presence and other forms of subjectivity, by attending closely to what is given subjectively.

Let me just add that one can find the being of the person only by attending closely to the subjective pole of consciousness and by avoiding a one-sided preoccupation with the object-directedness of consciousness. If one thinks that personal consciousness is nothing but its directedness to objects and overlooks the self-presence of the person, then one will overlook the experience from within which we can have of the more-than-conscious being of the person.

4. Another argument for the necessity of distinguishing in the person between being and subjectivity

There is another, entirely different argument for this being of the person, and I want now to introduce it into the discussion. It is not based on the investigations of Chapter 3, as the previous argument was, but on ideas that belong to Chapter 7.

It starts from a certain fact, first recognized by Socrates, about moral good and evil. In teaching that it is better to suffer than to commit injustice (see above all the *Gorgias*), Socrates teaches that nothing is so ulti-

---

6. Cf. the way in which Stephen Schwarz reaches the same conclusion in his *The Moral Problem of Abortion* (Chicago: Loyola University Press, 1991), especially Chapter 7, where he develops the distinction between being a person and functioning as a person.

mately harmful for a human person as doing wrong. Being the victim of the worst wrong is as nothing when compared to the harm inflicted on oneself as a result of committing some wrong. It defiles the soul so grievously that it is for Socrates a wonder that it does not destroy the soul as a similarly grievous bodily disease kills the body. (The soul must be indestructible and immortal, he argues in *The Republic*, X (608d–611a), to be able to endure moral evil in this life without being destroyed by it.) I assume with Socrates that moral evil is an incomparable evil for the human soul, and that one can as truly say that it is an incomparable evil for the human person. He teaches nothing more than what everyone of us knows when our conscience accuses us, namely that the gain we have from our wrongdoing is no compensation at all for the guilt that now afflicts us in our innermost parts, and that we would do anything to be free of it. I also assume with Socrates that doing the just thing is supremely beneficial for human persons, entirely surpassing any non-moral benefit of which they would be capable.

Now I argue that if persons really could be reduced to their subjectivity, it would be impossible to maintain this fundamental ethical insight of Socrates. To complete this argument I need only one further fact, an entirely non-controversial fact, namely that persons who do wrong commonly do not experience themselves as harmed or do not experience the harm to themselves in proportion to its seriousness. Given this fact I say that, if persons had no being beyond their conscious experiencing, they could not fail to experience that harm to themselves which is the supreme harm that can afflict them. How could this exist "objectively" and without being experienced? Of course if the harm lay in the fact that punishment is coming for the wrongdoing, then the harm could exist objectively. But the idea of Socrates, and the insight of each of us, is that moral harm to oneself is nothing imposed on us from without but is rather something springing up within us. How can it fail to be experienced subjectively in a being that is nothing but subjectivity?

I can readily admit that all kinds of facts could characterize persons (whom we assume to be nothing but subjectivity) without them being aware of the facts. For example, some persons could resemble others without any awareness of the resemblance. They may conform to or violate certain rules without experiencing the conformity or violation. Or again, general facts about consciousness in its relation to the brain, or simply in itself, could characterize persons without them knowing it. But I speak here of what is good for persons and bad for them, and in fact of what is supremely good and bad for them: how can this fail to be experienced subjectively from within? Such an "objective harm" would seem to be as absurd as an "objective pain," which would exist without anyone suffering from it. It follows that, since wrongdoing is not always experienced in all the harmfulness that it really has for me, I as person am more than my conscious experiencing. There must be a being of myself that can be really harmed even when the harm does not subjectively register in me. This being is, of course, not the body of the person, for the body is not a possible subject of moral guilt or of other moral predicates; no, this more-than-conscious being is found *within* the person, it is found at the center of personal selfhood. This being is expressed in the "soul" of which Socrates speaks, and we have to find a place for it in our concept of the person.

There is no point in objecting to the argument along the lines of the first objection to our previous argument, that is, there is no point in saying that the harm to the person is nothing but the violation of some standard or norm. Such a violation would at most explain the moral wrongness of an action—not really explain even this, in my opinion, but at least plausibly explain it—but not even plausibly explain the *harm for me* accruing from the wrongdoing. For this harm does not lie in a relation of my action to a norm, but in the relation of my action to my very self. Such an objection would try to explain in extrinsic terms that which is entirely intrinsic to the person.

Even if wrongdoers come to recognize the harm to themselves and to experience it, they are quite aware of having to distinguish between this experience and the harm they experience. They will for instance be aware that the depth of their experience of the harm to themselves will vary considerably from one time to another, though the harm itself that they experience is not subject to any such variations. This means that it would be no argument against my position if someone were right in saying that a criminal can never be entirely and at every level of his being unaware of the unsoundness in himself as person. The very fact that this moral unsoundness, and in and through it the part of the person that is unsound, can be very incompletely experienced, means that this part of the person has a depth of being that does not exhaust itself in being consciously lived through.

5. Responses to the reasons given for reducing persons to subjectivity

We return to the three reasons given at the beginning of this chapter for reducing persons to subjectivity, replying to each of them on the basis of the investigations just concluded.

ad 1. I grant that for a human person there is, existentially, hardly any difference between being entirely annihilated and being forever deprived of consciousness while remaining in existence with the being of the person. I would in a sense retain nothing by retaining my being if I irretrievably lost all consciousness. We have only to consider the self-possession of persons, which is an aspect of their being ends in themselves; it would remain utterly dormant or potential if they never consciously exercised it, as by being consciously present to themselves and consciously disposing over themselves. It is clear that subjective life is *the principle of actualization* for persons; without conscious experiencing and acting, persons remain in an utterly dormant condition. And yet, important as it is to recognize the supreme importance of personal consciousness, without which there is no actualization of the person, it is in my view no less important to recognize the being of the person, without which there is no person to actualize. *The task is to understand the unity of being and consciousness in the person and not to take the easy way out asserting the one at the expense of the other.*

ad 2. The "coinciding" of being and consciousness in the human person is not to be understood as a reduction of being to consciousness. It is, instead, the interpenetrating of distinguishable moments. With the talk of "coinciding" I simply want to express a relation of personal consciousness to personal being that is fundamentally different from, and fundamentally closer than, a relation of personal consciousness to some object of consciousness. Personal consciousness *actualizes* the being of the person, rather than merely *faces* this being as its object. But as we have come to understand in the previous pages, this *actualizing* precisely presupposes the more-than-conscious being of the person that we have tried to bring to evidence.

ad 3. We have to distinguish two different ways in which being in the person can remain "outside" of personal subjectivity. (1) It can remain outside in the sense in which, for example, the brain and the internal organs remain outside of subjectivity. These can never be subjectively lived through; they can get no closer to subjectivity than by being the objects of intentional acts of the person or by being causal conditions for these acts. (2) Personal being can remain outside of subjectivity in the sense that it is not awakened but is capable of awakening. The reason adduced in the third objection against the substantiality of the person is tenable only as long as one confuses (2) with (1), and takes (1) as the pattern for all being which is not reducible to subjectivity. One would indeed propose an impossible mix of subjectivity and substantiality if one were to identify the latter with the brain; for the brain remains forever outside of subjectivity in sense (1)—otherwise we would experience our brains in the intimacy of our self-presence. Once one thematizes (2) and distinguishes it from (1), there need be no further conceptual difficulty with the substantiality of the person.[7]

It is remarkable how St. Thomas Aquinas ascribes substantiality to the person in such a way as to avoid insinuating any thing-like substantiality incompatible with personal subjectivity. He thinks of the reflexivity that we see in all the forms of subjective life, such as in self-presence and self-determination, as being already established in the substantial being of the person. This is why he recognizes in the soul not only a certain *conversio* or *reditus ad seipsam,* or bending of the soul back upon itself when it knows itself, but also a purely ontological bending of the soul back upon itself, as we can see from his distinction between a being bending back upon itself *secundum substantiam* (in its substance) and bending back upon itself *secundum operationem* (in its acting), and also from his statement that the *conversio ad seipsam* in acting is possible only if the acting being has this *conversio* in its very substance.[8] In other words, when we think about the substantial being of the person, we have to think of it as in some sense already having (before it is subjectively actualized) those structures that show themselves in subjectivity.

It follows that I have no difficulty accepting the Boethian definition of a person as "*an individual substance* of a rational nature." I have cleared away the last obstacle to accepting it: I have shown that it does

---

7. Observe that I do not follow those who conceive of the substantial being of the person as unchangeable throughout the life of the person. Though I recognize, as explained above, that this being is the ground of the oneness of a person throughout stronger and weaker conscious conditions, I also recognize that, since it is subject to being actualized, it must undergo a certain kind of change.

8. Aquinas, *In librum de causis*, lectio XV, especially n. 305.

not need to be understood as excessively cosmological and that it is open to all that I would want to add about personal subjectivity. We saw above that the idea of personal selfhood that emerged in Chapters 1 and 2, centering as it does around the person belonging to himself, seems almost to coincide with the idea of Aristotelian substance, or rather it seems to be substance raised, as it were, to the highest power. We are now entitled to go on and embrace the Boethian definition; no personalist sensibilities, no concern for the mystery of personal subjectivity, has any right to hold us back.[9]

6. Consequences for the question of the beginning and ending of personal selfhood in each human being

I propose now to ask about the beginning in time of each human person. With this I turn for a moment from discussing the intension of personhood—what personhood is—to discussing a certain question about its extension—which beings are persons.[10] I raise this question because of the tremendous ethical consequences that follow from the answer to it, and also because the results of the previous section have put us in a position to offer an answer. By pursuing this question a little we also hope to develop our understanding of these results.

If one reduces the person to subjectivity, then it is easy to determine in principle when persons come into existence: they come into existence with the beginning of subjective life. The only remaining question is when in fact subjective life begins, but the principle determining their beginning is clear. One sees without difficulty the ethical consequences of such a position. Whenever exactly subjective life begins, it does not seem to begin in the zygote that issues from conception or in the early embryo: these, therefore, while undeniably human beings, cannot be

9. Here in the question on subjectivity and substantiality I part company with thinkers such as Scheler to whom I am otherwise close. Nor do I share the view of Josef Ratzinger that it is specifically pre-Christian to think of persons in terms of substance and that in Christian thinking about personhood the substantial conception of personhood, as in Boethius, has to give way to a more existential conception. Ratzinger, "Concerning the notion of person in theology," *Communio* 17 (1990), 448–449. I do not see that there need be any such antithesis between a substantial and an existential understanding of personhood.

10. Though the present study deals primarily with the intension of personal being, this is not the first time we touch on the extensional question. At the end of Chapter 3.6 I dealt critically with Scheler's thesis that collective persons are no less truly persons than individual persons—clearly a thesis about the extension of personal being.

human persons, and so the direct destruction of them does not fall under the moral prohibition of killing innocent persons.[11] One finds something similar at the other end of the life spectrum: the irreversibly comatose, apparently lacking any subjective life, must be dead as persons and be alive only in some sub-personal, merely biological sense, so that the direct destruction of them also escapes this prohibition.

But for us who have made the fundamental distinction between *onto-logical personal selfhood* and *the selfhood lived through in self-presence and in other forms of subjectivity*, the question as to the beginning in time of each human person is not so easily answered. Why should not the person in his substantial being exist in advance of any self-presence or other form of subjective life? Indeed, what would prevent the person from existing from conception? I will now explain briefly why, given our results in the previous section, *it is entirely possible* that each human person exists already as the single-cell zygote resulting from conception.

The argument for this possibility has two parts. We first argue for it *ex parte personae humanae* (from the nature of the human person), and then complete the argument by proceeding *ex parte conceptus humani* (from the nature of the human fetus).

1. Let us go back to our experience of our own personhood. We found that we can exist as persons while having very little of the actuality of personal life. Now why should we not be able to exist as persons while *entirely* lacking the actuality of personal life? There is fortunately no need to discuss this question in the abstract, for we in fact do sometimes exist as persons while entirely lacking the actuality of personal life: we exist this way in all dreamless sleep and in every dreamless coma. The being of the person that we know in ourselves before and after the dreamless sleep can only be assumed to continue in existence while we sleep. We cannot of course experience this continuing in ourselves, but once we have distinguished the substantial being from the subjectivity of the person, we understand that this being cannot come and go as subjective states come and go. The only reasonable assumption we can make, then, is to assume that we continue to be a person throughout the times we lack all consciousness.

And now we ask: if it happens again and again that I exist as person while deprived of all personal consciousness, why may it not be that I

---

11. This is exactly the argument of H. T. Engelhardt in his well-known paper, "The Ontology of Abortion," *Ethics* (April, 1974), 217–234.

existed as person even before personal consciousness had developed in me? Why may it not be that I was already present in my body as soon as it began to exist and to develop? This would be impossible if I as person were nothing but conscious self-presence and other forms of subjectivity; since the embryo, prior to the development of the brain, lacks conscious self-presence, it would have to lack personhood as well. But since I as person am being as well as consciousness, it is entirely possible that my personal being was already embodied in the embryo, long before the awakening of personal subjectivity.

2. But on closer inspection it is only part of this possibility that has been established; I have only showed this possibility *ex parte personae humanae*. But what about *ex parte conceptus humani?* There may be nothing in the human person preventing the embryo from being a person, but might there be something in the embryo preventing it? Of course it seems that the human embryo and the adult human body are the same living being at different stages of development, and this makes it only natural to assume that the embryo is a person. But let us beware of reasoning too abstractly. There is a plausible objection against this presumption; it is the philosophically most challenging reason that can be advanced against recognizing personhood in the earliest embryo.

This objection says that the capacity of the embryo for twinning (or recombining) shows that it cannot possibly be the body of a person. We might of course simply bypass this whole issue by taking "embryo" in the narrow sense in which it is sometimes contrasted with pre-embryo (which comprises zygote, morula, blastocyst); for twinning is no longer possible in the embryo so understood. But I am willing to take "embryo" in the broader sense in which the zygote represents the first form of embryonic life, and to offer, on the basis of my previous investigations, some remarks on the objection, even if I cannot deal with it here as fully as it deserves.

It is at first not quite clear what the argument here is. One possible reading of it is that if the zygote is a person, then twinning must involve the splitting of a person, which is an impossibility. This is indeed an impossibility that seems to be related to the incommunicability of the person discussed in Chapter 2. But it is far from clear why, on the assumption, twinning could only be the splitting of a person: why could it not be a form of asexual reproduction, such as occurs in many subhuman organisms?

The argument seems to become stronger when taken in a more Aristotelian sense: as long as the zygote has a divisibility and a fusability entirely foreign to incommunicable persons, it is not suited to be the body of the person; only when it gains a greater stability and unity as *this* organism, or, in other words, a greater individuality, a stronger incommunicability, does it become matter capable of being informed by a personal soul. To such an argument I respond that *even the adult human body lags far behind the person with respect to indivisibility and unfusability.* Consider the partially fused bodies of grown Siamese twins; there is no comparable partial fusion on the level of personhood; the bodies show a lack of inner unity which is impossible with persons. And yet no one doubts that the partially fused bodies are the bodies of persons who are not in the same way partially fused.

But I can make my point just as well by referring to completely normal human bodies. Every such body has a genetic "duplicability," and is in fact genetically duplicated whenever it has an identical twin; but each person is so incommunicably himself as to exclude absolutely any such duplication of himself, as we saw in Chapter 2. There cannot be two copies of the same person as there are two copies of the same body. If, then, the bodies of adult persons are, with respect to incommunicable being, much weaker than the persons themselves, why may not even the zygote be the body of a person? I grant that the discrepancy with respect to individuality is greater between zygote and person than between adult human body and person, but where is the evidence that this greater discrepancy is so great as to render the zygote strictly incapable of being the body of a person?

We can find, then, nothing in the human person as person preventing the zygote from being a person, nor is there anything in the zygote preventing the zygote from being a person. With this double approach we can establish the possibility of the person existing even as an embryo in its earliest stage of development.

The argument proceeds simply by recalling how the human embryo is related to the full-grown human body that develops from it; it becomes this body while remaining the same organism. Few deny that the zygote—in contrast to the haploid gametes from which the zygote derives—is, as organism, identical with the fully developed human body, differing only as to stage of development. Is it not natural to assume, and indeed to assume as the most natural assumption that we can make in this matter, that I, who now live and act as an incarnate person, began to exist when my body began to exist?[12]

---

12. Let the reader beware of making the plausible objection based on the recent discussion of brain death; with such a move he is likely to commit a *petitio principii.* I

This is as far as I propose to carry my treatment of the beginning in time of each human person, for the next step in developing my position would lead far beyond the scope of this chapter. The next step would be to investigate the incarnate condition of the human person to which I just referred, and to come to grips with the various dualisms of person and nature that are often taken for granted in this discussion. According to most of these dualisms, the person is related to his body as to a mere thing that he uses, whereas according to the position that I would develop, the person is incarnated in his body, which can in various ways be incorporated into his subjectivity and thus made to share in it. Now if I recognize the incarnate condition of my subjectivity, then it is far more natural to assume that I began to exist when my body began to exist than it is to recognize this on the basis of the dualism, which expresses a far-reaching estrangement of the person from his body.[13] But the embodiment of the human person is a subject for itself, which I do not intend to deal with in this study according to its importance in the philosophy of the person.[14] All the same, I hope to have contributed something to the question of the beginning in time of each human person, and to have thereby developed the fundamental distinction between the ontological being of the person and the subjective life of the person.[15]

---

refer to the objection that when the physical basis for consciousness has been irreversibly destroyed, the person must be gone, even if the body remains alive; and that if bodily death and personal death do not coincide, then neither must conception and the beginning of a new person coincide. But at the beginning of this argument one commonly assumes the very reduction of the person to personal consciousness that I have been arguing against. For why does one see evidence of the death of the person in the destruction of the organ on which consciousness is based? Commonly for no other reason than that one sees nothing more in the person than consciousness. Current opinions on brain death, then, which posit living human bodies that are not persons, far from constituting an objection to my position, are (many of them, at least) called into question if my argument is successful.

13. I have developed more fully the argument for the personhood of the human embryo in my "The Personhood of the Human Embryo," *Journal of Medicine and Philosophy* 18 (1993), 399–418.

14. I will have something more to say about it in Chapter 8.4 when I discuss the unity of person and nature in human persons.

15. With this result I find myself yet again in complete agreement with Quiles and his insistential philosophy of the human person. In his "La Esencia del Hombre," *Antropologia Filosofica In-sistencial* (Buenos Aires: Editiones Depalma, 1983), see his section 5, "La in-sistencia como estructura metafisica y como conocimiento," 333–335.

PART II

Selfhood and Transcendence

Cui [legi] qui non parebit, ipse se fugiet ac naturam hominis
aspernatus hoc ipso luet maximas poenas.

—Cicero

It could seem, considering the matter in the abstract, that human persons, if they have the selfhood and solitude that I have claimed to find in them, can live as persons only in a world of which they are the center and the measure. It could seem that the incommunicability of each person implies that each has his or her own truth and that persons cannot live under one truth that is the same for all. It could seem that the freedom of persons implies that each is a law unto himself and that persons cannot live under one moral law that binds all in the same way, and that their task in the moral life is not to be objectively right in thought and action, but to be genuine, true to themselves. It could also seem that the only way to understand other persons is to understand them as they understand themselves, and never to subject them to the judgment of any higher truth or law. Have not many modern philosophers tried to revive the teaching of Protagoras, that man is the measure of all things, precisely on the grounds that any human being undergoes violence if the measure of being and truth is outside of himself, and that he undergoes the most grievous violence possible if the measure lies in God?[1] If I talk

1. For a perfect example of such a thinker see Hans Kelsen in his essay, "Relativism and Absolutism in Politics and Philosophy," *What is Justice?* I (Berkeley, 1957). Kelsen argues that the object of knowledge, if it is understood as being known on its own terms and as it is in itself, tyrannizes over human beings just like a totalitarian dictator tyrannizes over his subjects, and that it has to be destroyed in its independence from our minds and understood as depending on them in order to be made compatible with our freedom; nor is it any accident that he appeals explicitly to Protagoras.

of human persons transcending themselves towards a reality beyond themselves, of being raised above themselves by participating in it, as by taking delight in beings according to their intrinsic worth, I seem to be proposing what amounts to heteronomy.

On the other hand, I have taken for granted up until now that transcendence does indeed belong to the human person, and that the full existence of persons, the full development of their selfhood and solitude, is possible only through participation in other beings. How do we reconcile this presupposition with the apparent tendency towards autonomy in our account of selfhood?

CHAPTER FIVE

Subjectivity and Objectivity

I have already introduced the idea of *intentional* acting in the sense of Brentano. We saw that every intentional act involves a polarity of subject and object and has, therefore, both its subjectivity and its objectivity. I then set aside the latter in favor the former; now I return to the objectivity, or object-directedness, or transcendence, of personal consciousness. I will study it first in its own right, and then in its relation to selfhood and subjectivity.

1. Persons as subjects of intentional acts

We saw that intentional acts live from a conscious relation to some object and cease to be themselves without this conscious relation. Thus the act of perceiving ceases to be the act of perceiving apart from something perceived, and the act of grieving ceases to be itself apart from some sad event that motivates it, and so on. This object-reference in any intentional act constitutes the innermost form of the act.

We can be intentionally related even to ourselves, but in this case we have to put ourselves in front of ourselves, becoming both subject and object of the same relation. This self-relation, of which more below, is altogether different from the one I call self-presence, and in Chapter 3.1 I went to some trouble to show the difference, thinking that the subjectivity of self-presence, with which I was primarily concerned in that section, could not be understood without understanding the difference. It will be recalled that in one of my arguments I said that an intentional relation of me to myself would divert me from the performing of other intentional acts; since our experience shows that self-presence causes no such diversion but, on the contrary, gives us the inner resources for performing intentional acts more authentically than ever, I concluded that self-presence is not rightly identified with an intentional relation of me to myself but must be an entirely different kind of self-relation, a subject-to-subject self-relation.

Let us now carry farther the analysis of intentionality so as to unfold further the dialectic of selfhood and transcendence in the human person. I want to introduce into our investigation the fundamental distinction between intentional and non-intentional conscious experiences.[1]

Let us begin by distinguishing intentional acts from body-feelings. The experience of bodily fatigue is not an intentional act, as we see clearly as soon as we sense the absurdity of saying that my bodily exhaustion is *about* something or other. I experience my body in bodily fatigue, but not as object; I seem instead to experience it subjectively, in a way analogous to my experience of myself in self-presence. My fatigue has its bodily causes, but these are never to be confused with intentional objects, for they need not be experienced at all (not even in the "subjective" way in which I experience my body) while I experience fatigue. The experience of fatigue is indifferent to my being aware or not being aware of the causes of it: the experience loses nothing by my ignorance of them, even as it gains nothing by my awareness of them. An intentional experience, by contrast, such as complaining about my fatigue, collapses and becomes impossible as soon as I am unaware of its intentional object. And further: my awareness of the causes of my fatigue is a new conscious act in relation to the fatigue; it is not the very form of the experience of fatigue. But in the case of an intentional experience my awareness of the object is not superadded to it, but *is* the intentional experience, or at least is the most basic part of it.[2]

---

1. Although Brentano failed to make this distinction, and in fact denied it, beginning with Husserl all of the phenomenologists made it. I am here particularly indebted to von Hildebrand, who offers a masterly study of intentionality in his *Ethics* (Chicago: Franciscan Herald Press, 1972), Chapter 17.

2. An interesting example of the distinction being recognized within analytic philosophy, apparently without the aid of any phenomenological authors, is found in John Searle, *Intentionality* (Cambridge, 1983), 1: ". . . on my account only some, not all, mental states and events have Intentionality. Beliefs, fears, hopes, and desires are Intentional; but there are forms of nervousness, elation, and undirected anxiety that are not Intentional. A clue to this distinction is provided by the constraints on how these states are reported. If I tell you I have a belief or a desire, it always makes sense for you to ask, 'What is it exactly that you believe?' or 'What is it that you desire?' . . . But my nervousness and undirected anxiety need not in that way be *about* anything."

The same analysis might be given of a mood such as a drug-induced euphoria; it is not a body-feeling, being a more psychic feeling, but it is just as little an intentional experience as the bodily fatigue. It forms a sharp contrast with the gladness motivated by something perceived as positive and good; the perceived positivity is the intentional object, and the gladness the intentional act. The drug that induced the euphoria can be unknown to me even as I feel high, and my euphoria goes no higher if I happen to learn of the drug. But if I do not know of the motive of my gladness, I experience no intentional gladness at all. The euphoria may of course influence other experiences that are intentional, or even give rise to intentional acts I would not have performed without the euphoria: but in itself the euphoria is non-intentional.

It is a particular merit of von Hildebrand's analysis that he recognizes another kind of non-intentional experience in all *consciously experienced drives and instincts,* such as in the experience of being hungry or thirsty. These resemble intentional experiences through their directedness towards that which satisfies the instincts, such as food and drink. But the consciously experienced instincts have causes that need not be known by the experiencing person; thus the hungry person need know nothing of the drop in blood sugar that causes his hunger. But the "cause" of the intentional act cannot remain hidden to the acting person. In fact, von Hildebrand says that not only the cause, but even the activity of the cause causing, is consciously lived in the case of intentional acts, so that the causing can be said to pass through my conscious center, as when I experience the sad event motivating my grief.

It follows that an intentional act unfolds entirely within the conscious acting of a person and that no part of it is withdrawn from his conscious acting. Non-intentional experiences, such as feeling fatigue, are indeed conscious, but some essential part of them, such as their causes, lies outside of that which we consciously experience. Perhaps the reason for this difference is that we speak of *acting* only in the case of intentional acting; a non-intentional experience is not an acting at all but only an enduring or an undergoing. Acting begins and ends in the conscious experience of the person; but the more passive forms of experiencing may be grounded in the world of causes lying "outside" of consciousness.

It is now clear why one speaks of the transcendence that is achieved in all intentional acts. Persons can hardly be said to transcend themselves in their non-intentional moods and body-feelings, seeing as they remain in these immersed in their own consciousness. Their only link with the world beyond their consciousness is a causal link; they undergo in themselves the effects of causes that are outside of themselves, but they need have no consciousness of the causes themselves or of the causality exercised by the causes. In a sense they experience only themselves. But in most intentional acts there is a conscious encounter with something beyond one's consciousness; in them one can experience more than oneself, or more than oneself as affected by something else; one can directly experience this something else, and how it affects one. It follows that persons achieve a transcendence in intentional acts that is proper precisely to their intentionality and that is impossible in the non-intentional experiences. Even in performing intentional acts directed not to another being but to oneself, one achieves something like this transcendence, experiencing oneself not subjectively from within, but objectively from without, thus experiencing oneself in a sense as other and so transcending oneself even in relation to oneself.

There is another aspect of the transcendence achieved in intentional acts, especially in the cognitive ones. Husserl observed that to insist on the intentionality of cognition is to break with the so-called image-theory of cognition, according to which we cognize something by having a mental image of that thing impressed on our minds. This would mean that the direct object of our cognizing is the image, which exists in a sense *in* our minds—as if the object of which the image is an image were itself beyond the reach of our direct cognition and could only be inferred as the cause of the image. To understand cognition as intentional is to say that in cognizing something we do not just undergo a mental effect of it while it remains hidden from us, but we reach beyond our consciousness and the effects wrought in it and can directly apprehend the object of our cognition. With this we see in a new way how transcendence is of the very essence of intentionality.

This transcendence is raised to a higher power in the case of that cognition which qualifies as *knowledge,* in which we apprehend some being as it really is, according to the truth about itself. But we are not yet ready to examine such further perfections of transcendence; for now we speak only of intentionality as it is found in both successful and unsuccessful attempts at knowing or at performing other acts.

Those who are aware of the contributions of Husserl to the theory of intentionality should note carefully the fact that I do not, as Husserl in his later philosophy did, understand intentional acts as acts that *constitute* their objects, investing them with whatever meaning and form are proper to them. An intentional act can be entirely receptive, it can be a conscious taking in of an object disclosing itself as it is in itself and on its own terms; those who hold the strictest philosophical realism are entitled to speak of the intentionality of our contact with being. Of course, the claims of philosophical realism represent a question of its own; I only mean that these claims are not excluded by the very form of intentional acting. The subject-object polarity of intentional acting does not by itself imply any predominance of the subject over the object. I could perhaps say it like this: "intentional" does not express an acting that is more masculine than feminine. Of course, if the intentional subject were completely passive in relation to its object, it would fall back into a causal dependency on the object, and then the subject would no longer really be a subject in relation to the thing, nor would the relation any longer be an intentional relation. But there is an active receiving that in no way compromises the receiving as a radical receiving.[3] It is all-important to stress this openness to receptivity that characterizes our concepts of intentionality and of objectivity, otherwise the intentionality of personal consciousness will seem to preclude much of the transcendence that is in fact proper to it.

When I spoke in Chapter 1.3 about "understanding the point" of an act so as to have it as an act fully our own, I was for the most part referring to what has now been explained as the intentionality of an intentional act; I was emphasizing the understanding we have of the relation between the object of our act and the act itself. (I say "for the most part," because we will see directly in the next section that "understanding the point of an act," while comprising all intentional acts, extends beyond them, being also found in certain acts that can be called neither intentional nor non-intentional.)

Important as the distinction between intentional and non-intentional is, one should keep always in mind that in this book we have come to the intentionality of consciousness from our study of subjectivity. We are, therefore, above all struck by a certain opposite that intentionality forms to subjectivity. In the subjectivity of our intentional acts we are anchored in ourselves, immersed in ourselves, living out of ourselves; in the intentionality of them we go out of ourselves and take things as outside of ourselves, over against ourselves, relating ourselves to things in a cer-

---

3. Von Hildebrand argues in many places for our capacity to perform actively receptive acts that are truly receptive; the interested reader might begin with the distinction that he draws within intentional acts between *cognitive acts* and *responses* (op. cit., 195–97).

tain "external" way that forms a contrast with all subjective experiencing of ourselves from within ourselves.

2. Persons as objects of intentional acts

We have been considering persons as the performing subjects of intentional acts; we have now to consider them as the objects towards which such acts can be directed. When in the title of this chapter I speak of the "objectivity" of personal selfhood, I mean not only the capacity of living in object-directed (that is, intentional) acts, but also the capacity of receiving such acts.

Scheler thought that to objectify persons is to lose them as persons. Thus he held that the *only* appropriate way to experience other persons is the non-objectifying way, whether of empathy and sympathy or of experiencing others as co-subjects.[4] This would imply that the present discussion of the object-directedness of consciousness is limited to our conscious relation to non-persons.[5] That would in turn mean that the focus of this chapter is much narrower and of much less importance for a philosophy of the human person than it seemed at first. I claim, however, that the opposite is the case; I claim that much of our relation to other persons unfolds in the subject-object polarity of intentional acting, and that this can occur without any depersonalization of them. Indeed, I claim that there is a rich dimension of personal and interpersonal life that would not be possible without a certain objectifying of persons.[6]

4. Scheler, *Formalism in Ethics and Non-formal Ethics of Values* (Evanston: Northwestern University Press, 1973), 386–393.

5. In his important study, *Der Andere: Studien zur Sozialontologie der Gegenwart* (Berlin: Walter de Gruyter, 1977), Michael Theunissen argues that authentic interpersonal relations are never lived in the subject-object polarity of intentional consciousness. His position derives in part from thinking of intentionality as it is presented in the late philosophy of Husserl, where it takes on a positing, constituting function that can only impede the openness and receptivity of the interpersonal. But it may be that he also neglects the considerations that I am about to offer. This work of Theunissen has been translated into English, but with the unfortunate omission of certain valuable chapters: *The Other: Studies in the Social Ontology of Husserl, Heidegger, Sartre, and Buber* (Cambridge, MA: MIT Press, 1986).

6. The reader will see that the discussion that we are about to enter upon is akin to the discussion in Chapter 3.3, where I asked whether it is possible to philosophize about subjectivity. But here it is not just a question of the objectifying act of philosophizing, but of all possible objectifying acts directed to persons.

Before giving my reasons for holding this and clarifying the sense in which I hold it, I want to try to give an account of the truth in Scheler's position. When persons join together as co-subjects of the same act, as when they grieve or rejoice *miteinander,* together with each other, thus giving rise to what I called collective subjectivity, they surely do not encounter each other in the polarity of subject-object. They encounter each other indeed; they do not remain in their own experiencing as they do in any non-intentional experience, with their relation to the other amounting to only a causal relation; no, they are consciously present to each other, and may well be exercising significant self-transcendence in achieving this presence. And yet it is not a self-transcendence lived in the form of a subject-object polarity; it is instead something like a sub-ject-subject relation to the other.

We get the same result if we think about experiencing the other with sympathy in the sense of *Nacherleben* or *Nachfühlen.* To the extent that we enter into the subjectivity of others, experiencing them as they ex-perience themselves, we come into contact with them not just as objects of our experiencing, but as subjects of their own experiencing. Perhaps I have to say it more carefully like this. Insofar as we are conscious of the difference that always remains between ourselves and the others with whom we sympathize, there is some subject-object polarity in our rela-tion to them; but insofar as we experience them subjectively, from within themselves, sharing in the way they experience themselves, we seem to stand in a relation to them which seems precisely to lack the subject-object polarity. It is hard to avoid speaking of something like a subject-subject relation to the other. Now this is a relation in which we tran-scend ourselves, and in fact transcend ourselves in a particular way; in empathy and sympathy we break out of our immanence and enter into the world of others. And yet we have here a self-transcendence that can-not be fully explained in terms of intentional acts. This is why I re-marked above that the transcendence we were studying in connection with intentionality is not all of the transcendence of which we are ca-pable.

And so Scheler is surely right insofar as he holds that we can ap-proach others without taking them as the objects of our intentional acts, and he is right again insofar as he sees certain personalist excellences in the encounter with others precisely in the non-intentional way of sym-pathy and empathy. But he seems to assert these truths in an extremely one-sided way when he claims that such a "subjective" encounter with others is the *only* mode of encounter worthy of them as persons.

For it is undeniable that we often put ourselves in front of ourselves as our own objects, as when we examine ourselves, critically testing our own motives and intentions. There need be nothing disordered about this relation that we can have to ourselves, as we can see from the fact that much truth about ourselves commonly comes to light only in objectivizing ourselves. There is in fact a whole dimension of self-possession to be gained through this objective self-knowledge. Perhaps I could also mention here certain kinds of humor and irony we can have in relation to ourselves; they presuppose some act of objectifying ourselves and at the same time they are all-important for the soundness of our personal existence.

But if we are right to make ourselves an object for ourselves, then surely we are right, or can in principle be right, to put other persons in front of ourselves as our intentional objects. Sometimes we test critically their motives and intentions, testing whether these are in order, whether they are in the truth (sometimes we even do this at the request of others). In such testing we are not trying to experience them as they experience themselves, but are trying to discern whether they experience themselves in accordance with the truth about persons. Unless we hold to the extreme Protagorean relativism according to which each man is the measure of reality for himself, then such critical testing will be in principle legitimate in relation both to myself as well as to others.

Indeed, there is a kind of "proof" that can be offered for the legitimacy of taking persons as objects of certain intentional acts. Everyone knows that others can see in me what escapes me and thus they can enable me to find far more in my self-examination than I could have ever found by myself. But if others were always only understanding me as I understand myself, avoiding on principle any critical assessment of me—presumably so as to be "non-judgmental" in relation to me—then they would leave me confined within my natural limits and would do nothing towards helping me to surpass these limits and to surpass myself. They would just reflect back to me what I am already experiencing subjectively, and would not help me to enlarge the depth and breadth of my subjective experience. If the prophet Nathan had just tried to feel himself into the mind and feelings of King David, he could not have helped David to discover a truth about himself that David had repressed. And if David had not been willing to step out of his solidarity with himself and to make an object of himself, looking at himself for a moment as Nathan saw him and recognizing himself in that other whom Nathan described to him, he would perhaps have never broken through to repentance. My view of another as object can have its own truth, and indeed a truth that the other has to receive from me; such a view need not, therefore, have anything to do with depersonalizing the other.

This holds not only for the faults but also for the excellences of others. The moral excellences of another can be experienced by me in a way in which they cannot be experienced by the person who has them. If I know another person only through his self-experience, my experience of his excellences will be as limited as his is, and I will lose an opportunity for knowing him that only I have, precisely as one who is other than he is and who can know him differently than he knows himself from within himself. Perhaps we also have to say that the excellent person in large part receives such knowledge as he has of his own excellences from those others who reflect them back to him as only others can. Again we see that there is a way of objectifying others without depersonalizing them.

The same thing is found in our experience of communities. Consider my experience of living in a community from within it as a full member of it, as when I live in the United States, speaking its language as a native speaker, living in its traditions, etc. Now a non-American can either try to feel himself into my experience as American, or he can stand firmly in his own position as non-American and look at me and my national community from his point of view. If he looks at me in this latter way, seeing me as a foreigner, my community and I will present to him an aspect that has its own truth. There is something in the way in which the American nation presents itself to the Frenchman or the German that is not found in the self-experience of the American nation. It comes not from sympathy and empathy with Americans but from taking them as objects of certain intentional acts. Americans need to know about this aspect; they will know themselves better if they know how they appear to non-Americans who see them as foreigners.[7] They should be willing to be objectified for the sake of bringing to light this aspect of truth about themselves.

Let us make an analogy with the knowledge I have of my body. I experience my body from within; it is an experience that only I can have of my body. Others can try to feel themselves into this body-experience of mine. But there is something else they can do: they can see me as a

---

7. If there is any merit in what I am saying here, then it is no accident that the greatest study of the American character was written not by an American but by the Frenchman, Alexis de Tocqueville.

bodily being that is over against themselves, or in other words, they can see me as I appear to them. With this way of looking they do not necessarily objectify me in a depersonalizing way, because what they see in me has its own truth. I need to receive this truth from them in order to know my bodily being fully. How much would be missing from my experience of my body if I never knew how my face looked to another! How much would be missing from my self-experience as person if I never knew how I presented myself to others!

What would Scheler say in response? How would he defend his thesis that persons can be known as persons only by entering with sympathy into their subjectivity? He would say that you can indeed refer to human beings as objects of your intentional acts, but that your act never attains to the others precisely as persons. You can reach the bodily being of the others, you can reach their psychic life, much of their feeling-life, even the psychological egos of the others; but you cannot reach their very personhood, or their personal selves, which always remain hidden from the intention of any objectifying act and which are always accessible only by means of *Nachfühlen*.

To this I would reply that Scheler can in this way call into question at most some of the evidence adduced in the foregoing pages. Thus he might say that irony towards oneself always refers to some limit in one's psychophysical makeup but not in one's very being as person, and that the self-objectifying that goes into irony is not really an objectifying of oneself as person. But for the most part such responses are unconvincing. Consider our sense of our moral faults as well as of our moral strengths. Recall all that was said about the role that certain objectifying others play in mediating to us the truth about who we really are in a moral respect. Surely our moral substance belongs to us not just as psychophysical human beings but as persons, precisely as persons. What was it if not a properly personal failure that Nathan confronted David with? (All of Chapter 7 is dedicated to unfolding this connection between moral worthiness and person—a connection that Scheler affirms no less than I do.) It follows that the objectifying acts of others can indeed reach us as persons, and that the self-objectification that others enable us to perform does indeed let us gain an objective relation to ourselves *as persons.*

I conclude, then, that others experiencing me as their object, or me experiencing others as my objects (in our particular sense of intentional object) plays a large legitimate role in the interpersonal life of human beings, and that the transcendence achieved in intentional acts includes much, though not all, of our interpersonal life.[8] In fact, I go farther and claim that by relating to another as my intentional object I am as far as could be from interfering with authentic interpersonal relation with this other; it is rather the case that I thereby make possible a whole dimension of the interpersonal. We can understand how it is that we serve as the "custodians" of the truth about each other as persons and mediate to each other the truth about ourselves only if we recognize the legitimate way in which we can objectify each other.

The reader will now see that I never intended the discussion of "sharing in the subjectivity of others" in Chapter 3.6 to be anything like a complete survey of the interpersonal; all that I said there needs to be completed by what I have just said about relating to others precisely *not* by just sharing in their subjectivity but also by taking them as the intentional objects of certain intentional acts.

It follows that "to make an object" of a person in my sense is *not* equivalent to "making an object" of another in the sense of depersonalizing the other, treating him or her more like a thing than a person. I can put a person in front of me precisely as person. Of course, with the person in front of me I am more exposed to the danger of depersonalizing the other; there are all kinds of way of seeing a person "from the outside" that lead to a distortion or caricature of the person. The personhood of the other is more sure to be experienced by me when I encounter the other as subject. But the other can also be experienced subject to object, and in fact this objective experience has its own perfection, as we have seen, and it would in no way be desirable to experience persons always only in the subject-to-subject form.

3. The dialectic of selfhood and transcendence in intentional acting

In what follows I will distinguish between *subjective selfhood* and *objective selfhood,* the former expressing the selfhood that is lived in the subject-subject relation to myself, the latter expressing the selfhood

---

8. When authors such as Ferdinand Ebner express their enthusiasm for the interpersonal by saying that one person should always take another person only in the second person (grammatically speaking) and that it is never right to take the other in the third person (*Das Wort und die geistigen Realitäten,* paragraph 14), they seem to exaggerate wildly, and burden their many deep insights with untenable claims. When we make another the object of our act we commonly take the other in the third person, and this can be done without any least depersonalization of the other, as I have just explained in the text.

that is lived in the subject-object relation to myself. *Subjective selfhood,* then, is equivalent to what I mean by *subjectivity.*

Subjective selfhood. It is clear that the subjectivity of persons is far more properly actualized in intentional than in non-intentional experiences. Of course, even the latter have their own subjectivity and self-presence (insofar as they are conscious experiences), but we become far more authentically present to ourselves in the simplest intentional act. It seems that we have to gather ourselves into ourselves and to dwell with ourselves in putting something in front of ourselves as our intentional object, whereas in the absence of an intentional object we are not driven back into ourselves. Without any intentional act we cannot be with ourselves as we are with ourselves in the simplest intentional act; any deeper subjectivity in ourselves requires the objectivity of intentional acting. I might also express this by saying that all intentional acts distinguish themselves from non-intentional experiences by presupposing, and also engendering, far more self-presence.

Let us try to understand this in terms of the distinction between person and nature as I made it in Chapter 1.3. I said that person is the principle of acting through oneself *(per se agere)* and nature the principle of being acted upon, undergoing *(aguntur).* Now it is clear, as we have already had occasion to observe, that all non-intentional experiences are only undergone, they happen in us and to us, but we do not perform them, acting through ourselves in them. This is why no one would think of calling a body-feeling or a mood or a felt instinct by the name of "act"; non-intentional experiences are never ways of acting but only ways of being acted upon, and so they belong not to person but to nature in our being. By contrast, all intentional experiences are acts; in them we act through ourselves. Sometimes we can see in another only instinctual striving and we cannot "find" the other as person; we can explain in terms of natural causes all that we see in the other. But then we catch sight of some intentional act in the other, and this gives us the sense that it is no longer just the species-nature of the other acting through him but that it is *the other himself, the other as person* who has begun to show himself. Nature has begun to give way to person, and being possessed by another has begun to give way to self-possession. And it is not only in *volitional* intentional acts that we act through ourselves; we act no less through ourselves in cognitive intentional acts. Thus an act of understanding, for example, does not befall us, it does not happen to us; we perform it. It is no less an act than the most deliberate choosing.

Objective selfhood. I have been speaking of the selfhood achieved in the subjectivity of intentional acts, that is, in the self-presence of these acts. But we should not overlook the selfhood that I achieve *when I make myself the object of my act.* I have already spoken of the legitimacy of certain ways of objectivizing ourselves.

Whenever, for instance, I remember my past, and attempt to interpret its meaning and to evaluate it in terms of a higher law, and also whenever I try to communicate it to another in words and sentences, I perform certain intentional acts towards myself. It is true that I experience my past from within as only I can experience it, that is, subjectively. But my attempt to understand my past, and certainly my attempt to see it as others see it, is more than a subjective relation of me to myself; in this attempt I also bend back on myself as on an intentional object. Persons are by no means related to themselves *only* subjectively, *nor is it in the least desirable that their whole self-relation should be subjective; the fully awakened self-relation of a person is also objective, that is, involves all kinds of self-directed intentional acts.* And it seems to be precisely the moment of transcendence in intentional acts, and the particular distance that I take to the objects of my acts, that makes self-directed intentional acts so important for the achievement of the self-possession in which persons ought to exist.[9]

Indeed, the reflexivity so characteristic of personal existence, expressed in persons belonging to themselves, being handed over to themselves, being a problem for themselves, is perhaps lived just as truly in the objective as in the subjective self-relation. I cannot possess myself as person only in my subjectivity, even if it is ever so recollected; full self-possession presupposes that I also stand over against myself, transcending myself toward myself, and facing myself as the intentional object of all kinds of acts.[10]

---

9. Notice that "self-possession," which has hitherto expressed a subjective self-relation, now is extended also to express an objective self-relation, that is, a relation to oneself as object. It does not, however, seem natural to extend "self-presence" like this, and so it will continue to express only a subjective self-relation.

10. I might in this connection recall Scheler's profound discussion of our ability to get free from the weight of our past by a certain kind of remembering of it. "Die gewusste Geschichte macht uns *frei* von der *Macht* der gelebten Geschichte." See "Repentance and Rebirth," in *On the Eternal in Man* (Hamden, CT: Archon Books, 1972), 40–41. Of course, this can hardly be reconciled with Scheler's teaching that persons can never be made objects; what he says here in effect is that it is a certain objectifying of our past that frees us from its weight.

Though I am at the moment calling attention to the objective self-relation, I want to say that the fullness of personal existence requires *both* the objective *as well as* the subjective self-relation. If the subjective prevails in a person at the expense of the objective, then that person suffers a certain loss of personal awakedness; the reflexivity of personal existence remains underdeveloped; we could say that such a person has "life" at the expense of "spirit." If, on the other hand, the objective self-relation prevails in a person at the expense of the subjective, then that person suffers from a certain excess of reflection; the surging up of the deeper sources of personal life is interfered with, and he exists "sickled o'er with the pale cast of thought."

It is also important to recall here all that was developed in the previous section: the truth about myself, as I put it, presents itself first of all to other persons, who reflect it back to me. I have already explained why such truth is apprehended by others in intentional acts directed to me and why it is not apprehended by them in their attempts at sympathizing with me. I receive this truth from others only by sharing in their intentional acts directed to me, that is, by objectifying myself as they objectify me. If I do not receive from them this truth about myself, my self-possession remains fundamentally deficient.

It seems that the objective self-relation has a certain interpersonal dimension that the subjective lacks. In the latter we live in a certain solitude; in the former we receive ourselves reflected back from others.

To conclude. We can say that intentional acting develops the selfhood of persons in two directions. By transcending myself towards the object of my intention, I am gathered into myself subjectively. But when this object is myself, so that I transcend myself towards myself, I also gain a certain objective self-possession. In other words, in self-directed intentional acting, persons take possession of themselves one time through the subjectivity of their acting, and a second time through the objectivity of it.

There is more to say on selfhood and intentionality, but I propose to defer it until I have developed further the transcendence that we achieve towards an object in an intentional act. If we examine more closely this transcendence of the human person in relation to intentional objects, we will discover a still more fundamental transcendence at its basis, and only this will let us do full justice to the selfhood and subjectivity of intentional acting. What is this more fundamental transcendence?

4. The transcendence towards a certain infinity which encompasses and conditions the transcendence of intentional acting

Various thinkers have pointed out that there is not only the transcendence achieved in being directed to some object; there is also the further transcendence achieved in surpassing the object. We can catch sight of this surpassing by noticing a *restlessness* that we feel in relation to the objects of consciousness, a restlessness typically expressed in the raising of questions about them. It was, I think, Lonergan who said that when an animal has satisfied all its needs it goes to sleep, but when a human person has satisfied all his needs he asks a question. We are never content just to see some object, but we wonder what lies behind it. We cannot look at a wood or an ocean without wondering what is in it. We cannot encounter a limit without wondering what lies on the other side of it. We cannot perceive an object without wanting to know whether it is the greatest of its kind, and if not, what the greatest is. We cannot perceive an object without wondering if it *really* is as we perceive it; we cannot escape the question of what things are in themselves; we cannot escape making statements about things and inquiring into the truth or falsity of our statements. We cannot live with the blunt givenness of an object without asking why it is as it is, and why it is at all; we cannot escape the question of the causes of things. It is hard for us to look at a thing without wondering how different it might have been, or might yet become. In a word: we cannot just take the objects of our experience for granted and live in an unquestioning solidarity with them; we have to put them in question in the most various ways, and in this sense we are always surpassing them, or transcending them.

It is often pointed out that we break away from biological and other needs when we put things in question; that with this questioning we wonder about things in an entirely non-pragmatic way and not just in their relation to the satisfaction of our needs. It is one thing to wonder whether this animal here that I would like to eat is worth the effort of chasing, and it is another thing to wonder where the animal came from, or what species it belongs to: it is the latter kind of questioning to which I am referring. And I want to say that in and through this questioning we transcend our biological and other needs and become free for things in their own right.

Philosophers have tried to explain this insatiable questioning in human persons; indeed, it is in accord with this very questioning that they should seek some further explanation of it. Many of them have said that we all carry inside ourselves an idea of infinity, of infinite fullness. It is this sense of infinity that makes us always reach beyond any object of our experience, finding quickly its contingency and its finitude, which we sometimes feel with keen disappointment, as if we had expected to find in the object all the infinity of which our minds are possessed.

Sometimes these philosophers point to the *passion for ultimacy* that is so characteristic of persons, who desire nothing so much as some truth or meaning that is in its validity not just relative to some time or place but is really, absolutely valid, or valid with an unsurpassable validity. It is a question of a *metaphysical passion,* which prevents alive and intact persons from living and moving and having their whole being in the relativities of innerworldly life. They want at least some share in ultimate truth so as to have a basis for some ultimate commitment. The many forms of idolatry into which human persons are always falling show that they would rather satisfy this need of theirs for ultimacy in a disordered and unworthy way than to let it go unsatisfied. It is this passion for ultimacy that makes us put into question the things of our experience and to reach beyond them as soon as we run up against their finitude.

If I read him correctly, Karl Rahner with his well-known theory of the *Vorgriff auf das Sein* (preapprehension of being, as it is usually translated) is one of the recent representatives of a long tradition that explains this deep-seated restlessness of human persons in terms of a certain infinity of which we are possessed. He says that this infinity is not like another object of experience, but is stirred up in us only in connection with our experience of particular objects. Once stirred up it provides us with a kind of background or frame of reference for experiencing them; inserted in this frame of reference they become questionable for us in the most various respects, often leaving us dissatisfied, driving us beyond them in search of more.

Rahner has given an original account of the place of the *Vorgriff* in the activity of abstracting the general form out of particular things. He says that we can abstract the form only because we perceive the concrete object of our perception as limiting the form, as being only one of many possible instantiations of the form. Rahner inquires into the condition for the possibility for this experience of the concrete being as a principle of limitation on the essence or form, and he answers by saying that we cannot turn to the concrete object except by reaching beyond it to a kind of infinity of being. It is by considering an object on the background of this unthematic apprehension of infinity that we grasp the potentially limitless communicability of the form or essence, in contrast to the incommunicable particularity of the concrete object; but to grasp this is to abstract the general form from the concrete particular.[11] If we lacked this sense of infinity we would presumably live completely contented with the thing in its particularity and would lack the inquisitiveness that makes us ask what in the object can be repeated in other objects. Rahner's theory of abstraction has the advantage of showing that our sense of infinity not only serves to "relativize" things, inflicting on us a sense of their finitude, but also to bring to light things (such as the universal form) having a certain affinity with this infinity.[12]

Rahner proceeds to identify this infinity with God. Of course other thinkers, such as Kant, recognize something like this infinity and its unsettling effect on our experience of objects, but they try to explain it without assuming any transcendence towards God. Kant explains it quite immanentistically in terms of the three Ideas of Reason, one of which is the Idea of God, and in terms of the "regulative" function that they exercise towards the objects of experience. Kant's Idea of God is a heuristic principle generated by Reason, having nothing to do with any intimation, however vague, of the reality of God Himself; thus for him the whole principle of our always reaching beyond the things of our experience *lies altogether in human reason itself.*

Before responding to Kant we should notice that he does not adequately account for the facts of our world-openness. Kant imposes a limit on this activity of always reaching beyond: he limits it to the realm of things we experience within space-time. But we can undeniably reach beyond the whole realm of space-time; we can put it in front of us, put it variously into question, and so take a position above it. Kant himself takes a position above it when he contrasts it with the noumenal world. Our world-openness does not only generate an insatiable reaching beyond things *within* space-time, it also makes us reach beyond spacetime altogether.

11. By the way, given the investigations of Chapter 2, I can hardly accept the idea that incommunicable particularity in a being is always only a principle of limitation. I do not venture to say whether Rahner commits himself to this idea.

12. Rahner first presented his theory of abstraction in his first work, *Geist in der Welt* (Munich: Kösel Verlag, 1957); one can find it recapitulated in *Hörer des Wortes* (Freiburg: Herder, 1963), especially in Chapters 3–5.

But how can I show with Rahner and against Kant that we are right to give a religious interpretation to our world-openness? I would explain it as follows. If we hold on other grounds, on grounds independent of the theory of intentionality, that God exists and that we human persons are grounded in God, and further that we are capable of some experience or knowledge of God, then it becomes natural to recognize in the sense of infinity conditioning our experience of things a certain presence (an unthematic presence, Rahner says) of God in our conscious lives. One sees that the debate between Rahner and the likes of Kant is not to be decided here in the analysis of intentionality but in the philosophy of religion and in philosophical theology. I am here assuming the theism that can, as I think (despite Kant), be established in these other areas of philosophy, and I am using it as a principle for interpreting our sense of infinity. And I would think that even a Kant, once he does justice to the facts of our world-openness, would have to agree with me that, on this theistic assumption, my religious reading of our sense of infinity is the only reasonable reading of it. Needless to say, if this religious interpretation of our world-openness were more important for the present analysis than it in fact is, I would have to analyze it more closely.

Perhaps I should add that this infinity seems to possess us not only as something of which we are aware, but also as an *infinite capacity in ourselves*. It seems to be not only something beckoning to us from beyond, but it also exists as an infinite need in ourselves. Our relation to this infinity might seem more extrinsic than it really is if we were to neglect the way it forms our subjectivity.

Of particular interest for us in this study is that the things of which we are conscious undergo a fundamental modification as a result of the sense of infinity that possesses us and which we cannot help bringing to them. In a sense we can be said to be hardly aware of them as long as we take them for granted, finding them unproblematic, seeing them only in relation to our needs; we awaken to them and gain a spiritual distance to them by putting them in question in various ways, by inquiring into the truth about them, and also into their causes, and so detaching them from our needs. Indeed, it seems that the things of our experience do not really become *objects* of experience, are not really thrown up in front of us as intentional objects, nor do we really become *subjects* facing them, until we transcend them, reaching beyond them, seeing them against the background of this mysterious infinity. Thus the subject-object polarity belonging to intentional acting is to be explained not just in terms of the human subject and of the objects to which it turns, but also in terms of a certain transcending of these objects, a certain reaching beyond them towards an infinite fullness.[13]

With the higher animals I hesitate to speak of subject-object relations, and hesitate even more to speak of the subjectivity of the animals or of the objectivity of their world. Why is this, seeing that they undeniably perceive things around themselves and respond to what they perceive, and so seem to have some kind of intentionality? Is it not because they are presumably so immersed in their needs that they are incapable of the distance to things that comes from putting them into question and from inquiring into the truth about them?[14] Is it not because they presumably lack that sense of infinity which we find ineradicably inscribed in our consciousness? Perhaps it is this lack that, more than anything else, ultimately explains the absence of language among animals.

One sees that there is an objectivity of beings that has nothing to do with "reducing beings to manipulable things," but which is simply the form in which beings are experienced by an awakened personal spirit.

It follows that we human persons inhabit an entirely different realm than animals, even when we and the animals "see" and "hear" the "same" things. A number of contemporary philosophers have proposed to mark this difference by saying that we inhabit *the world,* while animals live only in an *environment,* or by saying, with greater precision, that we not only live in an environment but also inhabit the world, while animals are entirely confined to their environment.[15] Insofar as we experience the things around us in some relation to the sense of infinity that always

13. Rahner thinks that the activity of abstracting is not just *one* way of surpassing the objects of experience, but is in a sense the most fundamental way. He thinks that it is precisely when the mind experiences some thing with reference to some general form, as by predicating a general name of the thing, that the mind puts the thing in front of itself as its object.

14. Cf. Scheler: "The animal has no 'object.' It lives, as it were, ecstatically immersed in its environment which it carries along as a snail carries its shell. It cannot transform the environment into an object. It cannot perform the peculiar act of detachment and distance by which man transforms an 'environment' into the 'world'. . . . I might say that the animal is involved too deeply in the actualities of life which correspond to its organic needs and conditions ever to experience and grasp them as objects" (*Man's Place in Nature* [New York: Farrar, Straus, and Cudahy, 1962], 41).

15. On the world-environment distinction see Josef Pieper, "The Philosophical Act," Chapter 2, in *Leisure* (New York: New American Library, 1963); Martin Buber, "Distance and Relation," in *The Knowledge of Man* (New York: Harper, 1966); Max Scheler, op. cit., 35–55; Hans-Eduard Hengstenberg, *Philosophische Anthropologie* (Munich-Salzburg: Anton Pustet Verlag, 1984), 9–12.

wells up in our conscious acting, insofar as we break away from our biological and other needs, or rather detach the objects of our acts from our needs, putting them in front of ourselves and taking them as authentic intentional objects,[16] we inhabit the world, we show ourselves as world-open subjects, as a number of authors express themselves. But insofar as we experience things through our needs and so live in an immediacy with them which is like (though never exactly like) that of animals in relation to their surroundings, we live in our environment.[17]

One often characterizes the world as the totality of all that is, and thus it is said that, while there can be many environments, there is only one world. Environments are functions of biological needs, and they vary as needs vary. Environments extend as far as things that can satisfy my needs extend, and there they stop. But once I put things in front of me so as to be concerned with what they are in their own right, there is no natural limit to the things that interest me; my interest extends to all that is. This openness to the totality of all that is, we find expressed (among other ways) in the insatiability of human questioning. Aristotle must have been referring to it in his famous statement that the rational soul is in a certain sense all things.[18]

Of course we can get a multiplicity of worlds, and perhaps even as many worlds as persons, if we take world in the sense of the range of objects that a given person has detached from his needs and put in front of himself. Then we find that one person's world is richer or poorer than another's.[19] And yet this is a plurality of worlds that means something

---

16. Wojtyla sometimes speaks of a certain "superiority" to things that we can gain by aiming at the truth about them: "Far from being but a passive mirror that only reflects objects, man acquires through truth a specific ascendancy over them. This 'superiority,' which is inscribed into the spiritual nature of the person, is connected with a certain distance or aloofness towards mere objects of cognition" (The Acting Person [Dordrecht: D. Reidel, 1979], 159).

17. Hengstenberg has rightly stressed how different the animal environment is from the human environment; he has pointed out how the world-openness of human persons makes itself felt even in the pragmatic lives they lead in their so-called environments. For example, to satisfy our needs by means of technological constructions is to satisfy them as only world-open beings can; it is to give rise to an environment such as no nonpersonal animal inhabits. For one thing, human beings living in a technologically controlled environment lack the mute immediacy to their environment that animals have to theirs.

18. Aristotle, On the Soul, III, 8, 431b, 21.

19. I might here mention the possibility we have of deliberately abstracting from certain things in our world for the sake of focusing for a time on certain other things, as

different from the plurality of environments. For with worlds we have different participations in the one world, but environments are not related like this to "one environment"; there is no such thing as one environment in the sense in which there is one world.

People with "post-modernist" sensibilities will be wary of this talk about "totality" and about the oneness of the world. But of course I have in no way implied that we human persons can *encompass and exhaust* the totality of all that is, as if we had divine knowledge. I agree with all that Kierkegaard said against Hegelian rationalism. I just now mentioned the partiality of each person's participation in the world. And in fact we can live our world-openness in ways that have no threatening totalizing tendencies. Thus we can live it by the questions we ask. We can live it *even in our way of dwelling in our environment.* As soon as we understand our environment *as a mere environment,* as only one of the realms in which we live but not the only possible one, as soon as we sense its relativity and partiality, perhaps even to the point of feeling it to be confining, *we have already reached beyond it, taken a position above it, situated it in the world, in a sense relativized it,* and so transcended it as no animal can transcend its environment. Or is "post-modernism" a naturalism that would confine human beings in their environment and not even allow them to press against its limits?

We see, then, that the transcendence of the personal subject towards some object is not to be explained only in terms of the subject and of the object; there is a more fundamental transcendence towards a certain infinity in virtue of which we are world-open subjects; *this* transcendence is the basis for the transcendence achieved in any authentic intentional act.

5. *The dialectic of selfhood and transcendence in the world-openness of human persons*

As we know by now, in transcending ourselves towards an intentional object we do not simply forget ourselves as personal subjects; this self-transcendence always has its own subjectivity. Let us now inquire into the subjectivity of the new transcendence that has just come to light and which has shown itself to be ultimately a religious transcendence.

---

when a hiker looks at his surroundings only from an aesthetic point of view and deliberately sets aside all the non-aesthetic questions that might be asked of his surroundings. Here we have multiple worlds within the experiencing of one and the same person.

1. We can discern a "correspondence" between each person being a whole of his own and never a mere part (see Chapter 1.2), on the one hand, and each person being open to the totality of all that is, on the other. That we are wholes and not parts is somehow expressed and lived whenever we inhabit the world and do not let ourselves be confined by some environment. It is the mark of a non-person to have its whole being in some limited region of the world, whereas persons can surpass every regional limitation and live in openness to the totality. St. Thomas makes this point in arguing that God governs human beings for their own sakes (*Summa Contra Gentiles*, III, 112); one of his arguments is based on the fact that the soul, as Aristotle said, is in a sense all things. He seems to mean that world-open beings can only be persons, and must be treated as persons, even by divine providence.

2. How must human persons be if they are capable of detaching objects from their needs and putting them in front of themselves, and so living in openness to the totality of all that is? Josef Pieper has found a helpful approach to answering this question; I will now render his thought in my own way.

He observes that with all living beings we can distinguish between an inner side and an outer side. The inner side of a stone is just like the outer side of it, and so the term "inner side" does not express a distinct dimension of the being of the stone. But in the case of a living being there is a distinct dimension of the being that is well designated as its inner side. For every living being has a dynamic center out of which it relates itself to other beings. Now Pieper claims that the stronger the inner principle of a living being, the vaster the realm in which it lives. If the consciousness of an animal lets it inhabit a vaster and richer environment than the plant inhabits, this is because the animal consciousness is a far stronger form of inner-ness than the life principle of a plant.

Now if a being occupies not just an ever so vast environment, if it is capable of inhabiting the one world of all that is, then the living being must have an incomparable inner principle—it must have the inwardness of personal subjectivity. This is not just an inner principle that is stronger by degree than the inner principle of animal consciousness—just as the world is not a realm vaster only by degree than the environment. The world is a realm of another order, an absolute realm; and so the person, who can live in the world, has inwardness of another order, the inwardness of personal self-presence. Only an act issuing from this inwardness can attain to the world.

The more encompassing the power with which to relate oneself to objective being, the more deeply that power needs to be anchored in the inner self of the subject so as to counterbalance the step it takes outside. And where this step attains a world that is in principle complete (with totality as its aim), the highest possible form of being established in oneself, which is characteristic of spirit, is also reached. The two together constitute spirit: not only the capacity to relate oneself to the whole of reality, to the whole world, but an unlimited capacity of living and being in oneself, of standing in oneself as a being of one's own—the very traits which, in the philosophical tradition of Europe, have always been ascribed to being a person. To have a world, to be related to the totality of existing things, can only be the attribute of a being whose being is within established in itself—not a "what" but a "who", a self, a person.[20]

We could in fact "define" personal subjectivity in terms of our direct-edness to the totality; we could say that personal subjectivity is that depth of inwardness in a living being which opens the being to the absolute realm of all that is. It is impossible to do philosophical justice to personal subjectivity without referring to the world-openness of the person; it is impossible to live personal subjectivity authentically without living this world-openness. I agree with Karl Rahner when he says, "Being a person means: a subject possessing itself in the act of relating itself to the whole of being, and this both in knowledge and freedom."[21]

Notice that in Chapter 1.3 I asked how persons must be so as to act through themselves; now we ask how persons must be so as to be able to

20. Pieper, "The Philosophical Act," in *Leisure* (New York and Toronto: New American Library, 1963), 90–91. Since I have had to correct the English translation in a number of places, I give here the German original, which expresses a thought so important for our study of personhood:

Je umfassender die Kraft, sich auf die Welt des objektiven Seins zu beziehen, desto tiefer verankert das Widerlager solchen Ausgriffs im Inneren des Subjekts. Und wo ein prinzipiell abschliessesnder Grad von "Weltweite" erreicht ist, nämlich die Richtung auf Totalität, da ist auch die prinzipiell höchste Stufe des In-sich-selber-Gründens erreicht, wie dem Geiste eigentümlich ist. So macht also beides zusammen das Wesen des Geistes aus: nicht allein die auf das Totum von Welt und Wirklichkeit gerichtete Beziehungskraft, sondern ein äusserstes Vermögen des Wohnen in sich selbst, des In-sich-Seins, der Eigenständigkeit, der Selbstständigkeit—eben genau das, was in der abendländischen Überlieferung seit eh und je als Personalität bezeichnet worden ist. Welt zu haben, auf die Allgemeinheit der seienden Dinge bezogen zu sein—das kann nur einem in sich selber gründenden Wesen zukommen, nicht einem Was, sondern einem Wer, einem Ich-Selbst, einer Person (*Was Heisst Philosophieren?* [Munich: Kösel Verlag, 1963], 49–50).

21. "Personein bedeutet so Selbstbesitz eines Subjekts als solchen in einem wissenden und freien Bezogensein auf das Ganze" (*Grundkurs des Glaubens* [Freiburg: Herder, 1976], 41 [my translation]).

reach out beyond themselves towards the totality of all that is and in this way to put beings in front of themselves as the objects of their acts. Earlier we were inquiring into the immanence, now into the transcendence of personal acting. The remarkable thing is that we get the same answer to both questions; at the root of personal acting is the self-possession of the person, the standing of persons in themselves.[22]

3. The insight of Pieper is entirely verified in the experience of recollection. The more recollected I am and the more I dwell with myself subjectively, then the more I find myself transcending my environment, and indeed in the deepest recollection I find myself opening to God in the center of my being (this is why the most important discussions of recollection are found in religious authors). It is as if I cannot recollect myself apart from living my world-openness. Indeed, I typically achieve recollection in the first place by directing myself to certain objects, especially to things of ultimate importance, such as God, or my own death. I do not gather myself into myself by my own strength, but I receive the recollected unity of my being as a kind of reflex of my turning outward in world-openness. The transcendence of turning outward, far from violating my subjectivity, tends to recollect it.[23]

4. Without the transcendence whereby we surpass every finite thing towards something infinite, we would live in an unquestioning solidarity with things and with this we would live so close to them, so immersed in them, as to be hindered by them from acting through ourselves. The distance to them of which I just spoke would be lacking and so we would not be free in relation to them.[24] As the things of our experience get detached from our needs and become objects for us, we are brought to life as subjects called to live in freedom. In the following Wojtyla explains how in our relation to things experienced as good we can fall prey to a certain heteronomy exercised by the goods.

22. It is one of the many merits of Norris Clarke's *Person and Being* (Milwaukee: Marquette University Press, 1993) that he fully recognizes this dialectical relation between selfhood and transcendence, that is, the relation whereby selfhood and transcendence, for all their appearance of excluding each other, in fact condition and perfect each other. He proposes to express this interpenetration of apparent opposites by his term, the *dyadic* structure of the human person.

23. Scheler speaks of the *Sammlung* out of which persons put things in front of themselves as their objects (*Man's Place in Nature*, 40).

24. Rahner often expresses a similar thought, as in the following: "We said that man does not stand in an environment as a passive part of it, but that he stands as self-subsisting before a world of objects as things in their own selves. This allows him to return into himself, to be self-subsistent in knowledge" (*Hearers of the Word*, reprinted in McCool, ed., *A Rahner Reader* [New York: Crossroad Publishing Co., 1975], 57).

Truth is a condition of freedom, for if a man can preserve his freedom in relation to the objects which thrust themselves on him in the course of his activity as good and desirable, it is only because he is capable of viewing these goods in the light of truth and so adopting an independent attitude to them. Without this faculty man would inevitably be determined by them: these goods would take possession of him and determine totally the character of his actions and the whole direction of his activity. His ability to discover the truth gives man the possibility of self-determination.[25]

There is something surprising about the threat to our self-determination that Wojtyla has in mind here; it is not a threat that comes from coercion or from foreign influences, but from the good itself that we will; even this good can determine us to the detriment of our self-determination. What is this "truth about good" that enables us to stay free in relation to good and to assert ourselves in relation to it? It is nothing other than good as it presents itself to us after being detached from our needs, that is, good according to what it really is: good as it presents itself to world-open spirits. We have already seen how the "truth about" any thing expresses not the environment but the world.[26] By reaching beyond particular goods towards a veiled infinity, we break a kind of spell they may have cast on us, breaking out of a natural immersion in them; we gain a certain spiritual distance to them, and so are enabled to take up a position in which we can determine ourselves in relation to them rather than being determined by them.

Here we have a transcendence which, even though it is ultimately a religious transcendence, has no least taint of heteronomy about it; for it is a transcendence that mediates to us our freedom in relation to finite beings.

5. If we recall our distinction between subjective selfhood and objective selfhood, then we have to recognize that it has so far been only the former that we have put in relation to the self-transcendence of world-openness. But the objective self-relation, discussed in section 2, also owes its very possibility to world-openness. Only if I live that insatiable

25. *Love and Responsibility* (New York: Farrar, Straus, Giroux, 1981), 115. I might have quoted from *The Acting Person* (chapter 3, sections 7 and 9, and Chapter 4, section 3), but I am particularly taken by the way the matter is expressed in this earlier work of Karol Wojtyla.

26. In my "Dialektyka podmiotiowosci i transcendencji w osobie ludzkiej" ("The Dialectic of Subjectivity and Transcendence in the Human Person"), *Ethos* (1988), n. 2/3, 57–65, I try to explain what Karol Wojtyla means by "the truth about good," and I try to explain it in terms of the openness of the human person to the totality of value and of being.

restlessness in relation to myself, only if I know how to put myself ever and again into question and to transcend myself ever and again, only if I can objectify myself as only a world-open being can objectify, only if I turn to myself with the passion for ultimacy: only then can I gain the objective selfhood of which I spoke.

6. Finally, without the world-openness proper to persons we could never encounter other human beings as persons. Consider Guardini's description of this encounter.

> The first step toward the "Thou" is that movement which means "hands off" and clears the space in which the person's capacity of serving as his own purpose can be realized. . . . Personal love begins decisively not with a movement toward the other but away from him. . . . I release the being which at first I regarded only as an object, and consider it as a self meeting me from its own center, permitting it to become my "Thou". . . .[27]

In this detachment of the other from my needs and projects so as to enter with sympathy into the inner center of the other, to understand him as he is in his own right, on his own terms, as he is for himself, we readily recognize a certain freedom for which we are empowered by our world-openness. It follows that all of the rich subjectivity and intersubjectivity of the interpersonal, of which I said something in Chapter 3.6, is grounded in the transcendence of world-openness. But not only this; there is also the interpersonal dimension based on a certain objectifying of other persons; this, too, is rendered possible only by our world-openness, or more exactly by the spiritual "distance" that we can gain to other persons through our world-openness.

If, then, one denies our transcendence towards the totality and if one encloses human beings in their environment, then one abolishes the very possibility of authentic interpersonal relations.

Let us conclude. Personal selfhood is a selfhood that empowers persons to transcend themselves. It can awaken and can be expressed only in self-transcendence and it cannot be lived and expressed apart from self-transcendence. A human person deprived of all intentional acting is not yet subjectively alive; a human person who lives in unquestioning solidarity with things, immersed in them, unable to put them in front of himself and to live at a distance from them, is also completely unawakened in his selfhood. Given the investigations of this chapter, I

27. Guardini, *The World and the Person* (Chicago: Regnery, 1965), 127.

would propose to "define" a human person as a subjectivity existing in openness to a certain infinity and therefore facing an objective world; and in this way I would bring the transcendence of intentional acting into the very idea of personal being.

CHAPTER SIX

Selfhood and Transcendence in Relation to the Good

We now turn our attention to those acts in which persons have to do with good and bad. I will distinguish different kinds of goodness and, corresponding to these, different kinds of interest in the good, looking, of course, for that interest that best expresses the power of persons to transcend themselves. Having found the most significant transcendence of human persons in relation to the good, we will proceed to explore the subjectivity of it.

1. Value and response to value

There are many things which take on for us a certain character of goodness as a result of satisfying us, of being agreeable to us. One has only to think of the appeal that water has for the thirsty, flattery for the vain, gossip for the curious. As soon as these things cease to be satisfying, they lose this character of goodness, and perhaps, if we find no other goodness or badness in them, stand before us as neutral, indifferent, lacking any appeal at all for us. The agreeableness of all these things is not simply *found*, as if it existed independently of being experienced, but exists only in the experiencing of those persons for whom such things are agreeable; remove these persons, or remove just their experiencing these things as agreeable, and the things lose the goodness of the agreeable. And so we can say that we make ourselves the measure of goodness insofar as we experience things as merely agreeable; we enclose ourselves in a realm that is relative to us, existing only for us.

But we find in our experience another and very different axiological aspect of the world. We find many things whose goodness is independent of our satisfaction. Take the datum of goodness that more than any other belongs to this study, the worth or value of the human person; no one who experiences this could think that it is relative to someone's satisfaction, as if the value of a human person existed only as a result of the person being experienced as agreeable, and vanished as soon as he or she ceased being experienced in this way. If this value exists at all in persons, then it exists independently of the agreeableness persons can have for others; persons have it in themselves and not just in the experiencing of others. We can reach the same result by considering that it belongs precisely to the rightly understood autonomy of persons that they have not only their being in themselves, but have as well their worth in themselves. They would be thrown back into the most extreme heteronomy if the structure of their worth, their ontological nobility, answered to the model of the merely agreeable. We will follow von Hildebrand in calling by the name of *value*[1] this goodness just described, which is precisely not relative to our satisfaction and which presents itself as inhering in the being that possesses it.[2]

1. Many of the readers to whom I address myself will agree with me about the existence of an absolute goodness but they will dislike the term "value" as a way of expressing it. They typically say that value presupposes a valuer and can therefore only express relative goodness. I would say to them that there is far more expressive power in the English word, value, than they realize, and that there is no good reason to abandon it to the value subjectivists. We can try to revive that sense of value which Shakespeare expresses in *Troilus and Cressida* when he has Hector say (II.1):

> But value dwells not in particular will;
> It holds his estimate and dignity
> As well wherein 'tis *precious of itself*
> As in the prizer [my italics].

Or we can try to revive that sense of value expressed by Oscar Wilde in his famous definition of a cynic: the one who knows the price of everything but the value of nothing. Or we can reclaim for our own that sense of value which C. S. Lewis expresses when in *The Abolition of Man* he speaks about, and argues for, "the doctrine of objective value" (29). By the way, those who are suspicious of the term "value" for the purposes for which I want to use it, are usually surprised to learn how prominent the Italian counterpart, *valore*, is *already in Dante*. Even in talking about God Dante often sets aside *buono* in favor of *valore* (many instances of this can be found in the *Concordance to the Divine Comedy*, Cambridge, MA, 1965). I insist, then, that there is nothing linguistically out of order in using value to express not relative or relational but absolute goodness; this is entirely in line with what it has meant for centuries. It is rather the subjectivist use of value that represents the dubious linguistic innovation, which should be resisted.

2. We follow here von Hildebrand, *Ethics* (Chicago: Franciscan Herald Press, 1972), especially Chapter 3, which contains perhaps the most important single contribution of

No one denies that things of value, when deeply experienced, can confer satisfaction, delight, happiness on persons; these positive results in persons in no way call into question the value-character of things. We only say that the satisfaction, delight, happiness that we experience in beings of value are not the principle of their value; their value is the principle of our satisfaction, delight, happiness.

Von Hildebrand has developed the concept of value by explaining why every being having objective value *calls for* a fitting response, or *is worthy of* being affirmed by persons. Thus, for example, every human person calls for or is worthy of a certain fundamental respect; or to offer another example, every morally outstanding person is worthy of a certain esteem; or again, God is worthy of adoration. One can as well say that what von Hildebrand calls a "value response" is *due in justice* to the being, so that I bring about a unique kind of disharmony between myself and some valuable being if I simply ignore it, or hold it in contempt instead of admiring it, or admire it less than it deserves, or for that matter more than it deserves. I am called to fulfill a certain justice between myself and every value I encounter. Notice that this meriting an appropriate response is something that characterizes only value; that which is good merely on the basis of satisfying me does not call for, or deserve, or merit any response at all. A thirsty person who perceives a pitcher of cold water as merely satisfying does not fail to give it its due if he or she, for whatever reasons, refuses to take any interest in the water. As far as this goodness relative to our satisfaction goes, it is entirely up to the arbitrariness of the person to drink or not; there is no response that is objectively due to the water, no response that ought to be given whether one wants to or not.

Value also has the power or authority to make actions right or wrong. Some of the wrong ways of treating persons from which we took our point of departure in Chapter 1 are wrong because they violate persons in their value or dignity. If persons have no dignity, then this wrongness

---

von Hildebrand to philosophy. I have discussed extensively his concept of value, and his contrast between value and the goodness relative to our satisfaction, in my "The Idea of Value and the Reform of the Traditional Metaphysics of *Bonum*," in *Aletheia* I/2 (1978), 221–336, especially Chapters 2 and 3, and also in my "Are Good and Being Really Convertible? A Phenomenological Inquiry," in *The New Scholasticism* 57 (1983), 465–500, especially section 1. On this contrast between the two fundamental kinds of good see also the profound but unjustly neglected study of Rudolf Otto, "Wert, Würde und Recht," in Boozer, ed., *Aufsätze zur Ethik* (Munich, 1981).

is an illusion; thus if a prostitute does not have the dignity of personhood, then the using of her for selfish gratification cannot be wrong. If the only goodness she has is relative to someone's satisfaction, one could never make sense of the wrongness of using her.

The reader may wonder how our understanding of value stands in relation to good or *bonum* in the Thomistic sense. Is value just a new term expressing what St. Thomas meant by *bonum?* No, value expresses an absolute goodness, or goodness in itself, whereas *bonum* expresses a relational goodness, a goodness that is *for someone* (this is why St. Thomas says that *bonum* always involves some *respectum ad aliud*). Of course *bonum* does not express a goodness relative to our satisfaction; it has a foundation in the nature of human beings and thus stands in contrast with this purely relative goodness. Like value it is an objective goodness, but it lacks that absoluteness ("goodness in itself") which distinguishes value. When we speak of the dignity of the human person, we do not speak of a *goodness for the human person,* but of a goodness that persons have in themselves. When we are moved by this goodness to respect persons, we are not exactly wishing them well or aiming at what is beneficial for them, and even less are we being moved by what is beneficial for ourselves, but we are esteeming them for what they are. *Bonum* is unsuitable for expressing the goodness in itself that we call the dignity of a person.[3]

We can enter more deeply into the nature of value by considering that all value has some aspect of beauty. It is not only aesthetic value but all value that is signed by beauty.[4] We can readily find this aspect of beauty in our example of the dignity of persons; we find it as soon as we express this dignity in terms of a certain ontological *nobility.* In fact, Plato and Aristotle come closest to value when they approach good under the aspect of beauty. Recall the famous passage in the *Gorgias* where Socrates catches Polus (474 b). Polus will not admit to Socrates that doing wrong is *harmful* to the wrongdoer, but he is led to admit that doing wrong is *base, ugly* (*aischron*, the opposite of *kalon*). To put it in my terms: since the two of them cannot agree concerning *bonum/malum*, Socrates shifts to value/disvalue; it is surprising that, as long as they take the disvalue of wrongdoing under the aspect of baseness or ugliness, they find it

---

3. I have discussed extensively the contrast between value and *bonum* in the two studies cited in the previous note.

4. See the discussion of this relation between value and beauty in von Hildebrand, *Aesthetik,* I (Stuttgart: Kohlhammer, 1977), Chapter 2, especially page 90.

easier to agree about the disvalue than about the harmfulness of wrong-doing.

There is something else about value which for our purposes we need to gather from authors like von Hildebrand. There are not only individual beings with their individual values; value is organized into a cosmos, an ordered system, which Scheler, von Hildebrand, and others express as the "world of values." We situate a value within the world of value when we speak of it ranking higher or lower than another value, as when we say that the value of a human person *ranks above* the value of a sub-personal living being. I will in Chapter 7 have the opportunity to discuss a certain superiority of moral values in relation to non-moral values of persons. Everyone knows what it means to say that the crimes of a Hitler are *worse than* the embezzlement committed by a bank teller and that they in fact represent evil *of a different and lower order.* Of course, I do not mean that any given value is always commensurable with any other given value, ranking above or below it in a way that can always be clearly measured, as if values had the clear and definite commensurability found among natural numbers. No, some values are clearly incommensurable one with another (some ethicians have recently pointed out that we gain a certain freedom in our choosing as a result of the incommensurability of the goods among which we choose). And yet we do not find a complete reign of utter incommensurability; we can still find enough hierarchical relations among values, and comparisons among them, to let us speak of the one world of value.

2. The transcendence achieved in the experience of value and in response to value

When we deal with persons (whether ourselves or others), or with any other being that has its worth in itself, and when we show respect for such beings because of their objective value, striving to give them their due and to fulfill justice towards them, then we are transcending ourselves. We are responding to and affirming a goodness which is what it is in its own right, and which measures us rather than is measured by us. On the other hand, we remain in our own immanence insofar as we are only interested in the merely agreeable. This is not the immanence of non-intentional consciousness, for the agreeable is a kind of intentional object even as our interest in it is a kind of intentional act. If I speak here of immanence, it is because our satisfaction is the measure of things merely agreeable and because we in a way bend things to ourselves in seeing in them only the goodness relative to our satisfaction.

One can understand the full measure of the transcendence of value response only if one realizes how I am here breaking with *eudaemonism.* I refer with this name to the teaching that each human being always aims only at his own happiness and in fact cannot act without making the attainment of his happiness the main point of his acting. This is a much stronger claim than is made in the thesis that all human beings desire happiness, which would not be eudaemonism as I will be using the term. Of course the happiness of the eudaemonist is not just the satisfaction of any urges or wants; the eudaemonist is not a hedonist. The eudaemonistic idea of happiness, as found, for instance, in Aristotle, is based on the real perfection of human nature, and thus the goods for which the eudaemonist lives are goods in the sense of *bonum* and not in the sense of the merely agreeable. And yet it remains the case that whoever lives as a consistent eudaemonist cannot achieve the transcendence of value response; such a one lives for his own happiness in such a way as to be prevented from giving things their due, affirming them for their own sakes.[5]

Will it be said that eudaemonists can be interested in the happiness of others and not only of themselves? Very well, but on what grounds is their interest extended to others? If on the grounds that they need the happiness of others in order to attain their own happiness, so that they desire the happiness of others under the aspect of promoting their own, then of course they do not transcend themselves towards others—indeed, as far as self-transcendence goes they might as well still be desiring only their own happiness. Or do they take an interest in the happiness of others on the basis of absorbing others into themselves, considering others as extensions of themselves? But surely there is no

---

5. A major medieval thinker who criticizes this eudaemonism in the vein in which I am criticizing it, is Duns Scotus. See above all his well-known distinction between the *affectio commodi* and the *affectio iustitiae* in his teaching on the will. Whereas the former refers to our natural inclination to desire our happiness, the latter refers to a higher and nobler capacity of the will, "by reason of which it [the will] is able to will some good not oriented to self" (*Ordinatio* III, suppl. dist. 26). See the texts of Scotus collected by Allan Wolter, *Duns Scotus on the Will and Morality* (Washington, D.C.: The Catholic University of America Press, 1986), 179–205. Wolter has often pointed out the deep kinship between Scotus's *affectio iustitiae* and von Hildebrand's idea of man's capacity for value response.

self-transcendence in attaining to the other by abolishing him or her as other! I will explain below how in my view we are able to take a truly self-transcending interest in the good of others; it will be an explanation that one could never get out of the eudaemonism of which I have been speaking.[6]

But I want to call particular attention to another, quite different respect in which the transcendence of persons gets lost in eudaemonism. To explain this I have to bring out the "cosmological" approach to man that typically underlies it.[7]

In this approach one observes the teleology in all living beings in the world, that is, the purposefulness of their instincts, which provide for the real well-being of the individuals as well as of their species. It is natural to think that with man it must not be different: his real well-being must be expressed in and promoted through the teleological structure of his being. When we see him desiring things that he takes as good, what is more reasonable than to think that the distinctive thing about man is that in him teleological drives become conscious? What is more natural than to think that these drives, when consciously felt and lived by human beings, become the desire for all that is beneficial for them, or in other words, become the desire for their happiness? But then the goodness that attracts and motivates human beings can only be some objective goodness, rooted in the objective well-being of individual human beings and of the human species; it can no more be a goodness detached from this objective well-being than the teleological tendencies in a subpersonal living being can detach themselves from its objective well-being. From this cosmological point of view, which relies heavily on analogies between plants and animals, on the one hand, and human beings, on the other, one cannot make sense of what I called above the goodness of the merely agreeable, which lacks any and every aspect of objective validity. One can at most admit that human beings sometimes deviate

6. Will one object that the transcendence of value response is possible only on the basis of *agape*, or Christian love, and that living on the level of eudaemonism is as far as "natural man" can go and is, therefore, as far as any *philosophical* study of human acting should go? We answer: can "natural man" not understand what it is to give another his due? There is, of course, a specifically Christian love that absolutely surpasses all "natural" love, but it seems that taking a value-responding interest in another, rather than seeing the other simply from the point of view of my happiness, belongs to both loves.

7. I continue using the terms "cosmological" and "personalist" in the sense of Wojtyla's essay, "Subjectivity and the Irreducible in Man," which I introduced at the beginning of Chapter 3.

from their real good in virtue of an error; but the good they pursue, one will insist, always retains for them the aspect of what is really good for them; the *kind of good* moving their will is still entirely objective, not indeed in the sense of value, but in the sense of *bonum*. It follows that human beings exercise no freedom in desiring happiness, or willing *bonum;* since the will is understood as a striving for perfection that has become fully conscious (hence the talk of the will as *appetitus rationalis,* or rational appetite), its object can only be the human *bonum,* just as the instinctive striving of animals aims at their animal *bonum.* Our freedom is, on this view, exercised in choosing this or that thing under the aspect of *bonum,* but it is not exercised in choosing *bonum* as the aspect under which we choose whatever we choose; the will is directed to *bonum* by its very nature, in advance of every act of personal self-determination.

But on the basis of von Hildebrand's groundbreaking distinctions regarding fundamental kinds of good, we can vindicate a dimension of personal self-transcendence which gets lost in this eudaemonistic scheme. The key to understanding this self-transcendence is, curiously enough, not the concept of value but rather the concept of the importance of the merely subjectively satisfying. Once we distinguish this kind of importance from *bonum,* then we understand that it constitutes an alternative to *bonum;* persons can pursue the merely agreeable while saying, and fully meaning, that they do not care whether the agreeable thing tends to their ultimate well-being or happiness. However surprising it may seem in the abstract, it is at the same time undeniable that my objective good can be entirely abandoned by me in favor of what is merely agreeable, and this not in the sense of erring about my objective good, but in the sense of recognizing this good and still turning away from it towards a good devoid of all claim to objectivity. We have only to free ourselves from the spell of certain cosmological analogies and to try to understand our relation to the good, not through these analogies, but through our lived experience of good: then we see that we do not desire all that we desire under the aspect of *bonum* but we can instead desire things under the aspect of being gratifying. This means that the will is not from the beginning and by its very nature directed to *bonum;* it is I who direct it to *bonum;* it is a fundamental task of my freedom to direct it to *bonum.* This in turn means that I have to transcend myself so as to live for *bonum;* I have to overcome myself, to rise above another kind of good which

8. The reader will wonder whether the position here criticized was held by St. Thomas Aquinas. It seems to me that it was. When he says, ". . . as the intellect of necessity adheres to the first principles, the will must of necessity adhere to the last end, which is

also attracts my will. Both this self-transcendence and this fundamental freedom typically get lost in the cosmological view of the will.[8]

Notice that this loss can occur even within a philosophy that recognizes value in our sense. Let us suppose that the human will were by its very nature tied to value and could not will anything except under the aspect of value; in other words, that the will were related to value in the way in which eudaemonists say the will is related to *bonum* or to happiness. This would require us to interpret even the merely agreeable as value, naturally as the lowest form of it. Something like this seems in fact to have been the position of Scheler. On this view, response to value does not involve any decision for value, for we are already directed to value by the very nature of the will, and we are prevented by its nature from willing anything but value. This means that our task in relation to value is simply to prefer the higher values to the lower ones. On our view, by contrast, there is a decision for value because there is an alternative to it. The merely agreeable is not a minimal form of value, it rather lacks entirely the *ratio* of value; it is a good relative to what we happen to need and to find satisfaction in, and so it lacks entirely the dignity of *real, objective* goodness.[9] It requires a fundamental decision to open ourselves to the goodness of value and to live for it; we can

---

happiness" (*S. T.*, I, q. 82, a. 1; translation of the Fathers of the English Dominican Province), he seems to imply that the will cannot possibly depart from *bonum* and happiness in favor of the purely subjective good of which von Hildebrand speaks. When he says that "nothing is good and desirable except forasmuch as it participates in the likeness to God" (*S. T.*, I, q. 44, a. 4, ad 3; same translators), he again seems to teach that the will responds only to that which has some aspect of real, objective goodness. Below we will quote C. S. Lewis saying, "When all that says 'it is good' has been debunked, what says 'I want' remains." I do not see that St. Thomas ever recognizes this arbitrary wanting that unfolds outside of all desire for good *(bonum)*.

9. How, then, would I answer the old question as to the object of the will if not in terms of value? I follow von Hildebrand in recognizing a certain positivity common to all the kinds of good, common to value, to the merely agreeable, and common to whatever other kinds of good one can distinguish. Von Hildebrand calls by the name of *positive importance* this positivity in virtue of which an object can interest us. Positive importance does not express a kind or category of goodness, but rather a trans-categorial goodness; *this* is the object of the will, that without which the will cannot be attracted or moved. Von Hildebrand also recognizes a *negative importance* as that trans-categorial badness without which the will cannot be repelled or moved to turn away. The object of the will, then, is a certain abstract goodness and badness; but this is an object of the will so broad as not to coincide with value/disvalue but to comprise it as only one of its kinds, thus leaving room for the choosing of value and so for a far more authentic self-transcendence in value response than can be explained from Scheler's point of view.

decide instead to live for the merely agreeable, centering our existence on ourselves and our gratification, and we can decide this in the full knowledge of turning away from everything having value. Indeed, this decision for or against value is an exercise of the most fundamental freedom of which we are capable. In value response we are not just living out the nature of the will, but we are choosing between value and another kind of good that we might have chosen in the place of value; as a result, we transcend ourselves in value response in a stronger sense than the eudaemonist can explain.

To summarize: in order to bring out the self-transcendence of the human person in value response, we contrast our position with that of eudaemonism in two respects. (1) Eudaemonism lacks the notion of value and value response; it does not get beyond *bonum* and the desire for my own good. (2) It lacks the contrast between *bonum* and the importance of the merely subjectively satisfying. In the first case, it cannot explain the transcendence of value response; in the second, it cannot even explain the transcendence achieved in desiring *bonum*. And even if a philosophy breaks through to value, thus surpassing eudaemonism, it still cannot do justice to the transcendence of persons in value response if it does not establish this contrast with the merely subjectively satisfying.

There is, however, still more to be said about this transcendence. We have now to explain why the fullness of it always involves some reference to what I just called the world of value. For instance, if someone sensed the dignity of persons and was somehow affected by it but made no effort to connect this sense of personal dignity with other experiences of worth that he or she has had with non-persons, and so did not even register the fundamental difference in value between persons and, say, plants, then we would say that such an experience of personal dignity, being so radically "unsituated," so completely unconnected with other values, is a value experience largely devoid of transcendence. Or suppose that someone deplored the absence of moral decency in another in the same way he deplored the absence of a musical ear in the other, that is, deplored both the one and the other absence with the same kind of regret, then again we would say that, though the regret may be a value-responding regret, the sense of value proportion is so disordered in such persons as to compromise the transcendence they might have achieved in either act of deploring. To take another example: if someone condemns the crimes of a Hitler, we will at first be inclined to see in his condemnation a real value response; but if we find that this person condemns *with the same ultimate indignation* the peccadilloes of some corrupt local politician, then the condemnation of Hitler seems to us to be undermined. This lack of the most basic proportion in this person's condemnations seems to us to spoil both of them and to prevent him from achieving in them any real transcendence towards that which is good or bad in itself. This transcendence requires that we love more that which is better, and condemn more that which is worse, and in general that we respond to different things in different ways.

We begin to see in the transcendence of value response the world-openness discussed in the previous chapter. Only a world-open being is fully capable of perceiving and responding to value; only a being that has detached the good from its needs, and can let it go to be what it is in its own right, is capable of being responsive to good in the sense of value. A person must be capable of reaching beyond goods and putting them into question and so of putting them in front of himself as something in their own right, in order to be capable of experiencing good in the form of value. Of course even the merely agreeable can be objectified like this; the merely agreeable that we know in the environment can be objectified in the world, as when we experience the agreeable *as merely agreeable* and as standing in contrast with objective goodness. But value seems to be able to be experienced only in the world; it seems not to exist for beings that are entirely enclosed in their environment; value response is possible only to world-open persons. Value response also has something of that totality to which persons are open; as I was just saying, the values to which we give authentic value responses are not taken in isolation but in relation to the whole world of value. It seems, then, that the sense of infinity of which we are possessed and in which we transcend ourselves makes itself felt here in relation to the good, opening us to the world of value and destining us to dwell in it.

Perhaps even now, before exploring the selfhood and subjectivity of value response, we can see in all such responses a revealing expression of personal being. In the following von Hildebrand connects personhood and transcendence, yet without appealing to personal selfhood to show the self-evidence of his claims.

Man cannot be understood if we interpret all his activities as manifestations of an automatic striving for self-perfection. So long as we are confined to this pattern, so long as we see man differing from other beings only by the fact that their objective teleological tendency assumes in him a character of consciousness, we overlook the real nature of man as a person. . . . [T]he specifically personal character of man as a subject manifests itself in his capacity to transcend himself. This transcendence displays itself above all in participation in the objective logos of being which takes place in knowledge insofar as our intellect conforms itself to the nature of the object, and which again takes place in every value response wherein we conform either with our will or with our heart to the important-in-itself. This kind of participation is absolutely impossible for any impersonal being.[10]

As I say, this is said without any reference to personal selfhood, and said convincingly; but the capacity for value response will become even more revealing of the human person if we now explore the selfhood and subjectivity of value response.

3. The selfhood and subjectivity of value response

We should not lose sight of the antagonist whom we constantly have in mind throughout Part II of this study: it is the philosopher who says that human persons suffer heteronomy if they understand themselves as subject to some higher truth about good, the philosopher who says that they can live as persons who are ends in themselves only if each is a law unto himself, having in himself the determining principle of any good and of any oughtness that he recognizes.

I want to admit and indeed to insist from the very beginning that there is one plausible way of avoiding heteronomy which is not open to us. We cannot say that such selfhood as we may achieve in value-response is the main point of value response. When we love what is lovable and show respect for what is worthy of respect, we are acting for the sake of the value and not, or at least not in the same way, for the sake of our selfhood (unless, of course, our act is a value-responding self-respect or self-love). If we begin acting with this self-referential intention, aiming at ourselves (rather like the person practicing some ascetic exercise is aiming at himself), then our response ceases to be a value response. What a value calls for from me is not my self-affirmation performed with reference to the value, but rather affirmation of the value for its own sake. And yet it remains true that the demands which the world of value makes of us do not inflict heteronomy on us, but rather engender the deepest personal life of which we are capable. We proceed now to show this.

The first thing to observe is that much of the discussion of the transcendence of value-responding persons was at the same time a discus-

10. Von Hildebrand, *Ethics*, 218.

sion of their rich subjectivity; we saw in effect that certain aspects of transcendence cannot be treated apart from their subjectivity. This was nowhere so clear as in our examination of the transcendence that persons achieve by choosing value and a life of value response and turning away from a life centered around the merely agreeable. To examine this transcendence was all one with examining the fundamental freedom of persons. The cosmological approach to the will, and indeed any approach that would tie the will only to objective goodness as its object, can no more do justice to the freedom of persons than it can to their transcendence in relation to value. The notion of value understood as a certain absolute goodness, far from implying heteronomy for the persons subjected to the demands of value, leads in fact, if only it is coupled with the contrast between value and the merely subjectively satisfying, to a new understanding of the fundamental freedom of persons.

By the way, further analysis would undoubtedly reveal that this fundamental freedom also includes what we called above (Chapter 3.2) subjective freedom. We stand before the task of choosing between being a person who respects value and gives it its due, and being a person who lives for his own gratification. We do not just choose between two kinds of good which present themselves in front of us, but between two forms of personal existence. In this latter choosing we dispose over ourselves from within ourselves, exercising our subjective freedom.

There was something else in our discussion of transcendence which has an implication for the subjectivity of value response. We said that we can be sensitive to value and capable of value response only on the basis of our world-openness, and that in fact we live our world-openness in a particular way in awakening to value. But we saw in the previous chapter that world-openness is a kind of transcendence with its own subjectivity, which Josef Pieper analyzes profoundly. It follows that this depth of subjectivity belongs also to value response.

Now we proceed to offering some new approaches to personal selfhood and to showing how it thrives in relation to value.

1. Understanding value and the internalization of value response. Only on the condition that my value response is based on *my own insight* into the value can I really transcend myself in the response. My response has to be preceded by some experience I have of the value and by some understanding of it (even if not a theoretically articulate understanding). If I am in my response just slavishly imitating some admired person but without having his or her value-understanding, or if my response is dominated by a compulsion to answer to the expectations of another, or if it is dominated by a superego, prompting me from within to do what I do not really understand, then, even if my response is objectively right, it is fundamentally deformed as value response and is harmed in its transcendence. Its objective rightness does not necessarily enable *me to transcend myself;* if I lack a certain subjectivity, namely my own insight into the value, then the rightness of the response passes over my head and the self-transcendence cannot occur. It is like the old distinction between a statement or belief that happens by chance to be true, and a statement or belief based on real knowledge: only in the latter can persons be said to transcend themselves.

There is, however, far more to be said about the role of value understanding in the internalization of value response. It does not suffice simply to say that the understanding on which my act is based must be *my own* and not someone else's. We have also to let the accent fall on the understanding *as understanding of value:* we have to focus not only on the immanent ownership of the understanding, but also on its transcendent reference. The idea that my response is *due in justice to a being in virtue of its inherent excellence or worthiness* provides me a reason for giving the response, a reason such as I can never have with regard to the merely agreeable, which only invites me and entices me but without ever laying any claim to my interest, without ever "saying" to me that it merits my interest or justifies it. It is this understanding that lets me appropriate as my own the value response, lets me understand the inner justice of it not as a foreign law but as my own law, lets me act through myself in the value response, willing it for myself, in my own name.

The desire for the merely agreeable does not seem to be exposed to the danger of heteronomy; the way in which this goodness depends on us and on the needs that we bring to things seems to exclude any harmful other-directedness in our interest in such goodness. And yet in willing and loving things with this goodness we cannot achieve the same subjective life and the same strength of selfhood that we achieve in value response, for *in the absence of any objective validity in the goodness and in the call for my response, we cannot have the understanding which value makes possible and so we cannot achieve the ownership of our response which is possible in value response.* We see, then, that the principle explaining my transcendence in value response—some value meriting my response—is at the same time, in virtue of the understanding that it grounds, the principle explaining the depth of my subjectivity in value response.[11]

Perhaps we can make here an instructive analogy. Let us go back to the traditional distinction between "theoretical" and "practical" reason. It has been well known since Plato that theoretical reason is most deeply satisfied when it *understands why something must be so*. If it looks out into the world and just bluntly observes that something is so as a matter of fact, it is far less satisfied; it longs for an understanding of the *reasons why*. There is a wonderful inwardness in all such understanding, which is undoubtedly why Plato was able to think that it is a kind of remembering. Now it seems that by grasping the value-point of an act or action our practical, or moral, reason is deeply satisfied in an analogous way. We are not drawn off of ourselves towards that which is outside of us, but we have the principle of our action within ourselves, so that our acting is never so much our own as when we act out of a strong sense of our acting being due to some value. Despite all the transcendence of value experience and value response, value does not weigh heteronomously on us, but our response to it, performed in the consciousness of being objectively justified, indeed of being objectively required, is entirely our own act, so that we stand with our whole selves in the response to value. It is as if the inwardness of rational insight that we find in theoretical reason, corresponds in practical reason to the inwardness of internalized norms of good and bad—as if the inwardness of "remembering" necessary truth corresponds to the inwardness of conscience.

In Chapter 1.3 we saw that an act can be performed by me as my own only on the basis of my own insight into the point of the act; we have just now been developing this idea in the setting of our relation to good and bad, trying to explain the particular point of an act which lies in the value to which it responds, and the particular perfection of owning the act that comes from understanding its value-point.[12]

---

11. Here again, as at the end of Chapter 1, we try to make personalist sense of the "rational nature" of man, so prominent in philosophical anthropology since Greek philosophy, so prominent, too, in some of the canonical "definitions" of personhood, as we have seen.

12. Perhaps our discussion throws some light on the teaching of St. Thomas Aquinas regarding the natural law and how it emerges from the eternal law (*Summa Theologiae*, I–II, 93). He teaches that the eternal law is impressed upon man by way of natural inclination and above all by way of reason; in both ways the eternal law ceases to be a law outside of man and it becomes his own law. When in the text I explore the under-

2. *The heteronomy that comes from living for the merely agreeable, and the autonomy that is possible in value response.* It is a universal human experience that whenever we live mainly for the sake of things merely satisfying, and offer no resistance to our cravings, urges, wants, we are soon dethroned as persons. We may find this strange if we consider it in the abstract, for we may at first think that, since our interest in the agreeable is not imposed on us from without but springs up within us, we act through ourselves when we live for the agreeable, which depends on us for its goodness. We may admit that there are *moral* objections to living mainly for our gratification, but will perhaps at first wonder what the *personalist* objection could possibly be, that is, wonder why we are dethroned as persons in seeking nothing but our gratification. And yet, as soon as we reflect less abstractly and more concretely, we all immediately understand the deep human truth of what Oscar Wilde said when he looked back on his own life of unbridled self-indulgence: "I ceased to be captain of my soul." Everyone knows that in living at the beck and call of one's latest strongest desires one loses the dominion over oneself which is due to oneself as person, and becomes a kind of cripple with respect to personal selfhood.

But it is different with our interest in that which is objectively good and worthy, for instance with our respect for persons. No one was ever so committed to the objectively good and worthy that he or she cried out in the words of Oscar Wilde, "I ceased to be captain of my soul." Though in affirming that which we understand to be objectively good we conform to an objective oughtness and strive to give things their due, we do not experience this oughtness as calling our sovereignty, our selfhood into question. We experience nothing depersonalizing in respecting persons and giving them their due, or in thanking our benefactors, or respecting the truth. Just the contrary: I gain rather than forfeit the captaincy of my soul in respecting and affirming the objectively good; I thrive as a personal self, as a being destined to act through itself. Von Hildebrand expresses well this fundamental contrast:

> The call of an authentic value for an adequate response addresses itself to us in a sovereign but non-intrusive, sober way. It appeals to our free spiritual center. The attraction of the subjectively satisfying, on the contrary, lulls us

standing of value that has the effect of internalizing in us the requirements of value, I am perhaps exploring what St. Thomas calls the power of reason in man to receive the eternal law into himself and to make it his own law, which is the natural law.

into a state where we yield to instinct; it tends to dethrone our free spiritual center. Its appeal is insistent, ofttimes assuming the character of a temptation, trying to sway and silence our conscience, taking hold of us in an obtrusive manner. Far different is the call of values: it has no obtrusive character; it speaks to us from above, and at a sober distance. . . .[13]

The difference between the two kinds of good and what each of them does to the human person has received a fine expression in Robert Bolt's play about the life and death of St. Thomas More, *A Man for All Seasons*. In one place Thomas More says to Norfolk: "I will not give in because I oppose it—I do—not my pride, not my spleen, nor any other of my appetites but *I* do—*I*! *(More goes up to him and feels him up and down like an animal.)* . . . Is there no single sinew in the midst of this that serves no appetite of Norfolk's but is just Norfolk? There is! Give *that* some exercise, my lord!"[14] As long as I am just living for the satisfaction of my appetites, I am unable to say "I," for I am not acting out of my very self, I am not acting as person, but am instead being acted upon by my appetites; but Thomas More, who is concerned with what is objectively good and lawful, gains a distance to his appetites so as to be able to say "I" and to act through himself. If only Norfolk were to act out of the same value-responding spirit of service to the good and worthy, Thomas could address him by his proper name, for then it would be Norfolk himself who was acting, that is, Norfolk acting in a properly personal way.

In order to throw into clearer relief this more authentic "I" that resonates with value, and the loss of this "I" when the merely agreeable takes over, we have to examine the case where the appeal of the merely agreeable and the call of value are experienced in conflict with each other within the same person. It happens all the time that to serve the intrinsically good we have to forgo certain gratifications. When we want to serve the good but at the same time are unwilling to forgo gratification, then we enter into a certain kind of moral temptation. Now whenever I yield to the temptation I always have the awareness, especially after yielding, of not doing *that which I really wanted to do,* or better, of not doing that which *I* really wanted to do;[15] I accuse myself of weak-

---

13. *Ethics*, 38–39.

14. Robert Bolt, *A Man for All Seasons* (New York, 1990), 123–124.

15. Needless to say, this talk of "failing to do what I really want to do" should not be understood in the sense of acting on the basis of an innocent mistake, as when a nurse dispenses a poison to a patient even after taking all reasonable precautions. If I speak in

ness and irresoluteness, and so of failing really to act through myself when I was called to act through myself. I suppose that no one has expressed more powerfully this being divided within oneself than St. Paul in Romans 7. "For I do not understand what I do, for it is not what I wish that I do, but what I hate, that I do" (15). "Now if I do what I do not wish, it is no longer I who do it, but the sin that dwells in me" (20). "For I am delighted with the law of God according to the inner man, but I see another law in my members, warring against the law of my mind. . . ." (22–23). St. Paul goes very far in expressing the loss of selfhood that results when my craving for gratification becomes lawless, saying even that it is no longer I who act but something else in my being which acts, something which inhibits my "inner man." This almost suggests that I am not really responsible for my lawless activity since its principle is outside of my real self; of course St. Paul resists this suggestion, and teaches that we are blameworthy for seeking lawless gratifications.

There is a passage in Shakespeare which seems to constitute a difficulty for our analysis. When in *Richard III* the two murderers go to kill Clarence, and the Second Murderer begins to get qualms of conscience, he says:

> I'll not meddle with it [conscience]: it makes a man a coward: a man cannot steal, but it accuseth him; a man cannot swear, but it checks him; a man cannot lie with his neighbour's wife, but it detects him: 'tis a blushing shame-faced spirit that mutinies in a man's bosom; it fills one full of obstacles; it made me once restore a purse of gold, that by chance I found; it beggars any man that keeps it: it is turned out of all towns and cities for a dangerous thing; and every man that means to live well endeavours to trust to himself and live without it. (I.4)

This almost sounds as if it were the merely agreeable that people really want, with the demands of the objectively good and worthy amounting to nothing more than an annoying interference. The solution of this difficulty can be found in what was said about experiencing value for ourselves and in this way internalizing our service to value. When the demands of the objectively good and worthy get detached from the experience of the good and worthy, when they become norms that have lost for

---

the text of a certain *involuntariness* in my choosing the merely agreeable over value, then I have to be understood as referring to a very particular kind of involuntariness (something like Aristotle's *akrasia*), as different as could be from the involuntariness born of invincible ignorance.

us their root in value, then they can only appear to us as all too many arbitrary oughts and ought-nots, as conventional restrictions on our behavior, and then they will quite naturally be nothing but annoying extrinsic constraints for us, as they are for the Second Murderer; they will be far from specifying that which we, we ourselves, really and most authentically want. We can make norms and laws our own, internalizing them, willing them for ourselves, only by renewing our sense of the values out of which they grow. Whoever has a lively sense of the value foundation of norms cannot possibly experience them in the external way expressed here by the Second Murderer.

By the way, the fact that the sentiment expressed by the Second Murderer has something definitely comical about it, presupposes that conscience, in its healthy functioning, is precisely not just an extrinsic constraint on our acting.

After Clarence has been murdered, the Second Murderer feels his conscience revive, and says:

SECOND MURDERER. A bloody deed, and desperately dispatch'd!
How fain, like Pilate, would I wash my hands
Of this most grievous guilty murder done!

FIRST MURDERER. How now! what mean'st thou, that thou help'st me not?
By heaven, the duke shall know how slack you've been.

SECOND MURDERER. I would he knew that I had sav'd his brother!
Take thou the fee, and tell him what I say,
For I repent me that the duke is slain.

We can assume that the Second Murderer, with the blood of an innocent man fresh on his hands and his victim dying at his feet, is overcome by a strong sense of the value and dignity of a human being. He experiences the wrongness of murder inside himself, in his conscience, and not at all as an extrinsic constraint.

We have now found one of the deepest sources of the fear of heteronomy: one despairs of the understanding of value (because one despairs of the very existence of value) that enables persons fully to own the acts in which they live a value-responding commitment to good. In the place of the cosmos of values one sees only a number of norms and moral demands that cannot be fully understood. Subjecting oneself to these can indeed only be heteronomous.

3. The heteronomy of natural causes. Let us now examine with greater precision the way in which our acting through ourselves is undermined by living mainly for the merely agreeable and is enhanced by living for the objectively worthy. Kant speaks for many when he says that the reign of "inclination" in human persons is depersonalizing *because it subjects them to the heteronomy of natural causes,* which tend to displace the persons themselves as the principles of their acting. Only by acting not from inclination but from duty do persons recover their freedom and resume acting through themselves. But since these insights of Kant's are embedded in his so problematical ethical formalism, I propose to study them as expressed in another author. Let us see how C. S. Lewis in his potent little study, *The Abolition of Man,* explains the heteronomy that comes from living mainly for the merely agreeable.

In his Chapter 3, in which an important argument is developed with exceptional rigor, Lewis is writing against those who think that "man's conquest over nature" should now extend even to values, and that he should produce systems of values just like he produces new synthetic substances, so that he lives only by the values of his own making. Lewis then puts the penetrating question about the motivation of those who produce values: what motivates them? Values are not available to guide them; since they think that all values worth living by will *result from* their work of value-production, they cannot be guided by them in deciding how to carry out this work. Will they be left without any reason for doing anything, Lewis asks, and be unable to act at all? No, he replies, there remains one possibility: "when all that which says 'it is good,' has been debunked, what says 'I want' remains." For "what never claimed objectivity cannot be destroyed by subjectivism." These value-producers "must come to be motivated simply by their own pleasure,"[16] that is, by things merely satisfying, merely agreeable. But this means, Lewis argues, that they must fall under the influence of mere "nature" or of mere natural causes, "of heredity, digestion, the weather, and the association of ideas,"[17] for it is just such causes that determine much of what is agreeable for us. They must become slaves of the physiological factors that determine hunger, thirst, sexual desire; for these are the factors which determine the only kind of good that can play any role for them. So though they started with dominating nature, they end by being dominated by it; they reverse their whole project and undo it by extending it

---

16. C. S. Lewis, *The Abolition of Man* (New York: Macmillan, 1976), 77–78. Notice, by the way, that Lewis agrees with me in saying there is a kind of goodness that falls outside of all objective goodness, a kind of goodness that lacks any aspect of objective validity.

17. Ibid., 79.

even to values. This analysis is very compelling; everyone understands that it is entirely unworthy of us as persons to do the bidding of natural causes, and to be buffeted back and forth by them as they arise, and to have no ground in ourselves for offering them any resistance.

I take this "abolition of man by nature" to mean that natural causes in man take over to the point of replacing intentional acting with instinctual behavior. There is undoubtedly a tendency of the merely agreeable to drag us down to a subpersonal way of feeling and desiring and reacting. The spirit of value-response, by contrast, has no such tendency; the more awakened I become in relation to value, then the more my acting becomes intentional, authentically personal, and the more I free myself from the dominion of natural causes. This means that my interest in the merely agreeable is not an intentional act in the full sense in which value response is an intentional act; that there is a tendency of the former to fall back into the sub-intentional category of the instinctual (in the last chapter we studied this non-intentional form of striving). This certainly explains the distress of St. Paul, or of Oscar Wilde; the loss of their real selves comes from the fact that through their love of the agreeable they become creatures of instinctual drives.

And yet the reduction of person to nature, of human persons to creatures of instinct, of man to the animals is not as easy to carry out completely as Lewis seems to think. Persons are always reaching beyond the things that natural causes make agreeable to them, giving evidence of their world-openness even when they try to live outside of the *Tao*. Thus the way they always become bored with agreeable things and are insatiable with respect to them, always needing more of them and different kinds of them, gives evidence of a residual subjectivity that natural causes can never entirely extinguish, gives evidence of how great the difference between persons and animals is even when the difference seems to be being effaced. But this serves only to qualify the thought of Kant and Lewis, not to eliminate its contribution towards understanding the heteronomy that comes from the merely agreeable.

But it is important to see that Kant and Lewis are thinking of the merely agreeable or satisfying in only one of its main forms—in the form in which it tends to brutishness. If we bring in the old distinction between pride and concupiscence, then we can say that they are thinking mainly of concupiscence. But the envy of a Iago or the cruelty of a Goneril shows us a kind of interest in the merely subjectively satisfying that is nevertheless not a concupiscent interest. We do not find here the same tendency to let instincts take over; the person who is eaten up with envy, or is malicious, does not seem to us to be dominated by natural causes, or immersed in the environment. The desire that a Iago or a Goneril has for his or her own satisfaction need have nothing brutish about it; evil as it is, it may still be a desire expressing a certain world-openness and even a desire rooted somehow in the spirit, that is, a desire such as has no counterpart among the animals but such as may well have a counterpart among angels and devils.[18]

And yet even when I will in this more "spiritual" way that which is merely satisfying for me, I still have to say: I ceased to be captain of my soul. Thomas More mentions "my pride" among the factors preventing him from saying "I" in his acting. Iago can never say "I" as Thomas More can say it; Goneril can never be captain of her soul as a deeply value-responding person can be. For one thing, neither Iago nor Goneril can have any understanding of the justification of their desire for good; they are as far from this understanding as was Oscar Wilde in the days of his worst debaucheries. Only those who live in the world of value can have such understanding, as we have seen, and so only they can make their willing and desiring fully their own. But the loss of selfhood in the different forms of pride would require a closer investigation than I am prepared to undertake in this study.

4. Sick and healthy self-presence. We were just saying that our subjectivity is not simply extinguished when we live only for our gratification. Let us now make some observations about the self-presence of our subjectivity, and see how it varies according to the kind of good that interests us.

According to some penetrating analyses of Schopenhauer, a person abandoned to the merely agreeable *alternates between the pain of lacking certain satisfactions and the boredom that comes from having them.*[19] This latter point is of particular interest; when human persons live only for their gratification, they get bored by being gratified. How often have we expected to be fully happy in the attainment of some gratification and then, immediately upon attaining it, been surprised and disappointed

18. Cf. the lines spoken by Iago in *Othello,* I.iii, which I quote in the next chapter.

19. Schopenhauer, *The World as Will and Idea,* I, para. 56–59. By the way, Schopenhauer thinks that it is not just a few moral reprobates who are condemned to this alternation, but rather all human beings. This implies that the only kind of good that can motivate us is the merely satisfying.

by feeling a restlessness springing up in our innermost parts. This feeling gives evidence of our existing as world-open persons, as we observed above; it shows us always reaching beyond a given gratification and "relativizing" it. It is remarkable that even when we are living far below our personhood we give evidence of the infinity which possesses us and modifies everything we experience. Now boredom involves self-presence. It is a self-presence that causes pain; persons prey upon themselves in being bored, and desire nothing so much as to get away from themselves. This is why bored persons crave distractions, so as to lose themselves in things.

The subjectivity of value response, by contrast, does not involve boredom. No one has ever been oppressed with boredom as a result of living in a value-responding attitude towards the world, and of showing a value-responding reverence for being, and of living in the truth about good. Even if we did not receive all that we had hoped to receive from the encounter with some value, and even if we live our world-openness with regard to value, always reaching beyond it, still our disappointment never takes the form of boredom. Value tends to recollect persons, and in recollected subjectivity persons never prey on themselves painfully.

But it is easy to give an incomplete explanation of why we avoid boredom in value response. It is not enough to say that in the transcendence of value response we are drawn off ourselves and so prevented from preying on ourselves; after all, in simply distracting ourselves we are drawn off ourselves. One needs to see that those who live in the reverence of value response have their self-presence, too, and then to see the antithesis between this self-presence and the self-presence of boredom. Bored persons are pained by their self-presence, whereas value-responding persons are at peace in their self-presence, being glad to come to themselves as persons and to dwell with themselves in transcending themselves, exulting in their transcendent selfhood. Abandoning themselves to value they are secure in themselves rather than driven to flee from themselves. But the self-presence of boredom is not mediated by any transcendence; it comes from the lack of transcendence. It is the diseased self-presence that persons fall back into when they are insufficiently mediated to themselves by transcending themselves towards value.

One will notice that in value-responding persons there is a dialectical relation between subjectivity and transcendence, recollected self-presence growing in direct proportion to the self-transcendence they achieve in relation to the truth about good. But in persons who know only the agreeable and who suffer from boredom, subjectivity and transcendence simply exclude each other, the "transcendence" of distraction being sought for the sake of escaping from one's self-presence.

5. Value response in relation to myself. It seems undeniable that I transcend myself in all value-responding stances towards myself. In showing respect for myself I am measured by the truth about good no less than when I show respect for others; I am not the measure of this truth in relation to myself any more than I am the measure of it in relation to others. It is after all entirely possible to affirm myself in the spirit of an arbitrary wanting, of a selfish self-assertion; it requires no small self-overcoming to be ready to affirm myself as personal subject according to my real worth and dignity, and this whether I feel like it or not. On the way to a value-responding self-affirmation a person typically has to overcome just as much disordered interest in the merely agreeable as in making his way to a value-responding affirmation of others. Indeed, it takes nothing less than an heroic self-overcoming in order to will to be the self I am and to refuse all despair over myself.

This is a transcendence in which even the suspicion of heteronomy is untenable. How can I be drawn off myself heteronomously when I am affirming the worth proper to myself, the worth born of my personal selfhood (Chapter 2.6)? On the contrary, it is also clear that I take possession of myself in and through a value-responding acceptance of myself, thus enacting my selfhood in a unique way. If I am so attached to the merely agreeable that I fail to show respect for myself, or if I even hold myself in contempt, then I am divided against myself, I am estranged from myself, and so I fall away from authentic personal self-possession. How can I be said to live as one who is his own, if I do not recognize the dignity which I as person really have? How can I be in a position really to act through myself if I refuse this dignity in myself?

6. Value response and happiness. Suppose that the only relation of the human person to good is that relation which we have called value response, as if we were always, or at least ought always to be, affirming for its own sake that which is intrinsically good. We would all feel that such a teaching goes too far, that it introduces an objectivism which does violence to the subjectivity of the person, an objectivism reminiscent of the extreme altruism discussed above in Chapter 3.5. In our value-responding affirmation of the world we cannot simply forget ourselves and ignore all that might be good or bad *for us,* or all that leads to or leads away from our real happiness; this would be to lose ourselves in a heteronomous way in that which is good in itself.[20]

It is of course true, as we just saw, that value-responding persons will be sensitive to values existing in themselves as well as in others, and will thus respect and affirm themselves as persons no less than they respect and affirm others as persons. The transcendence of value response does not mean the extreme altruism of which we have spoken more than once; it does not mean being other-directed to the exclusion of being self-directed. But this attitude of value response towards myself would not entirely suffice to ward off the danger of a certain heteronomy, because from the point of view of value response the main thing is to recognize value wherever it is found, the difference between myself and others being in a certain sense accidental.

There is also the possibility of persons stepping entirely out of the attitude of value response by taking an interest only in things gratifying for them, as we have seen. In this new attitude they experience indeed things good for themselves and no longer good absolutely; but this goodness-for, based as it is on their gratification, seems to trivialize the subjectivity of the person. It seems that there must be a fundamentally more serious way in which the good is good for the person, turning its face, so to speak, towards the person, and that this more serious way has to be grasped philosophically if we are going to do justice to the subjectivity of the person in relation to the good.

Now what we are looking for is in fact found and is fully developed in the ethics of von Hildebrand: it is found in his idea that among the basic kinds of good and bad, or categories of importance, as he calls them, there is *that which is objectively good for the person and objectively harmful for the person.* There is not only the good in itself which von Hildebrand calls value and the bad in itself which he calls disvalue, nor is there only the merely satisfying and dissatisfying; there is also that which is objectively beneficial for the person or objectively harmful

20. Cf. von Hildebrand: "Yet in stressing that the value response is motivated solely by the value of the good and in distinguishing it as such from any mere striving for our own good, we in no way intend to oppose interest in the important-in-itself to interest in our own objective good. The nature of the value response in no way requires indifference toward our own objective good. On the contrary, such indifference is not only impossible, but it would be in no way more sublime. Later on we shall see that the value response and our deep, legitimate desire for true happiness, far from being antithetic, are organically linked" (*Ethics,* 218–19).

for him. When we deal with things objectively beneficial for us, or harmful for us, we have to do not just with the good itself, *but with the good as beneficial for us.* And yet the relation to ourselves is not gained by taking things as merely satisfying or dissatisfying for us. Thus, for example, my friendship with some worthy person is not just good because it gratifies some want or craving of mine, it is obviously good for me independent of my wants and cravings. But at the same time it is not simply good in itself, having only value in our sense of the term, because it is obviously also *good for me* and tends to my real happiness: it represents a third kind of good, *the beneficial good.* It seems that this kind of good was recognized in the Aristotelian tradition under the name of *eudaemonia,* or happiness understood as the all-encompassing well-being of the person. It is very close to the *bonum* of St. Thomas.

Von Hildebrand and Scheler and others think that this good has in a way been too prominent in previous ethical philosophy in that a kind of eudaemonism has often hindered the recognition of value and value response. But for their part they do not want the ethics of value and value response to ignore or belittle happiness and our desire for it; as I say, they want nothing to do with the extreme altruism or with any depersonalizing objectivism, which they want to avoid just as much as they want to avoid eudaemonism. Von Hildebrand has explored various ways in which the transcendence of value response forms a unity with the desire for happiness.

1. He extensively investigates the fact that value is one principal and indispensable source of our happiness, that we take delight in and are enriched by all that we experience and affirm as intrinsically worthy and splendid and precious. In a world deprived of all value, in a world in which the only good is the merely agreeable, there would be no happiness; instead of happiness there would be boredom unto despair. Von Hildebrand argues that precisely the moment of transcendence in value response is all-important for the happiness that we receive in it;[21] we exult in value because in value response we are caught up in a goodness that is what it is in its own right, and is independent of our arbitrariness. Without this transcendence, we prey upon ourselves in boredom, as we have seen. So we can say that value response is good for the human person. It seems that things good in themselves have a goodness that is more than goodness in itself; they give rise to a goodness for us who affirm them in a value-responding way. We would not be wrong to de-

---

21. Von Hildebrand, *Ethics*, 35–39.

tect here a fulfillment of the axiom *bonum est diffusivum sui* (good communicates itself to others).

2. Of particular importance for our purposes is von Hildebrand's understanding of the place of happiness *in our motivation*. He quite recognizes that we not only receive happiness in value response, but that we are right to desire this happiness. It is true that he cannot stress enough that value response must never become an instrumental means for happiness (as it does in the philosophy that I call eudaemonism), for then our value response loses its transcendence, and, in addition, the happiness eludes us, as everyone knows from experience. The desire to be happy must be in a sense secondary to the will to give value its due.[22] And yet he is at pains to avoid the altruism which would try to talk us out of desiring to be happy in value, or at least to make us ashamed of desiring such happiness.

3. It is very significant for our purposes that von Hildebrand goes still farther and says that the value-responding stance of persons toward the world, far from excluding their interest in their happiness, *in fact presupposes this interest; value response otherwise lacks its integrity as value response.* We would combat not selfishness but our very selfhood if we tried to suppress our interest in our happiness and to live exclusively in the attitude of value response: with diminished selfhood we would have a diminished power of doing any kind of conscious acting and so also of transcending ourselves in value response. Just as the one who has knowledge of some object is present to himself in the knowing and would destroy all conscious acting, knowing included, if he were to be so absorbed in the object as to extinguish his self-presence, so in a similar way the one who gives a value response also wills his own happiness, and he would destroy the very possibility of value response if he were to give himself to the value in such a way as to lose all interest in his own happiness. We see yet again the dialectical relation obtaining between selfhood and transcendence in our relation to the good.

4. Von Hildebrand finds even more of this dialectical relation in his analysis of certain kinds of love, especially the love between man and woman (spousal love) and the love of man for God. Here the desire to be happy in the beloved forms a particular unity with the will to affirm the

---

22. One of the profoundest studies of the complex relations between these two intentions is to be found in Aristotle's *Nichomachean Ethics*, IX, 8; 1168a–1169b. I do not follow here the critics of Aristotle who think he reverts in this passage to his eudaemonism.

beloved person for his or her own sake.[23] It is not as if we transcend ourselves only in this will, and do something different from transcending ourselves in desiring to be happy in the beloved person: rather, *to want to be happy in the beloved person is a particular way of giving oneself to him or her.* We make ourselves dependent on the beloved person in making him or her the source of our happiness; we put ourselves in need of him or her. This is not indeed exactly the same as affirming the beloved for his or her own sake; even with these kinds of love the desire for happiness is distinct from the value response. But it is a uniquely self-transcending desire for happiness, and this is why we say that it forms a unique kind of unity with the value-responding affirmation of the beloved. What especially concerns us is that by belittling my happiness and trying to be indifferent to it in the name of some altruistic ideal of pure and exclusive value response, I make myself incapable of this kind of self-transcendence. I can give myself to another in the sense of willing to need the other for my happiness, only if I am sensitive to my happiness and capable of desiring it. In this we recognize yet another aspect of the dialectic of selfhood and transcendence in our relation to the intrinsically good.

5. An entirely different relation between happiness and value response emerges if we consider how it is that persons are empowered by their happiness to live in a value-responding attitude. A deeply happy person is uniquely able to be awakened to value and to give it its due. We will return to this subject in the next chapter, where I will study Scheler's thesis that happiness is not only a fruit of value response, but also a source of it. If the fullness of subjective life that characterizes happy persons enables them to transcend themselves in value response, and in fact expresses itself in this transcendence, then the suspicion of heteronomy is once again dispelled.

We turn now to a particular aspect of all authentic happiness.

7. *Affectivity and value response.* We link up with the rich work of Scheler in *Formalism in Ethics* and especially of von Hildebrand[24] on

23. Von Hildebrand holds that all love, whatever else it is, is a value-responding stance towards another person, that is, an affirmation of the other for his or her own sake. See his *Das Wesen der Liebe* (Stuttgart: Kohlhammer, 1971), Chapter 1.

24. Von Hildebrand, "Die geistigen Formen der Affektivität," in *Situationsethik und kleinere Schriften* (Stuttgart: Kohlhammer, 1973), and at greater length on the same subjects in *The Heart* (Chicago: Franciscan Herald Press, 1977), especially the first eight chapters.

the levels of affectivity in persons. They both resisted the reduction of all affective life to body feelings; they showed that in addition to body feelings there are also feelings that are fully intentional, and that in fact many of these exist only as value-responding feelings or affections. There is, for example, a delight in the beautiful which is, in their analysis, at once deeply affective as well as an authentic value response. It is a delight that we cannot possibly take in the goodness relative to our arbitrary pleasure; it exists only as a value response.

But in von Hildebrand the analysis goes further. He notices a striking difference within the sphere of value response between acts of willing an action and affective responses. While it is true that I commit myself in a morally decisive way in willing an action, thereby exercising my moral freedom in the action, there is nevertheless a deeper self in me that is engaged only in affective value responses. If I help another person with a beneficent action but remain affectively uninvolved in performing the action, then there is something of myself that belongs in the action but is painfully missing; it is a lack that can be supplied only by taking some delight in benefiting the needy person. Only through some such affective involvement will this person feel that I am really turning to him and giving something of myself to him. It is as if my real self lives only in a certain depth of affectivity. Von Hildebrand proceeds to distinguish those forms of affectivity which are particularly potent in expressing the innermost self of the person, such as feeling gratitude towards a benefactor, or taking delight in the presence of a friend, or being moved by the goodness of another; he speaks of the "tender affectivity" in which the most intimate self of a person lives and expresses itself. This is why persons are sometimes ashamed to show such feelings; they shrink from exposing what is so intimate in themselves. And yet persons do not really live as persons if all deeper affectivity in themselves remains completely undeveloped or repressed; their real selves remain buried.

The bearing on our present subject is this. Only value, especially under its aspect of beauty, evokes and engenders that deeper affectivity in which the most intimate selves of human persons live; the merely agreeable cannot evoke and engender it. The objectivity and absoluteness of value conjure up for many the specter of heteronomy; but if we consider the beauty of value, and consider also the relation between beauty and affectivity, then we see that there is something in the depth of personal subjectivity which responds only to value.

There is a kind of personalist objection that is commonly raised against affectivity. One says that affective experiences come and go outside of the freedom of persons; they are not subject to our freedom in the way in which our actions are. We often want to feel gratitude towards someone, and know that we ought to feel it, but we simply cannot feel it. On the other hand, it often enough happens that other feelings well up in us against our better judgment. It seems that we do not possess ourselves fully in experiencing affectively, and that it is, therefore, not as persons that we live and thrive in our affective lives.

One of the great excellences of von Hildebrand's work in this area is his response to the objection. He develops the idea, which has great general importance in philosophical anthropology, that we are capable, as he says, of *sanctioning* value responses that spring up on their own; through our sanctioning, these responses, which originate outside of our freedom, are incorporated into our freedom, so that we live fully as persons in them. Or to put it in the terms introduced at the end of Chapter 1: feelings which in their origin are akin to *nature* in man, to what happens in him, can be transformed from *nature* to *person* by the force of sanctioning. Von Hildebrand also discusses our capacity of *disavowing* other responses welling up in us.[25] In sanctioning, the person does not just act on the affective experience from without, as if it were the object of his intention; no, the person by sanctioning comes to live subjectively in the experience. This is why the sanctioning does not tend to blunt the affective force of the experience, and why the affective act is not controlled in such a way as to be weakened in its ardor. It is rather fully appropriated by the sanctioning person, taken into his freedom. And then it happens that he does fully possess himself as person in his most ardent affective joys and griefs. We say, then, not that human beings live as persons in affective experiences, or even in value responding affective experiences; we say that they live in sanctioned affective responses motivated by value.

We might add that it is not only value but also *bonum* (which always presupposes value) that can engender our deepest affectivity. In fact, the affective response of gratitude, which we have mentioned, only responds to something *objectively good for me;* without the thought of some benefit for me or for someone close to me, there is no gratitude. Or consider

25. The most extensive discussion of sanction and disavowal in von Hildebrand is to be found in Chapter 25 of his *Ethics*.

the joy over being delivered from some danger, or the dread of being abandoned to the danger; or consider the joy of attaining one's salvation, or the despair of ever attaining it—in each case one sees a deep affectivity which is engendered not only by value and the beauty of value, but also by something beneficial for the responding person.

8. *The unifying power of value.* We have already had occasion to mention the recollecting power that value exercises when it is encountered in the spirit of value response. Not many pages ago we were contrasting the recollection born of value response with the boredom born of a one-sided interest in the merely agreeable. Needless to say, it is not just any knowledge about value which recollects, but rather some lived experience of value. And the recollecting power of value varies according to the kind and measure of value. Thus the recollecting power of value is particularly potent when we have to do with some kind of *ultimate* value, with striving for that which is ultimately and absolutely good or avoiding that which is ultimately and absolutely evil, or when we glimpse through some particular value the whole world of value, the cosmos of value. The recollecting power of value also varies according as we experience value under the aspect of beauty, or under the more existential aspect that it takes on when it underlies something objectively good for us. It follows yet again, then, that value, understood in all its objectivity and absoluteness, "belongs to" personal selfhood; through value response it becomes a major source of recollected, or unified subjectivity.

There is another dimension of this unifying power of value. When von Hildebrand speaks in his philosophical sociology of the *virtus unitiva* of value,[26] he is aiming in the first place at the power of value to engender community among persons. His idea is that when a number of persons turn together to some value, they are unified in it in a way directly analogous to the way in which a single person is recollected in value.[27] Persons can form community in the good just like one person can be recollected in the good. It has been well known in Western philosophy ever since Plato that persons can come together and can form community in the name of the objectively good, and that they can be together in the good in a way in which they cannot be together in the merely agreeable. Everyone can easily verify this in his or her own experience. If you

26. See his *Metaphysik der Gemeinschaft* (Regensburg: Josef Habbel Verlag, 1955), Chapter 8, "Die *Virtus Unitiva* der Werte."
27. Ibid., 309.

have only sports in common with others, you can stand only in an extremely modest union with them, a union which is as nothing compared with the union born of sharing with them, say, a concern for ultimate philosophical truth.[28] We find here an "effect" of value on persons that has nothing to do with heteronomy. It is not exactly an effect that goes in the direction of autonomy either, for the effect is the formation of community. But when persons open themselves to each other, and form community among themselves, a community which is not a collectivity but an authentic *communio personarum* (communion of persons), then their selfhood is presupposed and lived. No one who realizes the community-generating power of the good could think that the good, when rightly understood, could do violence to persons.

4. The transcendence, including the religious transcendence, achieved in moral obligation

The transcendence of value response becomes potentiated, as it were, when value gives rise to moral obligation. The fear of heteronomy also becomes greater, as indeed does the appearance of heteronomy. But we, on the contrary, are drawn to explore this new dimension of transcendence in the hope of finding a new dimension of selfhood and subjectivity.

At the beginning of the present chapter we spoke of the fact that value deserves an appropriate response from us, or in other words that it *ought* to receive a value response from us. Now this ought is by no means the strongest ought that we encounter in our relation to good. The call to give to some beautiful thing the admiration it deserves has nothing of a *command* about it, and we would not speak of it as an *imperative*. But we do experience imperatives, and hence essentially stronger oughts than the oughts of value response. When Socrates realized that he ought not obey the court order directing him to arrest Leon of Salamis, whom Socrates thought was being arrested for the sake of being executed on politically trumped-up charges, he must have been aware—to judge by his unconditional refusal to participate—not just of any ought but of an imperative, or a command-like prohibition against cooperating in the

---

28. Von Hildebrand has made a particular contribution to this subject by arguing that there is a certain union of human persons in the good which is prior to the experience of this union; he says that in certain experiences of good we wake up to a solidarity with all human beings which we experience as already existing by the time we experience it.

judicial murder of Leon. We now ask how we can characterize the oughtness of a moral imperative.

We want to make our own an important distinction Kant introduced into moral philosophy: the moral imperative has a categorical character and is not merely hypothetical. To say that Socrates is hypothetically bound to refuse the court order would mean that Socrates can reach some goal that he has already set for himself only by refusing. Implied is that his obligation not to arrest Leon would cease to exist if Socrates gave up his goals. Thus if Socrates refuses to harm Leon because he hopes to have him as his student one day, then he could eliminate his obligation by giving up this hope. It follows that a hypothetical obligation owes its existence to some goal the obliged person has set for himself, and it goes into effect as soon as the obligatory action is recognized as necessary for achieving that goal. Kant added the important qualification that an imperative remains hypothetical even if the goal is one we cannot not set for ourselves, such as our own happiness, according to some philosophies. Thus if Socrates were bound to respect the life of Leon on the grounds that he would otherwise forfeit the inevitably desired end of his own happiness, he would still be only conditionally bound. In order to be not hypothetically but categorically bound, a person has to be bound without respect to his reaching any of the goals he has set for himself, whether these goals could as well have not been set or were inescapably set. This is clearly the kind of imperative that Socrates recognizes. He is not bound because the act of refusing to harm Leon is necessary for the reaching of some goal Socrates had set for himself; his being bound is not conditioned by any such goal; it is unconditioned, or categorical.

This is helpful, and it serves to show something of the transcendence achieved in responding to a moral imperative. For we can say far more properly of the categorical than of the hypothetical imperative that *it comes from outside of me and breaks in upon me.* The hypothetical imperative is still in a certain sense under my control, and is supported in being by my willing some end; the categorical imperative is completely independent of such willing, and has thus an objectivity that the other lacks. This is why it forces me to a greater transcendence than the other does.[29]

29. Cf. Josef Seifert, *Was ist und was motiviert eine sittliche Handlung* (Salzburg: Anton Pustet Verlag, 1976), 45.

We can, however, enter more deeply into the mysterious transcendence of being under a moral obligation. When we examine the moral imperative that Socrates must have experienced in the face of the unjust court order, which we too would have experienced if we found ourselves in a similar situation, then we find that this imperative is not entirely proportioned to the good of Leon's life but has *a mysterious ultimacy and unconditionedness.* Notice the highly significant fact that *our response to the imperative is an act of obedience, and includes in itself a gesture of submission.* The obedience could not possibly refer to Leon; Socrates neither obeys him nor submits to him in refusing to do him harm. It would be completely out of place, *indeed there would be something idolatrous in Socrates submitting unconditionally to Leon as he submits unconditionally to the moral imperative to do him no harm.* Nor does Leon think that he is being obeyed or submitted to when Socrates follows his conscience and refuses absolutely to do him any harm; Leon is glad to be the beneficiary of Socrates' refusal, but he knows that he is not the addressee of Socrates' obedience.[30]

As I say, this obedience goes beyond the transcendence of value response. As long as we are dealing with objectively good and worthy things in the realm of the finite, the ought which calls for our value-response, such as the response of admiration, is entirely proportioned to them, and shares in their finitude. Our responding refers precisely to the values, and is not made idolatrous by referring to them. Not only that, but our responding, such as our admiring, for all its transcendence, makes no gesture of submission or obedience.

This imperativity of moral obligation clearly requires some religious explanation; indeed, it seems impossible to continue to recognize it if one refuses any such explanation. Some thinkers such as John Henry Newman say that we can first experience moral obligation in its command-like force (Newman speaks of it as a "magisterial dictate"[31]) and can then discern God in it as its ground.[32] Other thinkers such as Elizabeth Anscombe hold that moral obligation in this strong imperative sense

---

30. The talk of obedience and submission also makes no sense when it is a question of a duty towards myself; I cannot obey myself. In responding with obedience to a duty towards myself, then, I have to do with something more than the objective worth of myself.

31. Newman, *An Essay in Aid of a Grammar of Assent* (London: Longmans, Green, and Co., 1898), 105.

32. I defended Newman's position in my "The Encounter of God and Man in Moral Obligation," *The New Scholasticism*, LX, 3 (1986), 317–355.

already presupposes God and so requires a belief in God in order to be experienced at all.[33] She would say that Newman argues in a circle by proceeding from imperative obligation to God, since he has to presuppose God in order to have imperative obligation. But she differs from Newman only regarding the order of our knowing, not regarding the order of being, that is, not regarding the inherently religious depth of imperative obligation. Indeed, even Schopenhauer, unbeliever though he was, saw this religious depth. He thought that Kant could talk as he did of moral duties, imperatives, laws, etc., only because he made far more Christian assumptions than he realized. He thought that these things would make sense only in a theological frame of reference.[34] He rejected them because he rejected the supporting theology. As far as I can see, almost everyone recognizes the religious dimension of moral imperatives, so much so that whoever wants to deny this religious dimension must deny that there are any moral imperatives, and/or must deny, like Schopenhauer, that God exists, but must under no circumstances admit the existence of moral imperatives; for with this admission one cannot long hold out against a religious interpretation of them.

Just a word on the relation between the encounter with God in moral obligation and the finite values (such as the life of Leon of Salamis) through which the obligation is mediated to us. It is of course not the case that God decrees that certain goods are to be respected, thus superimposing on them an imperative to respect them. None of the authors just mentioned invokes any such theological positivism in order to explain how moral obligation comes to be invested with religious significance. The connection is more intrinsic; a believer in God who under-

33. See her well known paper, "Modern Moral Philosophy," first published in *Philosophy*, 33 (1958), reprinted in her *Collected Philosophical Papers* III (Minneapolis: University of Minnesota Press, 1981), 26–42.

34. "This concept [duty] together with its near relatives, such as those of *law, command, obligation,* and so on, taken in this unconditional sense, has its origin in theological morals, and remains a stranger to the philosophical until it has produced a valid credential from the essence of human nature of that of the objective world. Until then, I do not acknowledge for it and its relatives any other origin than the Decalogue. In the centuries of Christianity, philosophical ethics has generally taken its form unconsciously from the theological. Now as theological ethics is essentially *dictatorial,* the philosophical has also appeared in the form of precept and moral obligation . . . separated from the theological hypotheses from which they came, these concepts [law, command, obligation] really lose all meaning. . . " (Schopenhauer, *On the Basis of Morality* [Indianapolis, 1981], 54; see the whole discussion 49–119. German: *Preisschrift über die Grundlagen der Moral* in *Sämtliche Werke* IV [Wiesbaden, 1950], 117–184).

stands the personhood of human beings will also understand without the aid of any special revelation that God must be present in a particular way in the requirement to respect persons. Religious depth is inherent in the moral relevance of a human person, and in fact it makes no sense to entertain the possibility of a divine decree which would revoke this religious depth.

But if we have directly to do with God in moral obligation, then we transcend ourselves beyond anything we achieve in relation to finite values. We respond here with an *ultimacy of commitment* unlike any commitment to good that has been previously discussed.

5. The subjectivity of responding to moral obligation

The suspicion of heteronomy is much greater with regard to imperative obligations than it is with regard to value. And the reason is not far to seek. It seems that the discrepancy between some finite good and the ultimacy of our obligation to respect it, introduces an element of blindness into our moral commitment; we seem to be bound to more than we can see or understand. It is only in accordance with our own analysis in the present and the previous chapter to say that any such defect of understanding compromises the selfhood and subjectivity of our moral commitment. And certain important authors confirm the fear of heteronomy in relation to moral imperatives. Thus Scheler rejects moral imperatives on the grounds that they have no intelligible value foundation and can only be obeyed blindly.[35] In this he is only following Kant, who, at least in the formalistic strain of his moral philosophy, had cut moral imperatives away from any value foundation. Scheler differs from Kant only in detecting the heteronomy of obeying formalistically conceived imperatives, but he agrees with Kant in thinking that moral imperatives can only be formalistically conceived, which implies that they can only be obeyed blindly.

Some of the authors rejecting moral imperatives assimilate them to the demands of the so-called superego, and include a critique of them in their critique of the superego. A superego arises when the directives of one's parents or of some other authority get internalized, so that one follows them on one's own without being monitored by the authority. If

35. Scheler, *Der Formalismus in der Ethik* (Bern and Munich: Francke Verlag, 1966), 199–203. English: *Formalism in Ethics* (Evanston: Northwestern University Press, 1973), 190–194.

one is called to account for some infraction of these directives, one does not call the directives into question, or act merely out of fear of the threatened punishment, but one is ashamed, and agrees with the authority that it was wrong to violate them. They take on for this person not hypothetical but categorical imperative force. And yet a strong superego can cause painful heteronomy in a person, because the norms and directives that are upheld by it are after all not entirely internalized; they are internalized without being fully understood, without being fully ratified by one's own insight, and hence are not really internalized. They remain somewhat outside of the person, so that conformity with them is burdensome. Well known is the experience of morally developing persons whose own moral insight begins to grow and in growing creates conflict with the demands of their superego. They are for a time divided within themselves, not daring to trust their new insight, perhaps even feeling guilty about breaking away from their superego. But if they live by their own insight they eventually grow out of the superego, replacing it with a mature conscience. They experience this growth as liberating; they have the awareness that only now are they leading their own moral life and are not just acting as the extension of others. Now the critics of moral imperatives say that it is precisely the imperatives which cause the element of blindness in the superego which makes it weigh as a burden on us. They say that the mature conscience, once liberated from the superego, knows only good and bad things, being drawn to the former and repelled by the latter without the crushing burden of a moral imperative.[36]

And yet a kind of antinomy seems to arise when we consider that other authors hold that the selfhood of persons is not burdened but is challenged and awakened by moral imperatives as by nothing else. When Thomas More says "I" so emphatically, he says it in relation not just to values alone but to values mediating to him what he experiences as an imperative obligation; it is this obligation which lets him get free of his pride, his spleen, and his other appetites so as to act supremely through himself. When in Chapter 3.2 we first introduced the idea of volitional subjectivity we referred to the experience in conscience of a moral imperative and discussed the power of the imperative to hand us over to ourselves in a unique way, challenging us to determine ourselves, and so

---

36. I have discussed the difference between superego and authentic conscience in my "Conscience and Superego: a Phenomenological Analysis of Their Difference and Relation," in DuBois, ed., *The Nature and Tasks of a Personalist Psychology* (Lanham, MD: University Press of America, 1995), 47–58.

making us quicken in our innermost selves. We observed that this subjectivity is expressed when people speak as if they would split apart if they were to act against their conscience and do what they know to be wrong.

This experience of quickening has been well described by von Hildebrand, who also stresses the paradoxical structure of it:

> A moral call is addressed to someone to intervene in a certain situation; perhaps another is in danger, or perhaps he has to refuse to do some evil which is asked of him. He grasps the morally relevant value, he understands its call, he is aware of the moral obligation, which appeals to his conscience. On the one hand, we have here a high-point of transcendence in the pure commitment to the morally relevant good. But on the other hand, this call, insofar as it is morally obligatory, pre-eminently contains the element of "tua res agitur" ("the thing concerns *you*"). In a certain sense this call is my most intimate and personal concern, in which I experience the uniqueness of my self. Supreme objectivity and supreme subjectivity interpenetrate here. One can even say that we have here the dramatic high-point of the "tua res agitur" in our earthly existence. On the one hand, I commit myself to something which in no way stands before me as merely "an objective good for me," but rather as something which appeals to me as valuable in itself; but on the other hand, since a moral obligation in its unique impact is here at stake, which is ultimately the call of God to me, my decision to follow the call or not, eminently reaches into the realm of my own life (*Eigenleben*). When the moral call is addressed to me and appeals to my conscience, then at the same time the question of my own salvation comes up. It is not just the "issue" which is at stake; I and my salvation are just as much at stake.[37]

We have to marvel at the "gentle strength" of moral imperatives: they are so demanding, so imperious, invested with divine authority, and yet, according to von Hildebrand, they do no least violence to the person, they do not terrorize him or manipulate him, but appeal to him where he is most a being of his own, eliciting his powers of acting through himself. They are also gentle in the sense that they can be ignored, and that it is easy to repress them.[38]

What are we to make of this conflict of opinions? Why did Scheler and others not recognize this congeniality of moral imperatives with the person? Did von Hildebrand and Newman and others overlook some

---

37. My translation from von Hildebrand, *Das Wesen der Liebe*, 274–5.

38. It goes without saying that the quickening of which I speak is not restricted to the person who is aware of being bound by an imperative, but extends to and in fact preeminently belongs to the person who accepts the imperative and wills to fulfill it.

blindness in which we live when we are bound by an imperative? The answer is not far to seek; the conflict of opinions is not difficult to explain. Von Hildebrand thinks that even in relation to moral imperatives we can act in a fully seeing and understanding way. Notice how he stresses in the passage just quoted the grasp of some morally relevant value as the basis for experiencing an obligation. Perhaps the reader will object that this grasp enables me to make my own only the ought of a value response but not the imperative ought of an obligation. It is true that von Hildebrand, who is clearly thinking of moral obligation in all its imperativity, does not mention any further value understanding. But it is not difficult to find this further understanding. There is some apprehension of God, however veiled and implicit, in every experience of an obligation as imperative. And it is an apprehension of God in terms of value. If God were apprehended only as powerful but not also as holy and so as worthy of our obedience, His presence in moral obligation would not serve to ground its imperativity, but would leave us still wondering where such imperativity comes from. And there is a further element of understanding, which we have already examined: we understand the intrinsic connection between the morally relevant value and the imperative obligation; we understand the connection between the finite value and the divine ground of obligation. When, then, we respond to an obligation with a certain ultimacy of commitment, our response remains within our value understanding and does not exceed it; our response is seeing and not blind. I would think that whoever follows me to this point will find no further difficulty in accepting von Hildebrand's account of the subjectivity and the objectivity of moral obligation.

Of course it happens all the time that our experience of moral obligation is not sufficiently supported by an understanding of the values in which it is grounded. An element of blindness can in fact enter into our experience of moral norms and duties. There really is such a thing as the superego. And as a result of this loss of value understanding, moral norms and laws really do become burdensome for us, seeming more to cramp our freedom than to liberate it. Then we say of them what the Second Murderer in *Richard III* says of conscience: "it fills one full of obstacles" (I.4). The fact that we all too often experience moral obligation in this way is the truth in Scheler and in the attempts to explain imperatives in terms of the superego. But the error in his view is to say that this unfreedom is of the very essence of the moral imperative; to have overlooked that there is an understanding of the moral imperative that lets us be never so free as in the will to fulfill it.[39]

There is something else to be said towards reconciling personal subjectivity and freedom with the weight of a religiously potentiated imperative. There is a way of showing that the religious potentiation is required by the subjectivity of the morally bound person. Here we show the reconciliation of the two terms by deriving the second from the first.

We know that all kinds of possibilities and powers in ourselves can awaken only in the encounter with another person. In knowing this we understand how fundamental it is to personal existence to live in communion with other persons. Is it possible, then, that we are really alone with ourselves, really in solitude, when we undergo that profound actualization of our personal being which occurs in being bound in conscience? Either we undergo this actualization under the gaze of, in the encounter with some person, or else the interpersonal is after all only accidental to personal existence and does not radically determine it. But if the fullness of personal existence achieved in conscience does presuppose another person, then which other person? It is a matter of empirical fact that we are often not in the presence of, are often not in touch with the person towards whom we act in fulfilling our obligation—Socrates is not in the presence of, does not encounter Leon in the act of refusing to do him any wrong (nor did Antigone encounter her brother, who was dead). And even when we do encounter the human person towards whom we act, and encounter him or her ever so closely, the question remains whether this person is really the one, and could ever be the one, who is present to us and enters into us and engages us in such a way as to effect that quickening of our personal being which occurs under the impact of a moral imperative. But if no human person can elicit this quickening, could it be a divine personal being? When under the impact of an imperative "the infinite abyss of existence" (Newman) is stirred up in ourselves, can we not catch a glimpse of a personal God as Him to whom this abyss of personal existence responds, as Him in whose presence it

---

39. In the following I think that Wojtyla, who is speaking precisely about moral obligation, means to affirm the power of value understanding to ward off heteronomy and to make us free: "The tension arising between the objective order of norms and the inner freedom of the subject-person is relieved by truth, by the conviction of the truthfulness of good. On the other hand, it is intensified and not relieved by external pressures, by the power of injunction or compulsion." *The Acting Person* (Dordrecht: D. Reidel, 1979), 166.

resonates? Does it not come very natural to speak of being "alone with God in conscience"?[40] Does not the solitude with respect to other persons which we experience as we enter into ourselves at a time of moral crisis, does not this solitude open up to an absolute person with whom we have to do? Does it not have to open up like this to religious transcendence, given the general truth that persons can quicken and thrive as persons only in intersubjectivity, only in communion with other persons? If we could elaborate and defend the answers we are suggesting to these questions, we would show how the term of selfhood and subjectivity requires the other term, the encounter with God, and we would thereby offer still further evidence for the paradoxical interpenetration of the two terms.

Aspects of selfhood that are lived in the experience of obeying a moral imperative. Now if the experience of being morally bound is really so deeply congenial to the selfhood of the person, as I have been arguing, then one might expect that I would consciously perform and live through my deeper being as person in this experience, and so get acquainted with this deeper being by probing the experience. Now this expectation is entirely fulfilled, and we propose to show it by drawing out a few of the fundamental truths about selfhood to which I can get closer by examining the experience of being morally bound.

1. In being handed over to ourselves in conscience, we experience our *real existence* as personal selves. Let us suppose that I am in a state of dispersion, lost in many things, so that I experience a certain dreamy unreality about myself. Suppose now that I am awakened out of this trance by the realization that I am morally bound to do something. With this I am thrown back on myself and feel the burden of personal existence thrust on me anew; I come alive as a personal self in a mysterious way. In experiencing this new life and energy in myself I experience the fact that I *really exist*. The dreamy unreality of myself gives way to a strong sense of my real existence, which may be expressed by saying "I" in a far more authentic way. Descartes said that we could come to encounter our real existence by starting from any conscious act at all; "I think," "I feel," "I imagine," or any other such conscious act will do in order to understand that "I am." But it has often been observed that we can reach a far more massive and convincing "I am" by starting pre-

---

40. Cf. the words of Vatican II: "His conscience is man's most secret core, and his sanctuary. There he is alone with God whose voice echoes in his depths" (*Gaudium et spes*, n. 16).

cisely from moral experiences, such as the experiences of obligation, guilt, responsibility, repentance. Thus Rudolf Otto proposes to improve on Descartes' *cogito ergo sum* with *peccavi ergo sum.*[41]

How could the moral imperative be doing violence to the person, when under the impact of the imperative I experience in a unique way the real existence proper to myself, living it from within, performing it and actualizing it?

2. In the experience of an obligation, especially one that has been potentiated and has taken on the ultimacy of an imperative, we not only experience the *esse* expressed by Descartes' *sum* but also the *ego* of the *sum*. It is hard to improve on these words of Rudolf Otto, which by the way lose none of their relevance for us by the fact that they refer to the experience of a guilty conscience, of a violated obligation.

> In our inner awareness nothing at all is ever given in the "impersonal" form such as "it is raining." . . . There is no mere "it is thinking" or a simply "cogitatur," but rather there is always only a cogito, or a cogitatur a me. It is the same with feeling and acting: all feeling and acting is always necessarily mine, yours, or his. In the case of the consciousness of guilt it is *my* consciousness. And the certainty and reality of a "my" never shows itself so clearly as in the "*mea* culpa, *mea* culpa, *mea* maxima culpa." Even if I otherwise strongly tend to put the I in question or to regard it as a mere form of changing contents of consciousness, and a form which can be removed— once I know that I am guilty, then all such phantoms are dissipated. Here I know, and know immediately, and know in the most definite way possible, that I am the guilty one, and that I am an I, and that this I is not a function of presentations but that they are rather a function of the I.[42]

When von Hildebrand speaks of the "tua res agitur" which belongs to the experience of an imperative moral call, he is referring to our sense that it is I who am called, that the call is mine. And when others speak of the *existential* character of the imperative, they are referring to the same thing.

3. A fundamental truth about persons is, as we know, that they possess themselves, that they are *sui iuris*, and exist in the form of self-belonging. This truth is deeply experienced and lived in the encounter with a moral imperative. How could I be handed over to myself and have to do with myself, determining myself so decisively in responding

---

41. "I have sinned, therefore I am." Otto, "Das Gefühl der Verantwortlichkeit," in *Aufsätze zur Ethik* (Munich: C. H. Beck Verlag, 1981), 147.

42. My translation of Otto, ibid.

to an imperative, if I did not experience myself belonging to myself and having a being of my own? Indeed, the experience of being bound in conscience is, as we came to realize in Chapter 3.2, one of the main sources for any study of subjectivity, self-possession, self-determination.

4. From here it is only a short step to the experience of my incommunicability as person, and also of my worth and dignity as person; this experience preeminently belongs to the encounter with myself in conscience. We are repeatedly overcome by a sense of being lost in the world, of being only one in a large population, or only one member in a large species, or of being infinitesimally small in relation to nature and the physical universe. Nothing is as powerful in reversing this sense of being lost, and in renewing in me the consciousness of being unrepeatable and of having a mysterious infinity in myself, as the experience of discerning an imperative moral call in my conscience. One should in this connection recall and meditate on the profound words with which Kant closes his *Critique of Practical Reason*.[43]

What interests us above all else is of course the fact that the experience of my incommunicability and of my worth as person goes as deep as it does only because of the transcendence I achieve in responding to the moral law with its categorical imperativity. This fact can be thrown into relief by contrasting the experience of responding to the imperative with the experience of my rights. In experiencing my rights, whether I experience their violation or whether I warn someone not to violate them, I experience my self-possession as person, for it is in this self-posses-

---

43. "Two things fill the mind with ever new and increasing admiration and awe, the oftener and more steadily they are reflected on: the starry heavens above me and the moral law within me. . . . The former begins from the place I occupy in the external world of sense, and it broadens the connection in which I stand into an unbounded magnitude of worlds beyond worlds. . . . The latter begins from my invisible self, my personality, and exhibits me in a world which has true infinity but which is comprehensible only to the understanding. . . . The former view of a countless multitude of worlds annihilates, as it were, my importance as an animal creature, which must give back to the planet (a mere speck in the universe) the matter from which it came, the matter which is for a little time provided with vital force, we know not how. The latter, on the contrary, infinitely raises my worth as that of an intelligence by my personality, in which the moral law reveals a life independent of all animality and even of the whole world of sense—at least so far as it may be inferred from the purposive destination assigned to my existence by this law, a destination which is not restricted to the conditions and limits of this life but reaches into the infinite." Lewis White Beck (tr.), *Critique of Practical Reason* (New York: Bobbs-Merrill, 1956), 166.

sion that they are grounded, as we saw in Chapter 1. I do not experience anything coming from outside myself but simply myself as one who belongs to himself. In experiencing a moral imperative, by contrast, I experience something breaking in on me from without and from above, and calling me to obedience; I experience a powerful element of transcendence, as we have been calling it. If my self-possession were the whole truth about me as person, and if demands for my obedience were unworthy of me as person, and if such transcendence caused heteronomy, then how explain the following fact: the experience of being morally bound is far more potent in renewing my sense of being an unrepeatable person with ultimate worth than is the experience of being the subject of rights. If I feel annihilated by the immensity of the physical universe, I may take a step towards recovering a sense of my personal being by recalling that in belonging to myself I am a subject of rights; but I will go vastly farther in recovering this sense of my selfhood and of my worth as person if some moral demand breaks in upon me, stirring up in me the inwardness of conscience.

We see yet again, as we saw at the end of the last chapter, that selfhood, foundational as it is in human persons, does not contain the whole essence of personhood. Transcendence is not heteronomy. Our selfhood is a transcendent selfhood. We possess ourselves in transcending ourselves towards value. Our self-possession is raised to a higher power when the transcendence is potentiated in moral obligation.

CHAPTER SEVEN

Moral Good and Bad

Sometimes we participate in value in the sense of responding to it; in the previous chapter I examined this participation and I tried to explore the selfhood achieved in it. But sometimes we participate in goodness in the different sense of *being ourselves good or worthy*. In the present chapter we will study this new kind of participation in value, giving particular attention to the subjectivity of it. With this I turn in the direction in which much of recent moral philosophy has turned, namely from ought, obligation, imperative towards moral goodness, moral value, moral virtue in the human person.

Back in Chapter 2 we discussed one fundamental dimension of value in human persons, the value rooted in the incommunicability of persons. Now it is another, no less fundamental dimension of personal value that I propose to explore in devoting the present chapter to moral value and disvalue in persons. At the end of this chapter I will set the two dimensions of value in relation to each other.

1. What is and what is not moral value and moral disvalue

Our natural point of departure is this, to grasp moral value as itself and nothing else, and to avoid conflating it with non-moral forms of goodness. It is not so easy to discriminate well between moral and non-moral, as one can see from the *Nichomachean Ethics* of Aristotle, who introduces all manner of extra-moral personal excellence into his discussion of the moral virtues. Take for example the virtue he calls magnificence, a virtue exercised by the very wealthy in disposing of their money. Aristotle calls the vice of excess in relation to this virtue by the name of vulgarity, which is committed when the wealthy spend their money in a tasteless way. But this excess seems to be more an aesthetic than a moral failing, giving evidence more of a lack of good taste than of a lack of moral decency. The virtue of magnificence seems to be more an excellence of aesthetic judgment than of moral goodness.[1] Or take the virtue that according to Aristotle is exercised in relation to joking lightly with others, the excess of which he calls buffoonery and the defect of which he calls boorishness. Most of us would say that Aristotle here is speaking about a social grace rather than about an aspect of moral integrity. Though this social grace may sometimes be grafted on to a person's moral character and may be expressive of it, we nevertheless often find that this social grace can be well developed even when it lacks much relation to the moral character of its possessor.

One can realize just how difficult it must be to make these discriminations if one recalls that Aristotle, who fails to make them, is the thinker who introduced new clarity into the theory of human goodness by attempting to distinguish for the first time between moral and intellectual virtue.

Kant made a considerable contribution towards grasping specifically and properly moral goodness when he pointed out that many excellent personal qualities are compatible with moral evil and can even enhance the virulence of evil, and that we must not be betrayed into taking their excellence for properly moral excellence. It is a good quality in a person to be able to deliberate calmly and coolly, but this is not intrinsically morally good, otherwise the evil of your crime would always be reduced, and never perfected, by planning it calmly; and yet its evil is undeniably perfected when you carry it out calmly and deliberately. Or consider the kind of self-control that a Iago has:[2] good as it is in the abstract to have such self-control, it is not good in Iago, who is a much

---

1. After all, Aristotle says, "The magnificent man is like an artist; for he can see what is fitting and spend large sums tastefully" (*Nichomachean Ethics,* 1122a, 34; Ross translation).

2. These words of his almost amount to an ode to the excellence of self-control: "'Tis in ourselves that we are thus or thus. Our bodies are our gardens, to the which our wills are gardeners; so that if we will plant nettles or sow lettuce, set hyssop and weed up thyme, supply it with one gender of herbs or distract it with many—either to have it sterile with idleness or manured with industry—why, the power and incorrigible authority of this lies in our wills. If the balance of our lives had not one scale of reason to poise another of sensuality, the blood and baseness of our natures would conduct us to most preposterous conclusions. But we have reason to cool our raging motions, our carnal stings, our unbitted lusts. . . " *(Othello,* I.iii).

more effective wrongdoer in virtue of his self-control. And so there arises for ethics the important task of finding those qualities of persons that are intrinsically and inalienably morally good, and always serve only to mitigate moral evil in a person, and are not "ambiguous" in relation to good and evil.[3] This is also important for our project: if we want to find the relation of selfhood and transcendence in possessing moral goodness, then we should look for it in that which is directly and properly morally good and not just morally good in some limited or derived respect.

Though it would exceed the limits of our study to try to develop this distinction fully, there is an aspect of it that is important for us to explore, namely the distinction between moral value and what we will call the "technical value of the human person." It seems to me that Karol Wojtyla refers to the same datum of technical value when he speaks of "personalist value,"[4] which we might have used interchangeably with "the technical value of the person," but which we will reserve for a somewhat different meaning to be introduced later. In making this distinction we will be led to understand the sense in which we can speak of the *transcendence* of the person who has and who grows in moral goodness.

In order to approach the technical value of the person we have only to return to the discussion of self-possession in Chapter 1. We know what it means to exercise our self-possession, to take possession of ourselves, to live as one who is *sui iuris,* who is an end in himself, and to act through ourselves. Now the more we do this, becoming, in the phrase of Oscar Wilde, the captain of our souls, then the more we grow in the technical value of the person. And so when we do not just repeat the opinions of others but form our own, when we refuse to put ourselves at the disposal of others in a servile way, but lead our own lives, when we do not live at the beck and call of each latest desire and craving that wells up in us but stand above them and exercise control over them: we exercise our self-possession and grow in this technical value. The more recollected we are, then, since recollection actualizes self-possession,

3. Von Hildebrand has made an important, though unjustly neglected, contribution towards carrying out this task in his *Graven Images: Substitutes for True Morality* (New York: David McKay, 1957), in which he examines all kinds of extra-moral values that bear some resemblance to moral values and are often confused with moral values. By working through his many concrete discriminations one can learn to refine and to develop one's sense for that which is specifically and properly moral.

4. Wojtyla, *The Acting Person* (Dordrecht: D. Reidel, 1979), Chapter 7, sec. 2. In what follows I am indebted to his discussion of personalist value.

as we saw, the more of this value we have. When Heidegger and others speak of the *authenticity* to which the human person is called, they seem to have in mind something very close to the technical value of the person; for to get free of conventional opinions, to lead one's own intellectual life and form one's own convictions, and to have the courage to be oneself and to profess them as one's own, is nothing but a certain perfection of personal self-possession. Just as there is the perfection of the eyes whereby they see well, and the perfection of the will whereby it is strong and resolute, and the perfection of the intelligence whereby it discriminates accurately,[5] so there is the perfection of persons whereby they possess themselves and stand in themselves and act through themselves; this perfection is the "bearer" of what I will call the technical value of the person.

Is the technical value of the person the same thing as moral value? It might at first seem so. For Socrates teaches that the epitome of moral excellence, justice, is that which makes the soul sound and healthy, and I just said that the technical value of the person is that which makes the person sound and healthy; and our "person," just like the Socratic "soul," is supposed to express that which is best and deepest in human nature. This technical value does not just make us good in some particular respect—good as a runner or good as a builder—but rather good as person, and this is just what many philosophers have said of moral value. And yet I hold that the technical value of the person *is not* moral value, and I think that the distinction is of the first importance for our purposes in this study, and indeed for any philosophical anthropology. We are especially interested in *a certain element of transcendence and participation* that characterizes our way of possessing moral value but not our way of possessing technical value.

1. The Kantian insight we were just discussing serves to show the distinction. A morally ugly insult can be delivered in a more or less authentic way, and the greater authenticity serves only to make it morally uglier. Authenticity, or strength of self-possession in persons, may have the function of simply perfecting the evil they think and do. Of course it also perfects the moral good they think and do; an act of gratitude, for example, is certainly weakened in its moral worth in propor-

---

5. These are examples of what von Hildebrand calls *technical value* (see his *Substitutes for True Morality,* 60–65). Whereas he limits himself to the technical values of different bodily senses and different spiritual faculties, I am trying here to find a technical value *of the human person as a whole.*

tion as it is performed in a merely conventional way, and is strengthened in proportion as it is performed as one's own act, authentically. Indeed, a *merely* conventional performance of the act of thanking may prevent it from having any moral worth at all. Nevertheless, this authenticity is morally ambiguous; it works on behalf of evil as well as of good. But that which is itself a form of moral goodness cannot serve the perfecting of evil in the morally good person; it would have to function always only as mitigating this evil. Therefore moral value is not the same as the technical value of the person.

2. One can distinguish this technical value from a corresponding technical disvalue, just as one distinguishes between moral value and moral disvalue; but the antithesis between value and disvalue has a very different sense in each case.

The technical disvalue seems to be ultimately only a lack of technical value. A person who is too dependent on his cravings and appetites, or too dependent on the opinions of his group, lacks a self-control or a self-possession that he as person ought to have, but he does not have a contrary opposite of self-control, or a negative counterpart of it. But what, one might object, if he wills to throw himself away as person; is this not a kind of negative counterpart to self-possession? Not at all; for such an act can be performed more or less authentically and thus may have considerable technical personal value. Of course it involves an irresponsible exercise of self-possession, but this need not hinder it from being a real and authentic exercise of self-possession. And so we hold that just as a will can fall away from the excellence of strength of will only by lacking strength, there being nothing more opposed to strength than weakness, which is a lack of strength, so a person can fall away from the fullness of self-possession only by lacking it. The traditional attempt to explain *malum* (bad) and *bonum* (good) in terms of *privatio* (privation) and *habitus* (having) seems to work quite well for technical value and disvalue.

But it does not work for moral value and disvalue. The evil of spitefulness or of cynicism, or of an arrogant scorn for the legitimate claims of others, is not just a lack, or even a conspicuous lack, of moral goodness—though it is that, too—but is antithetically opposed to goodness. Iago does not just lack moral goodness to an unusual degree, he is full of anti-goodness. Or consider the point just mentioned, irresponsibly disposing over oneself by throwing oneself away: this irresponsibility is not just the absence of responsibly disposing over oneself, which would be (to speak again with Kierkegaard) failing to will to be the self that one is; no, in addition to all such absence it is the opposite, the contrary opposite of such responsible self-disposition. I conclude, then, that the antithesis between positive and negative could not have one character with technical value and disvalue, and have another, more sharply antithetical character with moral value and disvalue, if they really were ultimately the same value/disvalue; therefore they differ.

3. We are entirely responsible for our moral value and disvalue, but we are not always responsible in the same way for technical value and disvalue. Thus there are persons who through their makeup are susceptible to being overly influenced by strong personalities; they may bitterly regret this weakness in their self-possession, but they just cannot help seeing things at certain moments too much with eyes of others. Or consider those persons on whom only a little pressure needs to be brought to bear before they "lose their head"; they too suffer a defect in self-possession, and so also in the technical value of the person, and yet they may really be incapable of ridding themselves of the defect. But one could never be helpless like this in the face of some moral deficiency in oneself, deploring it without being able to do anything at all about it. Perhaps we can say it like this, that moral value seems to belong to the person as person and so to be rooted in the freedom of the person, whereas technical value seems to be in part rooted in the psychic makeup and psychic soundness of a person and thus to depend in part on factors somewhat outside of personhood.

2. The transcendence achieved by persons in possessing moral value

An act has technical value in virtue of a certain relation to the person who performs it. Technical value comes from the act being the person's own, really deriving from him and from no one else. Moral value, besides needing this relation to the acting person, also comes from a certain objective factor that does not belong to the idea of technical value at all. Moral value comes from an act being in harmony with the goods to which it is directed, from giving them their due and "fulfilling justice" towards them, as we have seen. Thus if there is to be moral goodness in my thanking, I have to be mindful that it is only fitting and right to thank a benefactor and that I owe my benefactor in justice some expression of gratitude. But this concern with a fundamental justice is no part of the idea of authenticity or of any other aspect of technical value. Of course it is true that my self-possession remains stunted as long as I have no

interest in value and in what is due to it, living only for the merely agreeable, and that it is exercised and developed in a value-responding relation to being; to show this was the main point of the previous chapter.
And yet it remains the case that value response belongs to the idea of
moral value in a way in which it does not belong to the idea of the
technical value of the person. This is why the cultivating of my authenticity has a potential for egocentrically enclosing me in myself that is
quite foreign to the cultivating of moral value.

And yet the moral value arising in and through a value-responding
relation to the world is not reducible to the correspondence of my acting
with the demands of value. It is not like the legality of an action, which
is nothing other than the agreement of my action with some legal pre-
scription. When a person is enriched with moral worth he gains a qualitative fullness in himself which, though based on a right relation to value
and impossible without such a relation, is itself much more than any
such right relation.[6] I want now to call attention to a certain transcendence we achieve in possessing moral worth; corresponding to the transcendence of value response is the transcendence in the moral value
born of value response.

1. The technical value of the person seems to be in a certain sense
more "immanent in" persons than does moral value. In experiencing
this value we experience persons as beings who possess themselves, but
in experiencing moral value we encounter more, we encounter a content
of its own, something that is not simply transparent to the structure of
self-possession in persons. Of course we cannot experience the moral
value of a person without experiencing the person who has it and experiencing the value as a certain radiance of the person. As I have tried
to show elsewhere,[7] value qualities have such a dependency on the valuable being that they can never be apprehended through themselves but
always only on the basis of apprehending the valuable being. And yet
value qualities differ greatly in the way they express the being that has
value, as is shown precisely in the present discussion of personalist and
moral value. If we consider the moral value of reverence towards being,
of faithfulness to everything we have grasped as right and true, or the
moral value of loyalty to a friend, then it cannot be denied that in experi-

6. Scheler showed this brilliantly in *Formalismus in der Ethik und die materiale
Wertethik* (Bern and Munich: Francke Verlag, 1980), 173–210. English: *Formalism in
Ethics* (Evanston: Northwestern University Press, 1973), 163–202.

7. Crosby, "Are Good and Being Really Convertible? A Phenomenological Inquiry,"
The New Scholasticism, LVII/4 (1983), esp. section 2.

encing these values in another we do not just experience the self-posses-sion of the other, rather we also experience the other as enriched with "contents" irreducible to the structure of personal self-possession. We clearly experience the other, not as having a goodness all his own, but as "participating" in a realm of truth and goodness "above" his personal being.[8]

Perhaps I can clarify this way of distinguishing between technical value and moral value by using von Hildebrand's distinction between "ontological" and "qualitative" value. One of the things he says by way of distinguishing them coincides exactly with what I am here trying to say by way of distinguishing personalist and moral value.

> Moral values [to which von Hildebrand refers as examples of qualitative values] present themselves much more as something of their own, as some-thing more independent of their bearer and of the attitude which incarnates them than does the preciousness of the human person [an ontological value] with respect to the human person. The very fact that we are able to form a concept of the different moral values, that we have a name for generosity, veracity, humility, and so forth, testifies to this character of the qualitative values. We have no proper name to characterize the ontological value of the human person as such, but we must instead refer to the being which incar-nates this value. The nature of generosity or veracity or humility has a full *eidos* of its own. It is something definite which allows us to substantize

---

8. This is frequently expressed in the Bible, as in this passage from Isaiah 58:6–10:
> This, rather, is the fasting that I wish: releasing those bound unjustly,
>> untying the thongs of the yoke;
> Setting free the oppressed, breaking every yoke;
> Sharing your bread with the hungry, sheltering the oppressed and the homeless;
> Clothing the naked when you see them,
>> and not turning your back on your own.

Then he proceeds to speak about the goodness that arises in the one who does these things:
> Then your light shall break forth like the dawn,
>> and your wound shall quickly be healed;
> Your vindication shall go before you, and the glory of the Lord
>> shall be your rear guard.

And a little below he says:
> Then light shall rise for you in the darkness,
>> and the gloom shall become for you like midday. . . .

It seems to me that the mysterious light of which the prophet speaks can be at least glimpsed in our moral experience. And difficult as it may be to say exactly what we see in seeing this light, it is in any case certain that we do not just see the structure of self-possession in the other.

these values; whereas the ontological value of the person resists such a procedure and forces us to refer constantly to the person himself.

This becomes especially clear if we compare the ontological value of the will to the moral value of a *good* will. The moral value which we face when somebody refuses to enrich himself by betraying another person, or when he withstands torture rather than tell a lie, clearly differs from the ontological value of the free will as such. The ontological value of the will receives its *forma,* so to speak, from the will, and we have no other possibility than to refer to the will in order to distinguish this ontological value from other ontological values. The moral value of honesty, on the contrary, which shines forth from the will is in itself something clearly shaped, possessing a certain independence, having an essence of its own.[9]

The ontological value . . . is so closely connected with the respective being (in our example the human person) that it is impossible to describe the relation as a participation in the value; with moral goodness, however, we have a natural tendency to admit that the act of forgiving *participates* in the moral value of generosity and mercy. The ontological value is immanent to the being; but moral values transcend the being which is endowed with them.[10]

This element of transcendence and participation in moral goodness is really not so surprising if one recalls how moral value comes to be in a person. As we just saw, I become good as person not by turning in upon myself but by going beyond myself and affirming the objectively good and worthy according to what is due to it in justice. But in thus transcending myself toward value, do I not participate in the world of value? How can the value thus arising in me be entirely immanent in me, existing only as a function of my own perfection, when I gain this value by participating in a realm experienced by me as above and beyond myself?[11]

2. But the transcendence of value response, of course, goes only so far in explaining why morally good persons seem to participate in something above themselves. Let us try to go a little farther in sounding the depths of this participation. It seems to show itself in the fact that, as Kierkegaard understood so deeply, as person I am always only at the beginning of my moral existence, and that nothing is so absurd as the

9. Von Hildebrand, *Ethics* (Chicago: Franciscan Herald Press, 1972), 132–3.

10. Ibid., 138.

11. One sees, by the way, how misleading it can be to conceive of moral goodness as the health of the soul, in direct analogy with the health of the body, as the Greek philosophers constantly do. If one makes too much of this analogy then one is almost sure to lose sight of this so mysterious element of transcendence and participation in moral goodness.

idea of persons being finished in their moral existence, so that they have nothing more to become morally.[12] It has often been said in Western philosophy ever since it was first said by the Greeks, that the philosopher is one who loves wisdom without being able to possess it definitively and finally, that the philosopher can only reach out longingly for it and try to participate in it, and can never come to an end in striving for it. This seems also to be the way in which we are related to moral goodness: a human person who is finished in his moral striving is as absurd as a philosopher who is finished in his growth in wisdom. By contrast, the technical value of the person, when cultivated apart from moral value, has nothing of this inexhaustibility; while it can probably always be still greater than it is, it does not present itself as having a fullness to which we can only be related in the way of participation.

3. The following reflection leads us perhaps even more deeply into this mysterious element of participation in moral goodness. When we deeply experience the value of a morally outstanding person or a morally outstanding action, a certain awe-inspiring greatness seems to break forth and a mysterious solemnity seems to encompass the person and his action; he seems to take on a worthiness that bursts the contingencies of this world and intimates for him a fuller, more enduring existence beyond this world. Kant witnesses to this when he says that the moral existence of the person reveals that his destiny "is not restricted to the conditions and limits of this life but reaches into the infinite."[13] Newman expresses with great intuitive power this "intimation of immortality" in moral goodness.

> I mean, when one sees some excellent person, whose graces we know, whose kindliness, affectionateness, tenderness, and generosity,—when we see him dying (let him have lived ever so long; I am not supposing a premature death; let him live out his days), the thought is forced upon us with a sort of surprise; "Surely, he is not to die yet; he has not yet had any opportunity of exercising duly those excellent gifts with which God has endowed him." Let him have lived seventy or eighty years, yet it seems as if he had done nothing at all, and his life were scarcely begun. . . .
>
> Men there are, who, in a single moment of their lives, have shown a superhuman height and majesty of mind which it would take ages for them to employ on its proper objects, and, as it were, to exhaust; and who by such

---

12. This is one of the things that he seems to want to say in his reflections on Lessing in his *Concluding Unscientific Postscript* (Princeton: Princeton University Press, 1941), esp. 67–113.

13. For the entire passage in Kant see our last footnote in the previous chapter.

passing flashes, like rays of the sun, and the darting of lightening, give token of their immortality. . . .

There is something in moral truth and goodness, in faith, in firmness . . . in meekness, in courage, in loving-kindness, to which this world's circumstances are quite unequal, for which the longest life is insufficient, which makes the highest opportunities of this world disappointing, which must burst the prison of this world to have its appropriate range. So that when a good man dies, one is led to say, "He has not half showed himself, he has had nothing to exercise him; his days are gone like a shadow, and he is withered like grass."[14]

By contrast the technical value of the person does not seem to have this awe-inspiring greatness, or to be full of mysterious "intimations of immortality"; insofar as persons have this value they remain as it were within themselves, showing forth the self-possession that they have as persons, and they are not drawn beyond themselves to participate in a higher world.

4. But perhaps nothing shows so convincingly the moment of participation in moral value as its religious significance, which also serves to reinforce the contrast between moral value and technical value. It is a question of a religious significance which presents itself not to just anyone but only to a religiously awakened person, though not only to Christians.

Most believers in God understand that in becoming morally bad they estrange themselves from God. In being a moral failure, a moral disgrace, I do not just do what is irrelevant to my religious existence, but my moral failure has consequences for how I stand towards God. Believers never think that they can come to their prayer fresh from some crime, and, without repenting of the crime, without atoning for their guilt, hope to be heard in their prayer. Believers never think that God does not care about our crimes, as if their moral disvalue were simply irrelevant to our relation to God. All believers understand that our crimes and our guilt "displease" God, estranging us from Him and putting us in need of being reconciled with Him. I do not speak here as a Christian, saying what can only be understood on the basis of Christian faith; I am saying nothing Plato did not know and teach (as in his critique of Homeric religion). And the idea that lies so deep in our religious consciousness is not just that the commission of crimes violates divine laws, but that our

14. John Henry Newman, *Parochial and Plain Sermons* (London: Rivingtons, 1870), IV, 217–219.

moral unworthiness or disgracefulness cannot stand before the holiness of God—that there is an anti-holiness in moral evil that can only create enmity with the all-holy God.

Equally deep in our religious consciousness is the complementary idea that moral worthiness, moral dignity, moral greatness also affect our relation to God, but this time affect it positively, tending to put us in God's "favor," enabling us to become holy, and lending support, so to say, to all that we strive for through religious cult. This idea stands at the center of Rudolf Otto's analysis in *The Idea of the Holy*. He shows that while the holy is not simply reducible to the morally worthy, as Kant had thought, it nevertheless contains the morally worthy as an indispensable moment of itself, so that whoever is morally reprobate cannot be holy, and whoever is morally worthy is on the way to becoming holy. Being morally worthy, then, shares in the religious transcendence of being holy.

Notice that technical value is not full of religious significance like moral value. No religious person thinks that strength of self-possession by itself affects our relation to God for the better, any more than he thinks that bodily strength by itself affects it for the better. There is, then, a religious transcendence in moral value entirely lacking in technical value.

3. The interrelations of selfhood and transcendence in the goodness of morally worthy persons

One might have thought, considering the matter in the abstract, that being morally good, because of this moment of transcendence and participation, is something foreign to the human person, that it has no real root in the person, and is capable of being connected only extrinsically with the person. And so one might have thought that, of the two, moral value and the technical value of the person, only the latter can really belong to persons and be proper to them. One might have thought all this in the same abstract way in which one might have thought that moral imperatives, given their imperious binding force and their independence from the arbitrariness of the person, must be a cause of violence to the person. When, however, we consult more closely and more concretely our moral experience, we find our abstract expectations overturned.

1. One of the points of contrast that we made between moral value and technical value serves also to show that the former has a closer relation to our self-possession than does the latter. We said that technical

value and disvalue are to some extent *given to us* and are not subject to our freedom as moral value and disvalue are, depending as they do, at least in part, on our psychic makeup. We mentioned some instances of personalist disvalue that may be rooted in some psychic brokenness of a person and so be entirely beyond a person's control; but there are, of course, no such instances of moral disvalue. With this we do not deny the gift-character of all deep moral growth, which Scheler so stressed; but the given's of my psychic being and the gifts and graces received in my moral being are very different things.

It is for our present purpose highly significant that technical value, which centers around the idea of self-possession, is owned by us less perfectly than moral value, which does not in the same way center around the idea of self-possession; that moral value, for all its transcendence and participation, is more deeply rooted in our freedom than is technical value, which is a thoroughly immanent perfection of human persons.

2. While striving for the technical value of the person, it is entirely possible to achieve something of the inwardness of conscience. Suppose that I face a difficult decision, and that I am bombarded with all manner of conflicting advice from various people. I might withdraw into myself, saying something like, "But what do I, I myself, think about the alternatives I face? Enough of all these many voices—what does my own voice say? I can hardly hear it for all the clamor around me." With this I recollect myself in a certain way, entering into myself, though I may be aiming at nothing more than having my decision as my own, and may not mean to ask the question of good and evil with regard to my alternatives. But now let us suppose that I begin to try to visualize the moral value or disvalue of my alternatives, and to ask whether with any of them I might compromise myself morally; let us suppose that I realize the moral indecency of one of them, and realize how seriously I would defile myself by choosing it. No one who sympathetically feels himself into my conscience can fail to see: my interiority is immeasurably deepened as a result of turning like this towards moral good and evil, and I am enabled to recollect myself far more deeply than when I was merely concerned with my authenticity. By looking at my alternatives in moral terms I am not drawn off of myself in a heteronomous way, but am rather driven more deeply into myself and made to stand more in myself. That element of participation and transcendence in moral value seems, then, to be entirely congenial with the selfhood and subjectivity of the moral subject.

3. We can dig deeper and find the reason for this congeniality. It is one of the most elementary moral truths that in being morally good, human persons become good *as human persons;* they become good, not in some particular, "regional" respect, not good as carpenter, as surgeon, as musician, but good as human persons. Why would we say that these particular, or regional "goodnesses" are not forms of moral goodness? Precisely because they are particular and do not encompass the whole person so as to amount to *the goodness of the person.*[15] Socrates presupposed this in teaching that justice, which is for him the epitome of all moral excellence, makes the soul of the just person healthy and sound. Plato and Aristotle go beyond Socrates by trying to distinguish the parts of the soul and the right order among them which makes for moral excellence, and in this way they continue to understand moral excellence as an encompassing human excellence, forever to be distinguished from all regional goodnesses.

It seems that this encompassing (as opposed to regional) character of moral value can be found in our moral consciousness no less than the selfhood from which we took our point of departure in this study (Chapter 1). It is elementary that persons are ends in themselves and wholes of their own, as we saw; but it is really no less elementary that they become decent or indecent human beings according to what they make of themselves in their moral lives.

Our thought is not exactly that a morally good way of life is *good for man;* that is a distinct idea, which finds its own place below; the present point, that in being morally good the human person becomes good and worthy as person, is as such not a statement about what is beneficial for the person.

It is this simple human character of moral goodness, this fact that it belongs to the "vocation" of every human being, which explains why, as has often been observed, there is no such thing as a special expertise of ethical knowledge, nothing analogous to the special expertise of the carpenter, surgeon, or musician. Moral knowledge is available to all human beings in virtue of the task they all have of being decent, worthy human beings. There is no such thing as a body of moral knowledge unknown to everyone except a few specialists. Indeed, elementary moral knowl-

---

15. In a particularly convincing way Martin Rhonheimer brings this out in his "Gut und böse oder richtig und falsch—was unterscheidet das Sittliche?" in Thomas (ed.), *Ethik der Leistung* (Herford: Busse-Seewald Verlag, 1988), 47–76.

edge seems to be given to us in so intimate a way that we do not learn it at a definite point in time but seem always to have known it, and can never really forget it. This does not, of course, mean that everyone is capable of doing *philosophical ethics,* nor does it exclude the existence of expertise in ethical theory; but the ethicist only explores philosophically, but cannot materially add to, the pre-philosophical ethical wisdom of which every morally decent human being is capable. There is no more a body of moral knowledge reserved for a few specialists than there is a living of the moral life possible only to a specially trained elite.

It follows from this simple human character of all moral excellences that we as moral subjects should never become onesidedly preoccupied with the good results of our actions, becoming self-forgetful, for then we are liable to overlook our task of becoming a good and worthy human being in all of our moral action.[16] With this I enlarge a little on the personalist critique of consequentialism begun at the end of Chapter 3.5.[17]

As for moral disvalue and moral evil, we have to say that, insofar as a person has it, he or she is a failure as a human being. Such persons do not just lack what it would be desirable to have, but fail in their basic vocation as persons, as von Hildebrand puts it.[18] Socrates said that the soul of the unjust man is sick, like a body eaten up with leprosy or cancer.

And so it will hardly be reasonable to say that moral goodness, because of its element of transcendence and participation discussed in the previous section, is something foreign to personal selfhood, something that draws persons off themselves, inflicting heteronomy on them. To say this is to say almost the opposite of the truth. If we become good and worthy as persons by being morally good, then moral goodness, far from being something foreign to us as persons, belongs to the innermost existence of the human person. Instead of saying that moral goodness by its transcendence is harmful to selfhood, we should say that our selfhood is a transcendent selfhood; it is a selfhood that does not begin and end

16. Rhonheimer argues convincingly (64–72) that everyone who acts according to utilitarian, or consequentialist, principles, is open to this charge of self-forgetfulness.

17. Perhaps no one has unmasked this ethical self-forgetfulness as relentlessly as Kierkegaard in his *Concluding Unscientific Postscript,* Book II, Part II, chapter 1, "The Task of Becoming Subjective."

18. Von Hildebrand, *Ethics,* Chapter 15.

with selfhood, but is what it is as selfhood only through a certain transcendence and participation.

It is very different with the technical value of the person in the sense of mere authenticity, such as it might exist in amoral persons; this value does nothing to make them good and worthy persons. Even though authentic persons have developed themselves as persons by developing their self-possession in a certain technical way and have gained a goodness that belongs precisely to their personhood, they can still not be said to be *good and worthy as persons,* for this "justifying" goodness, as we might call it, is gained only in moral goodness. Or if we insist on saying that merely authentic persons are good as persons, then we have at least to notice that their goodness is a kind of technical goodness, and that we speak of the morally good persons as good persons in a fundamentally different sense, and in a far fuller and more proper sense.

We are now in a position to understand better the fact observed above, namely the fact that the interiority of conscience is so greatly deepened when one passes beyond a concern merely with one's authenticity and becomes concerned with one's moral worthiness.

We are also in a position to notice the emergence of a self-possession possible only in the moral life and impossible on the level of mere authenticity. If moral goodness makes me good as person, then I strive to become what I am when I strive to become morally worthy; but this is to strive to take possession of myself. Thus there is a certain self-possession that *results from* becoming morally worthy. The self-possession of technical value does not result from this value; rather this value results from self-possession, being nothing but the value of a certain technical self-possession.

4. In having moral goodness I am not only enabled to become what I as person ought to be; I also gain something that is supremely *good for me* and that secures my ultimate well-being, indeed secures for me a kind of salvation, which can be understood as salvation even apart from Christian revelation. This sense of an ultimate good for me is contained in the intimations of immortality which, as we saw, I have when I experience deeply moral goodness. In a directly parallel way moral evil not only estranges me from my vocation as human person; it is also harmful for me, it subverts my ultimate well-being, wounding me in my innermost self. This is the truth expressed by Socrates when he said that it is better for man to suffer than to commit injustice, by which he meant that there is no non-moral evil that harms man as grievously and as ulti-

mately as does moral evil. It is also the truth, or rather one of the truths, that he expresses by speaking of the just soul as healthy and the unjust soul as sick and diseased.

Moral goodness, then, for all its transcendence, is nothing foreign to me, but is rather, as the principle of my supreme well-being, supremely congenial to me. It is in fact far more congenial to me than the technical value of the person, for the person who has only technical value and whose excellence as person consists in nothing more than his authenticity, gains nothing of that supreme good for himself that comes from being morally good, nor of the self-possession that comes from the same source.

Here we find the person again exercising a fundamentally new dimension of self-possession; one can be said to possess oneself in one all-important way by possessing that which supremely benefits oneself. This self-possession is impossible on the level of the technical value of the person, which is not beneficial for man in the way in which moral value is beneficial.

All of the congeniality of moral goodness with the selfhood of the person which we are exploring in the present and in the previous point, was perhaps presupposed in our previous reflection on the congeniality of moral imperatives with the selfhood of the person. Why do I as moral subject wound myself so grievously in ignoring a moral call? Why do I flourish as person in fulfilling it? Because I become morally bad in ignoring it, and morally good in fulfilling it. We said that when persons enter into their conscience, they have to do with themselves and dispose over themselves in an unsurpassable way; this is because in conscience they choose between being good and being bad, that is, choose between being a good person and being a bad one, between salvation and damnation. We can now understand this better; we now see that the fulfillment of a moral imperative does not draw us off ourselves in a heteronomous way *for the very reason* that it raises for us the moral question, letting us become morally good, and all that is implied for us in this, in the fulfilling of it.

The reader will now understand better a remark I made back in Chapter 2.6 when discussing the dignity of the human person. I said that this dignity relativizes into a kind of insignificance those extraordinary excellences found in a few human beings, such as gifts of genius. But at the same time I said that personal dignity does not do the same relativizing work on the moral character of persons; we cannot say that it does not much matter whether human beings are good or evil as long as they are all persons having the dignity of persons. Our discussion in the last pages explains this. Persons are failures as persons by being morally indecent, and they suffer the worst possible harm to themselves by doing wrong. It is almost as if the tables are here turned, so that moral good and evil, far from being overshadowed by the dignity of persons, even tends to overshadow this dignity. Needless to say, this overshadowing is not to be understood in the sense that persons are only specimens of moral excellences and for this reason are failures as persons through their moral failures. I was in Chapter 2.6 strenuously opposing the idea that persons are specimens, and I am not now making any concessions to this idea. We will have occasion at the end of this chapter to see that the incommunicability of persons is revealed in a particular way by their moral worthiness, and that there is a profound material contradiction in the very idea of a mere specimen of moral qualities.

5. There is another aspect of the selfhood of the person which is expressed by moral goodness. Let us assume for a moment, counter to fact, that persons are capable only of particular, regional goodnesses, and that whoever strives for a more encompassing goodness can do nothing more than possess as many regional goodnesses as possible, that is, they can do nothing more than try to be good as carpenter, good as surgeon, good as musician, all at the same time. This means that they would lack any goodness simply as person. But then they would be abolished as persons; for if they are capable only of regional goodnesses (however many of them), then they must be only partial beings. Since they exist as beings of their own, as totalities in their own right, and never as mere parts, then they must be capable of some goodness that is not just regional, they must be capable of some all-encompassing goodness. They must be such that, when we ask for that which makes them good as persons, we get a different answer than we get when we ask about some particular, regional goodness. Moral goodness, then, in its power of making the person a good person, bears witness to the fundamental antithesis between "part" and "person," and reflects in the axiological order the selfhood previously studied in the ontological order.

This axiological expression of personhood becomes still more convincing if one considers the fact that each human person is called not to the one or the other but to all possible moral excellences. It makes no moral sense for me to say that I will limit myself, say, to justice, declining any interest in courage, or generosity, leaving these for others. Such

a division of moral labor is recognized as absurd by every morally awakened person, who is aware that the basic human vocation comprises all
possible moral excellences.[19]

6. How can this congeniality of moral goodness with the human person be experienced from within, how in other words can it be verified
subjectively? One of our answers is: in the experience of being deeply
happy in and through participating in moral goodness.[20]

One source of deep happiness for us is the world of value "outside"
of us; by participating in a value-responding way, we are happy in it.
This is the source of happiness I had in mind in Chapter 6.3.6. But there
is another source of happiness, of which Aristotle primarily speaks in
his philosophy of *eudaemonia,* namely the value and goodness *in ourselves.* We can be deeply happy (as distinct from being merely satisfied
or content) only by being good, and especially by being morally worthy.
It is not of course as if we made our goodness an object and then were
happy in admiring it; in this case our own goodness would not be an
essentially different source of happiness from the goodness in the world
around us in which we participate. The goodness of a happy person seems
to be experienced not objectively but subjectively, not from without but
from within, and to radiate or to diffuse itself through his consciousness, letting a kind of exuberant joy spring up in his innermost parts. We
quite recognize that this joy has other sources besides the goodness of
the happy person, sources outside of the person; we only say that one
source of it, which is particularly important for explaining its springing
up in the center of the person, is the goodness of the happy person himself. Who is there who, understanding something of this, would still say
that moral goodness, because of the way it transcends the selfhood of
the person, is foreign to the person? How can one of the main principles
of our deepest happiness be suspected of heteronomy?

One will also notice the deep affectivity that belongs to this happiness which is born of moral worthiness. I just spoke of the joy springing
up in the deeply happy person: what is this joy if not a profound affective experience? How can a person be deeply happy without being
affectively alive? But it is well known that in certain forms of affectivity

---

19. See von Hildebrand, *Ethics,* Chapter 15.

20. I say "deeply happy" with the intention of indicating that I mean by happiness
something fundamentally different from contentment. I mean to contrast happiness with
unhappiness in something like the way in which Scheler contrasts *Seligkeit* and
Verzweiflung in the profound passage in his *Formalismus in der Ethik,* 344–5. English:
Formalism in Ethics, 342–44.

the most intimate self of the person quickens, as we observed above (Chapter 6.3.7). It would not be difficult to show, though I will not attempt it here, that the different kinds of moral badness, whether in the form of pride or of concupiscence, inhibit in various ways the deeper affectivity in which the real self of the person lives. This would let us see again the complete congeniality of moral worthiness with personal selfhood.

Needless to say, the possession only of the technical value of the person has no power to release such affectivity, has no power to confer happiness and the experience of selfhood that goes with being happy. We have already mentioned that a person might exercise no little authenticity in the act of despairingly throwing himself away. It seems that the technical value of the person, considered in itself, is just as ambiguous with regard to happiness and unhappiness, as it is with regard to good and evil.

7. At the beginning of this study we spoke of the fundamental structure of self-possession, and then of the power which persons have, as a result of their self-possession, of acting through themselves. Now we call attention to the power of the deeply happy person, who is happy because of his goodness, to act through himself.

Let us distinguish two senses of the "motive" of our acting. There is motive in the sense of an object outside of us that elicits our acting, and there is motive in the sense of something *in* the person out of which he acts. Suppose someone helps his friend in need. The friend and his need form the motive for helping in the first sense of motive. The love for his friend that lives in the one who helps is the motive for helping in the second sense. We might express this second sense by saying that he helped his friend "out of love" for him.[21]

Now the deep happiness of which I am speaking, the happiness born of moral goodness, is a motive for our acting in this second sense. Scheler reflected profoundly on the spiritual resources for acting that only the happy person *(der selige Mensch)* has; he even went so far as to say that only this happy person is really capable of acting morally well. He challenged the usual idea that happiness only comes *after* morally good action as its reward, and showed that it also comes *before* morally good action as its source.[22] And this much seems indeed to be true in Scheler,

---

21. This distinction has been made by von Hildebrand, *Moralia* (Stuttgart: Kohlhammer, 1980), 217–19, as well as by Scheler, *Formalismus in der Ethik*, 346 (*Formalism in Ethics*, 344–45).

22. Scheler, ibid., 349–51 (English: 348–50).

that the happy person shows an exuberance in acting, a freedom and generosity and readiness to initiate, which flow from his happiness and do not just lead to it. It is as if the diffusivity of good, expressed in the axiom *bonum est diffusivum sui,* becomes the inner principle of the acting of the deeply happy person, who is happy because he is good. Now in understanding something of this exuberance in acting, we see the selfhood of the happy person in it; we see that the happy person has a heightened power of acting through himself. It is clear that persons who cultivate nothing more than their own authenticity and never transcend themselves so as to become morally good, know nothing of this power of acting.

It would be interesting to work out this heightened power of acting by contrasting it with other ways in which our power of acting can be enhanced. When, for example, I am not deeply happy, when I am instead in despair, then I may break out into feverish activity. Perhaps I want to justify myself through certain accomplishments, or simply to escape from the pain of despairing, according to the saying of Carlyle, "work and do not despair." My power of acting is heightened indeed, but not in such a way that I exercise my self-possession more perfectly and act more perfectly through myself. We have already spoken of an obsessive activity that eats up the self-presence in which the recollected person dwells and which is one main enemy of recollected subjectivity.

I now call attention to an extremely significant contrast between our present result and one of our previous results. Above we said that technical value of the person perfects moral value; an act has to be a person's own before it can take on all the moral value proper to it. Now we are saying something like this, that moral value perfects technical value; the structure of self-possession and selfhood, which is perfected in a technical way when one cultivates nothing more than authenticity, can flourish fully only if persons transcend themselves in moral goodness, aiming at more than authenticity and personalist value. Selfhood grows to its fullest proportions in the transcendent selfhood of morally worthy persons.

We need a term to mark this excellence of self-possession born of moral worthiness, and yet we do not want to use the term, "the technical value of the person," which should continue to express that excellence of self-possession that does not presuppose any moral worthiness. Let us, then, take the term "personalist value," mentioned above (it might have been used interchangeably with "the technical value of the person"), and let us determine it to express the excellence of the fullness of self-possession found in deeply happy persons.[23]

8. We are now in a position to resume the analysis of recollection and to mark two distinct forms of it. There is the recollection in which I achieve through my self-possession only the technical value of the person; and there is the recollection that presupposes moral worthiness in the recollected person and in which I achieve through my self-possession the greater value that we now call personalist value. We could call the former technical recollection, and the latter transcendent recollection. From the time I first spoke about recollection I often had in mind this latter form of it, possible only in one who participates in moral goodness.

We had occasion above (Chapter 6.3.8) to take notice of the *virtus unitiva* of value, of the unifying power which it exercises over persons by binding them together into community. We also saw that this unifying power is exercised in one and the same person: I can be unified from within through my relation to good, or in other words I can be recollected through this relation. Now this good in which I am recollected is not only some good outside of me that I love but also some good within me. All deeper forms of recollection seem to presuppose the moral worthiness of which we have been speaking in the present chapter; indeed, they seem to be ways of experiencing one's participation in moral goodness, or of experiencing something flowing directly from it. Just as all deeper happiness flows from it, so does all deeper recollection. The enhanced power of acting through oneself which I just pointed out in happy persons gives evidence of this deeper recollection.

It follows yet again that the transcendence of moral value is nothing foreign to our selfhood but rather serves to reveal our selfhood as a transcendent selfhood. That which recollects us deeply belongs to our personal selfhood, is absolutely congenial with it; if the recollecting principle is signed by transcendence in the sense explained, then so is our personal selfhood.

9. Let us return to that fundamental value which we studied in Chapter 2.6, the value human persons have through their incommunicable selfhood. The reader will recall that we distinguished two principal forms of this value: the dignity that a person has as person and that is in a sense

---

23. Though I have the term from Wojtyla, I do not claim to be interpreting him with the special meaning I have just given to it.

common to all persons, and the lovableness that a person has as this particular person and that distinguishes one person from another. In either case we have to do with a value that is not acquired but is given with one's very being as incommunicable person. Let us now inquire how moral value stands in relation to this *ontological value of the person,* as we might call it by way of marking its distinction from moral value. The expression, ontological value of the person, comprises both of the forms of personal value just distinguished.

It is not difficult to mark some fundamental differences between moral and ontological value. Moral value can become greater in a person, or become weaker; ontological value, being given with the very being of a person, does not seem to wax and wane like this. Moral value has a contrary opposite, which is moral disvalue, or moral evil; the ontological value of the person has no such contrary opposite, no negative counterpart. A being can get no farther from ontological value than simply lacking it (by which we mean not being deprived of it but only lacking it); there is no such thing as negative dignity or anti-dignity in a being. Of particular interest for us is the fact that the moral value of a person is not incommunicably the person's own in the way in which his ontological value as person is incommunicably his own; the transcendence of which we have spoken above means that moral value always surpasses the person who participates in it and that it can, therefore, in some way be participated in by other persons. Of course, each person has his or her own moral goodness, otherwise one could not explain how each has moral goodness in a different way, to a different degree, and mixed in different proportions with moral badness, nor could one explain how the loss of goodness in one person does not remove goodness from any other. And yet there is something about moral value, or rather about its transcendence, which makes us say that it is not each person's own in the sense in which the ontological value of the person is each person's own.

But for all these differences between these two dimensions of value in persons, they also form a unity that is very revealing for our present inquiry. Moral worthiness in a person seems in a way to *actualize* his or her ontological value as person, which is why we can recognize the ontological value far more distinctly in a morally worthy person. Perhaps we cannot recognize it at all without some understanding of the moral vocation of the person. Moral evil seems to annul this ontological value, or at least to tend to annul it. What serves to manifest more convincingly this ontological value in a person than the reverence, the truthfulness, the faithfulness of the person? Moral worthiness, then, takes up the ontological value, as it were, and perfects it. This is why no one who is generous and faithful and reverent seems to us to be a mere specimen of these moral excellences, or of humanity; no such person seems to us to be swallowed up by the immensity of space-time. On the contrary, nothing is so powerful in reversing the appearance of being an infinitesimally small speck and in coming to see another as if the only person, than to catch sight of his moral worthiness.[24] It seems that the same incommunicability that underlies the ontological value of the person is also expressed and actualized in moral worthiness.[25] This implies the deep congeniality of transcendent moral value with personal selfhood.

We can say the same thing from the point of view not of the ontological value of the person but of moral value itself. Moral value becomes individualized in each morally worthy person, so that each has moral value in his own unrepeatable way. We observed above (Chapter 2.5) that each person has his own way of being a human person, each being, as it were, a subspecies of human personhood that can exist only in himself. Perhaps it is the same with moral value, each person being a subspecies of moral goodness all his own. We quoted Maritain (Chapter 2.7) as saying that the saints precisely do not always act on a maxim that can be made a universal law for all persons but that each characteristically acts on a maxim all his own. Do we not find that to the uniquely personal maxim on which each of them acts, there corresponds the uniquely personal form of their moral goodness? Here we have the reason why there can be no such thing as a mere specimen of moral goodness: persons impress their personal incommunicability on their moral goodness, even as their moral goodness expresses their personal incommunicability. With specimens, by contrast, the universal that is instantiated bypasses, as it were, the incommunicable being of the specimen, or better, absorbs, or tends to absorb, this being into its universal self.

It follows that our account of the ontological value of persons given in Chapter 2.6 is incomplete, and would become erroneous if presented as complete. It has to be completed by some mention of the moral voca-

---

24. The famous words of Kant—I quoted them at the end of the last chapter—about the moral law and how it reveals a certain infinity in the human person, could easily be adapted to moral worthiness, which reveals the same infinity. I have shown in Chapter 2.3 that this infinity is most closely related to personal incommunicability.

25. One will of course not understand this if one thinks of moral worthiness simply in terms of *conformity with moral norms;* one has instead to think of a certain *qualitative plenitude in persons* which we express with the names of the different moral excellences.

tion of human persons.[26] Perhaps we could say it like this: above we approached the value of persons as a given, now we approach it as a task. Or: above we approached it *immanently* by trying to understand it through the incommunicable selfhood of persons; now we approach it more *transcendently* by trying to understand it through the moral vocation of persons. These are not two unrelated sources of the value of persons; if once we understand that our incommunicable selfhood is a transcendent selfhood, we will understand the unity of immanence and transcendence in personal value, and we will know how to recognize one and the same value under its different aspects. This unity gives new evidence of how congenial moral value, in all its transcendence, is related to the selfhood of human persons.

10. Throughout this study we have been sensitive to the danger of affirming selfhood in such a way as to undermine the bonds that unite persons in community. We have tried to bring to light not a monadic selfhood but a selfhood open to interpersonal union. This is undoubtedly the selfhood that emerges from our discussion of moral value. In most forms of moral excellence we are directed to other persons. A person has, of course, moral tasks in his relation to himself; this has been affirmed more than once, beginning with our first chapter. The famous Kierkegaardian analysis of despairing self-rejection as well as of a certain self-acceptance implies the fundamental moral importance of our stance towards ourselves. And yet the moral worthiness to which we are called requires other persons and can be lived fully only in a value-responding stance which includes them. Early on in this study we saw that respect for rights is possible only by one person in relation to another. Something similar holds for faithfulness; only if I practice it in relation to others as well as to myself can I grow into the full proportions of my moral calling. Some moral excellences make sense exclusively in relation to others, as, for example, gratitude.

Recall what was said above about the principle, *bonum est diffusivum sui,* namely that it is the principle of acting in deeply happy persons. Does this diffusivity not show itself primarily in relation to other persons? When the goodness of a person pours itself out, in what direction does it go if not in the direction of other persons? Take the person whose moral existence is formed by this diffusivity: is he not opened up from

26. If we speak of the dignity found in each person, then we have to speak not of the moral character of persons, which is different in different persons, but rather of the moral vocation of persons, which is the same in all persons.

the center of his being to others, and not just to others who have some claim on him?

Notice that the technical value of the person is not based on the selfhood that lives in relation to other persons, nor does it tend to open a person to others. It is based on a strength of selfhood that does not presuppose any value in the person. It is a more individual selfhood, which, while it enables a person, in virtue of his inner strength, to turn more adequately to others, lacks the dynamism of existing towards others that we find in moral value.

If, then, we think of personal selfhood in terms of interpersonal selfhood, it is clear that moral value, for all its transcendence, entirely belongs to human persons; it is nothing foreign to them, but it is the principle of their flourishing. We will return in our last chapter to this interpersonal dimension of selfhood implied by moral goodness.

PART III

Selfhood and Theonomy

Persona significat id quod est perfectissimum in tota natura.
—St. Thomas Aquinas

Our talk of selfhood in Part I will have seemed to some readers to go in the direction of absolute or divine being, and will have made them wonder whether human persons, if they really are ends in themselves and belong to themselves and even in a sense exist for their own sake, do not turn out to be divine beings. I seem to describe them in terms which really describe God. There are some philosophers (for instance, those who represent German Idealism) who do not hesitate to divinize or to absolutize human persons, and it is undoubtedly their sense of personal selfhood (among other things) which draws them in this direction. We ourselves, without of course ever calling human persons divine, said (Chapter 2.3) that each human person exists *as if* it had the divine in-communicability and so were the only person; we even ascribed a certain "absoluteness" as well as a certain "infinity" to persons, expressing ourselves in such a way that nothing but the quotation marks distinguished our talk about human persons from theological talk about God. It is now in Part III that I return to Part I and attempt to complete and balance our understanding of personhood by exploring the fundamental difference between human and divine selfhood. I might have addressed this question much earlier in our study, but it seemed to me that some of the results of our chapters on transcendence were needed for saying all that I want to say about the non-divine selfhood of human persons.

It may seem that in this last present part of this study I abandon the dialectical idea that kept recurring in the previous chapters. For in discussing the non-divine selfhood of the human person, I will bring out that which simply *limits* the selfhood of the person, and which shows the respects in which the person does not have supreme, divine selfhood; and the relation between two things whereby one limits the other is not a specifically dialectical relation. And yet even here we will also encounter dialectical relations which lead us deep into the mystery of human personal existence.

In Chapter 8 we will go as far as we can along the line of the non-divine selfhood of human persons, stressing our *dissimilarity* to God. In Chapter 9 we will balance and complete these results by considering how unexpectedly far the *similarity* of human and divine personhood extends. We call that which we will study at the end the *theonomy* of the human person.

CHAPTER EIGHT

Finitude

If I propose to characterize our personhood as non-divine, my first task is to say what I mean by God and in particular by divine selfhood. It is enough to think of divine selfhood in the terms in which we referred to it in Chapter 2.2, namely as the selfhood of a being that does not just have its nature or essence but which *is* its nature or essence, and which, therefore, possesses itself to the exclusion of other beings of the same nature. Another aspect of this supreme self-possession came to light in Chapter 2.4; we recognize divine selfhood in that being which *is* its own existence. The being that does not have its existence as given to it but that exists with an existence absolutely its own, so that it exists through itself and could not not exist—such a being possesses itself supremely. It has the divine selfhood, or supreme self-possession, of which I will be speaking, and this is the aspect under which I will begin to speak of God.

For most of the analysis of the present chapter, it is not necessary that my readers share my conviction that such a God indeed exists; even if God expresses for them nothing more than the idea of the highest conceivable selfhood, even if it expresses nothing more than an idea against which to measure human persons, they can still understand most of what I want to say about the non-divinity of human persons. They can understand that human persons are not divine even if they doubt whether any being is in fact divine.

Needless to say, I am not only concerned with establishing *that* we are indeed finite persons, but also and especially with finding the most revealing marks of our finitude and trying to understand the way in which these marks enter into and qualify our personhood.

1. A first sign of the finite personhood of human beings:
the plurality of persons, and in particular a certain partiality
of each of them

In Chapter 2.2 we drew the distinction between communicable and incommunicable within each person and analyzed the amazing "strength" of the incommunicable being of any person. A person does not just instantiate some communicable type or communicable traits; he has them as his own, incorporating them into his incommunicable selfhood. This is why other persons cannot replace a given person, even though they may share much that is communicable with him. This is also why (Chapter 2.3) a given person cannot be "relativized" by a large number of other persons, that is, reduced to a negligible quantity by them. Each exists, I said, *almost as if* he were the only person—so strongly is he incommunicably himself and not another. I said that all of this discloses to us in a particularly deep way the selfhood of human persons, which I could only describe as something "absolute" and "infinite."

And yet, for all the selfhood that comes to light in the incommunicability of human persons, I observed that human persons, *since they are not one but many,* do not have the greatest conceivable incommunicability. God incorporates His essence so strongly into Himself as to render it absolutely incommunicable in the sense of excluding the possibility of a second being like Himself, a second being that would in the same way incorporate into itself the same divine essence. This would be a being that would not just exist *almost as if* it were the only one of its communicable kind and makeup, but would be, and could only be, absolutely the only one. Such a being would belong to itself in a supreme way. For it is a weakness in the self-belonging of a being when its kind and makeup, for all of their rootedness in the incommunicable selfhood of the being, are nevertheless available to possible other beings (of the same kind and makeup), and can be "repeated" in them. We can say of a being in a far more proper sense that it "is itself and is not another" if it were the only possible being of its essence, than if other beings outside of it also share its essence, thus making something of its being exist, so to speak, outside of it. A being that supremely possessed itself would not just *share in* its own communicable nature and makeup, leaving room for others to share in the same nature and makeup, but would have *to be* its own communicable nature and makeup, excluding others of the same nature and makeup. Human persons, being many, do not possess themselves like this, but have a fundamentally weaker form of selfhood.

So far I have only said what is fairly obvious. We have now to reflect more deeply on the plurality of human persons, and in particular to try to understand in what sense there is a certain "point" or "purpose" or even "necessity" to this plurality.

A certain teleological point of the existence of many persons. Most of us have had the experience of marvelling at the gifts of some exceptional other, at his or her insights and excellences. We may be so taken by them and find them to be so far beyond anything of the kind that we are aware in ourselves or in others, that we are surprised when, turning from this gifted one to others, we discover that *they, too, have their proper gifts.* Our surprise comes from finding that, after all the excellence that had so impressed us in the first, *there is still room for so many other kinds of excellences among human persons.* While we were still under the impression of the first we tended to think that all possible human excellence must be of his kind, and that other human beings gain excellence in proportion as they approach his excellence. What we discovered was that there are innumerably many different kinds of human ability, excellence, wisdom, and the one whom we so admired did nothing more than ably represent one of them. We discovered a *partiality* that not even the ablest and worthiest and greatest human being can overcome. We experienced this partiality quite keenly if we, taken by the greatness of some one human person, tried to dwell only with this one and to be nourished only by this one, patterning ourselves only on him: we found to our surprise that this extraordinary person can be experienced as limiting and even as cloying and that there are always other persons who can give us what we need but could never receive from the one who had absorbed all our attention. We became aware of the *plenitude of personal riches* found in the totality of human persons, which no single human person can achieve, or even begin to achieve, in himself.[1] It is as if *the human person* contained so much, that *many human persons* are required to realize it all.

1. This suggests another approach to what we in the previous chapter called the inexhaustibility of moral excellence and moral worthiness. If moral goodness is really the goodness of man as person, then it belongs, and belongs preeminently, to the human plenitude of which we just spoke in the text. We are, then, not surprised when we find that this goodness is realized in any good person with the same partiality with which *the human person* is realized in any one person. This partiality manifests in a new way the

One will now understand what I mean in saying that there is a purpose or even a certain necessity in the plurality of persons. Given that each person has, even amidst the most remarkable realization of personal possibilities within himself, the partiality of which I spoke,[2] he could not possibly be the only human person; the partiality with which he realizes *the human person* in himself prevents him from *being* the essence of the human person, makes him only *share in* it, and establishes the possibility of other persons. It even "calls for" them, so that it would be unfortunate if he were the only one, if there were not also many others who might make their contributions to unfolding the inexhaustible riches of *the human person.*

It is different with specimens, each of which presumably embodies the whole idea or model that it instantiates. One specimen (such as a copy of today's newspaper) does not embody some aspect or dimension of the model that only it can embody and which all other specimens necessarily lack: there is instead a sense in which each specimen has all that any other specimen has, a sense in which each specimen represents its model in exactly the same way. Thus the idea or model multiplied in many specimens does not gain anything by the existence of many specimens; it is fully established in reality by just one specimen. But there is more of a "point" to there being many human persons: each unfolds or represents something in "the human person" that only it can unfold or represent; any one human person only begins the work of establishing "the human person" in reality; all of them together represent a fullness of human personhood that could never exist in only one of them. This means that there is a certain partiality of my being in relation to all other persons, a partiality that in specimens gives way to a certain wholeness of each specimen.

If now we consider the plurality of human persons not simply as a blunt fact but rather in the light of the deep meaning of it, that is, in the light of the partiality of each and of the need of being completed by many others, we can find in this plurality further evidence of the non-

---

inexhaustibility that I ascribed to moral goodness. (We return at the end of the present chapter to the partiality in the moral goodness of a human person.)

2. It seems that this partiality is all the greater as a result of a fact of which we took notice in Chapter 2.4, namely that the partial realization of *the human person* that a given person achieves in himself *can only be achieved in himself and cannot be repeated in others;* it is incommunicably his own. This is why, as we said, something of the human substance would be irretrievably lost if individual persons were simply annihilated.

divine selfhood of each human person. Let us ask: how could the being of supreme incommunicability, which exists through itself and which has its being as radically its own, have its essence so partially and have to look to other beings in order to find the completion of its essence and of the excellences proper to itself? How could it find, in a certain sense, the fullness of its own being outside of itself in others and yet at the same time exist through itself, standing supremely in itself? Things would be different if each human person realized in himself all the plenitude of the human person and differed only numerically from all the others, as with mere specimens. Then I would lose the present way of arguing from plurality to non-divine selfhood and would be left with only the previously mentioned way of arguing. But as it is, we can argue not only from the mere fact of the plurality of human persons, but also from a certain teleological "point" of their plurality, which implies a certain partiality of each of them.

The non-divine selfhood of human persons is revealed all the more forcefully if the plenitude of *the human person* should turn out to be such that no finite number of human persons can exhaustively realize it. For then the essence of *the human person* would transcend not only any given person, but the totality of all human persons. This would mean that any given person is even farther removed from *being* the essence of the human person (in the sense of absolute self-possession).

It follows from all that I have said about plurality and about the particular form of it that rests on a certain partiality, that I have to modify what we said above about each human person existing as if he were the only one, being unable to be relativized by all the innumerably many others. For in the partiality of each in relation to the totality of the others we encounter a certain smallness of each person. Of course it is a smallness understood in a personalist and not in a "cosmological" way, for it is not the smallness of man in the spatio-temporal universe, it is not any quantitative smallness, but is instead a smallness that belongs to human persons as persons. And yet it is a smallness and a partiality that imply the finitude of selfhood in human persons. This selfhood, amazing as it is, goes only so far; it is indeed opposed to being a mere part, but it is not opposed to having something part-like, or a certain partiality. As we probe it, it appears in its fundamental limits.

And yet we encounter here, just when we are exploring our non-divine selfhood, new evidence of the strength of our selfhood. For although no one of us human persons can *realize in ourselves* the fullness of the human person, we do not rest content with this partiality. We desire to surpass it, and *to participate in* the fullness of personal excellence through our relationships with other persons. Our partiality is not the final word for us; we still try to find a way towards the totality, even if this cannot be the way of fully realizing it in ourselves.

We have to face the question whether this criterion of finite selfhood coheres with the Trinitarian faith of Christians. One might argue that either this criterion is false or else this faith is false. If there are three persons in God, each of them divine, then plurality does not imply non-divinity. Or if it does imply non-divinity, then we have to conclude that the three divine persons—since they are three—turn out to be finite persons.

I would respond that, according to Christian faith, each divine person fully possesses the divine nature, each is as truly God as if the others did not exist. None of them merely participates in the divine essence; each of them *is* the divine essence. The plurality of persons that implies finitude is the plurality which prevents any of the persons from *being* its essence and which requires each of them to participate in its essence. A plurality that does not require participation—a plurality of persons that lets each of the persons *be* its essence—does not imply finitude. No one should claim to show how it is possible for each of plural divine persons to *be* its divine essence; understanding such a possibility seems to exceed altogether the reach of human reason. But the Christian affirmation of this possibility does not contradict what we have wanted to say in putting forward our first criterion of finitude.

Nor does it contradict what we wanted to say when we sharpened the criterion by pointing out the teleological point of many human persons. For there is no question of one divine person unfolding one aspect of divinity, with the other divine persons unfolding other aspects. If, then, the plurality found in human persons is connected with a certain partiality (in the sense explained) of each of them, and if the plurality found in the Christian God lacks any such partiality, then clearly the first plurality, which is especially revealing of finitude, is altogether different from the second one, and we can recognize the non-divinity implied by the first without having to call into question the divinity that Christian faith sees in the second.

2. Second sign of the finite personhood of human beings: their relation to time

Beginning in time. Each human person had a beginning in time; each of us once was not. I do not have to go back very far to find a time before I existed. This means that my present existence is what is called a *contingent* existence. There is no absurdity in my non-existence, seeing as my non-existence was once a fact. Thus even now, when I do undeniably exist, I do not exist necessarily; I could as well not exist. Some philosophers have said it like this: there is in my essence a certain indifference to existence, there being nothing in what I am that necessarily requires existence or that explains my existence, which is in some sense *given* to me.

With this I am forced to modify quite substantially what was said earlier about the belonging of persons to themselves, or about their self-possession. Of course, there is no denying that persons really do possess themselves and that they show this in a very revealing way when they act through themselves. And yet this self-possession is altogether limited if my very existence is not radically my own, if I could as well not exist, if the existence I have is in some sense given to me. I do not fully possess myself if I do not fully possess my existence. A being possessing itself without qualification would have *to be its own existence;* it would have to exist through itself, out of itself; it would have to be absolutely incapable of not existing. As a result, this being, which is commonly called an absolute being, could have no beginning in time, but must have always been. It is clear that my human selfhood is as nothing when contrasted with this divine selfhood. Indeed, one might wonder how a being that could as well not exist, that receives its existence from without, can be said to possess itself and belong to itself in the sense of a person; it would not have been at all unreasonable to think that only a being that possesses its existence in the sense of being its own existence can really possess itself as person. In other words, the weakness in our selfhood goes so far as to make it hard to understand how our selfhood can be, as it undeniably is, personal selfhood.

Enduring in time. One could press a skeptical doubt about our beginning, asking how we know for sure that we did not always exist. According to our critique in Chapter 4 of those who would reduce persons to their subjectivity, there is no absurdity in persons existing even though they have as yet no conscious possession of themselves. How do we know that we did not pre-exist our becoming conscious, and always pre-exist it, existing without beginning? And even if we have always existed with conscious self-presence, how do we know that we have not forgotten most of our previous existence, which for all we know may be without beginning?

But whether human persons had a beginning in time, they in any case *live and endure in time.* Skeptical doubts about *this* relation to time are entirely unreasonable; we experience our enduring in time in our self-presence. We are aware in ourselves that our being, as experienced subjectively in self-presence, does not remain but is ever passing away, not in the sense that we cease to be entirely, for we could not experience that, but in the sense that something of that being which we live through in the present *passes away, is irretrievably lost to self-presence, and is no more.* Let us be as skeptical as we will about our activities of remembering this or that in our past, we can never be skeptical about *the constant losing of something of ourselves that we live in self-presence.* Or let me express the matter by considering the eternal self-presence of God, who endures without losing what He once had, who endures without ever ceasing to be what He once was. Is it not certain that we do not endure like this, but that our enduring is such as always to render past what we now are in the present?

And of course in our non-eternal self-presence we also experience our openness towards the future; we know that much of our being is "not yet," that we are in the present not living through much that could be ours, and we know that if it is ever to become ours it can only become so in the future.

It is not difficult to see why this enduring of human persons in time implies a great distance of their selfhood from divine selfhood; this enduring implies a radical limitation of the belonging of persons to themselves. Insofar as their being is past and is no more, they do not fully possess themselves; and insofar as their being is future and is not yet, they do not fully possess themselves. It seems to me that Aquinas expresses this defect of self-possession with the greatest possible precision when he says: "Esse autem nostrum habet aliquid sui extra se: deest enim aliquid quod jam de ipso praeteriit, et quod futurum est."[3] By liv-

---

3. *In I. Sent.,* d. 8, q. 1, a. 1. I would translate as follows: "But our being has something of itself outside of itself: for something is lacking to it which has already passed away from it, and something which is yet future."

ing and enduring in time I exist *with something of myself outside of myself,* and as a result I do not fully possess myself. A being that is its own essence and that is its own existence can only exist in an eternal self-presence, existing with nothing of itself outside of itself. Between such a self-possessing being and us human persons there is a metaphysical abyss.

Edith Stein brings out another aspect of our temporality, which has the effect of further diminishing our self-possession. She says that the human person

> is confronted with itself as a living being which is present to itself, but which at the same time comes from a past and lives into a future—*he and his being are inescapably there, he is "thrown into being."* But that is the extremest antithesis to the sovereignty and self-sufficiency of a *being existing through itself.* And his being is one which surges up from moment to moment. It cannot "stop," for it cannot be "held up" as it passes away. *And so it never really comes into the possession of itself.* (The italics of this last sentence are mine.)[4]

She seems to be saying that not only do we as temporal beings exist with something of ourselves outside of ourselves, but this condition of existing outside of ourselves *is imposed on us.* We do not perform our duration subjectively, but we endure it, we are borne along by it, even to the point of being "thrown" into it. Even in the present, when we are not outside of ourselves but in ourselves, we find time surging up in us outside of our freedom. As a result, our self-possession is again revealed in its radical finitude. By contrast, God, existing in supreme self-possession, must not just be in eternity, *but must be His own eternity.* As Aquinas says, "no other being is its own duration, as no other is its own being. . . as He [God] is His own essence, so He is His own eternity."[5]

But let us take care not to exaggerate this loss of self-possession. I do not say that the human person exhausts his whole being in being "no more" and in being "not yet," as if the present were nothing but the line

---

4. E. Stein, *Endliches und ewiges Sein* (Freiburg: Herder, 1962), 52. The German text reads: the human person "findet sich als lebendiges, als gegenwärtig seiendes und zugleich als aus einer Vergangenheit kommendes und in eine Zukunft hineinlebendes vor—*es selbst und sein Sein sind unentrinnbar da, es ist ein 'ins Dasein geworfenes.'* Das ist aber der äusserste Gegensatz zur Selbstherrlichkeit und Selbstverständlichkeit eines *Seins aus sich selbst.* Und sein Sein ist ein von Augenblick zu Augenblick auflebendes. Es kann nicht 'halten,' weil es 'unaufhaltsam' entflieht. *So gelangt es niemals wahrhaft in seinen Besitz."*

5. *Summa Theologiae,* I, q. 10, a. 2.

dividing past and future. No, there is also an extended present, and in fact we can express the recollection of the person in terms of it; we can say that the more deeply the person recollects himself and strengthens his self-presence, the more of an extended present he comes to inhabit. In being unrecollected, he tends to live in the ever-vanishing present, but in coming to himself in the way of recollection he extends the present in which he lives; he gains a certain superiority to the flow of time, and resists the dis-integrating effect of it. Now if the human person could continue what he begins in recollecting himself, and could raise recollection to the highest possible power, and could live in a supreme recollection, then his present would become so strong as to absorb past and future, and his mode of duration would pass over into the eternal self-presence proper to God. But this of course is impossible for us; the strongest recollection gives us only a small island of presence; we remain forever encompassed by past and future. And so we remain fundamentally reduced in our self-possession.

And besides recollection there are other ways of taking possession of our past, and even of our future. We can recall our past, try to understand it, take responsibility for our past actions, stand by our past commitments; and we can anticipate the future, plan for it, make commitments to be fulfilled in the future, etc. The more deeply recollected a person is, the more he tends to try to encompass past and future in such ways, since he cannot encompass them by absorbing them into an eternal present. But all the different ways of taking possession of my past cannot get rid of the fact that my past life, even when I try to understand it deeply and to take responsibility for it, in a certain sense *is no more;* nor can my attempts to take possession of the future get rid of the fact that my future life in a certain sense *is not yet.*

We saw that since we have a beginning in time, we exist contingently. We now ask whether our existing and enduring in time also implies our contingent existence. Could a being that exists with something of itself outside of itself, exist through itself? Clearly not. If I really existed through myself and so existed in absolute self-possession, I would live in the duration of eternal self-presence. A being cannot be ever losing its being and ever awaiting it, thus existing in a certain sense outside of itself, and yet be supremely established in itself and exist through itself. Nor can a being be thrown into its duration and be borne along by it, and yet be its own existence. Since I endure in time I must exist not absolutely but contingently, and the weakness of my selfhood must include the weakness of contingent existence.

Once we see how human persons endure in time, the real question is not whether they are contingent, but rather how it is that their contingency does not go so far as to prevent them from being persons. How can a being stand in itself in the sense of a personal subject, and yet be ever losing and ever awaiting its being as a result of existing in time? How can a being act through itself in freedom, and yet be acted upon by present time welling up in it apart from its freedom?[6]

Notice that the so expressive phrase of Aquinas, "existing with something of one's being outside of oneself," can also be applied to an individual human person in relation to all other persons, and so can be used to articulate the previously discussed sign of our non-divine selfhood. The fact that my human nature is in some sense repeated in all other human beings means that it exists not only in me but also outside of me in the others. But this existing outside of me becomes much stronger and much more humbling for my selfhood, as soon as one considers the partiality of each human person and the "need" of there being many of them. For then what exists outside of me is shown to be not just that which exists in me as well, but that which, while belonging to my human personhood and unfolding the riches of what I am, *does not* exist in me.

3. Third sign of the finite personhood of human beings: they are "suspended" between potentiality and actuality

Persons experience their temporality whenever they strive to develop themselves, or, to express ourselves in Aristotelian categories, whenever they strive to actualize their potentialities. Let us examine the way in which human persons are "suspended" between potentiality and actuality, and let us do this not merely in order to develop the previously discussed criterion of non-divine selfhood, but above all in order to find a new criterion of it.

Any being which has some of its being in potency and has to gain it by actualizing itself, or which having actualized itself could yet revert, in at least part of its being, to potency or to some irretrievable loss of actuality, possesses itself in a non-divine way. A being does not possess

6. There are other facts about the human person's enduring in time that might be explored with a view to showing the contingency of the person. There is for instance the fact that Pascal so marvelled at, the contingency of the time at which I live. He means that there is no necessity why I should live at this time and not at another time, now rather than at some time in the distant past or at some still future time.

itself fully and exist absolutely through itself, if it has yet to become itself fully or could cease to be itself fully, and especially if it could be hindered by external factors from becoming itself fully or continuing to be itself fully. It is true that in actualizing itself a being does not receive its being from another, but rather draws it forth, as it were, from itself; but all the same, such a developing being does not possess its being as radically its own. Insofar as it is still in potency, it does not possess itself fully. And if it could lose any of the actuality of itself that it has gained, it also does not possess itself fully. An absolute being has to be conceived as always in possession of the full actuality of its being, as having none of its being only potentially, and as being incapable of declining into any potentiality, to say nothing of any irretrievable loss of actuality. A supremely self-possessing being can only be conceived of as a supremely actual being and without any defect in the actuality proper to itself.

Perhaps this criterion contains the previous one; perhaps we can say that as a being yields up its present to the past, it suffers an irretrievable loss of actuality, and that it is in potency with respect to the future. But there are many other kinds of actuality, de-actuality, and potentiality besides temporal actuality, de-actuality, and potentiality, as we shall see as we proceed to apply the present criterion to the human person.

Human persons fulfill this criterion, for they are constantly actualizing themselves out of a state of potency and are constantly in danger of losing to potency such actuality as they have. Let us return to the so deeply significant experience of recollecting oneself, and let us hold fast to the irreducibility of the being of the person to personal subjectivity (Chapter 4). If persons exhausted their whole being in conscious self-presence, then we would have to say that recollection enlarges indeed their being as person, but we could not say that it actualizes their being, that it actualizes what they in a sense already are. But as we saw, persons do not exhaust their whole being in conscious self-presence; we can and indeed must characterize their coming to themselves in recollection and their strengthening of their power to act through themselves, as an actualizing of what they potentially are. And persons can lose recollection as well as gain it, and in fact they are constantly losing it by falling into dispersion and passivity; but in losing it they fall away from the actuality of their being as person. Human persons have, then, precisely that relation to their actuality which fulfills this third criterion of non-divine selfhood: they are always striving towards it, and can lose it once they achieve it. In virtue of all the potentiality in their being they can be said to exist with something of their being outside of themselves. A being that exists through itself cannot have so precarious a relation to the actuality of its being.[7]

And there are other ways in which persons can actualize themselves and be deactualized besides through gaining and losing recollection. Thus there is the whole process of growth whereby an infant becomes a child and the child becomes an adult, and then there is the process of declining into senility. It is not just the human organism but the person who undergoes this growing and declining. This also shows his non-divine selfhood in the sense of our third criterion.

This way of showing the finite selfhood of the human person is not open to the skeptical doubt that was raised with regard to the human person having a beginning in time; for the coming and going of the actuality of my being is experienced in my innermost present consciousness. Whatever I was before I became conscious, and whatever I have forgotten about myself, I nevertheless experience in myself in the present that coming and going of actuality which implies my contingency.

I still have to show the full extent of the non-divine selfhood of human persons that is revealed by this criterion.

The potentiality in which a person exists can go very far; for the person can in principle exist, as I claimed in Chapter 4, apart from any conscious self-presence. If one considers how closely the structure of personal selfhood is tied to conscious self-presence, one sees how utterly latent, or dormant, a completely unconscious person is. It is astonishing that persons can be so radically separated from the actuality of their being, and thus so radically reduced in their self-possession, without ceasing to exist as persons.

But much more interesting is the following consideration. Putting aside the question of losing the actuality of their being, let us ask: could it be that human persons can never actualize themselves in such a way as to exhaust all potentiality in their being? If we think back to our investigations (Chapter 5) of the way in which persons are always surpassing themselves, and surpassing their surpassing, giving evidence of a mysterious infinite capacity in themselves, then the answer to our question can only be that there is no such thing in persons as a finished actualization of them. However much they become, they will always know

---

7. E. Stein, too (op. cit., 54), sees in the more and less of our self-presence *(Gegenwart)* a more and less of actuality, and she, too, takes this as evidence of our non-divine selfhood, and in particular of our contingent existence.

how to experience it as a confining limit and to be restless until they have surpassed it. But this call to surpass themselves, which is always renewing itself, reveals unfulfilled potentiality. This in turn means that an actuality in a person that would swallow up all potentiality, is as impossible as a natural number that is the greatest number and has no successor number.

Now if an absolute being, which possesses itself so as to exist through itself, could not possibly exist as not yet completely actualized, as we have already argued, even less can it exist as always striving for but never finally achieving, and indeed never even being able finally to achieve, the actuality proper to itself. For then it would be even more separated from the full actuality of its being, and its self-possession would be further weakened. Since human persons do strive for their actuality with a striving that can never be finally fulfilled and completed, a striving that is always surpassing whatever it reaches, they exist forever with something of their being outside of themselves, and so possess themselves in a radically finite way.

Let us set this contingent self-possession in relation to our discussion of the selfhood of the person in Part I. Though what I have just said does not call into question the fact that the person really is an end in himself and belongs to himself, it nevertheless modifies our understanding of this being an end in oneself. Having said what I said in Part I, I have now to say that human persons, as a result of this incurable lack of definitive self-possession, are as it were "weak" ends in themselves, ends in themselves only in a limited respect, and ends in themselves with a surprising resemblance to those beings that are not ends in themselves; in a word, they are utterly non-divine ends in themselves.

*4. Fourth sign of the finite personhood of human beings:
the unity of "person" and "nature" in human persons*

Agere sequitur esse; the activity proper to a being is proportioned to the metaphysical makeup of the being. This readily suggests a further sign of non-divine selfhood, which we can express in the terms of Wojtyla (which we made our own in Chapter 1.3): any being which can only undergo and endure what happens in it, which is only a subject of activations, that is, any being which cannot act through itself in freedom, can only possess itself in a non-divine way. A being so gathered into itself as to exist through itself cannot fail to be able to act through itself. There would be an absurd disproportion between the self-existence and the self-possession of God, on the one hand, and His acting, on the other, if He could always only undergo what happens in Him. Or we could put it like this: a being that has its being as radically its own cannot fail to have activity radically its own, and such activity can only be an acting through itself and not a mere undergoing of what happens in it. In a word, since God exists in freedom, any being that can only undergo and endure must be non-divine.

But this criterion, unlike the other criteria of finite selfhood which we are here discussing, does not apply to human persons; for human persons *can* act through themselves. A being would have to be fundamentally more non-divine than human persons if it were to be revealed in its non-divinity through this criterion. We are reminded again of the amazing extent of the selfhood of the person, precisely in the course of an investigation that is looking for the non-absoluteness of this selfhood.

But perhaps we are after all not so far from finding a new criterion for the finite selfhood of human persons. We have only to consider that the being which supremely possesses itself must *always only* act through itself and *never* merely undergo what happens in it. This can be understood through the axiom, *agere sequitur esse;* if a being possesses itself so as to exist through itself, if it has the supreme self-possession of being its own existence, then it has no basis in itself for something merely happening in it. In a word, God must not only exist in freedom, but be freedom through and through, without the admixture of any principle of enduring in itself; He must be pure selfhood and have nothing of "nature" in Himself. This implies the following criterion of finite selfhood: any being which is subject to enduring and happening in itself, and which is, therefore, less than pure selfhood, has a selfhood which, even if a personal selfhood, is non-divine selfhood.

Now it would seem that human persons clearly fulfill this criterion, for they do not have the being of pure selfhood, but they have within their being a principle of enduring; they are a composition of "person" and "nature," as we expressed it above. But this is not so unproblematical as it appears at first. Many thinkers do not stop with a distinction between person and nature such as we, following Wojtyla, have made, but go on to posit a dualism of person and nature according to which the whole essence of man lies in his personal selfhood, and everything in the way of nature lies, strictly speaking, outside of the human person. They say that nature in man is an object for persons and, like other objects, does not belong to subjectivity but rather stands over against it; so that nature, being the principle of happening and undergoing, belongs more to their environment than to their very being as persons. This means that whatever finite selfhood is implied by the principle of undergoing, does not necessarily "infect" the human person; that, in other words, our fourth sign of non-divine self-possession is inapplicable to the human person. Others hold the contrary; they say that this principle of enduring and happening *does* belong to our essence, and that there is therefore in our very being a principle that limits personal acting, and that as a result this principle, which they, too, often call the principle of "nature," gives further evidence of the non-divine selfhood of human persons.

Let it not be carelessly and hastily said that the former are simply reviving a "Cartesian" or "Platonic" dualism of body and soul. Their position involves indeed a certain dualism, but not exactly one of body and soul. For there is much in the life of the soul that is an undergoing and not a self-acting, as, for example, the affective experiences that simply befall us. These are reckoned to the "soul" by Descartes, but are reckoned to "nature" by Wojtyla and others. Furthermore, at the present day one typically holds the dualism of person and nature without basing oneself on any metaphysics of a substantial human spirit (which one would then proceed to relate only extrinsically to the human body); indeed, it is possible to hold it while at the same time maintaining a thoroughgoing materialism in one's theory of man. One typically bases oneself not on a Platonic or Cartesian metaphysics of spirit, but rather on something like the Kantian dualism, according to which the person, understood as the center of freedom, inhabits a noumenal world, while the human body and indeed everything making up "nature" in man belongs to a completely different realm, to a phenomenal world organized according to causal laws, so that what happens to him and in him does not really reach him as free person.

We can understand this dualism more concretely by understanding how it comes out of and underlies a certain way of life. Many want to extend the technological manipulation of the environment to man himself; this leads them to a dualism of man-who-manipulates and man-who-can-be-manipulated, which they then express theoretically in terms of the dualism of person and nature in man. But perhaps an even more helpful way of getting at the sense of the dualism of person and nature, as it is usually put forward today, is to consider the sexual behavior to which it typically corresponds.

Many say that the sexual encounters between men and women involve only the body and have no consequences for how men and women relate to each other as persons. They can confer any personal meaning they want on their sexual relations. They can decide that sexual union means only recreation, and forthwith it means only recreation. If they decide that it will mean something more, perhaps even express a permanent marital relation, then it takes on this further meaning. To object that sexual union means something independent of the meaning-conferring acts of men and women, so that to engage in sexual relations while intending something other than this objective meaning is intrinsically dishonest, and that the human person, by his subjective intentions, does not have the power to get rid of this dishonesty, is, one says, to fall prey to a "physicalist" ethics, and to let considerations of mere nature interfere with what is immeasurably higher, namely the intentions of persons. I mention these ethical questions of sexual ethics, not for their own sake, for the present study is not an ethical study, but for the sake of rendering more concrete the dualism of person and nature in man as it is usually maintained today; for it surely becomes more concrete when we see why it leads to, and grows out of, a very definite understanding of sexual behavior.

Our task is to show that person and nature form one being in man, so that we can show the non-divine selfhood of human persons by means of our fourth criterion. As long as nature in us is outside our being as person, then the non-divinity of nature has no consequences for the non-divinity of us as persons. Of course, I can do nothing more than offer a few ideas on the unity of person and nature in man; I cannot hope to do justice to so vast a subject, which is nothing less than the embodiment of persons.

1. If human persons really endure in time, existing with much of their being outside of themselves, as we saw, and if they are forever suspended between actuality and potentiality, as we also saw, then it would not be surprising if they also had in themselves a principle of undergoing and enduring. If they cannot live in an eternal self-presence, and cannot live in full actuality, then it would not be surprising if they could not live in the form of pure selfhood, being all person and having nothing of nature in themselves. We pointed out above a certain passivity in our way of experiencing the passing of time, which reminds us of the passivity of nature. Indeed, we might well wonder whether the previously discussed weaknesses in the self-possession of human persons do not *necessarily imply* that they must also have the "weakness" that comes of being a composition of person and nature.[8] If this implication in fact obtains,

8. It would not be to the point to refer to the idea of angelic persons, as if they, having no body, had no principle of nature in themselves, despite their being limited in

consider what follows. Assuming that plurality and temporality and potentiality really do characterize human personhood, entering into it and qualifying it as finite, then the principle of nature implied by these metaphysical notes must also enter into human personhood and qualify it as finite.[9]

2. Those who maintain the dualism of person and nature can hardly deny that man as person, precisely as person, undergoes all manner of things. If for instance we receive a strong blow on the head and lose consciousness, then our entire conscious life as person is suspended, and it is as persons that we suffer. One cannot say that as persons we remain unaffected and that it is only the sight of personhood that is obscured by the interference of outside factors. I can speak this way only about my losing sight of some *other person,* or of some other losing sight of me; but when it is my conscious relation to myself, my very self-presence, which is interfered with, then *I, I myself* am being impinged upon by the outside factors.

Now does this not imply some principle of nature in the makeup of the human person? If the human person were nothing but personal selfhood, if nature lay entirely outside of the person, belonging only to his environment, how could nature "reach" the human person so as to make him undergo the loss of consciousness as well as, in other cases, to undergo all kinds of passive experiences? Indeed, how could persons even be situated or embedded in an environment? If the whole being of persons lay in selfhood, they would lack any basis in their being for undergoing. This is why it is only natural, in philosophical theology, to remove all thought of enduring and undergoing from the life of God and to affirm the transcendence of God over the world. And so human persons, since they are subject to undergoing, show themselves to be more than personal selfhood; they must have a being that is reduced and di-

---

their self-possession. We have been careful not to reduce nature in man to the human body (though it also comprises the human body); and we do not see why there should not be a non-bodily principle of enduring, and in this sense a principle of "nature," even in angelic persons.

9. There is, however, one way in which I would emphatically *not* argue from the note of plurality to the inherence of nature in our human personhood. I would not agree with Aristotle and St. Thomas that it is only through the body that plural persons can come into being. The analysis I offered in Chapter 2.1 will suggest to the reader some of my reasons for not sharing this theory and not sharing the hylomorphism on which it is based.

luted by some principle other than selfhood, and what is this principle in us human beings if not what we are here calling nature?

3. Let us recall the "subjective" relation of persons to their bodies that we found in our exploration of subjectivity. We are not just related to our bodies as to objects in front of ourselves, which we experience as others, too, can experience them; we also experience our bodies from within, each of us experiencing his body as only he can experience it. The same holds for particular bodily events, such as hunger; I do not just experience hunger as an object *about which* I think, but also as something *in which I subjectively live.* This suggests a bodily dimension, and so also a component of nature, in our very being as human persons. But this is only a suggestion; we have here a subject that requires a closer examination than we can give it.

4. Much of what we experience as happening in us is capable of being intimately incorporated or integrated into the existence of the person. Wojtyla has studied this work of integration with special attention to the sexual energy of men and women. He has shown how the self-donation of spouses, which is preeminently an act of them as persons, can inform their sexuality, which is first experienced as a drive springing up outside of their freedom. Men and women can integrate their sexuality into their self-donation, not just in the sense of controlling and channelling it but of making it a medium for the enactment of their love, thereby gaining for its gesture of self-donation an entire dimension that it would otherwise lack. It is clear that in performing this work of integration the spouses do not use their sexuality as an object, but incorporate their sexuality into their subjectivity, and in fact incorporate it so intimately as to perfect the entirely personal act of spousal self-donation.

I want to call attention not only to the unity of person and nature in the case of such "personalized" sexuality but also to the prior unity of person and nature that renders possible in the first place works of integration. There must be some sense in which my sexuality, as part of "nature" in myself, already belongs to me as person, if I am ever to be faced with the task of incorporating it fully into my selfhood. And the disorder that arises in me when I exercise my sexuality without personalizing it implies that my sexuality, for all its character of nature, must, prior to all efforts at integration, be not outside of the personal being that I am, but rather inside it, already connected with my subjectivity.

Let this suffice on the unity of person and nature in man; perhaps I have shown enough of a unity to "implicate" the human person in the non-divine selfhood implied in nature. We are not pure selfhood, as God is; our personhood is diluted by nature, and is thus shown to be non-divine by our fourth criterion.

This criterion is connected with our first criterion, a certain partiality found in each human person. Are there not certain forms of partiality arising in us as a result of our being composed of person and nature? What about the distinction between man and woman, which is in part a bodily distinction? If our bodily being is not, as in the person-nature dualism, outside of ourselves as persons, if it belongs to our human personhood, then it is as persons that we are man and woman, and the partiality and complementarity of man and woman becomes a partiality and complementarity of us as persons. But all such partiality, as we already know, indicates non-divine selfhood.

5. Fifth sign of the finite personhood of human beings: discrepancies between being and consciousness

1. The results of Chapter 4 led us to distinguish between being and consciousness in the human person, and not only to distinguish them, but also to show that they exist in a state of partial separation, that is, that the being of the person always exceeds the consciousness of the person. In other words, the conscious self-presence of the human person, as it deepens through recollection, never entirely encompasses the being of the person, never exhaustively penetrates and illuminates the being of the person. When we are only weakly recollected, then the discrepancy between being and consciousness is great, and when we fall into dreamless sleep then we are all being and no consciousness. But even when we are deeply recollected we do not have the consciousness of being present to ourselves with our whole being, or even of approaching any such unity of being and consciousness; we rather become more keenly aware than ever of the mysterious extent of our being as persons, and of how much more we could yet become in our conscious existence.

Now this inalienable, insuperable discrepancy of being and consciousness in ourselves as persons implies a far-reaching weakness in our self-possession, and thus implies our non-divine selfhood. A being that supremely possesses itself so as to exist through itself must be consciously present to itself with its whole being; its being and its consciousness must coincide without residue and be one. The discrepancy between being and consciousness in ourselves implies that we exist in contingent and not in absolute self-possession. It goes without saying that even if we were *often* present to ourselves with our whole being and were only subject to the *possibility* of a separating of being and consciousness, and even if it were unlikely that this possibility would ever be realized, our self-possession would still be weakened so as to imply our contingency. It is just that our finite selfhood is revealed more clearly when being and consciousness separate in the way in which we find them separating in ourselves.

We can develop this idea into a *reductio* argument for our contingency. Let us assume we were absolute, and let us ask: do we have any awareness of existing through ourselves, do we consciously live through the act through which we exist? Are we aware of a source of existing in ourselves that is beyond the reach of the most threatening forces? It seems not; if Heidegger and others are right, then human persons all live in a deep fear of nothingness and of falling into nothingness. But then human persons would be absolute beings unaware of their self-existence, that is, of their absoluteness, and in fact they would be absolute beings who think they are contingent and who suffer the most painful anxiety because of this. They would be, then, absolute beings whose absolute being is "outside" of their conscious self-presence, and who therefore would have a fundamental weakness in the way in which they possess themselves. But beings who live in so reduced a self-possession can only be contingent beings. The initial assumption that we are absolute must be untenable, for the undeniable fact that we do not experience absolute existence in ourselves implies that we are not absolute but contingent, and so altogether non-divine.

2. But there is another and very different respect in which we find being and consciousness parting ways in ourselves. If the previous one was found in our subjective self-relation, then the present one is found in what I have been calling an objective self-relation, that is, a relation to ourselves as objects of our acts.

Many human beings do not even recognize themselves as persons, and they think of themselves as parts, or specimens, or the like. Or at least they are confused about their personhood, and to some extent or other understand themselves in a depersonalized way. If they do recognize their personhood, they will sometimes overlook their contingency and take themselves for absolute beings. Perhaps they will fail to understand the unity that person and nature form in themselves, and/or will fail to understand the discrepancy of being and consciousness in themselves (in the sense discussed above); then they will understand themselves in terms of an erroneous dualism of person and nature, and/or in terms of an erroneous reduction to consciousness. If they succeed in avoiding the dualism, they have only to be asked *how* two such apparently incommensurable principles as person and nature come to form one being, and then they are confronted anew with their ignorance about themselves, just at the moment when they might have thought they were beginning to understand themselves. And there are innumerable other questions about our selfhood and personhood that are difficult to answer on the basis of our experience of ourselves, such as questions about our ultimate origin or our final destination. But even questions about ourselves, the answers to which would seem to be closer at hand, cause us hardly less perplexity. Thus if asked whether masculine and feminine extend even to personal being so as to constitute two fundamental forms of human personal being, most people will at first be at a loss as to how even to frame the question so as to investigate it fruitfully; and those who can frame the question will not be able to agree among themselves on the answer. My point is not just that we get confused when we try to develop a philosophical account of our personhood; even pre-philosophically, while we try to remain close to the experience of living our own being, we are aware of much darkness in our understanding of who we are.

Now it would seem that all of this ignorance and confusion in which we live about who we are as persons gives powerful evidence of our non-divine selfhood. For this confusion implies a great weakness in our self-possession; we are outside of ourselves and estranged from ourselves, and are precisely not in possession of ourselves, to the extent that we are perplexed, or even in error, about who we are as persons. It would seem that a being which supremely possesses itself so as to be its own essence and to exist through itself, would have to possess itself by understanding itself through and through. The estrangement from ourselves that lies in our ignorance and confusion about ourselves is utterly inconsistent with absolute self-possession and gives powerful evidence of our non-divine selfhood.

6. Sixth sign of the finite personhood of human beings: the endangered condition of their freedom

In the fact that the human person can act through himself and determine himself in freedom, we can find nothing of our non-divine selfhood, as we have seen; a being that possesses itself so as to exist through itself must also act through itself and live in freedom. But there are certain circumstances of our freedom that give evidence of our contingency, such as the fact that, as we showed in our fourth criterion, the human person is not freedom through and through, as an absolute being would have to be, but also has a principle of nature, of enduring and undergoing, in his being. And now we come to something else about our freedom that reveals our non-divine selfhood; it is a certain weakness, or rather set of related weaknesses, *within* the exercise of our freedom.

1. Consider the fact that we often dread the task of acting through ourselves and we experience it as a burden to have to determine ourselves in freedom. We cannot endure the solitude in which we live when we live and act in a manner worthy of our selfhood. And so we try to escape from ourselves by distracting ourselves; we make noise, we become active, we are glad to be submerged in something vaster than ourselves. Now how can a being existing in supreme self-possession, so that it exists through itself, live in dread of its own self-possession and run away from the task of acting through itself? We see in ourselves a deeply wounded self-possession, which no one could possibly mistake for absolute self-possession.

2. But let us suppose a person who is willing to exercise his freedom and not escape from it; he, too, will very likely show a wound in his self-possession, as the following reflection shows.

I tried to explain at some length why we have to will what is good if we are going to use our freedom so as to thrive as persons. If we just abandon ourselves to the merely agreeable, then we cease to be the "captains of our soul" and are humiliated as persons; we have to will what is objectively good and worthy in order to gain possession of ourselves. But even when we understand this and want to commit ourselves to that which is objectively good, we nevertheless remain susceptible to the siren-song of the merely agreeable, and we are again and again betrayed into pursuing the agreeable at the expense of the objectively good. Let us resolve to serve the good as firmly as we will, still our freedom remains irresolute, vulnerable, and we experience the greatest difficulties in doing what we really want to do.[10] It is not that we are prevented from without from doing what we really want to do; the problem is in ourselves, within our very freedom, it is a problem of irresolution. We are constantly acting in such a way that, no sooner is an action over and done, than we wish it undone and are full of remorse over our inconstancy. Surely this reveals a tremendous weakness in our self-possession. A being that possesses itself in such a way as to exist through

---

10. Let us recall the powerful way in which St. Paul expressed this in Romans 7:15–24.

itself, could not be so divided against itself in its acting and face such difficulties in doing what it really wants to do.

3. This dividedness against ourselves does not only arise from our love of the merely agreeable; it is not always a matter of concupiscence, nor can it always be explained in terms of the tension between the life of the spirit and the body with all its "carnal stings" and "unbitted lusts." There is a dividedness at the very center of the life of the spirit, in the depths of the person. Kierkegaard spoke of it when in his analysis of despair he showed how each person has to choose between willing to be the self which he is, and refusing to be the self which he is (which is despair). Now the person who despairingly refuses to be the self which he is refuses to possess himself in a very important respect of self-possession. Just as a person has to know himself in order to enter into the full possession of himself, as we saw above, so he has to will himself, to affirm himself, to be happy in himself, in order to enter into the possession of himself. How could a being exist absolutely, in supreme self-possession, when it disowns itself and would be another self if only it could? Indeed, how could it exist absolutely if it is only capable of disowning itself? Even if it never does in fact disown itself, the mere possibility of this self-repudiation seems to imply a self-possession that forms a contrast with the supreme self-possession that is conceivable. Since we are capable of despair, and in the best of cases struggle against it, but are unable to affirm ourselves so as to extinguish the temptation to despair over ourselves, it follows that we must exist as non-divine persons.

7. Seventh sign of the finite personhood of human beings:
the unity of belonging to themselves and receiving
themselves as a gift

Let us return to the deep happiness born of the goodness of a person. I said in Chapter 7 that in being deeply happy we live and experience our selfhood and subjectivity in an incomparable way, and also our power of acting through ourselves. Now I add that the more deeply happy we are, then the more we experience our happiness, and our very selves, as surging up from beyond ourselves. The more deeply we come to ourselves and take possession of ourselves in being deeply happy, then, paradoxically, the more we experience ourselves as supported by something that is more than ourselves. And all the acts that we perform out of our happiness, all the acts of understanding, of deciding and committing ourselves, which are performed out of the inner fullness and inner freedom of happiness, are experienced as invested with this character of being our own but then again not entirely our own.

The experience of this character has to be distinguished from the experience of undergoing "nature" in ourselves, of which I spoke in connection with the fourth sign of finitude. For in undergoing "nature" we experience something originating outside of our freedom and possibly even threatening our freedom—in any case limiting it. But here we experience something which conditions our freedom from within, and conditions it more as we become freer. There is no paradoxical or dialectical unity of undergoing what happens in us and to us, and possessing ourselves in freedom; there is at first only an antagonism. But in being deeply happy we experience an amazing interpenetration of self-possession and a certain being given to ourselves from beyond ourselves. And yet this sense of the givenness of our being, different as it is from undergoing nature in ourselves and interwoven as it is with our self-possession, is also an experience of our non-divine selfhood. In being deeply happy I experience myself possessing myself but also not possessing myself.

Another such experience of not being completely my own can be found, paradoxically, in the deepest exercises of my self-determination. Let us think again of the fundamental option that Kierkegaard describes in his account of despair: the option whereby I choose either to be the self which I am, or refuse to be it. This choosing is normally carried out not in a single act, but in a lifetime of acting. But there are rare moments of greatly heightened freedom in which I am able, in a single act, to leap out of despair and to accept myself before God, or to throw myself into despair. These are fateful single acts in which I re-orient, as it were, my whole relation to myself and to God; what normally takes many acts repeated over a long time, is here accomplished in a single act in a moment. I am gathered up and handed over to myself for a fearful exercise of my self-determination. Now what I want to point out is that we cannot give ourselves the power to determine the whole direction of our existence in one decisive act; the mere fact that we want this power does not give it to us. The experience of having it, is not simply the experience of sovereignty and selfhood; it is rather the experience of sovereignty and selfhood interpenetrated by the experience of being raised above myself, of being empowered by some source outside of my freedom. And if I exercise my heightened powers of self-determination so as to turn away from despair and to will to be the self I am, then I experience myself as determining myself and at the same time as being supported by something not myself. Perhaps we could even venture to assert the general principle that the further a free act is from this supreme self-determination, the more the act is subject to my arbitrariness, and can be performed whenever I want to perform it (as the volition whereby I move a bodily limb); whereas the closer a free act is to this supreme self-determination, the more the performing of it, or rather the capacity of performing it, is withdrawn from my arbitrariness and is experienced by me as a kind of gift.

In moments of deep recollection we experience a similar sense of not being altogether our own. There are rare moments in which the present in which we live spreads out and deepens, letting us get far freer than usual from the transitoriness of temporal existence. This is a present in which, as we observed above, we can gain some intimation of what an eternal present might be. We are aware of living out of ourselves in a new dimension, of awakening to unsuspected powers of selfhood in ourselves; and yet the deeper the present in which we live, the stronger the sense of not being absolutely our own and of being grounded in sources outside of ourselves.

We find something similar in the deepest affectivity of which we are capable. It is especially von Hildebrand who has shown that persons are present in a unique way in certain affective experiences and stances. As I have already pointed out, he develops a contrast between willing with and without affective fullness. Thus we can will to benefit another, perhaps out of duty, but without taking any affective delight in the benefitting, or we can will to benefit the other precisely out of delight in benefitting him. Von Hildebrand says that in a certain sense we are far more fully present in the affectively strong commitment to the other than we are in the affectively dead commitment. The point in his analysis which is of particular interest to us is that this affective presence of persons in their acting is not directly subject to their willing; they may deplore their being affectively dead without having it in their power to give themselves affective life. There is an element of a gift in the ability to take delight in helping the person in need. And in general von Hildebrand finds that the deeper the affectivity, the stronger this gift-character. We can dispense with the gift and be in complete control of our acting only by paying the price of being affectively barren in our acting.

We have already observed the remarkable thing about the present approach to our finitude. In most of our previous considerations we have mainly brought to light the "antagonism" between our selfhood and the various circumstances of our finitude and contingency; now we get acquainted with a more dialectical relation between them, a relation in which our selfhood gets stronger in direct proportion to a certain "givenness" of our being. As a result of the interpenetration of human selfhood and givenness or giftedness which we have examined, we find that the finitude implied in the givenness seems to "infect" the human person in a particularly intimate way. When the factor implying the non-divinity of the person simply limits selfhood, the non-divinity seems to be more extrinsic to the person; but when the experience of selfhood increases with the increase of this factor, then the non-divinity seems to qualify the person more from within.

8. Eighth sign of finite personhood: selfhood awakens in the human person as a result of self-transcendence

Let us return to the dialectic of subjectivity and transcendence that we studied in Part II. One might at first doubt whether this dialectic implies anything non-divine, for it seems that even God's acting towards His creation must spring from, and be grounded in, and manifest His divine subjectivity and self-possession. And yet the dialectic of selfhood and transcendence *as found in human persons* gives undeniable evidence of their non-divine selfhood. For human persons *need* to transcend themselves so as to realize themselves. With us human persons selfhood does not always ground the act of self-transcendence, but needs this act for its perfection. But it seems inconsistent with the absoluteness of an absolute being to have any such need—to have to go beyond itself towards other beings so that, returning to itself, it can come into the full possession of itself. This would be a dependency on them that would imply a very imperfect self-possession. Since we frequently do live in this dependency on other beings, we must exist as non-divine persons.

Our need for self-transcendence shows itself already in the way in which consciousness awakens. It seems that we first go out of ourselves towards the objects of sensation and only then return to ourselves with the beginnings of conscious self-presence. The same holds for the higher operations of the person; we do not always act out of the fullness of our selfhood when performing acts of knowing and willing objects, or of exercising our world-openness towards the totality, or of giving the good its due. Rather we come to ourselves and gradually take possession of ourselves in and through performing such acts, and without performing them we remain unawakened in our personal existence. The same holds for the interpersonal, as we have stressed more than once; I find myself *in* turning to the other as Thou, and not before. We said that the other whom I encounter can mediate me to myself in a way in which I cannot mediate myself to myself. In a word: in very various ways we do what no absolute being could possibly have to do, namely to go out of ourselves so as to gather ourselves into ourselves.

The non-divinity implied in the necessity of this going forth is all the greater if we factor in the *contingency* commonly found in my encounter with some being. I mean that there is no strict necessity in me encountering some other person who mediates me to myself; it could have been that I would have never met him and that I would have remained without the growth in personal life that was possible for me through him. The distance to supreme self-possession is even greater when we consider this contingency of my meeting those who enable me to grow through transcending myself.

But we should once again (cf. the beginning of Chapter 6.3) take care to avoid saying, or even implying, that the whole *raison d'etre* of our transcending ourselves towards other beings is to gain the fullness of subjectivity that results from turning to them. If it is something of intrinsic value and goodness to which we respond, and if we are really to transcend ourselves in relation to it, then we have to respond in the consciousness that our response is due to the object, that the object calls for our response—and then we are not simply responding for the sake of developing our subjectivity. If we are fulfilling a moral imperative in acting towards some being and are conscious of obeying the imperative, then even less can our turning to the object be interpreted simply in terms of developing our subjectivity. We have to do justice to the full extent of our transcendence so as to be able to take the full measure of our non-divine personhood. It seems that our finite personhood is all the greater if we do not just use beings for coming to ourselves as persons, but have to take them seriously in their own right and can come to ourselves only as the subjective reflex, as it were, of giving them their due.

It is helpful here, as it has so often been helpful in this study, to consult our experience of recollection. While we can take a step towards recollecting ourselves by trying to get a direct hold on ourselves, it is only a step. We have already seen that we cannot generate the fullness of self-presence and self-possession directly out of ourselves, but also have to turn towards something, typically towards some question of ultimate importance, such as my death, or towards some existential truth, or towards God. We have to expose ourselves to the recollecting power of some such thing, and only in the encounter with it do we become more deeply recollected. But a being that possesses itself so as to exist through itself would have the full possession of itself out of its own resources, and could not possibly depend on its relation to other beings in order to come to itself.

We might recall here the world-openness of the human person. Persons need to exercise their world-openness in order to come alive as the totality that each of them is. As long as they live only in the environment or in some limited region of existence and fail to turn outward to things as they really and ultimately are, they remain cramped and confined in their personal existence; they cannot come alive as ones who have a being of their own and who exist as a world for themselves.

Again we can appropriate the expression of St. Thomas that we human beings exist with something of ourselves outside of ourselves. This time we interpret his expression like this: I find outside of myself the sources for living as person; I draw on these sources, transcending myself, and I receive ever fuller personal life as a result.

We have to take care not to exaggerate the awakening of selfhood as a result of self-transcendence. It is after all also true that I act out an inner fullness and strength that precedes the acting. When I recollect myself so as to face some difficult decision, I aim at first recovering inner strength and only then acting out of it. The truth is that both movements are found in the existence of persons: awakening as a result of acting, and awakening so as to be able to act. And the movements are dialectically interrelated. When persons act morally well, they build up moral being or character in themselves as a result; the moral being did not precede the acting but followed on it. But it is also true that moral being in a person, once established, becomes for its part a source of moral acting. And yet this source of acting, just when it grounds acting, depends on the acting it grounds; for if it is not exercised, it is lost. Thus moral being or character needs acting, as for its origin, so for its continuance. If we are at present stressing all that depends in the person on acting, then only because this is what implies non-divine personhood; in no way do we deny the many ways in which persons act out of an inner abundance.

9. The finite personhood of human beings as shown in their moral existence

We said at the end of the last chapter that persons cannot be understood only in terms of selfhood, but must also be understood in terms of their moral vocation. Personal selfhood can only be understood if it is referred to the moral vocation of persons. We become ourselves fully not only by becoming strong in our selfhood, but also by becoming morally worthy, and the one becoming does not simply coincide with the other. So far we have considered the non-divine personhood of human beings mainly by exploring their non-divine selfhood. It is only natural to complete our reflection on our non-divine personhood by considering our non-divine moral existence.

By divine moral existence I mean the goodness of a being that does not participate in goodness but that *is* its own goodness. This is what seems to correspond in the order of goodness to absolute existence in the order of existence. I need not insist that there really exists such a being; it suffices for our present purposes to consider the idea of supreme goodness and to show how great the contrast is between it and such moral goodness as we human persons are capable of.

We do not need to look for entirely new signs or criteria of non-divinity; we have only to apply to our moral existence some of the ones elaborated in the course of this chapter.

Let us return to the plurality of persons. On closer inspection the real criterion of finitude turned out to be this: a human person *is not* human nature but only participates in it; he can be one of many as a result of only participating in his nature. It is not difficult to see that a person has exactly the same relation to his moral goodness; no one of us *is* his moral goodness, we only participate in it. Think back to the transcendence of moral goodness discussed in Chapter 7.2. We saw that a person's moral goodness, though in one sense his own, in another sense (which we tried to explain) transcends him, rather as the wisdom sought by the philosopher transcends him and cannot be definitively possessed by him. If a morally worthy human being *were* his own goodness, then there would be no basis for this experience of transcendence, which implies that we only participate in goodness.

Next, we might return to the *partiality* of human persons, also discussed in connection with the plurality of persons. We saw that each human person has something incommunicably his or her own, so that the irretrievable loss of a human person would leave a gap in the world that could never be filled by any subsequent person. We also saw that this incommunicable something in each person stands in a relation of complementarity with the incommunicable something in all other persons, so that they all form a unity to which each makes an irreplaceable contribution: hence the talk of a certain partiality of each person. But surely this incommunicable something includes a moral component; each person is called to be morally worthy in an unrepeatable way, as we remarked at the end of the last chapter. We find this entirely verified in morally outstanding persons and in the saints; in each case we find that moral stature expresses incommunicable personhood. The so winning moral integrity of St. Thomas More is as unrepeatable in another as is his very person. It could hardly be otherwise given that persons are perfected as persons precisely in their moral worthiness, as we saw. It seems, then, that just as there is a fullness of human personhood that needs very many persons for its realization, so there is a fullness of human moral goodness that could never exist in one person but also needs many persons for its realization. It follows that human persons, as in their selfhood so also in their moral existence, are signed by a certain partiality.[11]

We might also return to the particular mixture of potentiality and actuality that we found in human persons. Of particular importance is the inescapability of living in this mixed condition, that is, the impossibility of us ever being all actuality and no potentiality. This impossibility is entirely verified in the moral life. Morally worthy persons only participate in moral goodness, as we just said. This means that morally worthy persons are *always* striving and are *never* finished, just like the philosopher in relation to wisdom. We do not just mean that the morally good person can always become better; this gives only a quantitative sense of unfinishedness, which as we saw is found even with personalist value. We say something quite different in saying that moral goodness has an inexhaustible fullness, which can only be related to in the way of participation. But then see what follows for the moral potentiality and actuality of human persons: they are not just *sometimes* in potency, rather they *always* exist in the tension towards an actuality that they can *never* finally and definitively possess. This lack of complete moral self-possession is not just a temporary lack, but an incurable lack.

11. There is, however, one kind of partiality that is out of the question. As we saw in Chapter 7, it makes no moral sense for human persons to specialize in one virtue to the neglect of others, such as specializing in justice to the neglect of truthfulness or chastity. There is a unity to the fundamental moral virtues such that each of us is called to cultivate all of them. And yet it seems that even among the morally serious persons who really do cultivate them all, we find that one has what the other lacks, and that they all complement rather than duplicate each other. This partiality, of which I speak in the text, goes, then, in a different direction from the partiality of one virtue in relation to the others.

Our reflection has much to gain from a subjective turn, that is, from considering the moral life as experienced from within. In this experience I find the following remarkable fact: as I grow morally, and become more of a person who is good as person, and become more and more deeply happy, I do not experience myself as approaching the limit or the end of my moral potentiality; *just the contrary, I experience how much more I could yet become.* It is as if the greater the actuality I achieve, then the more I reach beyond that actuality, experiencing it as a limit to be surpassed, and so the greater the potentiality of which I become aware in myself. This is why Kierkegaard says that it is a very superficially led ethical existence that thinks of itself as finished, and why he says that the deeper a man's ethical existence, the stronger his sense of being only at the beginning of his ethical striving. Hence the well-known fact that it is often the most developed moral personalities who pass the severest judgments on their moral condition. The morally worthiest persons have the strongest sense of the finitude of their moral stature.

As for the finitude revealed in the discrepancy of being and consciousness in human persons, the reader will recall that one of our arguments in Chapter 4.4 for this discrepancy was taken precisely from our moral experience. We said that the harm we inflict on ourselves in wrongdoing is usually not experienced in the form of a suffering proportionate to the harm; that the harm has a being of its own which surpasses the subjective experiencing of the wrongdoer. It is surely also true that the benefit to the person that comes from loving the just thing has a being of its own that almost always surpasses the subjective experiencing of the lover of justice. Since this discrepancy between being and subjective experiencing implies finitude, as we argued above in section 5, it follows that our ethical existence is signed by finitude.

I spoke in section 6 of the endangered condition of our freedom. Given that the moral condition of a person grows out of his freedom, and that without freedom persons do not even inhabit the moral universe, it follows that such moral worthiness as we are capable of is also endangered. The factor that shows the non-divinity of our selfhood also shows the non-divinity of our moral existence.

But in the case of our moral existence there is a particular danger deriving from the particular kind of negativity that belongs to moral evil. Moral evil means not only limited moral goodness, or even deficient moral goodness; it means a kind of anti-goodness, as we saw in contrasting it with the technical disvalue of the person. If moral goodness makes us worthy human beings, investing us with a fundamental soundness in our personhood, then moral evil, by contrast, tends to make us unworthy, unsound, indecent human beings. With moral evil we are exposed to the danger not just of deficient fulfillment of our personhood, but of a kind of anti-fulfillment.

In section 7 above I spoke about how we experience ourselves as not being entirely our own and how this is mysteriously interwoven with our deepest experiencing of ourselves as being our own. Much of what I said was taken from our moral existence; all in one I argued for the finitude of our selfhood and for the finitude of such moral worthiness as we can achieve. The same holds for the criterion of finitude articulated in section 8: in explaining how it is that human persons need self-transcendence, I mentioned that fact, well known since Aristotle, that moral character arises in us only as the result of actions in which we give the good its due.

But there is one evidence of our finite moral being that I cannot conveniently bring under any of the criteria of finitude discussed so far. I refer to the encounter with God in moral obligation as discussed in Chapters 6.4 and 6.5. Here we find ourselves quickening as persons by living a certain moral obedience that must ultimately be an obedience to God. This means that there is a radical moral dependency on God at the center of our moral existence. Perhaps we can even detect in the religiously potentiated experience of moral obligation something of our being metaphysically grounded in God. Perhaps the total claim on ourselves that we feel in conscience would not be possible if we did not exist through Him. In any case, we find that in being morally bound we are not absolutely our own; we stand in a moral dependency incompatible with existing through ourselves. A being called to moral obedience cannot *be* its own nature nor can it *be* its own goodness.

Let us conclude our meditation on the non-divinity of the human person, even though there are other evidences of it besides the ones that we have considered (one of these further evidences will come to light in the next chapter). I think that it constitutes an indispensable completion of all that was said in Part I about the selfhood of the person, and that we can no longer be suspected in the least of divinizing or absolutizing the human person. Whatever selfhood we find in the human person, and however amazing its extent, it is clearly a non-absolute, finite selfhood. Indeed, the non-divinity of this selfhood goes so far that we have again and again had to wonder why this finitude does not eliminate the selfhood and the personhood of human beings.

And yet, at the same time, the personhood of human beings receives a certain defense as a result of this stress on its finitude and non-divinity; only by affirming the finitude of human persons can we hold fast to the fact that human beings are indeed persons. What stands behind this paradoxical affirmation? If the human person were absolute, then each individual human person would inevitably be reduced to the status of a mere part. The reason is simply that the Absolute Being can only be one, as already Plato and Aristotle knew and as we ourselves were able to establish in reflecting on the divine incommunicability. Since there is not one human person but rather many of them, and since God can only be one, we could identify human persons with God only by making them parts of one being; but as we saw, as parts human beings are abolished as persons. But if human persons are recognized as non-divine, and if one makes a point of affirming their finitude and contingency, then there is no problem about their plurality. We are subject to no pressure to make them parts of any totality; we are free to grant them the space they need in order to be self-possessing persons.

CHAPTER NINE

The Image of God in Human Persons

I now propose to complete the reflection of the previous chapter on the dissimilarity of human persons and God by reflecting on the similarity of human persons and God.

What I mean by God has become more definite as we proceeded through Chapter 8. Each time we elaborated some respect in which human persons are precisely not divine, we elaborated the divine that they are not. Thus God must be one and must not exist as one of several; otherwise He would be non-divine for the same reason you and I are non-divine. He must be without beginning in time and also without temporal duration; otherwise He would be non-divine just as we are. And so on. The underlying idea, which I varied and unfolded, is that God cannot be God if He exists with anything of His being outside of Himself. He must possess Himself supremely, being His own existence and being His own essence.

It may at first glance seem that God, on this understanding of who He is, must be utterly beyond human persons and that there is little to say about the similarity obtaining between Him and them. But let us look more closely.

1. Personhood as a "pure perfection"

It will be noticed that among the many signs of our finitude discussed in the last chapter I did *not* mention our very personhood. I mentioned the temporality of our personhood, and the potentiality that always and inescapably encompasses us as human persons, and the component of "nature" that qualifies our human personhood, and some of the dependencies in which we as persons exist; but I never said that personhood as such, or any trait intrinsically connected with personhood, such as incommunicability, implies non-divinity. As far as the investigation of the previous chapter goes, *our human personhood* is limited in various ways, but *personhood as such* is not limited; or in other words, we human persons, limited though we are, are not limited because we are persons. If personhood as such were something which is itself non-divine, then this would have had to have been the first and most important thing to be said and explained in the previous chapter; all that we in fact said would be only secondary in relation to the intrinsic non-divinity of personhood itself. It is very important for the project of the present chapter, as of our entire study, that we were unable to find any such intrinsic non-divinity in personhood as such.

Indeed, we often noticed a kind of antagonism between personhood and the various circumstances of finitude, an antagonism that I expressed by saying that these circumstances would seem almost to abolish the possibility of persons, so that only the fact that they do indeed exist in such circumstances assures us of their possibility. Our thought here was not just that human persons fall short of divine personhood, with which we were constantly contrasting them, but that they seem to fall short of the minimal conditions for any personhood at all. But if there is such an antagonism between personhood and the leading circumstances of its finitude, then personhood is not itself intrinsically finite.

We can express it more positively like this. Personal being seems to require, as its natural mode of existence, absolute self-existence. If a person is distinguished by the fact of his belonging to himself, then a person does not really exist, or at least does not exist properly and authentically, until he exists through himself; but this is to exist absolutely. If we say that a person exists through another, we seem to be taking away what we had affirmed when we said that as person he belongs to himself. Further, a person who is through and through person would have to have that incommunicability in virtue of which he would be the only possible personal being; otherwise he does not have, at least not properly and authentically, the form of personhood. Thus the supreme selfhood of which I spoke throughout the last chapter seems to be the natural element, so to say, of a person. This undoubtedly explains why we have so often spoken of the person in terms that seemed more properly theological than anthropological, and why I have had constantly to guard against the appearance of absolutizing human persons. This also explains that antagonism, as I called it, between personhood as such and the various circumstances of finitude which characterize human persons.

We could also say it like this. The idea of divine being and the idea of personal being seem in a sense to coincide; the idea of personal being seems to contain nothing that was not found in the idea of divine being, and the idea of divine being seems to contain nothing that was not found in the idea of personal being. Both ideas center around selfhood, self-possession, self-action *(per se agere)*. Take the idea of absolute self-existence and develop it in relation to duration, actuality, nature, plurality, conscious self-presence, inwardness: and what results is the idea of the person. Or take the human person, and remove all the circumstances of his finitude: what results is the idea of an absolute being, or of God. The removal of finitude from the human person does not leave us with nothing, or with a metaphysical monstrosity like an "infinite horse," it rather leaves us with supreme self-possession, in which we can recognize God under one aspect.

This is why the idea of a finite, non-divine person seems much more problematical to us than the idea of a divine person. Perhaps we could have never been sure that contingent persons are possible if we were not ourselves contingent persons, and if we did not find the hard facts in ourselves which let us argue: *ab esse valet illatio ad posse* ("from the being of a thing one can infer to the possibility of the thing"). But we have no such puzzlement with the possibility of God, nor are we reduced to *inferring* its possibility from its existence; even though God is in some ways so far beyond us, and never directly experienced by us in the way in which we experience each other, He is nevertheless vastly more intelligible for us than the idea of a finite person.

Personhood as a pure perfection. We can express our main thought in the terms of Scholastic philosophy and say that personal being is not a *mixed* perfection but a *pure* perfection.[1] A mixed perfection is one that is essentially tied to finite, non-divine being, so that it is abolished as the perfection which it is if it is separated from its finitude. Take, for example, resourcefulness and cunning. For a being capable of having these, it is surely a perfection to have them, it is far better to have them than to

1. Cf. Seifert, *Essere e persona* (Milan: Università Cattolica del Sacro Cuore, 1989), Chapter 5, in which the distinction between pure and mixed perfections is elaborated, mainly in dialogue with Duns Scotus, and in which the fundamental metaphysical importance of the distinction is shown. For our purposes it is enough to make the distinction as we do in the text, but Seifert develops it in various other ways as well.

lack them; and yet resourcefulness and cunning presuppose limited power and even vulnerability in their possessor, and all of this documents the non-divinity of the resourceful or cunning being. Remove this non-divinity, and you remove the frame of reference in which alone resourcefulness and cunning can exist. But other perfections, the so-called pure perfections, have no such intrinsic finitude, and instead become themselves more fully the more they are released from the conditions of finitude. In his famous "ascent to absolute beauty" in the *Symposium* Plato treats beauty as just such a pure perfection. The more beauty is freed from its finitude, freed for example from embodiment, from plurality, etc., the more it becomes itself as beauty; and it is supremely itself only as Absolute Beauty. We could almost say: the same procedure that destroys the very possibility of cunning, reveals beauty for what it really is.

Now it follows from our discussion in the previous chapter that personal being is just such a pure perfection; for it is cramped and cut short, so to speak, in human persons, seeming almost to be contradicted by the finitude of our personhood, and it manifests itself for what it really is, and shows itself in its fullness, only in God. The circumstances of our finitude—plurality, temporality, potentiality, person-nature composition, discrepancies between being and consciousness, endangered freedom, existing in dependency—are none of them *constitutive of personhood;* they only serve to establish *limited personhood.* A person lacking all these circumstances of finitude would not be prevented from being a person, but would, on the contrary, be enabled to be person without qualification. Some of these circumstances of finitude, such as existing in dependency, are so far from constituting personhood that they seem even to contradict personhood, as we saw. Others, such as person-nature composition, are very difficult to think together with personhood, even if they do not in the same way seem to contradict it. Almost every philosopher who recognizes personhood in human beings will admit that personhood can in principle perfectly well exist without any admixture of nature (in the special sense that I gave this term at the end of Chapter 1). Or consider the plurality of human persons which, as we showed, serves to "weaken" the incommunicability of each: there is nothing about incommunicable selfhood that requires such a "weakening" of it. When we look beyond the finitude of our incommunicability towards God, we do not look beyond the very idea of incommunicability towards that which has nothing to do with incommunicability; we look instead towards the fullness of it. God *is* His being and does not merely *have* it, and so must exist as the one and only God. But this means that God exists, not beyond all incommunicability, but with supreme incommunicability.

Perhaps we have here in the idea of a pure perfection the deepest explanation for the mysterious "fullness of the human person," as we called it in Chapter 8.1. I said that no one human person, nor even many human persons, can exhaust, or even begin to exhaust, the human person; however many persons there are, there is always room for indefinitely many others, each of whom unfolds yet another possibility of the human person, and none of whom duplicates any of the others. Now this mysterious transcendence of the human person over all the human persons who ever have been and who ever will be, becomes more understandable if personal being is indeed a pure perfection. It is clear that if personal being needs absolute self-existence in order to be itself fully, then personal being has a plenitude that is forever beyond all the finite persons of our world.

Moral goodness as a pure perfection. If human persons perfect themselves as persons by being morally worthy (Chapter 7), then it would seem to follow that moral worthiness is not a mixed but a pure perfection. For if personal being is a pure perfection, then so must be, one would think, the full actuality of it in moral goodness. Of course, all such goodness as we human persons have is signed by finitude; indeed, there are even certain forms of moral goodness that presuppose some non-divine possessor of them, such as asking for forgiveness. But in this respect goodness is in no different a position than personhood, which, as it exists in human beings, is also signed by finitude, and this in the most various ways, as we have seen. To say that moral goodness is a pure perfection is to say that the finitude that characterizes its realization in ourselves does not belong to its very idea, is not a condition for its very possibility, but is in a sense extrinsic to it. More positively, it is to say that there is a potential infinity in moral goodness, and indeed that moral goodness needs to exist *in a divine being which is its own goodness,* in order to be itself fully. St. Augustine gives expression to goodness as a pure perfection when he says in a celebrated passage (*De Trinitate,* VIII, 3): "This good and that good; take away this and that, and see good itself if you can; so you will see God. . . ."

But can we show on independent grounds that goodness is a pure perfection? Can we only derive this from the fact that personal being is a pure perfection, or can we show this in such a way as to lend support to our claim that personal being is a pure perfection? Plato must have thought that goodness no less than beauty was a pure perfection, otherwise his teaching about the supreme metaphysical position of the Idea of the Good would be impossible. He evidently came to this conclusion independent of any analysis of personal being, which is not to be found in his work, as I pointed out in Chapter 2.4.

We think that it is possible to gain a direct (non-inferred) understanding of moral goodness as a pure perfection. Of course, it is only possible if one works with an adequate concept of good or value. If one thinks of good as nothing more than a function of human need which comes and goes as human needs arise and are satisfied, then good is nothing but a creature of our finitude and is as unlike a pure perfection as could be. But I will continue working with the idea of objective value that I introduced and developed in Chapter 6.1 and that I was presupposing in discussing the dignity of persons in Chapter 2.6 and also in discussing moral value in Chapter 7.

Let us return to our point of departure in this book, namely to our moral consciousness. Consider the atheist who rejects God in the spirit of Ivan Karamazov or of Camus, saying that God could prevent certain terrible evils in the world but does not prevent them. They are saying that God lacks a goodness that He should have: but with this they imply, and imply quite rightly, that God is susceptible of goodness, which in turn implies that goodness is a pure perfection. If you think that goodness is a mixed perfection, that it makes sense only in the setting of finite being, then you will not complain that God lacks it, any more than you would complain that He lacks resourcefulness, or self-control, or for that matter venerate Him for having such things. God is simply beyond certain excellences. But many a morally conscious atheist will deny that He is beyond goodness. They think, of course, that He lacks goodness, but at the same time they think that goodness is relevant to God, and this suffices to indicate to us that they think of goodness, and indeed of moral goodness, as a pure perfection. They think that God lacks goodness, not because of any intrinsic finitude of goodness, but because of the choices God makes in relation to His finite persons; and they think that He could and should have made choices that would express goodness. Of course, I am not speaking here *only* of atheists, I am speaking of anyone who recognizes the question of theodicy, including those of us who deal with it as theists. My idea is that the evidence for moral goodness as a pure perfection is so deeply rooted in our moral consciousness that it is understandable from very many points of view, even from the point of view of many an atheist.

It is remarkable that we do not have to show that God really exists and that He is supremely good; we can show that moral goodness is a pure perfection by means of insights that even atheists have. We and they can agree about a certain "potential infinity" of goodness, and this suffices to show that we have here to do with a pure perfection.

We can also find something for our question in our concrete moral experience. Let us return again to the experience of being morally bound in conscience, and let us assume the religious interpretation of it proposed in Chapter 6.4. The God who gives an intimation of Himself in conscience, the God of whom we catch a glimpse in experiencing the imperativity of moral obligation, is no value-free God, is no God beyond good and evil, but is a God absolutely "committed" to the good and who presents Himself as unsurpassably good. If He were any less than unsurpassably good, whence His "right" to bind us so authoritatively? Cardinal Newman speaks for all who deeply experience some intimation of God in conscience when he claims to find the divine holiness in conscience.[2] We might also recall here the brief exploration of our religious consciousness that we attempted at the end of Chapter 7.1. No religiously awakened person, I said, can do grievous wrong and think that his wrong remains outside of his relation to God, no more interfering with his relation to God than, say, some bodily defect; every religious person is aware that his wrong cannot "stand" before God and that it "estranges" him from God and that he needs to atone for it. But this implies goodness in God; the fundamental religious experience of the wrongdoer shrinking away from God would make no sense if God were altogether beyond good as He is beyond the cunning or the resourceful, if good were a purely finite category having no applicability to God. That moral goodness exists in God and is therefore a pure perfection, is the testimony of our moral and religious consciousness.[3]

With this we confirm the mysterious transcendence which in Chapter 7.1 we found in our experience of moral worthiness. The mysterious fullness in which we participate in being morally worthy, the mysteri-

---

2. Newman, *A Grammar of Assent*, Chapter 5, part 1.

3. The divine goodness is recognized in all "higher" forms of religious existence, according to the great study of Rudolf Otto, *The Idea of the Holy*. He shows that goodness is in fact a component of the holy; without a sense of the divine goodness a religious person can experience only the "numinous," but not the holy.

ous light breaking forth in the morally worthiest persons, the intimations of immortality surrounding them, this all becomes intelligible in a
new way if moral goodness is a pure perfection and if God is Goodness.

Now if we can in various ways understand that moral goodness is a
pure perfection without relying on the fact that personhood is a pure
perfection, then we can lend support to our claim that personhood is a
pure perfection. If that excellence which fulfills and perfects the person
is a pure perfection, can one perhaps argue that the personhood which is
thus perfected must itself be a pure perfection? But even apart from
such an argument, it is deeply significant for our present subject that the
primary excellence of persons is no less a pure perfection than personhood
itself.

God as exemplar and the human person as image. Let us conclude
the present section with a word on what follows for the relation between
God and human persons. Our examination of personal being as a pure
perfection discloses to us the exemplary causality that God exercises
towards human persons. It shows us that God is in unsurpassable fullness that personal being which all human persons have in a derived and
finite way, and that God is in unsurpassable fullness that moral worthiness to which all human persons are called. God and each human person
stand in a unique relation of *Urbild* (exemplar) and *Abbild* (image). One
sees why it is natural to speak here of a certain *theonomy* of the human
person; this expresses well the fact that each human person is *measured*
by God. I could also put it like this: there is a unique analogy between
each human person and God, an analogy in which God is the primary
analogate, and the human person the secondary analogate. Or I could
say, as I say in the title of this chapter, that there is a far-reaching "image" of God in human persons as a result of their personhood.

One might try to belittle the strength of this image. One might say
that we can find pure perfections in any and every finite being, and that
we can, therefore, say of any and every finite being that God is in absolute fullness what the given finite being is in a derived and diluted way.
Let us consider, for example, what it is to exist at all and not to be nothing. I shall assume that to exist is a pure perfection; that existence is not
tied to the frame of reference of contingency, but that even God exists,
and distinguishes His existence from that of all other beings by existing
without the limitations and restrictions under which they suffer, that is,
by existing with no adulteration of non-being, as Plato says in *Republic*
V, but with the fullness of existence, which means *being His own exist-*

ence. And so one can say that every stone and atom resembles God in the sense in which we were saying that each human person resembles God; every stone and atom has a resemblance with God based on a pure perfection, so that every stone and atom is in a partial and broken way what God is in absolute fullness.

We respond by saying that there is still an all-important difference between the way in which stones and atoms are images of God, and the way in which persons are images of God. The name of the pure perfection, being, is not the name of the nature of a stone or an atom; we reveal hardly anything about the specific nature of a stone (or of anything else for that matter) by saying that it shares in the pure perfection of being. When we speak more specifically about a stone, we are liable to express ourselves in terms of mixed perfections; indeed, "stone" expresses a mixed perfection. But the name of the pure perfection, person, is at the same time the most significant name of man; what other name could express the nature of man more deeply than the name of "person"? This name does not express some vast category containing human beings and many other beings as well: it expresses the *proprium* of our being, our innermost core. The same holds for the pure perfection, moral worthiness; it expresses the excellence not of many another kind of being as well as of ourselves, but of ourselves as persons. The image of God in human persons, then, is implanted more intimately in each human person than the reflection of God in non-persons is implanted in them.

The divine image in human persons may also differ in another way from the divine reflection in non-persons. The name "person" seems to be more expressive of God than the name "being." If this could be shown—we will not attempt to show it here—then it follows that God is imaged in human persons in a fuller, more revealing way than when He is reflected in non-persons.

In our discussion of the theonomy that comes from being measured by God as *Urbild,* we can also develop our understanding of the finitude of human persons. We are led to expect this by the very etymology of the word, theonomy, which was evidently formed to express a certain antithesis to autonomy. Human persons, for all their resemblance to God, still only resemble Him, and are in fact related to the Absolute Being as *Abbild* (image) to *Urbild* (exemplar). But no being having its nature only in a derived and very imperfect way and having the *Urbild* of itself outside of itself, can exist through itself. We have here a new and powerful evidence for the non-divinity of human persons, which ought to be added to the ten evidences of the previous chapter.

2. Deepening the thesis that personal being is a pure perfection by responding to the main objections that can be raised against it

1. Perhaps the reader will try to derive an objection from the seventh sign of non-divine personhood in the previous chapter. We expressed it like this: "experiences of us not belonging entirely to ourselves when we most belong to ourselves." My idea was that whereas some of the circumstances of our finitude simply limit our personhood and limit it more as they get stronger, others are such that the actuality of personal life increases as they get stronger. An example of the latter kind of circumstance of finitude would be what we called the gift-character in the deepest exercises of our freedom; as we saw, the deeper the self-possession and freedom, the greater this sense of a certain gift-character. One might object that personhood seems to be a mixed perfection if it grows and gains actuality in proportion as we live a certain way of not possessing ourselves. One might object that the marks of finitude should serve only to hem in and cut short a pure perfection; but if the relation between finitude and a perfection is a dialectical relation, then the perfection seems to be only a mixed one.

I would simply respond that this dialectical relation is in no way intrinsic to *personal being as such,* but belongs only to *human personal being.* Let us suppose that the divine freedom lacks this groundedness in something gift-like; let us suppose, as is surely the case, that in acting towards creation God acts out of supreme self-possession without any least sense of being mysteriously empowered by something above Himself. This unqualified self-possession would in no way make God depart from the idea of personhood; on the contrary, He would fulfill it more perfectly. He would not transcend personal being, but would have personal being in an unsurpassable way, or rather *be* personal being. It is, then, only in *the human person,* but not in *the person as such,* that we find the mentioned dialectic of freedom and gift-character.

2. One might raise an objection based on the vocation of human persons to interpersonal relation. One might point out that precisely our own reflections on the interpersonal have indicated that human persons do not enter into relation with others *only after* becoming complete personal selves. In this case interpersonal relation would in one sense be merely extrinsic to a person. We have seen that it is instead the case that

I come to myself not prior to but in and through transcending myself towards others and in and through receiving the transcendence of others toward me. I do not *first* possess myself and *only then* participate in the subjectivity of others, but self-possession can be fully realized only as a reflex of such participation (cf. Chapter 8.8). Not only that, but there is a truth about myself of which others precisely as others are the natural custodians, as we saw. In the most various ways others mediate me to myself. But in being thus ordained to interpersonal relation my personhood is ordained to a plurality of persons—the interpersonal requires at least two persons. But this means, according to the analysis of Chapter 8.1, that my personhood is intrinsically connected with finitude.

One could strengthen the objection by considering the moral goodness in which persons become themselves as persons. This, too, seems to require the interpersonal; the fullness of moral worthiness in a person seems to require the situation in which the person is an I facing a Thou. We need not go beyond the elementary respect for other persons from which we started in Chapter 1; in this respect there is often a moral worthiness, a moral splendor that would not be possible in a solitary person showing respect for himself. It follows anew that we are tied by our very personhood, or rather by that which perfects our personhood, to plurality.[4]

This objection does not turn, like the previous one, on the dialectical idea of personhood growing stronger as the notes of finitude become more distinct. It turns simply on the intrinsic connection between personhood and our first note of finitude.

Our response to the objection has already been prepared by the cautions we observed in discussing plurality in Chapter 8. We said that it is not plurality in the abstract that implies finitude, but only plurality as qualified in certain ways. For example, if each of several beings of a kind unfolds different possibilities of the kind, then they are several in such a way as to imply the finitude of each of them. Or if each of them is a distinct substance, then again they are many in such a way as to have to be finite through their many-ness. This means that the interpersonal is

---

4. I find that the thought on which the objection is based is expressed in a remarkable passage in Maurice Blondel, *L'être et les êtres* (Paris, 1935), 195–6, beginning with the sentence, "D'abord la personne n'est pas concevable comme une singularité unique." Blondel also mentions the essentially interpersonal dimension of moral goodness.

not "convicted" of finitude by the mere fact of its connection with plurality; for all we have said, it involves plurality without also involving
those qualifications that make plurality a criterion of finitude.

Of course, it is the Christian understanding of the Trinity which lets
us think more positively about the interpersonal existing without finitude or contingency; for in the Trinity there are three persons existing
not as finite but as divine persons. From the Christian point of view,
then, our vocation to interpersonal communion belongs no less to
personhood as a pure perfection than does our individual selfhood; the
image of God in human persons exists no less in the interpersonal than
in the individual aspect of personhood. Speaking as a philosopher one
may hesitate to affirm this, but whoever recognizes so much as the *possibility* of the one God existing as a community of persons can at least
recognize that plurality does not as such imply finitude, and that, therefore, the interpersonal as such also does not imply it.

But there is a way in which one can come surprisingly close to this
fundamental article of Christian faith without ceasing to speak as a philosopher. If we can establish beyond a doubt that personal being is a
pure perfection, then the interpersonal structure of personal being will
not count as a telling objection that requires an answer, *it will instead be
treated as something that enables us to expand our understanding of all
that is contained in the pure perfection of personhood.* That is, we will
argue that since personal being is a pure perfection, and since personal
being can be fully itself only interpersonally—and this not just in the
case of human persons but of any possible persons—then the interpersonal must belong to the pure perfection of personhood. This means that
there must be what we have called a "potential infinity" in the interpersonal, and that there must be something interpersonal in the supreme
personhood of God. That there are neither more nor less than three divine persons standing in the relations which are believed by Christians,
this surely exceeds all that can be understood by philosophy. But that
God cannot be a solitary person, that there must be interpersonal life
within God: this can be approached by philosophy. One has only to put
the understanding of personal being as a pure perfection together with
an adequate account of the place of the interpersonal in the fully developed existence of persons.

3. One commonly objects that the very idea of personhood seems to
imply some lack or deficiency in every person. For a person is a being
which in a particularly strong sense is itself and is not any other. Certainly among human persons we find that a given person becomes him-

self and no other as a result of having as incommunicably his own that which no other can have, and of necessarily lacking that which others have as incommunicably their own. It seems each human person owes his selfhood to a certain having and lacking. And so it seems that there is some lack inherent in the very idea of selfhood and solitude, which in turn implies that personhood is after all only a mixed perfection. One might try to add force to this objection by saying that the divine, infinite being must be supremely comprehensive, and that being "oneself and no other" expresses a mode of being too particular and exclusive to be divine and infinite. A person seems, according to the fundamental formula of personhood to which we committed ourselves in Chapter 1, to be necessarily "one being among others," and this is just what God in His infinity is not.

I can grant this much to the objection, that many of the ways in which a human person marks himself off against others give evidence of finitude and contingency. There are many selfish ways of standing in oneself and separating from others, there are also pathological ways of doing this, as in schizophrenia, but one should take care not to say that these are intrinsic to the selfhood and solitude of personal existence, for it is clear that a person can grow out of them without losing his selfhood, and in fact grows out of them by exercising his selfhood. But what about the partiality with which each human person embodies "the riches of personal being," as we expressed ourselves? Does each not distinguish himself from others by this partiality, in that each has what the others lack? And does this partiality, which belongs to our very being and does not derive from any fault, not reveal our finitude, as we ourselves argued above?

I would say by way of response that selfhood implies lack only among human persons, and that lack or deficiency does not flow from the very idea of personal selfhood. When in proposing the principle of identity we say that a being is itself and no other, we do not imply that there must in every case be other beings from which any given being distinguishes itself. God is Himself and no other in the sense that His incommunicability "destroys" the possibility of other Gods; as we saw, He *is* His divinity, having it as incommunicably His own, and so existing as the only possible God. God is in a supreme sense Himself and no other, since His incommunicability prevents the existence of any other God. Thus there need be no lack in God as there would be if another God had something as incommunicably His own; there can be no such lack, since there can be no other God. The unicity of God lets us see how selfhood can exist without any of that "mutual lacking" which characterizes selfhood among human persons.

Of course, there also exist contingent persons "outside" of God; you and I are persons who are not God. But this fact that God is not us human persons, need imply no lack in God. If God is related to us as *Urbild* to *Abbild,* then He has to be thought as having in divine fullness, or rather as *being* in divine fullness, that according to which we exist in a finite and contingent way. The lack would seem to be all on the side of the *Abbild* and not at all on the side of the *Urbild.*

4. The third objection can be cast in a more general form, and then we have a fourth objection, which merits a brief mention here. There is a deep-rooted tendency of the human mind to think that whatever exists as something definite and determinate, as this and not that, can only exist as limited. It is the tendency to think that the *determinate* is the same as the *finite,* or at least that it implies the finite. I say that this is a generalized form of the previous objection, because in a discussion of pure perfections it tells against not only personal selfhood but against all other pure perfections as well (with the possible exception of the perfection of existence). For it means that any quality which has a definite character or content, so that it is itself and is not to be confounded with any other quality, is by that very fact a limited quality. Thus, for example, goodness, since it can be contrasted with all the things different from goodness, must be finite. From this it follows that there are no pure perfections at all, unless perhaps the pure perfection of an undifferentiated *esse ipsum,* or being itself.

Since this objection is not directed specifically against personal being, and since the response to it does not necessarily require that we explore personal being more closely, we will not deal with it here. I will just mention one of the responses which Josef Seifert has given by going back to the Scholastic theory of the transcendental properties of being. One said within this theory *omne ens est res* and *omne ens est aliquid,* and taken together these mean something like, "every being is a definite something, is itself and no other." Since this was said within the theory of *transcendentals,* one meant that a being could not amount to a being without having some determinate content. If one identifies with finitude the transcendental determinateness expressed by *res* and *aliquid,* then one holds that the only possible real being is finite and that, therefore, the existence of God is impossible.[5] Thus any theist who recognizes

5. See Josef Seifert, "Esse, Essence, and Infinity: a Dialogue with Existentialist Thomism," *The New Scholasticism* (1984) 58, 84–98, where he develops a distinction

these transcendental properties of being must deny that the finite is one with, or necessarily follows from, the determinate.[6]

5. One could try to argue that moral goodness is a mixed perfection, and on this basis to suggest that personhood, given its particular relation to moral goodness, must also be a mixed perfection. Aristotle certainly treats moral goodness in this way when he contrasts it with intellectual excellence, which alone counts for him as a pure perfection. He says that moral excellence presupposes bodily appetites, the reasonable mastery of which gives moral excellence (*Nichomachean Ethics,* 1102b, 1103a); it follows that a non-bodily rational being is beyond the possibility of moral goodness and badness. This is why he says that the typical acts of moral excellence cannot be conceived among the gods, the only excellence conceivable in them being intellectual (*Ethics,* 1177–1178).

It is not difficult to show the inadequacy of such an understanding of moral virtue, especially if we look back to some of our results in Chapter 3.2 on what we called subjective freedom. That fundamental deciding about oneself of which Kierkegaard speaks presupposes no body, no unruly appetites; it is altogether conceivable in a non-embodied spirit, which—assuming it to be a finite spirit—could be as exposed to the danger of despair over itself as we are, and which could, therefore, be just like us in standing before the fundamental moral task of willing to be the self which it is. Such a spirit is as capable of moral goodness as of intellectual goodness. But this implies that moral goodness is not tied to having a body, and with this we clear away the reason given in the objection for taking moral goodness to be a mixed perfection.

Again: if we think of the virtue of reverence, or of love of truth, we have to do with virtues that presuppose no embodiment at all, and which can in fact be exercised in purely contemplative ways, so that as moral virtues they share in all of that dignity which Aristotle reserves for the intellectual virtues. We would say to Aristotle that moral virtue, if understood rightly in all of its forms, is no more tied to our embodiment than is intellectual virtue, which Aristotle himself treats as a pure perfection (though of course without expressing himself by means of this concept).

---

between *Abgrenzung* (delimitation from others) and *Begrenzung* (limitation), and shows that the former can exist without the latter.

6. With great intuitive force C. S. Lewis captures the fundamental metaphysical difference between the determinate and the finite in his *Miracles,* Chapter 11. This passage deserves to be recognized as a classic contribution to metaphysics.

Still other objections might be raised to personhood being a pure perfection, but perhaps I have found and dealt with the weightiest ones.

In defending our thesis that personal being is a pure perfection we have responded to thinkers such as Averroists, German Idealists, Schopenhauer, and others, who hold that the distinct individuality of human persons is a kind of human appearance, or is valid only among the relativities of finite being, and that at the level of ultimate reality this distinctness vanishes and gives way to a oneness that excludes a plurality of incommunicable persons. If personal being is a pure perfection, then it not only exists at the highest level of being, but exists most properly at that level, existing in only a derived way in the realm of finite persons.

3. Some consequences for human knowledge that follow from this theonomy of the human person

On the basis of what has emerged regarding the theonomy of the human person, we can not only (1) come to know God through knowing the human person, but can also (2) come to know the human person through knowing God.

1. As a result of the fact that human persons are images of God, or in other words that God is the norm and measure of human persons, there must be a way of developing our knowledge of God through our knowledge of human persons.

Let us suppose that the idea of God is for us still only an abstract idea; that it seems to us to be a construction of philosophical theologians, an idea the inner unity of which escapes us, and that we cannot even make out what might be meant when one says something such as that "God is His own essence," or when one speaks of "the eternal present" in which He exists, or of His transcendence over the world. And let us suppose that we want to grasp this inner unity and render the idea of God more concrete to ourselves, or in other words that we want, in the well-known terms of Cardinal Newman, to go beyond a merely *notional* apprehension of God and attain to a *real* apprehension of Him. Surely there is hardly any more promising approach than to try to understand God through the human person. How better make sense of God being His own essence, and hence being the only God, than to consider the unrepeatability and the incommunicability of human persons, and the way in which each person exists as if the only person, and so to find even in ourselves something that in a way foreshadows the divine self-possession and the divine unicity? As for the eternity in which God exists, we can get a kind of glimpse of it in moments of deep recollection, for hardly anything is so characteristic of deep recollection as an extended present. As I already remarked, we understand in such moments that if the present in which we live were to extend itself without restriction, then our mode of duration would pass from time over into eternity. Or what about the transcendence of God over the world, and the insistence of theologians that God is not in the world, not even as the most important and most powerful being in it, but has to be conceived as entirely beyond the world? In discussing person and nature in the human person, we saw that we ourselves, insofar as we are persons called to live out of our inwardness, begin to transcend the world, but do not transcend it entirely because of the moment of nature in our being, which lets us be acted upon by other beings. From here we can gain some understanding of why a being which is all person and no nature at all, which is pure inwardness, would transcend the world in a radically different way than we do.

It seems that the concreteness which the idea of God can in this way gain for us need have nothing to do with the concreteness of the anthropomorphic; we need not reduce the divine unicity to something human-all-too-human by approaching it from the incommunicability of human persons. It is rather the case that we are simply drawing the consequences of our being *theomorphic* beings. For if personal being is a pure perfection, and we are non-divine persons, and personal being is fully itself only in God, then it is philosophically altogether in order to try to draw out the lines beginning in our human personhood, and to try to apprehend God as the completion of that which begins in us as persons.

It seems that even elements of revelation can be clarified by recourse to the personhood we know in ourselves. When one looks in to the Trinitarian faith of Christians as expressed in the Athanasian Creed, one might desire to grasp better the unity of it and to apprehend it more concretely. To this end one would do well to consider the way in which—we were discussing this above—we human persons are ordered one to another, and mediate ourselves to each other, remembering that we do not first become intact, thriving persons and only subsequently turn to others, but rather gain ourselves in and through relation with others. Along this line we can go far towards understanding the metaphysical impossibility of a solitary person, and the metaphysical necessity of persons always only existing together with each other, even in God. This simple reflection already renders more concrete the three-in-one

Trinitarian faith of Christians. When one looks more closely at the articles of this faith, one finds still further elements susceptible of being rendered more concrete by thinking of human persons. Thus the radical relationality of each divine person—the first divine person, for example, does not have His personal identity prior to the fatherly act of generating a son, but He has it only in and through this act—can be helpfully approached by considering the radicality with which we human persons exist towards and with others (though of course we never exist with them in such a way as to form one being with them).

Here is another example of how Christian revelation can be fruitfully approached through analogy with the human person. The Christian God is eminently a "living God," *Deus videns et vivens*. As Pascal says, He is not just the God of the philosophers but the God of Abraham, Isaac, and Jacob. He chooses whom He will, He hardens whom He will. He speaks when He will, then He hides Himself for as long as He will. He flares up in anger, and then remembers mercy. Many people can see in this living God of Christian revelation only anthropomorphic color and imagery; they think that God cannot *really* be like this. The analogy with persons requires them to consider whether there may be more literal truth in this living God than they think. For persons are not just instances of general types but are incommunicable individuals, as we know; they do not unfold only according to the general laws of the types to which they belong, but each is also, in the sense explained in Chapter 2.7, a law unto himself. The apparently anthropomorphic passages in Judeo-Christian revelation in fact convey to us the personhood of God; the "living God" of revelation is a personal God. The free electing and the free rejecting on the part of the Judeo-Christian God is just the kind of divine life that expresses divine personhood. These deeds of God prevent the human mind from staying with a onesidedly essentialistic understanding of God, as if the ways of God could be entirely understood in terms of divine names such as powerful, knowing, just, etc. In God there is not just an eternal divine essence which, if only we understood it better, would render God's deeds entirely intelligible to us; in God there are incommunicable persons acting in freedom.

Of course, the human mind will often fail to discriminate well between what belongs to a pure perfection as such and what belongs only to the human realization of it, and will in this way be betrayed into some anthropomorphism. Nor should we deny the perpetual danger that the human mind runs of failing to do justice to the fundamental metaphysical distinction between finite and infinite, between contingent and absolute, between being that shares in its essence and being that is its own essence. And yet it remains the case that one can suspect anthropomorphism where there is none, where there is in fact a revelation of God as personal.

These are meant only as a few hints as to how the knowledge of God might be rendered more concrete on the basis of our knowledge of our own personhood. There is no other being in the realm of our direct experience which can compare with the human person in mediating to us this more concrete apprehension of God.[7]

2. We now ask whether we ever get to know ourselves as persons, or at least deepen our understanding of ourselves as persons, on the basis of knowing God. In other words, does our knowledge ever proceed, not from our personhood to God, but from God to our personhood? Such knowledge would constitute a very significant experience of our nondivinity. God can presumably know Himself through Himself; He would be abolished as God if He had to consider Himself in the light of another in order to know Himself as God.

Without understanding that personal being is a pure perfection, we cannot understand ourselves adequately as persons, we cannot experience fully, nor can we account for, the mysterious ultimacy of our being, the unsurpassability of existing in the form of a person. But we cannot understand personal being as a pure perfection without relating it to God. For the very idea of a pure perfection is that it needs the divine infinity in order to be itself fully. Just as mixed perfections make no sense apart from finite being, to which they are intrinsically tied, so pure perfections make full sense only in reference to God. If, then, we were to abstract completely from God in our metaphysics of the human person, we would be unable, strictly unable, to understand that amazing ultimacy—I even wants to say, "absoluteness"—which belongs to our personal being.

7. We might add that the knowledge of our own personhood can enrich our theological knowledge in other ways than rendering it more concrete. For instance, in Christology one has put the question whether God really assumes our humanity in Christ; one has asked this in light of the fact that personhood, which is at the center of our humanity, is divine and not human in Christ. Christ seems to be more divine than human as a result of being divine in both person and nature, and being human only in nature. But if we consider that our human personhood is, as a pure perfection, *already in a certain sense divine,* and that we exist theomorphically as a result of existing as persons, then the divine person in Christ does not appear to be so foreign to human personhood as it may at first seem.

It would be a mistake to think that this ultimacy and unsurpassability of our personhood is nothing other than the *relation* of analogy between the human person and God; no, it is an ultimacy entirely intrinsic to, immanent in the human person. It is fully *revealed* only when we set ourselves in relation to the divine *Urbild* of our being; but that which is revealed is not just a relation in which we stand towards God, but something of our own.

There is perhaps a more general consideration that helps us understand this element of theonomy in our gaining knowledge of ourselves as persons. Since our personhood is so "reduced" and "diluted" by our finitude, as we saw, it may be that only some glimpse of personal being in its absolute fullness lets us awaken fully to personal being in ourselves. There may be some analogy to this cognitive process in the way in which we cannot recognize a badly drawn geometric figure for the figure which it is, until we are reminded of the figure in its ideal purity and perfection. Perhaps one will object that we can surely understand something of our personal being without any reference at all to God. Let us grant it; it is nevertheless the case that one in general understands better some species or some perfection by considering it, not in its weakest and most inauthentic specimens, but in its most complete and perfect specimens. Thus one can make more progress in understanding what love is by considering love not as distorted by selfishness, sensuality, possessiveness, etc., but in its noblest and purest forms. We might recall here the claim of Plotinus that we can come to understand temporal duration in the light of the supreme duration which is eternity.[8] Now in somewhat the same way one can make more progress in understanding who we are as persons by considering not just our diluted and restricted personhood but the supreme personhood of God.

It can hardly be denied that certain Christian thinkers have been enabled to do more justice to the interpersonal nature of man by thinking

---

8. He says at the beginning of his treatise on Time and Eternity: "We begin with Eternity, since, when the standing Exemplar is known, its representation in image—which Time is understood to be—will be clearly apprehended—though it is of course equally true, admitting this relationship of Time as image to Eternity the original, that if we chose to begin by identifying Time we could thence proceed upwards by Recognition (the Platonic Anamnesis) and become aware of the Kind which it images." Plotinus, *The Enneads,* tr. MacKenna (London: Penguin, 1991), III, 7, 214. And so with regard to time and eternity he recognizes the same two possibilities for our knowledge that we recognize with regard to the human person and God: in both cases we have two terms, each of which can be known in the light of the other.

of man in relation to the interpersonal Trinitarian life of God. It is not that their Trinitarian faith enables them to recognize the interpersonal at all, but it enables them to do more justice to the depth at which we exist towards and with other persons, and it leads them to an understanding of the impossibility of a solitary person. Of course, the reverse relation also obtains, as we just said above: we can approach the interpersonal life of God through our own interpersonal life. The relation runs in both directions, starting with man and leading to God, and starting with God and leading back to man.

This partial dependency of our self-knowledge on some partial knowledge of God is very expressive of the theonomy of the human person. Even though the human person exists as a being of his own, and even though nothing is closer to him than his personhood, and even though his personal subjectivity lies at the very center of his being, he nevertheless recognizes himself fully as person not directly through himself, but in part through his relation to and his encounter with God. When it comes to our knowledge of other aspects of our own being, we do not find this theonomy. Thus we do not, it seems, need any reference at all to God in order to understand that we have a body.[9] But precisely our personhood, where we are most ourselves, seems to need this reference in order to be known fully. The theonomy of our knowledge of ourselves as persons seems to be strongest precisely when it is a question of coming to know, not what is on the periphery of, but what is at the center of our personhood.

But there is another and more existential form of this theonomy of knowledge. I am thinking of the way in which we become aware of our personhood in the living encounter with a personal God. To believe that I am known by God, willed by Him, called by name, taken seriously by Him, held accountable by Him, is to have an overwhelming experience of personal selfhood. Perhaps the impact of Christian revelation on our experience of our personhood is above all to be explained in terms of such encounters. We have spoken about the encounter with another human person, who can mediate me to myself: what will the encounter with the Divine Person not do for my self-understanding as person? We have gotten a glimpse of the answer in discussing (Chapter 6.5) the experience of personhood that goes with the religiously potentiated conscience. We can hardly do justice to this subject here, but we did not want to leave it unmentioned.

9. Different, of course, is the case of understanding the place of the body in the makeup of the human person; this perhaps has a certain theological foundation.

If there is any merit in these thoughts on knowing ourselves as persons through knowing God, then we are in a position to respond decisively to an atheistic thesis of Feuerbach and Nietzsche. They say that by considering man with reference to God we drain man of his being, strength, dignity; we transfer all of this to God, who grows great at man's expense. Thus they think that we have to become atheists if we are going to affirm man in all the being, strength, and dignity proper to him. But I respond that if it is the personhood of man that is revealed by seeing man in relation to God, then this "humanistic atheism" collapses. For personhood means precisely existing in freedom, existing as one's own end, having not price but dignity. To experience one's personhood more deeply is not to have one's being and dignity drained away; it is to grow in the sense of one's being and dignity. The effect of seeing ourselves in relation to God is not to be humiliated, reduced to nothing; it is to be confronted with the fact that as persons we are immeasurably more than we could have imagined or thought.

Conclusion. Let us bring this study to an end by considering how the *Abbild-Urbild* relation between human persons and God challenges a certain modern sensibility about human existence. Many think, and feel as well, that the realm of human existence is an entirely secularized, finite realm, that we live and move and have our whole being amid the relativities of existence. Even our personal being, in which they too perhaps recognize the selfhood and solitude of which we have spoken, seems to be thoroughly stamped by this finitude and relativity. Insofar as they still speak of God they say that He is utterly beyond us, incomprehensible to us. Perhaps He makes Himself felt enough for us to experience the finitude and relativity of our existence; they are ready to admit that this way of experiencing ourselves and our world presupposes some apprehension of God, however hidden, however implicit it might be. But for the rest He is hidden, they say, and gives no more positive disclosure of Himself. And so they fear God as one who, in His otherness, could be a source of heteronomy for us men.

But our reflection on the pure perfection which lies in our personhood as well as in moral worthiness, and on the analogy obtaining between ourselves and Him, and especially on the similarity implied in this analogy, shows an amazing "principle of continuity" between ourselves and God, so that we can gain knowledge of Him through ourselves and of ourselves through Him. What I am here suggesting is verified in a certain experience that is widely had by religious people. They speak of a mysterious familiarity, or kinship, or consanguinity, which they experience in God, and which they experience together with the hiddenness and mystery of God. If God really is in absolute fullness that which we human persons are (and are called to be) in a finite and contingent way, then it is entirely understandable how religiously awakened persons would have this sense of God as not only profoundly other, but at the same time as mysteriously familiar.

Bibliography

Anscombe, G. E. M. "Modern Moral Philosophy." *Philosophy* 33 (1958): 1–19. Reprinted in *Collected Philosophical Papers*. Vol. 3. Minneapolis: University of Minnesota Press, 1981.

Aquinas, St. Thomas. *In Librum De Causis.* Lectio XV, n. 5. Edited by Ceslai Pera, O.P. Turin: Marietti, 1955.

Aquinas, St. Thomas. *On The Truth of the Catholic Faith (Summa Contra Gentiles).* Bk. 3, chaps. 111–114. Translated by Vernon J. Bourke. Garden City: Image Books, 1956.

————. *Scriptum Super Sententiis Petri Lombardi.* Book 3. Edited by Maria Fabianus Moos, O. P. Paris: P. Lethielleux, 1933.

————. *Summa Theologiae.* Pt. 1, Q. 29. Translated by Fathers of the English Dominican Province. 2nd edition. London: Burns Oates & Washbourne, Ltd., 1926.

Aristotle. "Nicomachean Ethics." In *The Basic Works of Aristotle,* edited by Richard McKeon, 935–1112. New York: Random House, 1941.

Bolt, Robert. *A Man for All Seasons.* New York: Vintage Books, 1990.

Buber, Martin. "Distance and Relation." In *The Knowledge of Man.* Edited by Maurice Friedman and translated by Maurice Friedman and Ronald Gregor Smith. New York: Harper & Row, 1966.

————. *I and Thou.* Translated by Ronald Gregor Smith. New York: Charles Scribner's Sons, 1958.

Clarke, S.J., Norris. *Person and Being.* Milwaukee: Marquette University Press, 1993.

Crosby, John. "Are Good and Being Really Convertible? A Phenomenological Inquiry." *The New Scholasticism* 57 (1983): 465–500.

————. "Conscience and Superego: A Phenomenological Analysis of their Difference and Relation." In *The Nature and Tasks of A Personalist Psychology,* edited by James DuBois, 47–58. Lanham: University Press of America, 1995.

————. "Dialektyka podmiotiowosci i transcendencji w osobie ludzkiej." (The Dialectic of Subjectivity and Transcendence in the Human Person). *Ethos* 2, no. 3 (1988): 57–65.

————. "The Encounter of God and Man in Moral Obligation." *The New Scholasticism* 60, no. 3 (1986): 317–355.

————. "The Idea of Value and the Reform of the Traditional Metaphysics of Bonum." *Aletheia* 1, no.2 (1978): 221–336.

————. "The Personhood of the Human Embryo." *Journal of Medicine and Philosophy* 18 (1993): 399–418.

Engelhardt, H.T. "The Ontology of Abortion." *Ethics* (April 1974): 217–234.

Gracia, Jorge. *Individuality: an Essay on the Foundations of Metaphysics.* Albany: State
     University of New York Press, 1988.
————. *Introduction to the Problem of Individuation in the Early Middle Ages.* Munich:
     Philosophia Verlag, 1984.
Guardini, Romano. *Die Annahme Seiner Selbst.* Würzburg: Werkbund Verlag, 1960.
————. *Welt und Person.* Würzburg: Werkbund Verlag, 1965. Translated by Stella Lange
     under the title *The World and the Person* (Chicago: Regnery, 1965).
Hengstenberg, Hans–Eduard. *Philosophische Anthropologie.* Munich: Anton Pustet Verlag,
     1984.
Hölscher, Ludger. *The Reality of the Mind: St. Augustine's Philosophical Arguments for the
     Human Soul as a Spiritual Substance.* London: Routledge, 1986.
Kant, Immanuel. *Critique of Practical Reason.* Translated by Lewis White Beck. New York:
     Bobbs–Merrill, 1956.
————. *Foundations of the Metaphysics of Morals.* Translated by Lewis White Beck. New
     York: Liberal Arts Pres, 1959.
Kelsen, Hans. "Relativism and Absolutism in Politics and Philosophy." *What is Justice?*
     Berkeley: University of California Press, 1957.
Kierkegaard, Soren. *Concluding Unscientific Postscript.* Translated by David Swenson.
     Princeton: Princeton University Press, 1941.
————. *The Sickness unto Death.* Edited and translated by Howard V. and Edna H. Hong.
     Princeton: Princeton University Press, 1980.
Lewis, C. S. *The Abolition of Man.* New York: Macmillan, Co., 1976.
————. *Miracles.* New York: Macmillan Co., 1971.
Lynkeus [Josef Popper]. *Das Individuum und die Bewertung menschlicher Existenzen.* Dresden:
     Verlag von Carl Reissner, 1910.
Maritain, Jacques. *Existence and the Existent.* Translated by Gerald Phelan and Lewis
     Galantiere. New York: Doubleday, 1948.
————. *The Person and the Common Good.* Translated by John Fitzgerald. New York: Charles
     Scribner's Sons, 1947.
Newman, John Henry. *An Essay in Aid of a Grammar of Assent.* London: Longmans, Green,
     & Co., 1898.
————. *Parochial and Plain Sermons.* Vol. 4. London: Rivingtons, 1870.
————. *Sermons Preached on Various Occasions.* London: Longmans, Green & Co., 1900.
Ortega y Gasset, Jose. "Ensimismamiento y alteracion." In *Obras Completas.* Vol. 5. Madrid:
     1958.
Otto, Rudolf. "Das Gefühl der Verantwortlichkeit." In *Aufsätze zur Ethik.* edited by Jack
     Boozer, 143–174. Munich: C.H. Beck Verlag, 1981.
————. *The Idea of the Holy.* Translated by John Harvey. London: Oxford University Press,
     1950.
————. "Wert, Würde und Recht." In *Aufsätze zur Ethik,* edited by Jack Boozer, 53–106.
     Munich: C. H. Beck Verlag, 1981.
Pieper, Josef. *Was Heisst Philosophieren?* Munich: Kosel Verlag, 1963. Translated by
     Alexander Dru under the title "The Philosophical Act." in *Leisure, The Basis of Culture.*
     (New York: New American Library, 1956).
Plato. "Gorgias." In *The Dialogues of Plato.* Vol 1. Translated by B. Jowett. New York: Random
     House, 1937.
Quiles, S.J., Ismael. "La Esencia del Hombre," In *Antropologia Filosofica In-sistencial.* Buenos
     Aires: Ediciones De Palma, 1983.
Rahner, Karl. *Geist in der Welt.* Munich: Kosel Verlag, 1957.
————. *Grundkurs des Glaubens.* Freiburg: Herder Verlag, 1976.

————. *Hörer des Wortes.* Freiburg: Herder Verlag, 1963. Translated by Joseph Danceel S.J. under the title *Hearers of the Word* in the Gerald McCool edition of *A Rahner Reader.* (New York: Seabury Press, 1975).

————. "Theology and Freedom." In *Theological Investigations.* Vol. 6. Translated by Karl and Boniface Kruger, 178–196. New York: Seabury Press, 1974.

————. "Über die Frage einer formalen Existenzialethik." In *Schriften zur Theologie.* Vol. 2. Einsiedeln: Benzinger Verlag, 1955. Translated by Karl H. Kruger under the title "On the Question of a Formal Existential Ethics" in *Theological Investigations.* Vol 2. (London: 1963).

Ratzinger, Joseph. "Concerning the notion of person in theology." *Communio* 17, no.3 (1990): 439–434.

Reale, Giovanni, and Dario Antiseri. *Il pensiero occidentale dalle origini ad oggi.* Brescia: La Scuola, 1983.

Rhonheimer, Martin. "Gut und Böse oder Richtig und Falsch—Was Unterscheidet das Sittliche?" In *Ethik der Leistung,* edited by Hans Thomas, 47–76. Herford: Busse-Seewald Verlag, 1988.

Richard of St. Victor. *La Trinité* (De Trinitate). Edited by Gaston Salet, S.J. Paris: Edition du Cerf, 1959.

Sartre, Jean-Paul. "La transcendence de l'ego, esquisse d'une description phénoménologique." *Recherches Philosophiques* 6 (1936–37): 85–123. Translated by Forrest Williams and Robert Kirkpatrick under the title *The Transcendence of the Ego.* (New York: Noonday Press, 1957).

Scheler, Max. "Die Stellung des Menschen im Kosmos." In *Späte Schriften.* Vol. 9 of *Gesammelte Werke.* Bern: Francke Verlag, 1976. Translated by Hans Meyerhoff under the title *Man's Place in Nature.* (New York: Farrar, Straus, and Cudahy, 1962).

————. *Der Formalismus in der Ethik und die materiale Wertethik.* Vol. 2 of *Gesammelte Werke.* Bern: Francke Verlag, 1966. Translated by Manfred Frings and Roger Funk under the title of *Formalism in Ethics and Non-Formal Ethics of Values.* (Evanston: Northwestern University Press, 1973).

————. *Wesen und Formen der Sympathie.* Vol. 7 of *Gesammelte Werke.* Bern: Francke Verlag, 1973. Translated by Peter Heath under the title of *The Nature of Sympathy.* (Hamden: Shoe String Press Inc., 1973).

————. "Reue und Wiedergeburt." In *Vom Ewigen in Menschen.* Vol. 5 of *Gesammelte Werke.* Bern: Francke Verlag, 1968. Translated by Bernard Noble under the title "Repentance and Rebirth." In *On the Eternal in Man.* (Hamden: Archon Books, 1972).

————. *Ressentiment.* Translated by William Holdheim. New York: Free Press of Glencoe, 1961.

Schopenhauer, Arthur. *On the Basis of Morality.* Translated by E.F.J. Payne. Indianapolis: Bobbs-Merrill, 1965.

————. "Preissschrift über die Grundlagen der Moral." In *Sämtliche Werke.* Vol. 4. Wiesbaden: 1950.

————. *The World as Will and Presentation.* Translated by E.F.J. Payne. New York: Dover Publications, 1969.

Schwarz, Stephen. *The Moral Problem of Abortion.* Chicago: Loyola University Press, 1991.

Searle, John. *Intentionality.* Cambridge: Cambridge University Press, 1983.

Seifert, Josef. "Esse, Essence, and Infinity: A Dialogue with Existentialist Thomism." *The New Scholasticism* 58 (1984): 84–98.

————. "Essence and Existence." Pt. 1. *Aletheia* 1, no. 1 (1977): 17–157; Pt. 2. *Aletheia* 1, no. 2 (1978): 371–459.

————. *Essere e Persona.* Milan: Università Cattolica del Sacro Cuore, 1989.

———. *Leib und Seele*. Salzburg: Anton Pustet Verlag, 1973.

———. *Was ist und was motiviert eine sittliche Handlung?* Salzburg: Anton Pustet Verlag, 1976.

Sillem, Edward. *The Philosophical Notebook*. Vol. 1. Louvain: Nauwelaerts Publishing House, 1969.

Stein, Edith. "Die ontische Struktur der Person und ihre erkenntnistheoretische Problematik." In *Welt und Person*. Vol. 6 of *Edith Steins Werke*. Louvain: 1962.

———. *Endliches und Ewiges Sein*. Freiburg: Herder Verlag, 1962.

———. "Individuum und Gemeinschaft." *Jahrbuch für Philosophie und phänomenologische Forschung* 5 (1922): 116–283.

Theunissen, Michael. *Der Andere: Studien zur Sozialontologie der Gegenwart*. Berlin: Walter de Gruyter, 1977. Partially translated by Christopher Macann under the title *The Other: Studies in the Social Ontology of Husserl, Heidegger, Sartre, and Buber*. Cambridge: MIT Press, 1986.

Tinder, Glenn. *The Crisis of Political Imagination*. New York: Charles Scribner's Sons, 1964.

Von Hildebrand, Dietrich. *Ästhetik*. Vol. 1. Stuttgart: Kohlhammer Verlag, 1977.

———. *Das Wesen der Liebe*. Stuttgart: Kohlhammer Verlag, 1971.

———. "Die geistigen Formen der Affektivität." In *Situationsethik und kleinere Schriften*. Stuttgart: Kohlhammer Verlag, 1973.

———. *Ethics*. Chicago: Franciscan Herald Press, 1972.

———. *Graven Images: Substitutes for True Morality*. New York: David McKay, 1957.

———. *The Heart*. Chicago: Franciscan Herald Press, 1977.

———. *Metaphysik der Gemeinschaft*. Regensburg: Habbel Verlag, 1955.

———. *Moralia*. Stuttgart: Kohlhammer Verlag, 1980.

———. *Morality and Situation Ethics*. Chicago: Franciscan Herald Press, 1966.

Weil, Simone. "Human Personality." In *Selected Essays, 1934–1943*. Chosen and translated by Richard Rees, 9–31. London: Oxford University Press, 1962.

Wojtyla, Karol. *The Acting Person*. Translated by Andrezej Potocki. Vol. 10 of *Analecta Husserliana*, edited by Anna -TeresaTymieniecka. Dordrecht: D. Reidel Publishing Co., 1979.

———. *Love and Responsibility*. Translated by H. T. Willetts. New York: Farrar, Straus, Giroux, 1981.

———. "The Personal Structure of Self Determination." In *Person and Community: Selected Essays*, translated by Theresa Sandok, 187–195. Vol. 4 of *Catholic Thought from Lublin*, edited by Andrew N. Woznicki. New York: Peter Lang, 1993.

———. "Subjectivity and the Irreducible in the Human Being." In *Person and Community: Selected Essays*, translated by Theresa Sandock, 209–217. New York: Peter Lang, 1993.

Wolter, Allan., ed. *Duns Scotus on the Will and Morality*. Washington D.C.: Catholic University of America Press, 1986.

Index

JOHN F. CROSBY

THE SELFHOOD OF THE HUMAN PERSON

It is often said that "each person is unique and unrepeatable" or that "each person is his own end and not a mere instrumental means." But what exactly do these familiar sayings mean? What are they based on? How do we know they are true?

John F. Crosby addresses these questions by unfolding the mystery of personal "selfhood." He stands in the great tradition of Western philosophy, but he is also greatly indebted to more recent personalist philosophy, especially to the Christian personalism of Kierkegaard and Newman, and to the phenomonology of Scheler and von Hildebrand. As a result, Crosby approaches the subject much as Karol Wojtyla does in his philosophical work; he enriches the old with the new as he explores the structure of personal selfhood.

Crosby sheds new light on the incommunicability and unrepeatability of each human person. He explores the subjectivity, or interiority, of persons as well as the much-discussed theme of their transcendence, giving particular attention to the transcendence achieved by persons in their moral existence. Finally he shows how we are led through the person to God, and he concludes with an original and properly philosophical approach to the image of God in each person.

Throughout his study, Crosby is careful not to take selfhood in an individualistic way. He shows how the "selfhood and solitude" of each person opens each to others, and how, far from interfering with interpersonal relations, it in fact renders them possible.